FOREST PARK

CAROLINE LOUGHLIN AND CATHERINE ANDERSON

FOREST PARK

The Junior League of St. Louis and University of Missouri Press, Columbia, 1986

St. Louis WELCOME HOME Reception TO Col. CHAS. A. LINDBERGH FOREST PARK — JUNE 19TH 1927.

Copyright © 1986 by the Junior League of St. Louis
St. Louis, Missouri 63117
Library of Congress Catalog Card Number 86-1376
Printed and bound in the United States of America
All rights reserved.
Second printing, 1987

Library of Congress Cataloging-in-Publication Data

Loughlin, Caroline
    Forest Park

    Bibliography: p.
    Includes index.
    1. Forest Park (Saint Louis, Mo.)—History.   2. Saint Louis (Mo.)—His-
tory.   I. Anderson, Catherine   II. Junior League of St. Louis.   III. Title
F474.S27F675   1986   977.8′66   86-1376
ISBN 0-8262-0605-0

(photocredits on last page)

☞ This paper meets the minimum requirements of the American National Standard for
Permanence of Paper for Printed Library Materials, Z39.48, 1984.

ACKNOWLEDGMENTS

Producing a book such as *Forest Park* requires the support of many organizations and corporations.

Ralston Purina Trust Fund

is a primary underwriter and helped make the book a reality.

The Junior League of St. Louis wishes to thank all those who helped its members with the work on this book.

Among those who were especially helpful were James Neal Primm and Howard S. Miller, who gave many helpful suggestions for improving the text. James D. Cherry, Glen E. Holt, and John Lark gave much initial encouragement and advice. The staff of the St. Louis Department of Parks, Recreation and Forestry, especially directors George M. Kinsey and Nancy E. Rice, were also extremely helpful. The management staffs of the *St. Louis Post-Dispatch* and the *Globe-Democrat* were extremely generous with their time, files, and photographs.

Others gave us special access to research materials that are not ordinarily open to the public, especially the Barnes Hospital Public Relations Department, Erwin R. Breihan and George K. Hasegawa at Horner & Shifrin, Inc., Robert T. Briggs at the St. Louis Science Center, Mr. and Mrs. Edward H. Cunliff, Charles H. Hoessle, Director, and the staff of the St. Louis Zoo, Laclede Gas Co., Peter Langston at the St. Louis Area Council of the Boy Scouts of America, Roy Leimberg at Pitzman's Company of Surveyors & Engineers, the Muny (Municipal Theatre Association), Ward S. Parker, Viola E. Pollak, John C. Shepherd, William T. Stewart, Henrietta Lubke Taylor, Frank A. Thompson, Jr., Alexandra M. Usher, Norbury L. Wayman, and Margaret J. Witherspoon.

There were many people who helped with various aspects of the book. Especial thanks goes to those who helped do the research, especially Charles E. H. Luedde, Cathryn K. Mollman, and Linda S. Penniman; Philip H. Loughlin for his photographic work, and R. E. Klockenbrink and William E. Mathis for help in reproducing photographs.

Many shared their knowledge with us, especially William H. Albinson, Mary M. Bartley, Gerald D. Bolas, Dennis A. Bolazina, Raymond L. Breun, Anne F. Dillon, Jean E. Durham, William B. Faherty, S.J., Nancy Fields, the Reverend William E. Gillespie, David M. Grant, Cornelia L. Hath, Rita Houghasian, Berl Katz, Charles M. Kindleberger, Mary Jane Kirtz, Barbara Kodner, Charles P. Korr, Kay Kramer, Susan R. Lammert, Richard Longstreth, Eugene J. Mackey III, Lucille McClelland, David W. Mesker, John H. Poelker, Jane Pratt, Robert E. Reed, Sally K. E. Reeves, Frederick Roos, Elizabeth Schmidt, Jerry Schrier, Martin Schweig, Jr., Quinta Scott, Robert Charles Smith, Carolyn Toft, Leroy Tyus, Blondale Wingo, and Alexander Yard.

Those who were especially helpful at public collections were Beryl Manne, Victoria Witte, Carl B. Safe, and the staffs of the AAA Automobile Club of Missouri, the Library of Congress in Washington, D.C., the Mercantile Library, the Metropolitan Sewer District, the Missouri Botanical Garden library (particularly Constance P. Wolf), the Missouri Department of Conservation (particularly Larry Belusz and David Tylka), the Missouri Historical Society (particularly Helen M. Backer, Katharine T. Corbett, Duane Sneddeker, Jean Streeter, and Carol Verble), the New York Public Library, the St. Louis Art Museum (especially Ann Abid), St. Louis City Hall (at the Archival Library and the offices of the Board of Public Service, Recorder of Deeds, and Register, and particularly the late C. H. Cornwell at the Municipal Reference Library), the St. Louis County Library Headquarters, the St. Louis Police Library, the St. Louis Public Library (particularly Joan Collett, Head Librarian, and Julanne Good), the St. Louis University libraries, the School Sisters of Notre Dame (Sister M. Dionysia Brockland), the Smithsonian Institution, the State Historical Society of Missouri, the U.S. Department of the Interior Geological Survey EROS Data Center in Sioux Falls, South Dakota, the University of Missouri-St. Louis archives and library (particularly Anne R. Kenney), the Washington University libraries.

Any others who preserved books, newspapers, pictures, and other materials and who cataloged and indexed them to make the information available deserve credit for helping to make this book.

To all of the others with enthusiasm for Forest Park and for this book who encouraged us to continue even when the task seemed overwhelming, we give special thanks.

★   ★   ★   ★   ★   ★

The following members of the Junior League of St. Louis helped with this book:

Katherine Altvater, Beverley Amberg, Catherine Anderson, Louise Angst, her mother, also Louise Angst, Kathleen Armstrong, Ann F. Babington, Linda Benoist, Diane Bofinger, Marie Bone, Joy Burns, Doreen Cherry, Mary Ciapciak, Virginia Curby, Cheryl Davis, Sharon Dougherty, Jill Dowd, Cicely Drennan, Melanie Fathman, Anne Flora, Margretta Forrester, Eleanor Frederich, Lucie Garnett, Louise Gazzoli, Deborah Godwin, Margaret Ann Goffstein, Dudley Grove, Kathleen Hamilton, Schuyler Herbert, Leslie Hibbard, Katherine Hibbitts, Elizabeth Higginbotham, Judith Hinrichs, Ellen Honig, Suzanne Jones, Martha Jordan, Margaret Kahle, Concetta Kirchenbauer, Neela Kottmeier, Nancy Kurten, Katherine Law, Noel Leicht, Louise Lonsbury, Caroline Loughlin, Dorothy Loughlin, Ann Lucas, Jane Luedde, Anne McAlpin, Elizabeth McDonald, Eugenia McKee, Kathleen McQueeny, Jane Mitchell, Mary Beth Paynter, Carol Perkins, Mary Jane Pieroni, Jane Piper, Christine Pirrung, Mary Beth Powell, Diana Rawizza, Emily Reynolds, Patricia Rich, Judith Sandler, Susan Schmidt, Kathryne Sheldon, Kathleen Sherby, Alice Sherwood, Joan Smith, JoAnn Smith, Katharine Smith, Deirdre Sullivan, Kristi Vaiden, Patricia West, Ruthann Wolff, Lana Yunker, and Judy Zach.

February 1, 1986

CONTENTS

INTRODUCTION

For generations, large urban parks have shaped the growth of major cities and brightened the lives of their citizens. This book is about such a park—Forest Park in St. Louis, Missouri.

St. Louisans care about Forest Park. For more than a century they have used it, loved it, and argued about it. The park has been a part of many of the city's major achievements and problems.

The founding of Forest Park was part of the national movement for large urban parks. As Gunther Barth wrote in *City People*, this movement briefly united groups that usually opposed each other—businessmen interested in the rise of real estate values or the flow of visitors, politicians seeing a source of jobs for the unemployed party faithful, reformers seeking physical and moral relief for the poor from the squalor of the cities and a method of weaving the city's new-comers into the social fabric, and landscape designers planning works of art. These groups joined to establish the parks, until disagreements about how the parks should be used set them to wrangling again.[1]

This book grew out of such a disagreement—the heated discussion that followed the 1976 R/UDAT (Regional/Urban Design Assistance Team) visit described in Chapter 8. At the request of the St. Louis Chapter of the American Institute of Architects (AIA), members of the Junior League of St. Louis began an independent study of Forest Park. During that research, Junior League members looked at the history of the park to gain some perspective on current controversies. Valuable information was available in park administrators' reports, issued annually from the park's opening through the middle 1960s. Trips to the park revealed current conditions. Local news-papers had covered the park extensively, and their articles, editorials, and letters to the editors were enlightening. But no complete history of the park existed, though such a book would give a framework for understanding current problems.

The questions park planners, administrators, and users were trying to answer in the 1970s and 1980s weren't new. They had been asked repeat-edly during the period covered by this book (1876 through 1976, with glances back to cover the es-tablishment of the park and forward to cover dis-putes that continued past 1976). Traffic has been a problem since the beginning. Fast driving, through traffic (both east-west and north-south), inadequate park road maintenance, and the lack of public transportation have been the source of complaints since the 1870s. Parkgoers' misuse or abuse of park facilities, measures to make park-goers safe (and to make them feel safe), disagree-ments about what structures the park should contain, the issue of who should pay for park fa-cilities and how much—all were hotly debated before 1900. Increasing use and development in, around, and beyond the park have brought differ-ing values into sharper conflict as the space filled up and uses collided.

Several strong men and women have left their stamp on Forest Park as various individuals and groups, including the courts, have made deci-sions about the park. Their decisions have re-flected financial pressures as well as different ideas about what the park should be—an oasis of urban tranquillity, a center for athletic contests, an edu-cational resource, or a social gathering place. Everything that St. Louisans take for granted about the park, including its very existence, has been the subject of often bitter dispute that might easily have had a different outcome.

Disagreements about Forest Park were often part of larger struggles for political power in the St. Louis region. Changes in life in the United States have inevitably affected Forest Park—inventions such as the bicycle and the automobile, the growth of recreation, periods of political corruption, financial depression, prohibition, or war. This book, however, considers outside influences only as they have affected the park. It looks at the park from the viewpoint of St. Louis's business and political leaders, and of Forest Park's administrators, neighbors, and users, concentrating on activities that attracted large numbers of people, made major changes in the park or its usage, were controversial at the time, or are the subject of current debate.

Controversy has sometimes obscured the fact that Forest Park has been successful in accomplishing much that its early proponents intended. It has raised real estate values and attracted visitors, been a source of jobs, become a place of beauty, and served as a common meeting ground for the people of a diverse city. Over the years park officials have largely succeeded in creating a park for everybody, though distance, racial regulations, and admission fees have restricted use at times.

Since the 1870s St. Louisans have been proud of Forest Park, whether or not they lived in the city or used the park. As early as the 1890s, Forest Park's size, location, and varied attractions made it unique in the region and nationally recognized. Planners in the 1970s and 1980s discovered that many people strongly resisted any suggested change. Anything someone recommended was loudly opposed by someone else whose favorite corner of the park would be affected. Financial problems remained.

Yet, amidst the problems and controversies, Forest Park has continued to be a remarkably successful attraction. Those who wish to protect and improve it can be guided by the successes and failures of Forest Park's first century in deciding how best to manage the park through continuing change.

People have cared about Forest Park, and they still do. Those who care about Forest Park and also understand its story can help to make its second century at least as successful as its first.

1

IN THE BEGINNING (1870–1876)

What the people want is a park that . . . the laboring man can reach without spending the whole day in the attempt, and that can be surrounded by . . . [the] residences . . . [of] men of taste and means.—Alonzo W. Slayback, 1873

I present to you, the people of the County of St. Louis, your own, this large and beautiful Forest Park for the enjoyment of yourselves, your children and your children's children forever. . . . The rich and poor, the merchant and mechanic, the professional man and the day laborer, each with his family and lunch basket, can come here and enjoy his own . . . all without stint or hindrance . . . and there will be no notice put up, "Keep Off the Grass."—Chauncy F. Shultz, June 24, 1876

Forest Park officially opened to the public on Saturday afternoon, June 24, 1876. The Civil War had ended twelve years earlier. The United States was celebrating the hundredth anniversary of its independence with a Centennial Exposition in Philadelphia. Ulysses S. Grant was president; there were thirty-seven states in the union. George A. Custer would be killed the following day at the battle of the Little Bighorn. The fastest trains achieved an average speed of twenty-five miles per hour.

Trains to St. Louis from the east used James B. Eads's Great Bridge, opened two years earlier, to cross the Mississippi River on their way to the new Union Depot downtown (replaced in 1894 by Union Station a few blocks away) (Fig. 1-1). Under the bridge, paddle-wheel steamboats made their way up and down the river. The 1870 census, widely disputed but never revised, had listed St. Louis as the fourth largest city in the country behind New York, Philadelphia, and Brooklyn (still a separate city) and ahead of Chicago. The Democratic party was holding its national convention in downtown St. Louis in June 1876 (Fig. 1-2).

Forest Park was in St. Louis County, almost two miles west of the St. Louis city limits, a forty-minute carriage ride from downtown. Despite the distance, the *Globe-Democrat* reported,

"A vast concourse of people, estimated at 50,000" came to the park for the opening-day ceremonies, by train and by carriage, at a time when the city population was between 300,000 and 350,000.[1] "It seemed," the paper said, "as if all the carriages and buggies in the city, public and private, were on the grounds." The train ride from Union Depot, on tracks opened less than a week before, took about twenty minutes. Although the ceremonies were not scheduled to begin until four o'clock, trains full of people left Union Depot every half hour beginning at eleven o'clock. A line of more than a hundred carriages brought the special guests, many of them delegates to the Democratic National Convention. The lieutenant governor of New York, senators from Wisconsin and California, Missouri Gov. Charles H. Hardin, St. Louis Mayor Henry Overstolz, and Chauncy F. Shultz, presiding justice of the St. Louis County Court (the chief executive of St. Louis County), were all there.

Nature seemed, the *Dispatch* said, to have intended the spot for a park. The gentle slopes provided a variety of scenery. Sport fish jumped in the park's clear streams, such as the River des Peres. The forest that gave the park its name was "indescribable in its loveliness. The large trees stand as nature planted them, . . . [and] cool

1-1. James B. Eads's Great Bridge (later known as Eads Bridge), drawn in 1875 by Camille N. Dry. After the bridge officially opened on July 4, 1874, railroad lines from the east entered St. Louis for the first time.

winds play and sing with invigorating grace to those who seek . . . a retreat from the oppressive heat of the city" (Fig. 1-3).

Around the park, the land was mostly farmland, with clusters of houses along Clayton Road and some industry along the Missouri Pacific Railroad south of the park. Kingshighway, then called King's Highway, ran east of the park, with a jog that gave the park a projection in its southeastern corner; and Skinker Road edged the park on the west. Neither road was even graveled. To the north and south, no road divided the park from the surrounding land.

The opening-day crowd gathered near the new wooden music stand to be entertained by Frank Boehm's band, playing a program that opened with the "Forest Park Quickstep" and in-

cluded selections by Verdi, Donizetti, and Bach. The park administration had supplied numerous benches and free ice water, a welcome touch on a day when the temperature downtown exceeded 90 degrees, according to A. S. Aloe, optician and mathematical instrument maker. Soon, from the nearby speaker's stand, men began praising the park and reviewing the struggle to establish it, a struggle that, because of major setbacks, had lasted from as early as 1863 until November 1874.

The story of Forest Park may have begun in April 1863 at Tower Grove, the St. Louis County residence of Henry Shaw, a wealthy retired merchant and enthusiastic amateur botanist who had established a botanical garden and opened it to the public in 1859. Frederick Law Olmsted, on

1-2. The Democratic party held its national convention in St. Louis in 1876. Many of the delegates attended the Forest Park opening-day ceremonies on June 24, 1876.

leave as architect-in-chief and superintendent of New York's Central Park, was in St. Louis as secretary of the U.S. Sanitary Commission, a private organization dedicated to improving conditions for Union soldiers. While he was in St. Louis, Olmsted called at Shaw's house and botanical garden, and the two men almost certainly discussed large urban parks.[2]

Less than a year later, in February 1864, the Missouri legislature authorized St. Louis voters to approve a Central Park for their city, created a board of commissioners for the park, and instructed the commissioners to select a site west of the city containing not more than 350 acres. The board included three city officials ex officio and four citizens. For the first board, the law named the citizens—John H. Lightner, a merchant and

an official of St. Louis County; lawyer and financier William M. McPherson; engineer James B. Eads; and Henry Shaw.[3] The commissioners elected Lightner president, and on March 25, 1864, Lightner announced that the park would be bordered on the south by Laclede Avenue and on the west by Kingshighway with the exact boundaries to be settled in negotiation with property owners. Mayor F. W. Cronenbold announced that the election necessary to approve the park would be held in less than two weeks, on April 4, 1864. Some St. Louisans supported the proposal saying, "New York has her Park, Brooklyn a great Park, Baltimore a Park nearly as large as the Central Park of New York, and our neighbor, Chicago, has commenced a Park. Let us not lag in the background." Others opposed it on the grounds

1-3. Sport fish jumped in the River des Peres, one of Forest Park's prime attractions in the 1870s. The river's repeated floods posed problems for park administrators for years.

1-4. Hiram W. Leffingwell's persistence resulted in a major park for St. Louis but no profit for him.

that the city should not make such a major commitment until the Civil War was over and conditions more settled. In addition, some said, the location would benefit McPherson, who owned land nearby, but not the city's poor who "will rarely take the time to go four miles in the country to breathe the pure air."[4] McPherson denied that he hoped to gain from the park location, but the voters overwhelmingly rejected the proposal, and there the matter rested until 1870.

In October 1870 Hiram W. Leffingwell, who had been in the real estate business in St. Louis for more than twenty-five years, revived the idea (Fig. 1-4). One of Leffingwell's earlier projects had been the founding of the town of Kirkwood in the early 1850s, shortly before the Pacific Railroad (later the Missouri Pacific) linked the site to the city. He had also been responsible for laying out Grand Avenue as a wide drive in 1852, when it was still outside the city limits. In late 1870 Leffingwell invited reporters from all the daily

papers as well as influential citizens, including Congressman Erastus Wells, to hear about his plan for a 3,000-acre park to extend west about three miles from Kingshighway.[5] Henry Shaw had recently donated more than 275 acres to the city for Tower Grove Park, but many agreed that St. Louis needed a larger park to provide a refuge from the heat, noise, smoke, and filth of the city. Every up-to-date city needed such a "breathing space," which would also, they believed, increase real estate values.

Under Missouri law at that time, the park could be established only by the state legislature; so in January 1871 Leffingwell arranged for the introduction of a bill authorizing the area he called St. Louis Park. Opposition to the scheme developed quickly. The park was too big, some said, and too far from the city. Others objected to financing by a special tax on property around the park. Henry Shaw, Thomas Skinker, Charles P. Chouteau, Robert Forsyth, Charles Cabanne, and other owners of property in the taxing district signed a resolution calling the tax "an act of injustice and robbery" and an "attempt to force from the county a compulsory donation of a park to the great city of St. Louis." Various alternate proposals were made for smaller parks, ranging from three parks of 300 acres each to one park of 1,680 acres. Some suggested that the idea should be approved by the taxpayers, a vote proponents wanted to avoid because of city voters' rejection of Central Park and two other park proposals. The legislators listened to delegations from St. Louis supporting and opposing the bill but adjourned without taking action (Fig. 1-5).

The following year park supporters tried again. In March 1872 the legislature established Forest Park with a law that would be declared unconstitutional a year later. The law, which did not require voters' approval, named fourteen Forest Park commissioners with power to issue bonds and to buy the land. Although supporters had reduced the size of the park to 1,370 acres from their previous 3,000-acre proposal, they had retained the financing method, a special taxing dis-

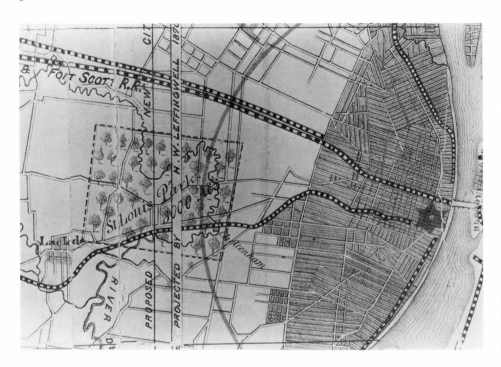

1-5. Leffingwell's 1871 proposal for the 3,000-acre St. Louis Park failed to pass the Missouri legislature, making the 1,370-acre Forest Park seem small in comparison.

trict outside the city limits. If the city limits were extended, that tax would be deducted from city taxes.[6] At the same time, the legislature created a park named Northern Park, with a similar tax district. A few days later the legislature extended the city limits to include all the land in the Forest Park and Northern Park tax districts.

Despite the changes from Leffingwell's original proposal, opposition continued, claiming that the park was still too big, its 1,370 acres much more than the 840-acre Central Park that satisfied the much larger city of New York. It was too far away and could only be reached by those wealthy enough to own a carriage, since there was no public transportation to the park in 1872. Property owners in the park district still opposed the special tax. Thomas Skinker, who had opposed the 1871 bill, was enraged. Charles P. Chouteau, his sister Julia Maffitt, and others filed suit to have the 1872 bill declared unconstitutional. Although the circuit court ruled against them, the Missouri Supreme Court announced on the last day of April 1873 that the Forest Park Act was unconstitutional because of the special tax district. (Al-

though the Northern Park district had not been challenged by the court case, it was subject to the same legal objections as the Forest Park district).

During the year the case was in the courts, however, the Forest Park commissioners, led by Chairman of the Executive Committee Leffingwell, bought more than half of the land for the park, including Skinker's land, giving bonds as payment.[7] In June 1872 the Forest Park commissioners entertained Skinker, Erastus Wells, U.S. Senators Carl Schurz and Francis P. Blair, and numerous other prominent citizens with a *Fête Champêtre* (outdoor feast) on the park grounds, near the "golden waters" of the River des Peres, demonstrating the park's beauty and the commissioners' success in acquiring the land (Fig. 1-6).[8]

The commissioners also worked to remove the objection that the park was only for the rich by negotiating for public transportation to the grounds. In early July 1872 they were able to announce that the St. Louis County Railroad Company would build a narrow-gauge track and run trains at least every quarter hour at a round-trip fare not to exceed twenty cents. While such a fare

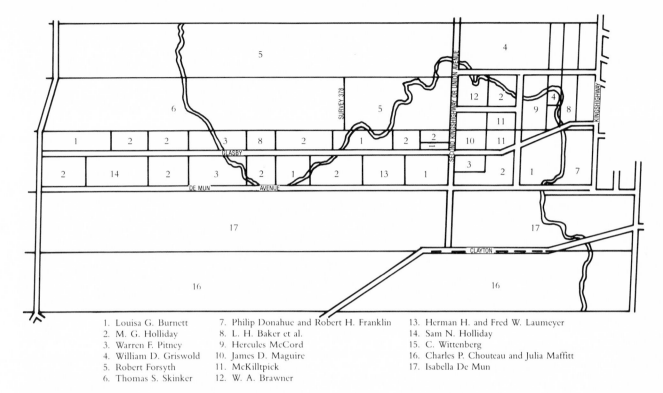

1. Louisa G. Burnett
2. M. G. Holliday
3. Warren F. Pitney
4. William D. Griswold
5. Robert Forsyth
6. Thomas S. Skinker
7. Philip Donahue and Robert H. Franklin
8. L. H. Baker et al.
9. Hercules McCord
10. James D. Maguire
11. McKilltpick
12. W. A. Brawner
13. Herman H. and Fred W. Laumeyer
14. Sam N. Holliday
15. C. Wittenberg
16. Charles P. Chouteau and Julia Maffitt
17. Isabella De Mun

1-6. Charles P. Chouteau and his sister Julia Maffitt, Isabella de Mun, Thomas S. Skinker, and Robert Forsyth owned much of the land in the proposed park.

would be beyond the means of many, it was still an improvement over the necessity to take a carriage to the grounds.

The new park was a selling point for nearby property. Land nearby, according to the *Democrat* (merged with the *Globe* in 1875), offered the advantages of a "suburban home, free from the noise and bustle, dust and smoke of the city." Leffingwell advertised an auction of "322 Very Large Lots" in his new Forest Park Subdivision, which did not actually touch the park. Other agents mentioned Forest Park in advertising lots for sale in the new Bartmer's Subdivision, the existing Aubert Place, and Olive Street Grove, though none actually bordered the park. The *Democrat* urged buyers to act without delay, "The rapid advance in prices of all properties in the immediate vicinity of the large parks in all our chief cities, has invariably given a rich return to the shrewdness of those who bought early."[9] One

fourteen-acre property in the park district sold for $42,000 just before the bill passed and $80,000 just after. The *Republican* reported that before the law was struck down, Leffingwell's firm had negotiated sales of more than $1,650,000 worth of property citywide because of the new park.

The court decision against the park act invalidated most of these sales, which had been contingent on the law's constitutionality. The decision also voided the commissioners' purchases of land for the park, which had been recorded in the city's official deed books and could only be reversed by a court judgment against the Forest Park commissioners. The court had found, however, that the board of commissioners had never existed as a legal entity so there was no one to sue. Landowners were left holding worthless bonds issued by the nonexistent commissioners and supported by an illegal tax.[10]

The extension of the city limits was also "in

a very considerable muddle," the *Democrat* said, since the extension was defined by the very park districts the court had found unconstitutional.[11] City Counselor Edward P. McCarty advised Mayor Joseph Brown that the boundary extension was still valid. Others disagreed. Property owners in the annexed area, including Skinker, called for repeal of the extension, since they did not wish to be in the city without the parks. In February 1874 the legislature settled the argument by repealing the extension.

The *Democrat* reported that some people "felt that the Supreme Court had acted rather hastily." Park supporters requested a rehearing from the supreme court, but in early November 1873 the court rejected the request.[12] The legal remedies available to park supporters had been exhausted, and the 1872 Forest Park Act was dead.

The courts, however, seemed to encourage park advocates to try again, stating, "There is no question as to the desirableness of public parks in the vicinity of large cities," and "cities may be permitted to establish and maintain parks for the convenience and use of the public."

Park proponents, many of them prominent business and professional men, held several meetings and considered a variety of sites. Lawyer Alonzo W. Slayback, who, with his brother, would later establish the annual Veiled Prophet celebration, told a meeting at Côte Brilliante School, "What the people want is a park that . . . the laboring man can reach without spending the whole day in the attempt, and that can be surrounded by . . . [the] residences . . . [of] men of taste and means." The benefits would be great to the "throngs of visitors" who would "acquire health and strength by breathing the pure air." Real estate agent Andrew McKinley, citing the example of Central Park, told the group, "In the course of fifteen years the increased value of the surrounding property would return the cost of the park three times over in taxation." Streetcar magnate Erastus Wells and others reported during a meeting at Uhrig's Cave beer garden, "St. Louis is growing so rapidly . . . as to require immediate

action. The property which can now be bought for hundreds of dollars per acre, will in a few years cost . . . thousands and tens of thousands." Park advocates urged Mayor Brown to support their plan for two parks, one in the vicinity of the original site for Forest Park and another farther north, "connected by a grand boulevard extending to the cemeteries and the river." The mayor replied, "Every one wants a park near his property and a boulevard in front of his door," and said that if the plan for the two parks were adopted, "the people in the southern part of the city will complain."[13]

In 1874 the Missouri legislature passed three acts to establish three parks in St. Louis County: Carondelet Park in the south, Forest Park in the center, and O'Fallon Park to the north. The Forest Park Act, signed by Gov. Silas Woodson on March 25, 1874, established a public park "for the people of the county of St. Louis"[14] (which included the city of St. Louis) in exactly the same location as the 1872 park. The act authorized the county court to purchase all the land in the park (except the right-of-way belonging to the St. Louis County Railroad Company) and to issue thirty-year bonds to a total of $1.3 million, with interest at six percent. The bond proceeds were to be used for the purchase of park lands with any balance for park improvements. Instead of the special tax district, the law instructed the county to collect an additional county-wide property tax of one-half mill per dollar valuation to pay the interest and principal on the bonds, and for park improvements. The act provided for seven commissioners: three appointed by the county court, three appointed by the mayor of St. Louis and confirmed by the city council, and the presiding justice of the county court. No popular vote was necessary to approve the park and none was taken.

Most of the decisions affecting organization of the park were made by two different governmental agencies with similar names: the St. Louis County Circuit Court (the circuit court), a judicial body, part of the Missouri state court system;

1-7. The railroad tracks in Forest Park as they appeared in the mid 1970s when they were one hundred years old. Reaching an agreement with the railroad companies about the construction and operation of the line occupied much of the time of the Forest Park Commissioners in 1875.

and the St. Louis County Court (the county court), the legislative body that governed the county (the individual members of which were referred to as county justices, with a presiding justice). On April 27, about a month after the bill passed, the county court ordered County Surveyor Julius Pitzman to make a plat showing the correct boundaries of the park and of all the parcels of land in it.[15] On May 25, Pitzman delivered his report. The park consisted of 1,371.75 acres, more than 46 acres of which already belonged to the county in the form of public roads. The four largest parcels were owned by Thomas S. Skinker, Isabella de Mun, Charles P. Chouteau and his sis-

ter Julia Maffitt jointly, and the estate of Robert Forsyth, who had recently died. Chouteau was still opposed to the park and sued to have the new law declared unconstitutional. The reasons for his opposition are no longer clear. Perhaps he wanted his land to remain rural; perhaps he thought he could make more money from his land another way; or perhaps he didn't want decisions about the city his family had founded to be determined by real estate interests.[16]

Although the county court learned in early June that Chouteau was going to contest the constitutionality of the new Forest Park Act, it continued with its plans. The county chose as its commissioners Hiram Leffingwell and Peter G. Gerhart, both of whom had been commissioners under the 1872 act, and John O'Fallon Farrar. The city appointed Andrew McKinley, Ansyl Phillips, and John J. Fitzwilliam. They were sworn into office in June.

Of the six appointed commissioners, three were in the real estate business—Leffingwell, McKinley, and Gerhart. Of the remaining three, Phillips was a commission merchant (a type of broker), Fitzwilliam was a banker, and Farrar attended to various business interests, including real estate. The political sector was also represented. Gerhart had been a member of the city council from 1866 to 1868 (and would be again in the 1880s). The presiding justice of the county court was, of course, an elected official. When the commissioners took office, the presiding justice was banker Joseph O'Neil. Later, businessman Chauncy F. Shultz replaced O'Neil.

At their first meeting, on June 17, 1874, the commissioners elected Andrew McKinley president and Ansyl Phillips vice-president. McKinley, who was in his late fifties, had lived in St. Louis for more than twenty years, working as a lawyer and in real estate and insurance. During the next two years, he seems to have devoted himself to the park almost full time, overseeing all the planning and construction. The commissioners hired Charles Bland Smith as secretary, a position he had held under the 1872 act.

At about the same time that Charles Chouteau and Julia Maffitt filed suit to challenge the constitutionality of the new park act, William D. Griswold and other landowners sued to establish the legal ownership of the lands that the 1872 commissioners had bought before the act was found unconstitutional. With the agreement of the parties, the circuit court judge refused to hear either case so the cases could be combined and a

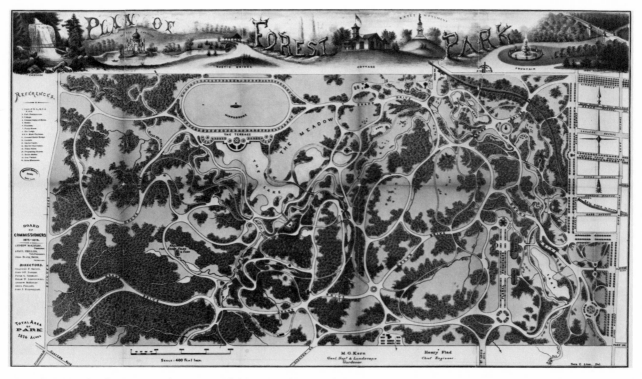

1-8. The 1876 plan for Forest Park. Because of shortages of time and money, the commissioners were unable to supply some of the planned features, such as the Cascades, pictured at the upper left.

prompt appeal could be made to the Missouri Supreme Court. Park supporters wanted the cases decided by the supreme court before the next session of the legislature so the lawmakers could make any necessary amendments to the act.

The strategy worked. On the last day of November 1874 the supreme court announced that the act was constitutional and returned to the circuit court all questions of land ownership and value.[17]

The 1874 act establishing Forest Park provided for a group of three appraisers to set the value of the land. The appraisers, Theophile Papin, John G. Priest, and Charles Green, and their secretary, Julius Pitzman, had begun work in May 1874 but had stopped because of the lawsuit. On January 9, 1875, the circuit court appointed the same three men as its appraisers.

After visiting the park site and hearing testimony on such matters as the vein of coal under the land, the appraisers advised the circuit court and the county court that the land to be bought included 1,326.009 acres (slightly different from Pitzman's earlier figure) worth $799,995, an average of about $600 an acre. The value varied from under $400 an acre for the Skinker tract, which was cut by the River des Peres and was remote from the city, to more than $3,000 an acre for some small parcels at the eastern end of the park along Kingshighway. Some of the landowners received significantly less than they had from the 1872 commissioners.

After the appraisal, the county court ordered $800,000 of the park bonds sold. The county treasurer paid the proceeds to the circuit court, which distributed the money to the sellers, giving title to the land to "the County of St. Louis and the people thereof" subject only to the right of way granted to the St. Louis County Railroad Company.

The 1874 Forest Park Act did not result in major real estate activity around the park as the 1872 law had. The panic of 1873, caused in part by similar real estate speculation nationwide, had led to a recession that continued past 1876.

Later, after the park was a success, various stories were told about its purchase. One of the sons of Justice O'Neil said in 1913 that O'Neil had bought an option on the park lands, using his own money, to prevent purchase of the land by speculators after the 1872 law was declared unconstitutional. The option, if it ever existed, was never exercised since O'Neil is not mentioned in the appraisers' report.

Nicholas M. Bell, a young state legislator who lived until 1931, longer than the major figures in the park's establishment, later said that he had persuaded Forsyth, who in turn convinced Skinker, that the park would increase the value of their remaining land outside the park and that they should support it. Skinker then reportedly said to Forsyth, "This is going to be the most beautiful park in America. We'll never live to see it, but Nick will."[18] However, Bell was not given

1-9. The Forest Park Commissioners intended Forest Park to be a driving park, as illustrated by this drawing by Camille N. Dry for an 1876 report to the St. Louis County Court.

credit for Skinker's change of heart at the time, and the story contained several inaccuracies.

Much later, after Bell's death, people said Leffingwell only wanted the park to increase the value of land he owned nearby. This story, too, appears unlikely. Leffingwell was a promoter who proposed schemes for improvements throughout the St. Louis area, from Grand Avenue to Kirk-wood. He surely expected to profit, as an agent, from real estate sales all over the city that would be generated by the new park. But Leffingwell's motives were not publicly questioned in the 1870s, as William McPherson's had been in the 1860s. The letters to the newspapers protesting the financial arrangements in Leffingwell's park bills alleged that the city was unfairly benefiting at the expense of the county, not that the park was a scheme for private gain. In fact, Leffingwell's 1870 plan was for the city to buy more land than was needed for the park, then sell the surround-ing land as lots, allowing the city to reap the major profit for the taxpayers. In any case, by the time Forest Park was legally established, financial hard times had ended the speculative real estate frenzy. Whatever his intentions, Leffingwell did not profit from his idea and his work, but St. Louis received a major park.

By the time the Missouri Supreme Court upheld the second Forest Park bill, Leffingwell was sixty-five years old. He seems to have been content to let McKinley take the lead in working on the new park. Afterward, Leffingwell left the real estate business and, after a few years, moved to Florida, where he died in 1897 at the age of eighty-eight. Ironically, various park facilities later bore the names of Bell and O'Neil, but none carried Leffingwell's name.

As the appraisers finished their work, the commissioners began theirs. They negotiated with railroad companies, authorized a plan for the park, and set men to work. The law establish-ing Forest Park provided that the St. Louis County Railroad Company could use the right-of-way it had been granted before the property became

1-10. The statue of Edward Bates was dedicated on opening day. It was moved to a different location in the park in the 1930s. In this photograph, taken in the 1980s, there is a small plaque dating from the park's centennial in 1976.

park land under certain regulations, including a requirement that the commissioners must ap-prove the grade of the line through the park. The company had not built the planned narrow-gauge track, presumably waiting until there was a park to generate traffic. The St. Louis, Kansas City and Northern Railway Company, later part of the Wabash Railroad, also wanted to use the right-of-way (Fig. 1-7).[19]

On August 11, 1875, the two railroads and the Forest Park commissioners signed an agree-ment covering the use of the right-of-way. The agreement reduced the width of the right-of-way from seventy feet to forty-two feet and regulated in detail the construction and operation of the railway line "to prevent unnecessary noise or in-

1-11. The Cabanne house, near Kingshighway, served as the park's headquarters building for a short time, then was torn down about 1882.

convenience to the public" and to protect "the landscape beauty of the Park." As part of the continuing struggle to provide public transportation to the remote park, the commissioners required that the St. Louis County Railway Company provide a stop at the park and contribute $3,000 for construction of a depot.

Since the St. Louis County Railroad Company did not begin construction within ninety days as agreed, it lost all claim to the right-of-way, leaving the St. Louis, Kansas City and Northern Railway Company the holder of the right-of-way and owner of the tracks it had built. The line was completed in 1876 and was the railroad used by thousands on opening day. However, the Kansas City company was not bound by the agreement to build a depot, so there was no shelter at the park stop.

In addition to negotiating with the railroad companies, the commissioners authorized a plan for the new park, to "preserve the natural beauties of the ground, so that it will always appear in fact as well as in name a forest park," they told a reporter from the *Republican*. Such a plan would prevent expensive mistakes caused by following

"every chance whim or passing fancy of the future." They intended to provide for all social classes: "Here the rich man may drive his fine turn-out . . .; here the poor man may wander at will under the trees, and his children sport as much as they please . . . without fear of a policeman hustling them off the grass."[20]

On January 1, 1876, the commissioners gave the county court a report of more than a hundred pages describing the actions and plans of the commissioners, including an extremely detailed list of the property held by the various departments. (It showed the three spittoons, two erasers, and two paper clips held by the engineering department) (Fig. 1-8).[21]

In the report, Maximillian G. Kern, Forest Park superintendent and landscape gardener, described the plan. Kern was a European-trained landscaper, one of the few in the United States. He had studied in the German town of Tübingen, where he was born and where his uncle was a professor of botany. He then worked as a gardener at the royal gardens in Stuttgart and on the landscape staff of the Tuileries Gardens in Paris. From there he probably went to Cincinnati, and he was almost certainly the author of *Practical Landscape Gardening*, a book that Olmsted admired. In St. Louis, Kern had developed Lafayette Park and would later design parks at the Compton Hill and Chain of Rocks reservoirs and oversee the landscaping of Portland and Westmoreland places.

The commissioners had considered inviting plans from "the most eminent landscape gardeners in the country,"[22] but had dropped the idea, perhaps to save time and money, or perhaps because they decided that Kern was the best man available. In fact Kern drew the plan in consultation with Commission President Andrew McKinley, and Chief Engineers Julius Pitzman and later Henry Flad, assisted by park draughtsman Theodore C. Link.

Pitzman, Flad, and Link were all German-born engineers. Pitzman was in his late thirties. He had served as county surveyor, had gone to Europe in 1874 to examine its great parks, and later laid out many St. Louis subdivisions, including Portland and Westmoreland places, where he again worked with Kern. Flad, who was about fifty, had assisted Eads in construction of the Great Bridge and was elected president of the St. Louis Board of Public Improvements after his Forest Park service. Link was the youngest, in his early twenties. He later designed a number of St. Louis buildings, including Union Station and some of the Washington University Medical School buildings.

Kern told the county court that some of the features of the plan were financially impossible at the time. He had included them only to stimulate interest in various possible uses of the park. The park was designed as a driving park for carriages, with winding roads disclosing a new view around each curve (Fig. 1-9). At frequent intervals, the roads provided openings, called concourses, "as congregating and resting places, from which the most attractive views can be enjoyed," probably the source of the name for Concourse Drive. The drives would take advantage of the park's natural beauty and of new natural-looking structures and gardens that workmen would create. Develop-

ment of the scenery near the drives was to be guided by the "new art . . . of *Landscape Gardening*" to achieve a "diversity of effects of tints and color, and of light and shade" united into "one harmonious whole." The design included eleven artificial lakes and ponds covering a total of more than forty acres. A driver could also enjoy the straight boulevard to be opened parallel to Kingshighway, or speed around the one-mile Hippodrome racetrack "designed in accordance with the most approved rules of the turf."

The eastern section of the park, nearest the city, would be "the congregating and rambling grounds of the masses," with "play grounds properly fitted out and guarded." This section should also be a place of elegance, "brilliantly lighted during the early hours of the night." The floral promenade, planned for the southeastern portion of the park, could some day be joined by a floral conservatory, an aquarium, a music pavilion, and "an elegant museum, of art and science." Just west of the floral promenade, Kern wrote, a zoological collection of interest to the youngsters of St. Louis should soon be available free of charge. An entrance fee, however nominal, would decrease the collection's value as "an institution of public instruction and amusement."

As the plan was being drawn, work began. There was immediate interest in establishing the police force in the park to ensure that "no malicious trespassers commit any depredations to the beautiful growth of forest trees." The *Republican* reported, however, that the entire force was "a single unpretentious guardian and a crow-bait horse."

Soon three hundred men were at work clearing the lands, which had been forests, commons, orchards, coal mines, cultivated fields, and the Cabanne Dairy Farm, owned by Joseph Cabanne until he sold his land to William Griswold in 1871. In the eastern and northern sections of the park, the men tore down fences, barns, and shanties, removed trees to break up straight planted lines, and planted grass seed in the fields of the Forsyth farm. Squatters, evicted from the land,

1-12. The park keeper's house in the 1970s. The building, new in 1876, served first as a headquarters building, then as a residence for park officials, and then as an office building.

moved to shacks south of the park. In the western portions of the park, the men cleared trees from the virgin forest that had given the park its name, to make room for roads and to open scenic vistas. Columns of smoke and fire from burning stumps and other debris showed St. Louisans that work was under way.

The workmen built the wooden music stand and some small shelter buildings and prepared the site for the statue of Edward Bates, the St. Louisan who was Abraham Lincoln's attorney general (Fig. 1-10). Originally intended for Lafayette Park and completed several years before, the statue had not been erected because the sculptor's fee had not been paid in full. The commissioners paid the balance to buy the statue for Forest Park.

Primarily, the commissioners gave priority to administrative buildings and roads. A new frame boarding house near the southern edge of the park housed the large labor force. Robert Forsyth's house became a restaurant called the Cottage. The Cabanne house, in the former dairy land near the eastern edge of the park, provided office space during construction of the new headquarters building, a solid structure of brick on a stone foundation (Fig. 1-12). After the headquarters building was completed, the Cabanne house was torn down (Fig. 1-11).[23]

The park work force built all the roads except the boulevard near Kingshighway, which was built by the lowest bidder, Jerry Fruin and Company. McKinley reported that the cost of constructing gravel roads was about $16,000 a mile. Along the roads were drain pipes covered by gutters. The road system included eight rustic bridges over the River des Peres, one iron and the rest of wood, and a railroad viaduct over the main drive.

The lakes were all artificial. They were five feet deep and filled through pipes with water from the River des Peres, from the Cabanne Spring, and with storm water runoff from the park, all propelled by a steam pump and controlled by a system of valves. Park engineer Henry Flad reported that the water supply would soon be insufficient, an assertion that proved correct.

Two other problems plagued commissioners for years to come—Clayton Road and the River des Peres. Clayton Road, through the southeastern section of the park, was a major thoroughfare, since there were no roads along the northern or southern boundaries. St. Louis County farmers used the road to bring wagonloads of hay and produce into town, not the kind of traffic the commissioners wanted in the park. Kern reported in 1876 that he "confidently hoped" Clayton Road would soon be removed from the south-

eastern section of the park, but it wasn't. Union Avenue no longer crossed the land north to south, as it had before the park was established. Traffic went either to Kingshighway or to Skinker Road. These two roads seem to have absorbed the traffic easily, at least for a time.

The River des Peres, Kern said, was a "wild and uncontrollable prairie stream, sufficiently strong to float a stern-wheel steamer at certain times, at others almost devoid of water." Park commissioners would complain of flooding by the River des Peres until it was put underground in the 1920s.

The county court tightly controlled park funds, requiring a warrant explaining in detail the reason for each expenditure of more than $500. The county counselor ruled that the county court could refuse to make payments approved by the park commissioners. In fact, however, the park commissioners seem to have been more prudent managers than the county court. A citizen's committee chaired by Walter C. Carr investigated park finances and reported that "the money spent on work in the Park had been judiciously used." The most controversial expenditure was the payment of $7,000 to the county counselor for his legal work in connection with the park, an expense approved by the county court, not the park commissioners.[24]

Still, the money available was being spent quickly. Of the $1.3 million authorized by the state legislature, more than a million dollars had been spent by January 1876, including almost $800,000 to buy the land. Roads, bridges, walkways, lakes, and construction near the railroad line had cost more than $136,000, buildings about $9,000, and the Bates statue $3,000. The commission estimated that more than $150,000 worth of improvements were still needed, for which more than $40,000 had already been committed.

The park tax was not yet available, and much of it would be needed to pay the principal and interest on the bonds. Except for about $2,000 in park income, mostly from the sale of hay and wood from the park land, the money came from the park bonds, which were sold as funds were required.

St. Louisans did not wait for the official dedication of the park to begin their visits. Many came to inspect the work in progress. As opening day approached, interest grew. Two weeks before the opening, visitors attended a concert held to test the acoustics of the new bandstand. The next day, a Sunday, an unusually large crowd went to the park, according to the *Democrat*, though "the heat was a trifle excessive."[25] On June 20, 1876, four days before the park officially opened, the new railroad through the park made its first run, an excursion for the officers of the railroad company and other prominent citizens. The company provided an hour-long carriage ride through the park, past the statue of Edward Bates, shrouded until opening day, past the music pagoda, to the Cottage restaurant, and then back to the waiting train.

Much had been accomplished by opening day. Nineteen miles of driving road and twenty miles of "promenade walks" were usable, though only five miles of road and three miles of walk-way were complete (Fig. 1-13). The road bridges were in place, but the tunnel and viaduct to separate the drives from the railroad tracks were still under construction. The Hippodrome racetrack awaited "young bloods and lovers of horse flesh." The artificial lakes were full and appeared natural. Scattered around the park were numerous kiosks, pagodas, and other buildings, including the wooden bandstand, entirely surrounded by an artificial lake and accessible by bridges. The headquarters building was open, complete with a basement for use "as a calaboose for refractory visitors."

Commission President Andrew McKinley reminded the opening-day crowd of the long struggle for the park and praised the work of Kern, Pitzman, Flad, and Link. Then everyone

1-13. Many parkgoers reached Forest Park on horseback or in a carriage.

moved a short distance to witness the unveiling of the statue of Edward Bates. Chauncy F. Shultz, presiding justice of the county court, said:

> I present to you, the people of the County of St. Louis, your own, this large and beautiful Forest Park for the enjoyment of yourselves, your children and your children's children forever. . . . The rich and poor, the merchant and mechanic, the professional man and the day laborer, each with his family and lunch basket, can come here and enjoy his own . . . all without stint or hindrance . . . and there will be no notice put up, "Keep Off the Grass."

The park would not, however, belong to the people of St. Louis County much longer. Its ownership would soon change and the Forest Park commissioners be put out of office by the separation of the city of St. Louis from St. Louis County.

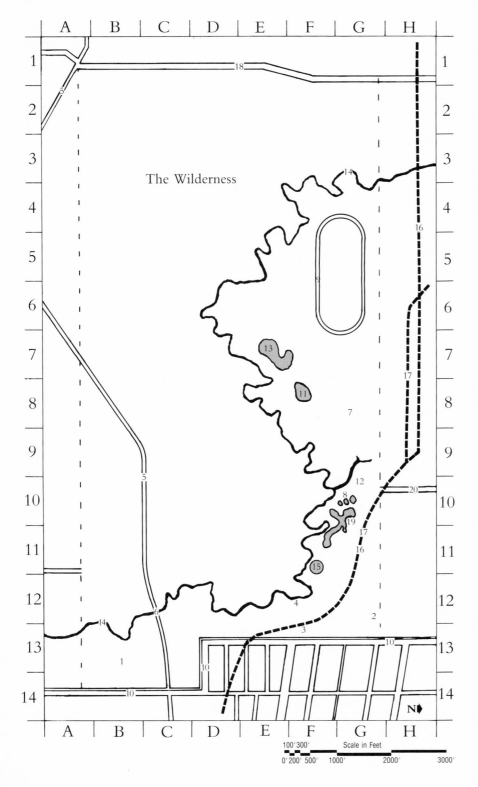

PARK LOCATOR MAP*
(1876–1885)

1. Bates, Edward, statue, B-13
2. Blair, Francis P., Jr., statue, G-12
3. Cabanne House, F-13
4. Cabanne Spring (probable location), F-12
5. Clayton Road (later Avenue), A-1 to C-14
6. Clayton Road bridge, C-12
7. Cottage restaurant (first location formerly Forsyth farmhouse), G-8
8. Fish hatchery lakes (original), G-10
9. Hippodrome racetrack, F-6 to G-4
10. King's Highway (later Kingshighway Boulevard), A-14 to H-13
Music pagoda (bandstand), see 11, F-8
11. Pagoda Lake, F-8
12. Park keeper's house (headquarters building), G-10
13. Peninsular Lake, E-7
14. River des Peres, A-13 to H-3
15. Round Pond (later Round Lake), F-11
16. St. Louis County Railroad (proposed), D-14 to H-1
17. St. Louis, Kansas City and Northern (later Wabash, then Norfolk and Western) Railroad, D-14 to H-6
18. Skinker Road (later Skinker Boulevard), A-1 to H-1
19. Sylvan Lake, F-11 to G-10
20. Union Avenue (later Union Boulevard), H-10

*No reliable maps were available for these years. Unverifiable items, such as park roads, were not included on this map.

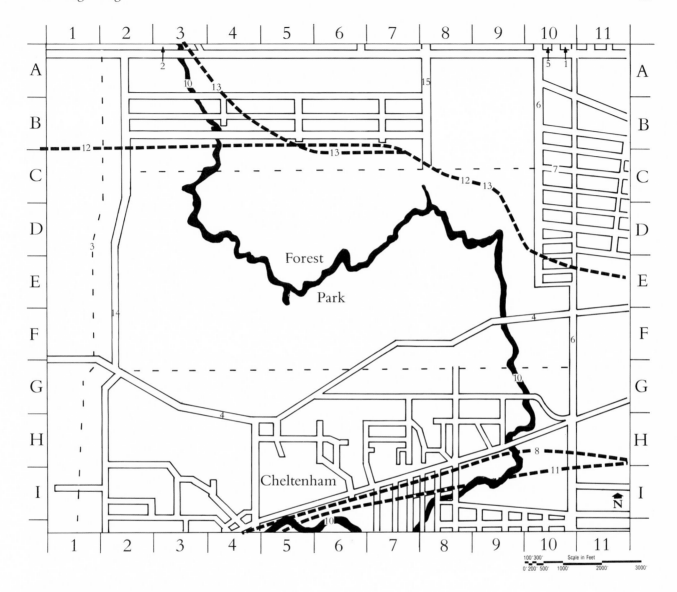

NEIGHBORHOOD LOCATOR MAP
(1876–1885)

1. Aubert Place, A-10
2. Bartmer's Subdivision, A-3
3. City limits (1876 and after), A-2 to I-1
4. Clayton Road (later Clayton Avenue), G-1 to F-11
5. Forest Park Subdivision, A-10
6. King's Highway (later Kingshighway Boulevard), A-10 to I-10
7. Lindell Avenue (later Lindell Boulevard), C-10 and 11
8. Missouri Pacific Railroad tracks, I-4 to H-11

9. Olive Street Grove, A-11
10. River des Peres, A-3 to I-5
11. St. Louis and San Francisco Railroad tracks, I-5 to I-11
12. St. Louis County Railroad route, proposed (later Rock Island Railroad tracks), C-1 to E-11
13. St. Louis, Kansas City and Northern (later Wabash, then Norfolk and Southern) Railroad tracks, A-3 to E-11
14. Skinker Road (later Skinker Boulevard), A-2 to G-2
15. Union Avenue (later Union Boulevard), A-8 to C-8

2

DIVORCE AND SEPARATE MAINTENANCE (1876–1885)

I am aware that in times of diminished revenues the parks are apt to be looked upon by many as . . . a . . . luxury . . . dependent upon the crumbs that fall from the municipal table, but the city must soon display greater liberality . . . for . . . this step child of the city government, or our public parks will ere long show traces of wear and neglect.—Park Commissioner Eugene F. Weigel, 1882

Between 1876 and 1885, Forest Park changed very little physically, though its legal and financial arrangements changed radically. When the city of St. Louis and St. Louis County separated, the city took over Forest Park, abolishing the Forest Park Commissioners and the Forest Park tax. At the same time, the city extended its boundaries past the park. As the city struggled to provide services like water, sewers, and streets to the new area, parks were a low priority, especially the large, remote ones such as Forest Park.

A new Missouri constitution, adopted in 1875, contained a section the *Dispatch* called "The Municipal Divorce Bill," which defined a procedure for the separation of city and county, after years of conflict over numerous issues. The voters of St. Louis and St. Louis County could elect a board of thirteen freeholders "to propose a scheme" of separation. The constitution stipulated that if the city and county separated, the city would take over the parks and the park tax and assume the entire county debt. The city could choose to extend its boundaries past Carondelet, O'Fallon, and Forest parks. The freeholders were elected on April 4, 1876, and were required by the constitution to finish the plan before July 4.[1]

The question of city boundaries was very controversial. Freeholder Dwight Collier argued for the extended boundaries, saying that a little town would grow up around Forest Park so that when the city later annexed the area, as it would

surely do, the streets wouldn't join easily. The *Globe-Democrat*, on the other hand, argued that extension of the city "into the wilderness is a piece of folly which will ruin the most flourishing municipality in the country." David H. Armstrong told his fellow freeholders that he opposed taking in "divers and sundry corn-fields and melon-patches" since the current city limits could "accommodate a city the size of London."

The boundary question was one of the last to be decided as the board hurried to meet its July 4 deadline. In an apparent rush, the Forest Park Commissioners opened the park on Saturday, June 24, even though their work on the park wasn't complete, perhaps in a effort to convince the freeholders that the park should lie within the new city boundaries. The *Globe-Democrat* described the park as "by no means in a finished condition," and Commissioner Chauncy F. Shultz said that "the rude condition of many portions of the Park show that much remains to be done." Whatever the reasons, two days later, on Monday, the board of freeholders voted to extend the city limits to include the area around the park.

The board of freeholders produced two documents: The Scheme of Separation of St. Louis City and County, and a new City Charter. On August 22 the scheme of separation was submitted to the voters of the entire county; the charter only to the voters within the enlarged city limits. At first it seemed that the scheme of separation

2-1. Racing buggies like this one may have been used at the Hippodrome track in Forest Park in 1877.

had been defeated. However, after charges of widespread voter fraud, the Missouri Supreme Court ruled on April 26, 1877, eight months after the election, that both the scheme and charter had been adopted.

Forest Park became one of sixteen city parks, administered by the city park commissioner, who was appointed by the mayor. After the court decision, several months passed before the separation was complete and all the new city officials appointed. From the court decision in April until the new commissioner took office in September, all of the city parks were administered by Theodore C. Link, who had served as Forest Park draughtsman under the Forest Park Commissioners. The first park commissioner appointed under the new charter, lawyer Eugene F. Weigel,

took office in September 1877, and served until 1887. Although Andrew McKinley, president of the Forest Park Commissioners, lived in St. Louis until his death in 1889, he was never again active in park administration.

People continued to enjoy Forest Park as they had before the separation, despite its remoteness and relative lack of facilities. Until the summer of 1885, the only public transportation to Forest Park was on the trains that stopped just outside the grounds, trains operated by the Wabash Railroad after 1879 (Fig. 2-2). The *Globe-Democrat* said, "The fact that [Forest Park] lies beyond the reach of all streetcar lines has thus far prevented its becoming a popular institution." The Sunday crowd consisted "almost entirely of people in vehicles and on horseback."[2]

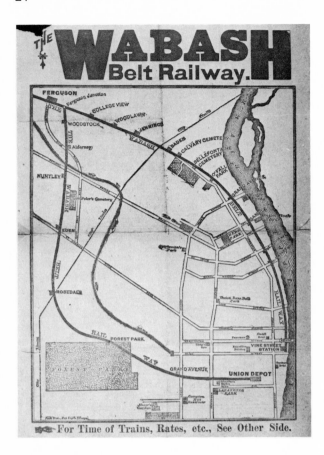

2-2. Wabash Railroad route some time between 1879 and 1894. Until 1885 the trains offered the only public transportation to Forest Park.

Even for people who drove, the trip to Forest Park was difficult. The best road to the park, Lindell, was a dirt road until the late 1880s, and Park Commissioner Weigel reported that "the drive to Forest Park on a hot afternoon against the scorching sun is anything but pleasant."

Still, in good weather St. Louisans braved the drive to reach the park's green shade. One Sunday the *Republican* reported that "throughout the entire day there was a steady stream of vehicles winding through the roads of the park to its remotest recesses, and there was probably no time from two in the afternoon until six when there were not several thousand people in the park." Even those not wealthy enough to own a

carriage could rent equipment for a drive to the park. The *Globe-Democrat* noted:

> The high and the low, the rich and the poor, the banker and the mechanic, alike enjoy the exhilarating effects of a drive, and it is no very uncommon sight to see the mechanic whizzing by the monied monopolist. . . . On Sunday every clerk who has $5 to spare has a rig out, and gets a week's enjoyment in one day.

Forest Park was the usual destination. The Forest Park drives also attracted the "young lady pupils" of a riding school that was "aiming to make riding a popular amusement" in St. Louis (Fig. 2-3).[3]

At the Hippodrome, the park's one-mile racetrack, visitors could watch races that the *Republican* called "little trots between gentlemen's roadsters," and "a test of speed between horses that are owned and driven on the road by private individuals" (Fig. 2-1). But, the paper emphasized, "No betting . . . is permitted, and those who at first opposed the races at the park now take as much interest in them as anyone else." Sometimes the racers competed for trophies, such as the Greeley cup, "an elegant $200 silver cup, offered by Mr. Chas. B. Greeley" beginning in June 1877. After races in October 1877 and May 1878, the track was apparently not much used.[4]

Forest Park was also the site of large picnics in these years. Schools, churches, fraternal organizations, and other groups made arrangements with the railroad for special car accommodations and obtained picnic permits from the park commissioner. For the fiscal year that included the summer of 1881, Weigel issued forty-eight permits to groups such as Soulard Market Mission Sunday School, Lafayette Park Presbyterian Church, St. Bridget's Church, Lincoln Public School, Shaw Public School, the Order of Foresters, and the Turner Association.

The Turner Picnic, for example, attracted more than five thousand members of the Turner gymnastic societies who had come from as far as New York and New Orleans for several days of games and competitions in June of 1881 (Fig.

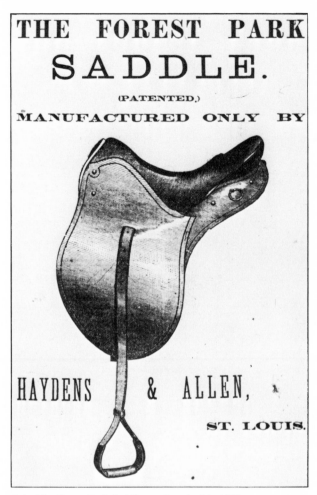

THE FOREST PARK
SADDLE.
(PATENTED,)
MANUFACTURED ONLY BY

HAYDENS & ALLEN,
ST. LOUIS.

2-3. The Forest Park Saddle as advertised in 1879.

2-4). After the games at the Agricultural and Mechanical Fair Grounds (which later became Fairground Park) and a parade downtown, the *Globe-Democrat* reported, "the men . . . crowded into the cars of the Wabash line that were to take them to the pleasure grounds of Forest Park."[5]

Celebrating the Fourth of July in Forest Park became a St. Louis custom. According to the *Globe-Democrat*, however, the celebration in 1879 was "a fiasco." "Train after train came in, but no audience." Perhaps nobody went because the celebration was sponsored by the Prohibitionists.[6]

By 1883 Forest Park and Creve Coeur Lake in western St. Louis County were, the *Post-*

Dispatch reported, the most popular destinations for those leaving Union Depot. "Extra trains were put on, and all the coaches that could be begged, borrowed or bought were pressed into service; yet it was literally true that you could not see the trains, as they moved out, for the people. They hung on cars from every projection. . . . The crowd was [one of] the largest that ever left the Union depot on a Fourth of July."[7]

On the Fourth of July the following year, 1884, Commissioner Weigel noted that "as many as twelve different schools and societies" had picnics in the park, including Zion Hope Sunday School, Martha Washington Council, Cottage and First Swedish M. E. Sunday schools, and the Secret Bumble Bee Club. "All were easily accommodated in different parts of the park, so as not to interfere with each other."[8]

With the separation of city and county, the area of the city more than tripled, from 17.98 square miles to 61.37 square miles. The new city charter had abolished the special Forest Park tax, so funds came from a city budget already stretched to provide city services to the vast new area. Funds for parks, especially Carondelet, O'Fallon, and Forest parks, were a very low priority. Mayor Henry Overstolz said in 1877 that he would consider selling portions of the three large parks, which the city neither wanted nor needed, if real estate prices improved from their depressed condition. Henry Flad, president of the board of public improvements, defended the large parks. Flad, who had served as Forest Park chief engineer under the commissioners, became the first president of the board of public improvements in 1876 and held the position until 1890. In that position, he worked to provide streets, wharves, drinking water, and electric lights for a growing city, leaving his stamp, the *Post-Dispatch* said, on "a thousand improvements all over the city," including Forest Park. Flad pointed out to Mayor Overstolz in 1878 that a growing city should own more park land than it currently needed in order to provide for future generations.[9]

2-4. The Turner games at the fairgrounds attracted competitors to St. Louis from around the nation. More than 5,000 men enjoyed a picnic in Forest Park afterwards.

Although Forest Park retained all its land, it did not receive a share of the revenue proportionate to its size, as Weigel concentrated on finishing the landscaping of the small, more accessible parks. Forest Park, with more than three quarters of the city's park acreage, received less than one quarter of the city's park expenditures throughout this period. At first work was financed entirely from the $45,000 remaining from the sale of Forest Park bonds and collection of the park tax, transferred from the county to the city and credited to a Forest Park fund. Late collections of the park tax added more than $15,000 before 1879, but were insignificant after that. Commissioner Weigel stretched these funds as far as he could, reserving, he said, "a large portion . . . for future emergencies." Small amounts of Forest Park revenue came from the sale of wood, hay, and ice, and from payments for the privileges of watering horses and selling refreshments. Beginning in 1882, Weigel discontinued the previous practice of selling ice from the lakes, leaving the surface intact for skaters.[10]

After the funds transferred from the county were exhausted, Forest Park was included in the city park appropriation. The funds were always inadequate. In 1882 Weigel reported that the city spent less money for the maintenance of 1,800 acres of park land than it had for 80 acres before the separation. He realized, he wrote, that parks were likely to be considered a luxury, "dependent upon the crumbs that fall from the municipal table." Without more money, however, they would soon show signs of neglect.[11]

Commissioner Weigel did the best he could with the sums available. In October 1877, soon after he took office, the *Republican* reported that the "condition of neglect into which Forest Park has fallen [during the uncertainties surrounding the court battle over the scheme and charter] has attracted general attention and regret." After an inspection visit, Weigel increased the labor force to thirty. The men cleared undergrowth, removed dead wood and stumps, and filled up more than sixty coal pits and air holes left from coal mining under the land in the 1850s and 1860s. After the initial cleanup, the work force concentrated on the 500-acre "wilderness," the forest in the western and southwestern portions of the park. By 1880 the wilderness had been cleared of underbrush, decreasing the danger of forest fire, and giving young trees a better chance to grow.[12]

2-5. Getting a drink at the Cabanne Spring, probably before the 1879 installation of a steam pump.

In addition to clearing the wilderness, Weigel concentrated his funds on maintaining the park roads. The rustic wooden bridges, admired on opening day in 1876, needed constant repairs. In 1884 Weigel considered that some of the bridges had "become so unsafe that they must be rebuilt or entirely closed to the public." [13]

One bridge, the Clayton Road bridge, was not Weigel's responsibility. As a major connecting link between the county and the city of St. Louis, the road was the responsibility of the city street commissioner. In September 1878, the street commissioner barricaded the bridge and declared it unsafe, arousing the suspicions of St. Louis County farmers that their rights to haul loads through the park were being denied. The bridge was shored up temporarily until construction of a new twenty-foot-wide stone and iron bridge in 1881–1882. [14]

The roads and gutters had to be weeded. Roads periodically needed to be regraveled. In dry weather, park roads were sprinkled with water to reduce dust. As traffic inside the park increased, so did dust, and in 1884, Weigel re-

Forest Park Restaurant.

The most delightful resort about the city.

The Table is supplied with the choicest dishes, and the attention is always courteous. Parties from two up to twenty easily accommodated.

Prices not above those of first-class city restaurants.

C. W. HERBERT, Proprietor.

2-6. In 1881 C. W. Herbert unsuccessfully operated the park restaurant (called the Cottage) in the old Forsyth farmhouse. Charles Schweickardt's operation, beginning in 1885, fared much better.

ported, "the dust occasioned by the countless carriages and buggies is almost intolerable."[15]

As Henry Flad 'had predicted in 1876, the water supply soon proved insufficient for all of its uses—drinking, sprinkling the roads, watering the plants, and filling the lakes. Before the summer of 1879 the water system was expanded "so as to furnish good drinking water to the pic-nic grounds" (Fig. 2-5).[16] A steam pump lifted water from Cabanne Spring to a 5,000-gallon reservoir "protected by a rustic straw-thatched shed." From there the water fed three drinking fountains. The pump also filled the lakes through fountains. Hot weather, however, caused more water to evaporate than the spring could replace. Trees, shrubs, and flowers had to depend on rainfall because city water lines didn't yet reach the park. In droughts, such as the summer of 1881, many plants died.

In 1878 Weigel pointed out the difficulties of buying plants through the city's supply commissioner. Weigel sometimes accepted trees and shrubs that were "not what they should be" because he feared that by the time the supply commissioner had advertised and accepted new suppliers the planting season would be over. Forest Park had plenty of room to raise trees for use all over the city, and thus stretch the money budgeted for parks. By the spring of 1879 Weigel had established a fifteen-acre tree nursery in Forest Park, "stocked with about seventy-five thousand young maples, elms, sycamores, lindens and box-elder, which were gathered . . . at but nominal expense to the city."[17]

The nursery did well. In 1882 it supplied replacements for all the trees that had died from drought in the city's parks, as well as trees for the

2-7. Philip Kopplin, Jr., left, worked for the Missouri Fish Commission (later the Missouri Conservation Commission) caring for the fish in Forest Park until his death in 1932. Then his son, E. Mortimer Kopplin, to the right, who had been his assistant, became hatchery supervisor.

2-8. This photograph of the statue of Francis P. Blair, Jr., was taken after 1904, when the land north of Forest Park had become a fashionable neighborhood.

grounds of the mental institution, poor house, city hospital, and courthouse. The nursery in Forest Park and the greenhouses in Benton and Hyde parks provided the park department with all its plants that year.

To supply facilities his budget didn't cover, Weigel turned to other sources of funds, especially two that would be important for the next hundred years—concessions and donations. Concessions allowed the city to provide park attractions without risking city funds. Indeed, the concessionaire paid the city for the privilege.

When the city took over the park, Mr. Aimee

Garnier operated the Cottage restaurant under a lease granted by the Forest Park Commissioners. After his lease expired June 1, 1878, the city approved a series of short-term leases. In the spring of 1880 the *Republican* announced that the restaurant was under new management "completely refitted and refurnished," and operated by a staff that included the former chief cook of the Southern Hotel downtown and the former manager of a racetrack restaurant in Chicago.[18]

But the operation did not prosper. In 1881 C. W. Herbert took over the restaurant lease but found himself in competition with E. R. James, who held a new concession, the right to sell candy, ice cream, popcorn, lemonade, and soda water at the picnic grounds. The city tried several different arrangements for the Cottage and the picnic grounds, none of which lasted more than a year, until a March 1885 ordinance awarded the restaurant lease to Charles Schweickardt, who held it for almost twenty years (Fig. 2-6).

Another attraction that didn't require city funds was the Missouri Fish Commission's fish-rearing operation in the Forest Park lakes. Although the commission did not pay for the privilege of using the park lakes, state funds supported its activities, which Weigel believed would prove "a source of amusement and instruction to the visitors." In 1879 the fish commission stocked one of the ponds with 250 German carp, imported from Bremen, Germany, and hired Philip Kopplin, Jr., to pump water for them (Fig. 2-7). (Kopplin's father had been overseer of the park work force as early as December 1877 and would later become Forest Park Keeper. As keeper he lived in the house inside the park's Union entrance, the structure the Forest Park Commissioners had built as their headquarters.) In early 1881 the city tried to persuade the fish commission to locate a major new hatchery in Forest Park but failed because of the lack of "plenty of pure, cold spring water." However, the commission stocked additional ponds.[19]

The carp spawned in the spring of 1882, and in the fall 11,500 young carp were removed from the lakes and distributed throughout Missouri. In February 1883 a new city ordinance granted the fish commission the use of the Forest Park lakes until January 1898. The fish commission could use any of the existing lakes in the park except the lake that surrounded the bandstand. In addition, the commission could build additional lakes with the approval of city officials. The city reserved the right to allow boating, but not fishing, on any of the lakes.[20] Kopplin continued to care for the carp, becoming acting superintendent of hatchery ponds in Forest Park in 1883 and superintendent in 1886.

Weigel tried to attract donations for the park, with little success. An 1882 ordinance authorized the park commissioner to accept donations, with the approval of the board of public improvements. Weigel reported that because his budget was so limited, he was unable to fund band concerts in the music pagoda. He asked for donations, but no donor appeared, so there were no regular band concerts in the park until the 1890s. Nor could Weigel persuade the Wabash railroad to provide a shelter to protect parkgoers from sudden thunderstorms while they waited for trains.

The only donation Weigel accepted for Forest Park before 1885 was the statue of Sen. Francis P. Blair, Jr., who had died in 1875 (Fig. 2-8). In 1876 the Forest Park Commissioners had told the Blair Monument Association that as soon as a statue was ready they would "gladly appropriate any suitable grounds that may be asked for." In 1883, after considering sites around the city, the association selected a Forest Park location, which Commissioner Weigel approved. The city appropriated $650 for the foundation, and the monument association supplied the statue, which was erected in 1885.[21]

Like the park, the land and the roads around the park changed little between 1876 and 1885. In 1878 the city street commissioner rejected a request for road improvement on Skinker because "a fully improved road will not be required for many years, if it ever is."[22] But the situation would soon change. As the city grew toward the eastern edge of Forest Park, city services reached the park, beginning in 1885, bringing major changes to the neighborhood and to the park.

3

MORE PEOPLE, MORE USES (1885–1901)

Access to all the parks has been rendered so cheap and convenient by increased . . . street railway facilities, . . . that now the humble pedestrian may enjoy an hour in the parks as cheerfully and often as the man who owns a carriage.—Park Commissioner Richard Klemm, 1890

With the extension of streetcar lines to the park in 1885 and a growing demand for active recreation, hundreds of thousands of people went to Forest Park each year to enjoy the old pastimes as well as many new ones. By 1901 the park had begun to live up to the plans of Andrew McKinley and M. G. Kern. As park advocates had intended, the park also began to influence its neighborhood, and the fashionable residences they had envisioned began to develop.

Four park commissioners worked to cope with this explosive increase in use. In an unsuccessful attempt to keep the parks out of politics, the 1876 city charter provided that a mayor had to wait until he had been in office two years before he could appoint a new park commissioner. When Republican Mayor William L. Ewing succeeded Independent Henry Overstolz in 1881, he kept Eugene F. Weigel in office. Democrat David R. Francis, however, replaced Weigel in 1887 with Richard Klemm, a German-trained engineer who had been a superintendent in the city street department. Mayor Edward A. Noonan, though also a Democrat, replaced Francis's appointee four years later with Jonathan P. Fechter, an active Democratic ward worker who, before he was appointed park commissioner, worked for a wholesale millinery company. Republicans Cyrus P. Walbridge and Henry Ziegenhein both appointed Franklin L. Ridgely, who served from 1895 until 1903. Ridgely had business experience, having been president of the Wiggins Ferry Company

and of the East St. Louis Connecting Railroad, and moved in St. Louis's elite business and social circles. As best they could, these park commissioners provided and maintained activities, facilities, and security for parkgoers, using public and private funds in a variety of combinations.

The first streetcar line, a horsecar, reached the northeastern portion of Forest Park in early June 1885, almost nine years after the park opened. The Wabash Railroad still ran from downtown to the park, offering five trips a day at a fifteen-cent fare, but the streetcars were much cheaper and easier to use (Fig. 3-2). They ran at least every half hour from 5:30 A.M. until midnight. The adult fare to the park was five cents; children were half price. Park Commissioner Klemm wrote in 1890, "Access to all the parks has been rendered so cheap and convenient . . . that now the humble pedestrian may enjoy an hour in the parks as cheerfully and often as the man who owns a carriage." An 1892 book, *St. Louis Through a Camera*, said, "every Sunday the . . . street car lines . . . are taxed to the utmost capacity to accommodate the tens of thousands" of passengers to Forest Park. By 1896 the seven streetcar lines that served Forest Park carried a total of more than two and a half million parkgoers a year. [1]

The streetcars quickly ended the complaint that the park was easily accessible only to the man who owned a carriage. Thousands of St. Louisans could now follow the advice doctors often gave for an ailing child—"take the child to Forest

3-1. Bicycling became a popular pastime in the park at the turn of the century. These wheelmen pose at the Blair statue on their way to St. Louis County.

Park, madame, medicine won't do it any good, it's air the little thing needs."[2] Often women and children spent an entire summer day there, joined in early evening by the men of the family when they finished their day's work.

Even five cents, though, was beyond the reach of the poorest (presumably those most in need of a "breathing place" away from the smoke, dirt, and heat of the city). So, during one unusually hot summer, as city residents literally died from the heat, the streetcar companies offered free transportation from the baking streets and brick buildings of the city to the comparative cool and shade of the park for children ten and under. The children, accompanied by an adult member of the family, could ride free upon presentation of a doctor's certificate, if they could afford to see a doctor.

In the 1890s park administrators succeeded where their predecessors had failed—in getting shelters for park travelers. Despite repeated pleas, the Wabash Railroad never built a shelter at its Forest Park stop. But when the city awarded streetcar routes to Forest Park, it required two companies (the Forest Park, Laclede and Fourth Street Railway Company, called the Laclede; and

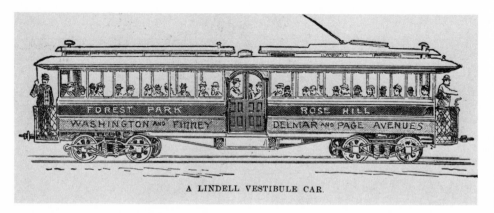

A LINDELL VESTIBULE CAR.

3-2. The first streetcar line reached Forest Park in 1885. By 1896 the seven streetcar lines that served Forest Park carried a total of more than 2.5 million parkgoers a year.

3-3. The Lindell Pavilion, which opened in 1892, provided shelter for streetcar passengers from hot sun or sudden showers. A portion of the tower still stood in the 1980s.

the Lindell Railway Company) to supply passenger shelters at their stops in Forest Park. Each company was required to spend at least $25,000 on its waiting room, which became city property as soon as it was constructed, though it continued to be named for the company that built it. The Lindell Pavilion opened by 1892 at the north central entrance to the park (Fig. 3-3). The Laclede Pavilion, at the northeastern entrance, opened in 1893. The architectural firm of Eames and Young designed both of the large open structures. In addition, Commissioner Ridgely reported the existence of a Missouri Pavilion, which seems to have been a less elaborate structure located in the southeastern corner of the park.

While thousands of people arrived at the park on the trains and the streetcars, others drove their carriages and buggies. Still others in the 1890s used that new method of transportation and nationwide craze, the bicycle, sometimes

called "the silent steed." Bicyclists, often called wheelmen though many were women, rode from downtown St. Louis to Forest Park, a distance of about four miles (Fig. 3-1). "The afternoon is the favorite riding time and groups of pretty girls may be seen dashing over the western approaches to the park, disappearing onto its shady lanes," the *Post-Dispatch* reported.[3] Riders who wished a longer ride would tour into the countryside of St. Louis County, going perhaps to Ballwin after meeting in Forest Park.

Cyclists conducted races, such as the 1894 Forest Park bicycle race, which were popular with participants and spectators. Cyclists came from as far away as Chicago to compete for the *Post-Dispatch* medal, made by the Mermod-Jaccard Jewelry Company, and other prizes, including four bicycles. The race was held annually for about three years and then periodically revived during the early 1900s.

3-4. A view in the middle 1970s of a footbridge built in the late 1880s to provide a pedestrian route into the park from the streetcar stop nearby.

The large numbers of pedestrians and bicyclists, added to the continuing stream of horses and carriages, soon made the park's road system inadequate. Commissioners Fechter and Ridgely requested funds for a separate bridle path, a bicycle path, and pedestrian walkways. The walkways came first, installed over a period of years, with footbridges where necessary (Fig. 3-4). After that the *Post-Dispatch* noted "the magnificent equipages of the wealthier classes, driving side by side with the humbler turnout of the middle classes, all watched by the poorest, who, with perfect independence, trudge on foot through the footpaths."[4]

At the same time, park officials worked to maintain the park's road system, gradually replacing the wooden road bridges with more permanent structures. These new bridges seemed to deserve names, instead of being numbered like the previous ones. So in 1892 Fechter named Carr Lane Bridge for William Carr Lane, the first mayor of St. Louis, and named the other bridges for heroes of United States history: Columbus, de Soto, Washington, Jefferson, Franklin, Lafayette, Steuben, and Lincoln. But in 1896 more than half of the roads in the park were still what Commissioner Ridgely called "mud roads," which were "very dusty during dry weather and almost impassable after a good spell of rain."[5]

And the cyclists were still on the park roads. Carriage drivers complained about bicycle riders on the roads, and cyclists complained about the roads. In 1895 a "meeting of wheelmen" in Forest

SCENE AT THE LINDELL BOULEVARD ENTRANCE TO FOREST PARK ON SUNDAY AFTERNOON.

3-5. The cyclists fill park roads in 1896. Blair statue is visible to the right, Laclede Pavilion to the left.

Park had called the city's attention to potholes and puddles in roads throughout the city. A street department employee agreed that bicycling required "a careful readjustment of old notions about what will do for a road."[6]

An 1896 ordinance provided some traffic separation by requiring "all persons driving vehicles of any kind on the park roadways, and . . . all persons riding horses, bicycles or tricycles . . . to keep to the right of the center" or risk a fine of five dollars to twenty-five dollars (Fig. 3-5).[7] Two years later cyclists had what they wanted—a cinder bicycle path. It opened May 7, 1898, with a bicycle parade to honor completion of the path, to thank the city for building it and to urge that the proceeds of the bicycle license tax be set aside for improvement and extension of park bicycle paths, a suggestion that was not adopted.

It was not enough, however, to supply ways for people to get to the park and get around in it. They wanted something to do when they got there. Besides bicycle riding, many parkgoers enjoyed other forms of athletics, which entertained both participants and spectators. Spectators could cheer local teams playing cricket, lacrosse, football, and baseball on the park's broad lawns, or watch tournaments in tennis or what the *Post-Dispatch* called in 1894 the "new fad of golf."[8]

Horse fanciers could participate in the revival of harness racing. More active parkgoers could play at lawn tennis or croquet or drive burros or ponies.

Horse racing at the Hippodrome had been available at the park since opening day, a tradition that the Gentlemen's Driving Club had revived in the 1880s. The private club used a half-mile speeding track inside the one-mile Hippodrome track and invited the public to attend harness races by trotters and pacers. In 1887 the city had agreed to construct the speeding track if the club would pay the cost of construction and maintenance, which it did. The driving club paid the city $500 to build the track and then $100 a year for maintenance. The city used all of the club's payment for work on the track, retaining nothing as rent for the use of park land. An 1894 ordinance removed the requirement for an annual club payment and opened use of the track to "all persons."[9]

Unlike the races sponsored by the St. Louis Agricultural and Mechanical Association at their fairgrounds (later Fairground Park), the Forest Park races were free of charge, the *Post-Dispatch* emphasized, and were also "free from that spirit which is fast relegating the turf to professionalism. It is not intended to imply that money

How the Lunch Was Served.

3-6. The ladies of the Lake Fund Lunch Association arrived in their carriages at ten o'clock every morning to prepare a hot lunch of sausage, bread, and coffee for the workers extending Peninsular Lake. The work, financed by money raised by the *Post-Dispatch*, provided work for the unemployed during the winter of 1893–94. The newspaper then referred to the lake as Post-Dispatch Lake.

never changes hands at Forest Park meetings—but bookmaking and systematic betting arrangements are entirely wanting there."[10]

The St. Louis Amateur Athletic Association (AAA or Triple A) was formed in 1897, ten years after the driving club moved into Forest Park. Commissioner Ridgely gave Triple A permission to use a portion of Forest Park near the racetrack. The group immediately built a clubhouse, tennis courts, a baseball diamond, and a nine-hole golf course. In many ways, the club's operation resembled that of the driving club. It emphasized amateurism and invited the public to attend, but not participate in, its competitions.[11] Both the Cricket Club and the Lacrosse Club also maintained grounds in the park. Another lawn was considered the YMCA ballground. These organizations, like Triple A, maintained their own facilities but paid nothing for the use of park land.

Ice-skating and boating occupied the park lakes, and a lake extension in the early 1890s provided more room. The 1890 ordinance that gave the Lindell Railway Company the right to run a streetcar line into Forest Park required the company to provide a passenger shelter at its stop and to pay $25,000 to share in the cost of enlarging the park's major lake "to a length of about three-fourths of a mile." Because boating was so popular, company officials later explained, they determined that the money was an investment in attracting people to ride the line. The company's share of the funds to build the lake extension was to be paid only after the city had appropriated its portion. By 1893 the company had built the car line and the shelter but hadn't paid for the lake extension, because the city hadn't provided its share of the funds.

The financial panic of 1893 gave the city another reason to want the lake extension, providing work for the unemployed (Fig. 3-6). Beginning in January 1894 the *Post-Dispatch* conducted a campaign to raise additional money for the expansion. The paper printed each donor's name and the amount of every gift. The streetcar company immediately pledged $20,000 and was released from its earlier obligation to the city.[12] Be-

3-7. After completion of the lake extension in June 1894, even more people could rent a boat to row. As this picture illustrates, many of the rowers were women.

fore the campaign ended, donations in addition to the company's money exceeded $19,000, at a time when $1.00 would buy fifty pounds of flour and a man's suit cost about $7.50.

City contract-letting procedures took so long, the *Post-Dispatch* explained, they would "defeat the purpose of furnishing employment to the unemployed through the hardest stress of winter." Instead, the city authorized three respected private citizens, Samuel J. Nicolls, Henry C. Haarstick, and Thomas O'Reilly, to contract to have the work done. Work began in mid-February. By the time the extension was completed in mid-June, about 6,000 men had registered for work, and the *Post-Dispatch* said, "not one dollar . . . went to a professional mendicant."[13] A balance of about $6,000 remained in the lake fund. In February 1895 the amount, together with accumulated interest at three percent, was spent to build a lake in Carondelet Park.

The expanded Forest Park lake was immediately popular, summer and winter. The conces-

sionaire who had offered boats for rent in the park for two years couldn't keep up with the increased demand, even in mid-September (Fig. 3-7). In 1894 thousands of people lined the lake shore, on foot and in carriages, and hundreds of others watched from their boats as Miss Tillie Ashley of New Haven, Connecticut, won a half-mile women's rowing meet.

Winter sports, too, attracted participants and spectators to the lake (Fig. 3-8). The *Post-Dispatch* reported that in one day in 1894, "Fully 25,000 skaters enjoyed the sport in Forest Park. . . . Hundreds of carriages were lined up along the banks of the lake to give their occupants a view of the . . . scene." That winter, park employees built a "monster toboggan slide" on a mound of stumps and branches left from construction of the lake. Sledders could then coast all the way to the lake and out on the surface of the ice.[14] Park employees used wire brushing to keep the ice in good skating condition and installed torches around the lake so skating hours could be extended.

3-8. Men, women, and children enjoyed skating on the extended lake, as illustrated by this 1894 drawing from the *Post-Dispatch*.

When the boat rental concession was relet in 1897, the city required that there be at least seventy-five boats, provided with an awning by day and a lantern by night, at a charge of not more than twenty-five cents an hour on weekdays and not more than fifty cents an hour on Sundays (Fig. 3-9). In winter the concessionaire could rent skates, but his contract required that he keep the lake clear of slush and snow for skating, freeing the park commissioner of that responsibility. The concessionaire was also required to supply a heated cloak room where he could charge not more than ten cents for taking care of coats. For these privileges, he paid the city almost $2,500 a year.

Other concessionaires rented "implements" for croquet, baseball, and lawn tennis.[15] William Pohlman, who operated a livery stable, had the concession to rent ponies and burros and carts for them to pull.

Observers at the time often commented on women's participation in active sports, as the healthy glow of perspiration replaced the previously fashionable pallor and languor (Fig. 3-10). In 1894 the *Post-Dispatch* reported that a "very pretty young woman . . . rows about indolently, as though it were difficult for her to propel her craft, but when another boat comes alongside she immediately challenges the occupants for a race

and frequently is the victor, even when her antagonists are athletic young men." And, in winter, there "were many ladies in [the] throng" of ice-skaters.[16]

Other parkgoers preferred quieter pastimes. Strollers enjoyed the trees and the formal plantings, or floral displays (Fig. 3-11). In 1892 Commissioner Fechter reported that about 50,000 plants were ready for the Forest Park display, which would be "very elegant and attractive."

At first, the plants for these displays came from greenhouses outside Forest Park. In 1890 Commissioner Klemm recommended moving the city greenhouses to Forest Park because the air was clean, and because of "the cheapness of fuel (furnished by wood from the park at no extra expense whatever)" and the availability of fertilizer from leaves and from the manure of the mules that worked in the park. The city built the first greenhouse in Forest Park in 1892 at a cost of $3,000. By 1897 all of the park department greenhouses had been consolidated into Forest Park.[17]

Park visitors could also watch Missouri Fish Commission employee Philip Kopplin, Jr., care for the fish in the lakes. The only change in the operation came in the late 1890s when the fish commission, in response to complaints from sports fishermen throughout the state, stopped stocking carp and turned to raising native United States fish such as black bass, crappie, and sunfish (Fig. 3-12).

Band concerts, too, were a popular attraction in the 1890s, paid for with both public and private funds. Beginning in the early 1890s the city appropriated money for regular weekly concerts, every Saturday from June through August. An ordinance required "not less than twenty-five skilled musicians."[18] Beginning in 1893, the streetcar companies and the operator of the Cottage restaurant provided additional concerts to attract more St. Louisans to the park. In the summer of 1896, in response to several requests, some of the city-sponsored concerts were held on Sundays, the working man's only day off.

3-9. Boats and boathouse on an unidentified lake in Forest Park, probably the newly extended Peninsular Lake. The numbers on the boats indicate they were the ones parkgoers could rent.

The 1875 park plan, which had emphasized floral decorations and provided for a bandstand, had also recommended a Forest Park zoo. By 1890 park department employees were caring for a North American animal collection in Forest Park that included Virginia deer, Canada geese, two prairie dogs, and a flock of California quail. Private citizens had donated all of the animals, as well as a large cage for the quail. The park department refused other offered animals, including bear cubs, raccoons, eagles, and owls, because of lack of space in the animal enclosure.

Park Commissioner Richard Klemm encouraged zoo supporters to form a society to help acquire American animals "in danger of being exterminated by the progress of civilization and the cultivation of the soil," especially buffalo (Fig. 3-13). The park was so big, Klemm said, he could build enclosures that would give the buffalo "an almost unlimited space, so as to bring them as nearly to a wild state as possible."[19]

Soon a herd of buffalo was on its way to St. Louis. The new group, the Forest Park Zoological Association, "put up at their own expense a very ornamental yard and old style block house" for the five buffalo, Klemm reported in early 1891, which soon became "an immense attraction to visitors."[20]

Mayor Noonan and private citizens, including brewer Adolphus Busch, George R. Thompson, and manufacturer N. O. Nelson, urged expansion of the collection. When the St. Louis Agricultural and Mechanical Association auctioned off part of the animal collection from its permanent fairgrounds in August 1891, Mayor Noonan instructed the new park commissioner,

3-10. Observers in the 1890s often commented on the number of women who participated in active sports, like this group playing lawn tennis.

3-11. The floral designs in Forest Park became more elaborate in the 1890s, such as the ones in this photograph at the base of the Blair statue, with the Laclede Pavilion in the background.

3-12. The Missouri Fish Commission shipped young fish all over the state in the railroad car *Benton*.

Jonathan P. Fechter, to bid for animals for the Forest Park collection. Fechter bought a herd of elk, Clint the dromedary, a sacred cow (zebu), and several others, but circus owners John, Charles, and Al Ringling outbid him for the yak. N. O. Nelson, treasurer of the Forest Park Zoological Association, accepted contributions to cover the $1,694 purchase price, and Mayor Noonan and the *Post-Dispatch* contributed $100 each. The dromedary walked to its new home, while the rest of the animals rode in large vans. All arrived in Forest Park on Friday, August 21, 1891, and were immediately on display, with new winter quarters planned. Unlike the fairgrounds, there was no admission charge at the new zoo, as Kern had planned, and it quickly became popular with adults and children.

After 1892 the city made no special appropriations for the zoological collection, and offers to donate animals were again declined. The *Post-Dispatch* commented in 1894 on the inadequacies of the animals' living conditions. Hyde & Conard's 1899 *Encyclopedia of the History of St. Louis*, which seldom criticized its subjects, noted that "limited appropriations for the maintenance and improvement of this [zoological] department have

prevented it from becoming what it was designed to be—a first class zoological garden."[21]

The city did manage to construct bear pits and animal houses in 1899 and 1900 and to relocate the deer park. In 1900 Commissioner Ridgely reported that the animals were healthier and better displayed in their new locations. By that time, the collection included several animals from outside North America, such as the dromedary and the "sacred cow" bought from the fairgrounds, and a small collection of monkeys, all cared for by park department employees.

Another private group was working to provide an art museum in the park. In 1875, at about the same time Kern was hoping for a museum in Forest Park, A. J. Conant was urging establishment of a public art museum. In 1881 the museum opened downtown, operated by the Board of Control of the St. Louis School and Museum of Fine Arts, a department of Washington University. Halsey C. Ives, museum director, was a Washington University faculty member.

In early 1897 the board of control decided to ask for permission to build a museum in Forest Park, and in March 1900 the board succeeded. There were three conditions: 1) the building

3-13. Enjoying a visit to the Forest Park zoo.

would become the property of the city, 2) the building would be governed by "the Board of Control of the St. Louis School and Museum of Fine Arts augmented by the Mayor, Comptroller and Park Commissioner of the City," and 3) the museum, which had charged admission downtown, would be open free of charge to the public at least "every Sunday afternoon from one o'clock to sundown." The building's board had the absolute right to choose a site in Forest Park, not subject to approval by the park commissioner or anyone else, though the board had little to fear from Park Commissioner Ridgely, who had business and social connections with many of the museum board members. While city officials sat on the building's board, they were in the minority, an arrangement that would later be challenged.[22]

The museum's site selection committee considered three possible locations for its new building in Forest Park, including one near the Laclede Pavilion and one near the Lindell Pavilion. The third, which the board selected, was the highest point in the park, on a hill later known as Art Hill. Plans for the museum were still incomplete in 1901.[23]

Not far from the site selected for the new art museum, the Cottage offered refreshments for hungry or thirsty parkgoers. In March 1885, only a few months before the car lines reached the park, a city ordinance granted Charles Schweickardt (who operated a downtown restaurant with a partner) a six-year lease for the Cottage. When the lease expired in 1891, it was extended for ten years, giving Schweickardt, by ordinance, the "exclusive

3-14. This building was the third to house the Cottage restaurant. The one that Schweickardt built in 1893 to replace the old Forsyth farmhouse burned, so he built this one to replace it.

LOADED TO THE GUARDS.

But the good boatman of Forest Park says he will come back for a ten years' extension of a soft snap.

3-15. This *Post-Dispatch* cartoon from 1894 commented on the City Council's terms for Forest Park leases. The papers in the boat include "No Inspection," "$40,000 Lake," "Soft Snap," "Good Thing," and "Contracted Till '97."

privilege of selling refreshments in Forest Park." The ordinance required Schweickardt to replace the former farmhouse with a new restaurant building costing at least $15,000, a building that would become the property of the city when the lease expired. Under the ordinance Schweickardt could also erect three ornamental refreshment stands, which he did, to serve those who didn't want a full restaurant meal.[24]

Construction of the new restaurant was delayed by a law suit that challenged the lease renewal, largely because it granted Schweickardt the right to sell liquor in Forest Park. The suit ended in 1893 when the Missouri Supreme Court refused to cancel the lease. In 1893 the new restaurant was complete, but on May 14, 1894, it burned down and another had to be built. Because of the delays of the lawsuit and the fire, the city granted Schweickardt a three-year extension,

which carried his exclusive refreshment privilege to the end of March 1904 (Fig. 3-14).[25]

Schweickardt attracted customers with a carousel, swings, and band concerts. He also hosted convention groups, like the Missouri Pharmaceutical Association, which in 1893 met downtown. The pharmacists took the streetcars to the park and assembled at the Cottage for their evening's entertainment "to combine business with relaxation."[26]

The Cottage and other concessions were evidently profitable enough to be a desirable political payoff, especially under the Republicans. The *Post-Dispatch* called the terms of the pony and burro contract with Republican Pohlman in 1894 under a Republican mayor "somewhat peculiar," since Pohlman was to pay no fixed amount, only a percentage of his gross based on his own sworn monthly statement. Although the ordinance for the lease of the Cottage in 1880 had provided for competitive bidding, Republican Schweickardt was given the lease by name in the 1885 ordinance passed under a Republican mayor (Fig. 3-15). The only extension granted Schweickardt under a Democratic mayor, in 1891, required him to build a new restaurant. Schweickardt was required to pay $1,000 a year for the Cottage lease at a time when the boat concession paid almost $2,500 a year. The *Globe-Democrat* commented that the lease payments were too low, and the *Post-Dispatch* called them "ridiculously small." Schweickardt confessed in 1903 that he had been the "go between and distributor of bribes" to four state senators. Although the Cottage lease he still held was not involved in the scandal, the *Post-Dispatch* asked, "Should a man of this kind be intrusted [sic] with public privilege?"[27]

It is at least possible that the board of the art museum paid some "boodle," as bribes were called, to get the right to build in Forest Park. Museum Director Halsey C. Ives had been a member of the city council when councilmen were often bribed to get bills passed. Ellis Wainwright, president of the museum's board of control from 1889 to 1905, was indicted in 1902 for

SCENE AT THE SALVATION ARMY CAMP AT FOREST PARK.

3-16. Bicyclists in their "bicycle suits" inspected the Salvation Army camp meeting in Forest Park in 1896.

connections with the boodling and stayed in Europe for almost ten years. When he returned to St. Louis in 1911 many of the witnesses had died and the charges against him were dismissed.

There is no evidence that any money changed hands while the city was considering the museum's request to use park land, but museum directors may have been forced to make such a payoff to convince the city to accept their gift of a new building. For whatever reason, the March 1900 city ordinance that gave the museum permission to erect a building in Forest Park, at its own expense, was unusually favorable. The art museum board had an unrestricted right to choose its site and design its own building. Ordinances passed at almost the same time required the streetcar companies, an industry in which boodle was common, to have the sites or the plans and specifications for their buildings approved by the city's board of public improvements.

But nobody publicly accused the museum of making a payoff nor did anyone object to the arrangement at the time. Many St. Louisans were probably grateful for the offer of a new museum building, as they were for the Zoological Association's donations and the facilities of the sports clubs. None of those groups, except the Gentlemen's Driving Club, had even bothered to obtain an ordinance authorizing its park activities.

· Crowds of St. Louisans went to Forest Park to celebrate holidays and special events in the 1890s. In the early 1890s the Fourth of July celebrations in Forest Park usually included baseball games and bicycle riding as well as picnics and a band concert concluding with Sousa's rousing "Washington Post March."

On Saturday, May 14, 1898, as patriotic fervor rose nationwide during the Spanish-American War, St. Louisans celebrated Dewey Day honoring Rear Admiral George Dewey, the hero of the battle of Manila Bay. Thousands of people came to St. Louis from surrounding towns and, although there were observances at other locations, most participants went to the Forest Park celebration, waving flags and carrying umbrellas for protection from the threatening weather. The St. Louis University cadets stood in formation near the speaker's stand, while the black cadets of the Knights of Pythias formed nearby. The *Globe-Democrat* said the crowd "applauded the patriotic utterances of a dozen speakers to the echo." However, the idea of

3-17. An officer of the Mounted Police District in 1891. In 1885 the city police department redrew its districts, assigning the entire area west of Grand Avenue to the Mounted Police District.

3-18. The Mounted Police Substation in Forest Park, constructed in 1890. It later served as a residence for park employees and briefly housed a meteorological observatory, far from the smoke and dust of the city.

changing the name of Kingshighway to Dewey Boulevard was quietly dropped.[28]

The patriotic fervor carried over to the Fourth of July that year. The mayor asked for contributions to the Forest Park Fourth of July celebration, which included speeches, music, baseball games, a cakewalk, and, of course, fireworks.

A different kind of special event was the Salvation Army camp meeting of 1896, which the *Post-Dispatch* called a "red-hot campaign against His Majesty, the Devil." Bicyclists came in their "bicycle suits," while nearby "a party of picnickers" tried to enjoy themselves despite the August heat (Fig. 3-16). A baseball practice and a tennis game "were going on jointly with the services all day Sunday."[29]

The large numbers of park visitors in the 1880s and 1890s and the new kinds of people that could reach the park caused trouble. Park administrators worked with the St. Louis Police Department to solve the problems but weren't always happy with the results. Beginning in 1885, the St. Louis police department's Mounted Police District covered the entire area west of Grand Ave-

nue, including Forest Park. The park commissioners considered this protection inadequate. In June 1885, a few weeks after the first horsecars reached Forest Park, Commissioner Weigel instituted a curfew in Forest Park "in the interest of morality." The *Globe-Democrat* reported sarcastically:

> Since the construction of a street-car line to the park the youths and maidens have been thronging the lawns and sporting under big trees, and missing the cars. Now the Superintendent of the park believes that moonlight and night are all bad for young folks, and so the park is to be closed after 11 o'clock, and the park police after that hour will start out and beat the bushes and blow horns to warn the lovers to hustle and get the last car for town. If the park is to be closed it will put a stop to moonlight drives and wild orgies on the lawns in early morning hours.

In 1888 Park Commissioner Klemm reported, "Forest Park is now a favorite resort, at all hours of the day, both week days and Sundays, of thousands of visitors, principally ladies and children. Except on Sundays, no protection is furnished beyond that afforded by the regular police-

3-19. The Mounted Police District station and stables, constructed in Forest Park in 1893–94, despite the vehement objections of Park Commissioner Jonathan P. Fechter.

3-20. The mounted police lined up in front of their new building.

man, whose beat includes the park, and also miles of territory about it" (Fig. 3-17). The park was, he wrote, "at the mercy of trespassers and the evil disposed" whose offenses included "wanton plucking of flowers," "fast driving," and the "taking away of plants and shrubbery." The building that had contained the "calaboose" on opening day was, by the 1880s, the park keeper's residence and so, presumably, not appropriate for even a temporary lockup. In 1889 Klemm argued that "in Forest Park, a police station with calaboose, is absolutely necessary to protect the valuable property from damage and respectable visitors from annoyance." So in 1890 the police department spent almost $5,500 to build a police substation in Forest Park (Fig. 3-18).[30]

To supplement the patrols of city policemen assigned to the park, in the early 1890s Commissioner Jonathan Fechter established a force of park police, paid from the Forest Park maintenance fund. After the park police had been on duty for a year, Fechter reported that "there has been less disorder in the park during the past year although it was visited by double the number of people during summer and winter." However, in the financial difficulties following the panic of 1893, he had to discharge the park police. After that, William Marion Reedy's magazine *The Mirror* complained of "indecencies and insults in Forest Park" by "loafers who have no other aim in life than approaching ladies who happen to be alone."[31]

Police protection in the area around the park

was also inadequate as the city grew. Although there was a substation in Forest Park, the mounted police station and stables were about two miles from the park's eastern boundary. In 1891 the police commissioners recommended construction of a police stable in Forest Park, "a portion of which on the southern line is unsuitable for park purposes, and could not be put to a better use." Commissioner Fechter disagreed strongly, calling the proposal "very objectionable" and not in the spirit of Kern's and McKinley's plan. The original park plan, Fechter said, "has been strictly adhered to with great care, and I do not believe that it can be improved upon."[32]

But Fechter had a very powerful opponent. The driving force behind the new building was the Superintendent of the Mounted Police Stables, Dr. William R. Faulkner. The *Globe-Democrat* called Faulkner the "police boss de facto." The *Republic*, formerly the *Republican*, reported that Faulkner was responsible for collecting political contributions from the police force and turning them over to the Democratic party. Fechter and the plan lost to Faulkner's political muscle. The municipal assembly appropriated funds for the construction of a new mounted police headquarters and allocated almost 20 acres of Forest Park for the building and for grazing lands for the horses.[33] The brick headquarters and stable building took a year to build and cost more than $46,000 (Fig. 3-19). The new road to the station was soon named Faulkner's Drive.

3-21. Sylvan Lake, a much smaller lake than the extended Peninsular Lake, reflected its boathouse, built in the rustic style also used for the zoo buildings.

The new headquarters building, completed in August 1894, did not solve the park's crime problems (Fig. 3-20). Forest Park Head Gardener John Moritz awoke one morning in 1901 to discover that thieves had loaded fourteen of the park's potted palm trees into wagons and driven away. The *Globe-Democrat* reported the same year on the "banditti of the River des Peres," three "barefooted urchins" who had attempted to rob "two nice little boys" and had forced them to swim fully clothed in the "slimy . . . River des Peres."[34]

After completion of the mounted station, the Forest Park substation became a house for park employees. Park Commissioner Fechter and the St. Louis representative of the U.S. Signal Service (soon to become the U.S. Weather Bureau) supervised establishment of a meteorological observatory in the tower of the substation, remote from the smoke and dust of the city. Outside the observatory, Fechter erected "a granite stone. . ., on which is inscribed the exact longi-

tude, latitude and altitude of the point on which it stands."[35] After the building was torn down some years later, the marker remained to puzzle future parkgoers.

As more St. Louisans went to Forest Park, their representatives in the city government managed to find more funds for it. Between 1885 and 1901 appropriations for Forest Park more than doubled, growing more than three times as fast as total park department funds, which in turn grew almost twice as fast as total city expenditures. The park department concentrated its funds on facilities like boathouses, small shelters, roads and bridges, water pipes, and electrical wires.

After city water lines reached the park in the late 1880s, city water bubbled from the ornamental and drinking fountains, filled the lakes, watered the plants, and sprinkled the roads (Fig. 3-21). Park employees connected the park's water system to the city's and installed a horse trough and six outlets to fill the carts that sprinkled the park

3-22. Westmoreland Place in the 1890s contained several of the city's most expensive houses.

roads. The spring, no longer needed for the lakes and fountains, was converted to a drinking water source, surrounded by rockwork, trees, and shrubs, and approached by a cinder walk. Even with the improved water supply, droughts like the record drought of the summer of 1901 killed large numbers of trees.

As electric lines reached Forest Park it converted to electricity, beginning in 1890. The *Post-Dispatch* explained in 1894 that the new lights were ugly, but they were all the city could afford.[36]

Growing numbers of employees worked to maintain the many new attractions. Between 1886 and 1902 the Forest Park payroll more than tripled from about $11,000 to $34,400. In 1899 Forest Park Keeper Philip Kopplin supervised 105 Forest Park employees; ten years earlier, there had only been fifteen. The number of gardeners increased from two in 1889 to twelve in 1899, including two who lived in the park near the greenhouses. Forest Park Keeper Kopplin also lived in the park, in the house at Union and Lindell. Zoo Keeper

Charles Angermeyer lived in the old police sub-station with his son Martin, a park laborer. Stableman Robert Brown lived in the park near the mules in his care. The payrolls may have been somewhat padded, as municipal payrolls often were at the time, but the numbers of employees were important to the park, and the park had become an important source of employment. Ridgely remarked in 1900 that a reduced park appropriation would mean the "laboring class will . . . suffer from the loss of employment."[37]

The crowds of parkgoers meant some changes in procedure. Commissioner Ridgely had to buy hay, he reported in 1900, because "the meadows, where we formerly obtained most of our hay for the park animals, are nearly all being utilized for recreation grounds." And the park, with more facilities, had more to lose from weather. Flooding by the River des Peres caused extensive damage to the bridges in 1892 and destroyed the Franklin Bridge in 1897. The disastrous tornado of May 27, 1896, which destroyed

3-23. The John W. Kauffman house covered the entire city block at the corner of Lindell and Kingshighway, across from the park, and included the largest private greenhouse in the city. The retired grain dealer and speculator spent $175,000 to $200,000 to build the house, which William K. Bixby bought following Kauffman's death in 1904.

Lafayette Park, missed Forest Park, but wind damage required repairs that consumed almost all the money appropriated for the park that year, preventing planned improvements.[38]

As the park began to fulfill its planners' hopes, the fashionable neighborhood that park proponents had envisioned started to develop, influencing Forest Park in unexpected ways. Those who could afford to escape the city's noise and dirt followed tree-lined Lindell Boulevard westward. Developers built expensive subdivisions north of the park by laying sewer pipes and building short, tree-shaded, dead-end streets, often with entrance gates.

One of the most ambitious of the real estate companies was the Forest Park Improvement Company. The company constructed sewer and water lines on its land and built what Park Commissioner Klemm called in 1889 "an excellent road on the north boundary of the Park from King's Highway to Union avenue."[39] This road, Park Road, was later considered an extension of Lindell. Immediately north of the new Park Road, on the company's land, Julius Pitzman laid

out Westmoreland and Portland places, and M. G. Kern landscaped them (Fig. 3-22).

Of the "Ten Costliest Private Residences" described by the *Post-Dispatch* in April 1894, five were on either Portland or Westmoreland Place—the houses of George L. Allen, William K. Bixby, William McMillan, and William H. Thornburgh, and the intended residence of John T. Davis, uncompleted at the time of his death. A sixth house, the residence of John W. Kauffman, occupied an entire city block on the corner of Lindell and Kingshighway, just around the corner from the private places (Fig. 3-23).

Attempts to create a real estate boom east of the park were not successful, probably because of the industrial district to the south. Although land was subdivided and offered for sale as early as 1885, by 1904, almost twenty years later, almost half the land was still empty.

Institutions used the land south and west of the park. Along the southern border a private company operated the Forest Park Highlands, which attracted generations of St. Louisans to the Forest Park vicinity. The Highlands opened in the summer of 1896 as a beer garden offering a min-

3-24. Advertisement for the scenic railway at the Forest Park Highlands, about 1897. L. A. Thompson invented the scenic railway, which thrilled passengers with views of the countryside and fast downhill rides, then whirled them into the tunnel where patches of darkness alternated with brightly lighted spectacular scenes.

strel show, comedy gymnasts, and "The 20th Century Comedian." The following year Anton Steuver bought the beer garden and changed it into a summer garden, or, as Steuver advertised, an "al fresco park . . . especially adapted for women and children."[40]

Steuver, a Democrat, had political connections and other business interests. His positions included brewer with the Home Brewing Company (whose bottled and draught beer were sold at the Highlands) and president of the Highlands Fire Clay Company, next to the amusement park.

Almost every year Steuver added something new for patrons of the Highlands, many of whom arrived on the streetcar (Fig. 3-24). The first year he promoted an amusement ride, the scenic railway and "high-class and refined vaudeville in Hopkins's new pavilion," managed by J. D. Hopkins.[41] Hopkins's first program on May 23, 1897, featured Marie Dressler, at prices ranging from ten to thirty cents.

Two different universities planned to move near the park in the 1890s, and one, Forest Park University, did. The school for women moved in 1891 from Kirkwood, the suburb Hiram Leffing-

well had developed, to a former cornfield next to Forest Park and changed its name from Kirkwood Seminary to Forest Park University.

Anna Sneed Cairns founded and operated the school. In addition to her work in educating women, Mrs. Cairns was a leader in both the prohibition and women's suffrage movements. The university consisted of three colleges (Forest Park College, the School of Art and Elocution, and the College of Music) as well as a preparatory school and served both boarding and day students (Fig. 3-25). Until the streetcar line reached the university in 1895, day students traveled by horses and "wagonettes," which crossed the park hourly to make connections with the streetcar line. The streetcar remained the best way to the campus from the city, since there was no road along the park's southern edge. When the city authorized Oakland Avenue in the late 1890s, the road ran west from the university toward St. Louis County, not east toward the city.[42]

The school took advantage of its location next to the park. Brochures told parents that their daughters would "spend the day in the invigorating air" around Forest Park "instead of the

3-25. John G. Cairns, the husband of the school's founder and operator, designed this Forest Park University building, which looked north into Forest Park.

smoke, dust and sewer gas of the city." "The boating, riding and walking in Forest Park," the school advertised, "the lawn tennis and croquet, furnish delightful recreation . . . and the end of the year finds [the students] blooming with health, instead of spiritless and pale, as is often the case with girls in the close and unwholesome air of cities."[43]

The other university, Washington University, decided to move west of Forest Park in order to consolidate its scattered departments, housed in various buildings downtown. In 1894 a syndicate representing Washington University bought approximately 108 acres of land at the northwest corner of the park. The university's move west was delayed, however, until after 1901.

The land just west of the park was still undeveloped and hard to reach, so there were large tracts of vacant land available for the university. Neither of the roads along the park's northern and southern edges ran from Kingshighway to Skinker Road, the park's western border, though by 1895 the streetcar lines extended to both of the park's western corners (Fig. 3-26). The Clayton and Forest Park line (later called the 04) opened on December 8, 1895, running a few blocks along the park from the northwest corner before turning west to Clayton. The Lindell line along the southern border of Forest Park also opened in 1895.

It wasn't easy to reach the planned campus from the county either. Wydown Boulevard was built on either side of the tracks of the car line in 1896. Forsyth Boulevard, a dirt road, was not opened from the county courthouse to the western city limits until 1899.

Increasing neighborhood development caused serious problems for the park. By 1894 the Cheltenham district south of the park produced more fire clay sewer pipe than any other district in the United States. Other industries grouped along the railroad tracks included the St. Louis Smelting and Refining Company. These industries were among the dirtiest of the time, and the smoke and sulfur fumes often blew into the park and damaged the trees.

Residential development north and northwest of the park, extending well past the city limits, polluted the River des Peres because the extension of city sewer lines fell behind the growth of residential districts. What Thomas Scharf had described in 1883 as "a romantic little stream" was, the *Post-Dispatch* reported in 1894, "practically nothing less than a monster open sewer, poisoning the air with the most dangerous corruption and menace to health known, the corruption of sewage." The paper reported that the animals in the Forest Park zoo and their visitors had to breathe "the thick, gummy exhalation from the sewer creek known as the River des Peres." City

3-26. View of Skinker Boulevard from Delmar Boulevard in the early 1900s, when it was still a dirt road.

3-27. View of the Forest Park bandstand, or music pagoda, after Mary J. Rankin donated statues of the four seasons in 1886. This picture of the wooden bandstand, built in 1876, was probably taken after renovation and landscaping done for the 1904 World's Fair.

3-28. The cover of sheet music published in 1892 shows favorite Forest Park attractions — the zoo, top (with its rustic buildings and fences), carriage and buggy drives, and boating on the lakes.

the driftwood and debris coming down the River des Peres from the county."[44]

Construction in these new neighborhoods damaged the park roads, too. Since nearby streets were impassable, Commissioner Ridgely said, he was "compelled to issue permits [to drive through the park from south to north] . . . to vehicles hauling building and other material to districts where building, street making, water pipe laying and sewer constructing are going on. The park roads, not made for such heavy traffic, are thereby worn out."[45] In the first twenty years the park was open, the road mileage in the park actually decreased from 19.66 miles in 1876 to 18 miles in 1897.

The western portion of the park, "the jungle" or, more often, "the wilderness," was still untamed. Laborers again cleared the wilderness, Commissioner Fechter reported in 1893, so that "ladies can now drive in the remotest rural lanes without fear of molestation." The *Post-Dispatch* described the area a year later, however, as one "of almost primeval wildness" where "tramps and vicious-looking men are often seen skulking through the shadows and dodging from sight in the underbrush." A parkgoer who left the paths got lost in the wilderness and discovered the "curious habitation" of a hermit who had apparently lived undiscovered in the park for years.[46]

Some park facilities were still missing in 1901. There was no bridle path. The children's playground Kern had envisioned was represented only by the carousel and swings at the Cottage. A newspaper letter writer in 1894 who signed himself "A Father" pointed out the need for "a house of public comfort for ladies and children" so they would not be "forced to return home before they wished on account of not having conveniences of this kind."

In 1886 Mary J. Rankin donated four marble statues, representing the seasons, for placement around the music stand, but otherwise donations lagged (Fig. 3-27). Commissioner Ridgely called on "our wealthy citizens" in 1896 to donate "fountains, bridges, statuary, monuments, etc."

Health Commissioner Max C. Starkloff reported that "the contaminating influence of the gases that arise from the river is certainly injurious to health." Because much of the sewage came from outside the city limits, city officials wanted the state to create a River des Peres sewer district so the county would pay "its just burden" of the expense of the needed sewers. In the meantime, city officials said, the use of the River des Peres for sewage was a "temporary expedient." The development also made the river's periodic floods even more damaging to park property. "The damage," Fechter commented, "is in most cases caused by

which his budget didn't provide. The *Republican* agreed in 1897, "Donations to our city parks are in order. . . . An Ordinance [the 1882 one] . . . is already in existence, though half forgotten."[47]

Still, Forest Park had come a long way since its "rude condition" of 1876. Park administrators had succeeded in stretching their budgets with private funds, both donations and corporate investments. Millions of St. Louisans arrived at the park every year through the new streetcar shelters. On Sundays, tens of thousands "spread themselves out over its beautiful expanse of green sward and forest trees," a guidebook reported. Some had picnics and others dined at the Cottage. They enjoyed the zoo, admired the flowers and statues, or listened to the band music. Others exerted themselves boating or bicycling. Some came for celebrations of holidays and special events. Sports competitions attracted others, to watch or to play. One page of the *Republic* in June 1901 listed horse and bicycle races, games of cricket and baseball, and tournaments in golf and tennis (Fig. 3-28).

By 1901 Forest Park had achieved national recognition as St. Louis's outstanding park. The national magazine *Harper's Weekly* called the park "the chief pride of the city." By then Forest Park was known internationally as the chosen location for the widely anticipated Louisiana Purchase Exposition, the St. Louis World's Fair.[48]

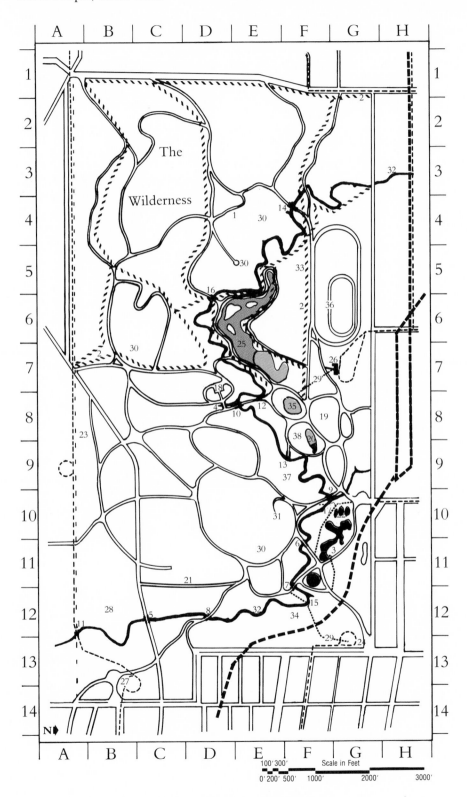

PARK LOCATOR MAP
(1885–1901)

1. Art Museum (approximate proposed location), D-4
2. Bicycle path (western half of park only, eastern half unknown), A-7 to B-1 to G-1 to F-8
3. Boat house, F-11

Bridges

4. Carr Lane, D-8
5. Clayton Avenue, C-12
6. Columbus, F-11
7. Franklin, F-12
8. Jefferson, D-12
9. Lafayette, F-10
10. Lincoln, E-8
11. Lindell Railroad, A-12
12. McKinley, E-8
13. Stable, F-9
14. Steuben, F-4
15. Suspension footbridge, F-12
16. Washington, D-6
17. Waterworks footbridge, F-10

18. Cottage restaurant (second location), D-7
19. Cricket field, F-8
20. Deer Paddock Lake (later Deer Lake), F-8 and 9
21. Faulkner's Drive, C and D-12
22. Fish hatchery lakes (original), G-10
23. Greenhouses and gardener's lodge, A-8
24. Laclede Pavilion, G-13
25. Lake extension, E-5 and 6
26. Lindell Pavilion, G-7
27. Missouri Pavilion (probable location), B-13
28. Mounted Police Station, B-12
29. Pedestrian walkways, F-7 and 8, G-10 to G-13
30. Picnic grounds (probable locations), B-7 to C-7, E-4 and 5, E-11
31. Police Substation (later residence and meteorological observatory with marker), E-10
32. River des Peres, A-13 to H-3
33. St. Louis Amateur Athletic Association (Triple A) Clubhouse (approximate first location), F-5
34. Spring, F-12
35. Spring, Summer, Fall, Winter, statues, F-8
36. Speeding track, G-5 and 6
37. Stableman's residence (probable location), F-9
38. Zoo (approximate location), F-8

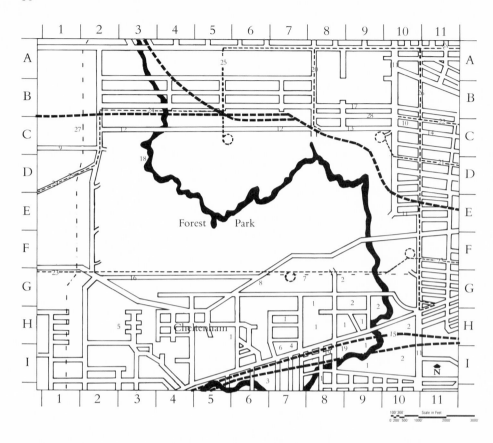

NEIGHBORHOOD LOCATOR MAP
(1885–1901)

Brick and Fire Clay Companies, 1905

1. Evens and Howard Brick Co., H-5 to I-9
2. Hydraulic Press Brick Co., G-9 to I-10
3. Laclede Fire Brick Company, I-6 and 7
4. Mitchell Clay Co., I-7
5. Missouri Fire Brick Co., H-2 and 3
6. Winkle Terra Cotta Co., I-7

7. Forest Park Highlands, G-7 and 8
8. Forest Park University, G-6
9. Forsyth Boulevard (later Forsyth Avenue), C-1 and 2
10. Kauffman (later Bixby) house, C-10
11. King's Highway (later Kingshighway Boulevard), A-10 to I-10
12. Lindell Avenue (Skinker Road to Union Boulevard, private street until 1909), C-2 to C-8
13. Lindell Avenue (Union Boulevard to Kings Highway, formerly Park Road, then Forest Park Terrace), C-8 to C-10
14. Lindell Boulevard (east of Kings Highway), C-10 and 11
15. Missouri Pacific Railroad, I-5 to H-11
16. Oakland Avenue, G-2 to G-6
Park Road, see 13, C-8 to C-10
17. Portland Place, B-8 to B-10

18. River des Peres, A-3 to I-5
19. St. Louis Smelting and Refining Works, I-8 and 9

Streetcar Lines, 1901

20. St. Louis and Suburban Railway Company, Forest Park Division, A-8 to C-8
21. United Railways Company, Central Division (formerly Forest Park, Laclede Av. and Fourth Street Railway Company), Laclede Avenue Line, C-9 to D-11
22. United Railway Company, Central Division (formerly Missouri Railroad Company, cable), Olive Street Line, C-10 and 11
23. United Railways Company, Lindell Division (formerly Lindell Railway Company), Chouteau Avenue line, G-1 to F-11
24. United Railways Company, Lindell Division (formerly Lindell Railway Company), Clayton Line, B-5 to E-1
25. United Railways Company, Lindell Division (formerly Lindell Railway Company), Delmar Avenue Line, A-11 to C-5
26. United Railways Company, Lindell Division (formerly Lindell Railway Company), Euclid Avenue Line, A-10 to H-11

27. Washington University site, C-1 and 2
28. Westmoreland Place, C-8 to C-10
29. Wydown Boulevard, D-2 to E-1

4

THE PARK AND THE FAIR (1901–1904)

This is our end and aim; not Forest Park for the World's Fair, not a sacrifice, but the World's Fair for Forest Park; for its perfection, its monuments, its permanent results in giving St. Louis a finished and central garden fully a generation ahead of its time.—Forest Park World's Fair Free Site Association, 1901

The Louisiana Purchase Exposition (the 1904 St. Louis World's Fair) changed much in St. Louis, especially Forest Park and the surrounding neighborhood. The debate over the use of about half of Forest Park for the fair (657 of the park's more than 1,370 acres) clearly illustrates St. Louisans' pride in and affection for the park.

Efforts to bring a World's Fair to St. Louis had begun well before the turn of the century. The St. Louis Agricultural and Mechanical Association had tried to promote an 1861 World's Fair on its grounds in the northern section of the city where it sponsored an annual agricultural and mechanical fair. In early 1870 a group had organized "in connection with the movement to procure a World's Fair in St. Louis." Attempts had been made to have the Columbian Exposition, celebrating the 400th anniversary of Columbus's discovery of America, in St. Louis, and an 1890 St. Louis ordinance offered Forest Park for that fair.[1] A delegation headed by Missouri Gov. David R. Francis, a former St. Louis mayor, went to Washington in 1890 for that purpose. Promoters of St. Louis for the fair published a map showing the population within 500 miles of the proposed cities, with, of course, the circle around St. Louis containing the largest total (Fig. 4-1).

After the Columbian Exposition was awarded to Chicago, St. Louis's traditional rival, St. Louis fair promoters tried again. Beginning in the spring of 1897 the Missouri Historical Society took Pierre Chouteau's advice and began serious consideration of methods of celebrating the cen-

tennial of the Louisiana Purchase of 1803. St. Louis civic, business, and labor organizations were invited to send representatives to a meeting in June 1898 to plan for the celebration. The *Post-Dispatch* reported after the meeting that a fair was the least likely celebration since there wasn't enough time left to create a fair that would equal or excel the Chicago fair held in 1893. The proposal most participants favored was a riverfront park containing a public museum and occupying the ten blocks south of the Eads Bridge from Third Street to the river (later the site of the Jefferson Expansion Memorial National Park). Pierre Chouteau, whose father Charles P. Chouteau had opposed Forest Park in 1872 and 1874, favored a park a few blocks farther west, "in the heart of the city," but that site was considered unlikely because of the high cost of the land.[2]

But Francis, whose term of office as governor had ended in 1893, was determined to have a fair (Fig. 4-2). Francis had served as mayor and governor and was a wealthy and successful businessman, one of the small group of men who made things happen in St. Louis. In January 1899 he led the St. Louis delegation at a meeting in St. Louis of representatives of all the Louisiana Purchase states. After Francis addressed the delegates, the meeting unanimously decided on a St. Louis World's Fair, though some had earlier favored other plans. The next day an executive committee was appointed, and David R. Francis became chairman.

This time, efforts in Washington were suc-

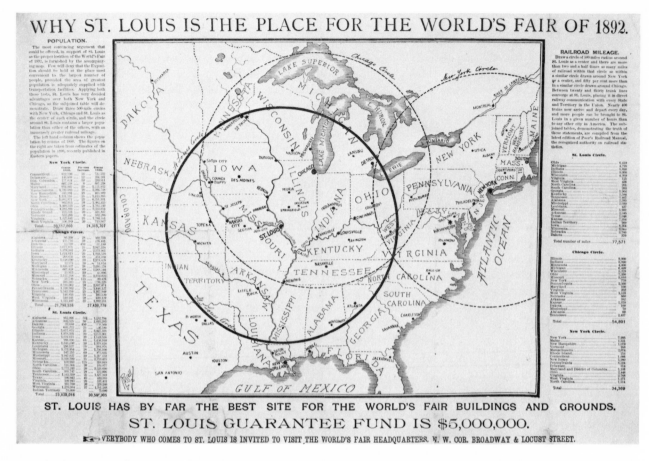

4-1. This flyer promoted St. Louis as the site for the Columbian Exposition of 1892, but St. Louis lost the contest for that fair to Chicago.

cessful. In June 1900 Congress authorized $5 million from the federal government if the city of St. Louis would also appropriate $5 million and if another $5 million could be raised by popular subscription (Fig. 4-3). By March 1901 the conditions had been met, and the federal appropriation was authorized. In April the World's Fair supporters incorporated as the Louisiana Purchase Exposition Company (LPEC) and in May elected Francis president.

In early 1901 the St. Louis Municipal Assembly considered a bill to offer the three largest city parks (Carondelet, O'Fallon, and Forest parks) as sites for the fair. Even after the bill was amended to exclude Forest Park, Republican

Mayor Henry Ziegenhein vetoed it, perhaps because he opposed closing portions of any park to the public, even temporarily, or perhaps to thwart Francis, a Democrat.

In April 1901 a new mayor, Rolla Wells, son of streetcar magnate Erastus Wells, took office. Rolla Wells was a prominent businessman and a longtime friend and ally of Francis, so Francis and the other LPEC directors tried again. In May 1901 a committee of the house of delegates held a public hearing on a bill to offer for the fair all of Carondelet Park or O'Fallon Park or the western half of Forest Park. Francis testified in favor of the bill; he pointed out that Chicago had offered all of its parks for the Columbian Exposition and urged

4-2. David R. Francis, a former mayor of St. Louis and governor of Missouri, was determined to bring a World's Fair to St. Louis.

business leaders supported, asserted that the fair directors had already decided to use Forest Park and said, "Charges ought to be brought against a man who would chop down its trees, and he should be sent to the penitentiary."

Hiram Phillips, president of the board of public improvements, replied that the bill "requires the World's Fair commissioners to place the park in the condition in which they found it when they are through with it. . . . If D. R. Francis and the World's Fair people wanted my house for two years and promised to return it in good condition they could have it."[3]

The committee recommended the bill to the house of delegates, which passed it at a meeting attended by so many of the bill's supporters that they were allowed to overflow from the visitors' galleries onto the chamber floor. The city officially adopted the ordinance on May 16, 1901. The *Globe-Democrat* remarked approvingly that because the city was allowing fair promoters to use one of the city parks, instead of having to buy or lease land, they could "head off all attempts to corner the real estate market against them."[4]

Despite, or maybe because of, Ziegenhein's charges that Francis and his associates had already chosen Forest Park, an elaborate site selection procedure began soon after the ordinance was official. In late May 1901 the LPEC directors asked for suggestions for sites that included at least 700 acres and could be enlarged to 1,000 or 1,200 acres. Probably Francis and his associates did prefer the Forest Park site, though some of their West End neighbors wanted to keep the fair's bustle and crowds out of their quiet neighborhood. However, Francis said he was willing to consider any reasonable offer of land and financing that was made for another location.

The president of the St. Louis Chapter of the American Institute of Architects, William B. Ittner, urged a site that could be connected by a system of boulevards with the major sights of the city. The president of the St. Louis Architectural Club, G. F. A. Brueggeman, gave the LPEC di-

prompt consideration since there was not much time left for building the fair. Herman W. Steinbiss, Secretary of the Building Trades Council and an LPEC director, testified that while labor interests were divided on the issue of the location of the site, they supported the bill.

Opponents of the bill concentrated their protests on the use of Forest Park. E. H. Bickley told the committee that Forest Park "should be preserved as a Sunday promenade for visitors to the city." He also pointed out that the use of a park might be illegal because the city charter required a vote of the people before any park land could be sold or leased. H. C. Koenig, president of the southside Tenth Ward Improvement Association, said, "My heart bleeds at the thought of destroying Forest Park." Ex-Mayor Ziegenhein, who tended to oppose anything Wells and the other

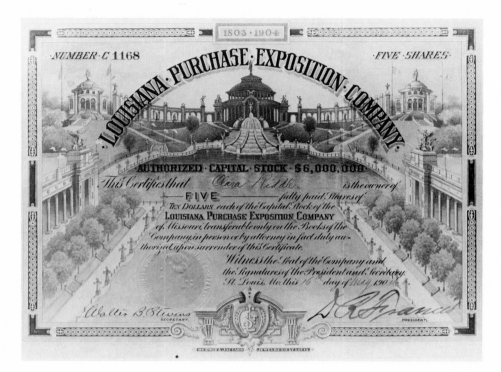

4-3. The Louisiana Purchase Exposition Company (LPEC) raised $5 million by popular subscription by selling "share certificates" like this one, signed by David R. Francis, president, and Walter B. Stevens, secretary.

rectors drawings of suggested boulevard systems. Others recommended a site with a variety of elevations and with plenty of water. The fair directors said they would also consider transportation facilities for both freight and people, and such factors as sewers, cost of the land, and the character of the buildings on the surrounding land. Finally, since it was planned that some of the fair buildings would be permanent, it was necessary to consider the suitability of the site for such improvements. In all, seven sites were considered for the fair (Fig. 4-4).

The executive committee of the LPEC was responsible for selecting the site and devising a general plan for the fair. Members of the committee visited all seven sites beginning in late May, accompanied by city officials. Then the committee met in its downtown offices to hear representatives of each site. For both the site visits and the hearings, Forest Park was considered last.[5]

The site visits were quite extensive. The visit to Forest Park, for example, was hosted by representatives of a group called the Forest Park World's Fair Free Site Association, including Judge John H. Terry, L. C. Irvine, F. E. Niesen, Luther H. Conn, E. J. Spencer, H. P. Taussig, and Frank H. Gerhart, son of Peter G. Gerhart who had served as Forest Park Commissioner under both the 1872 and 1874 acts. The trip included a view of the park from the tower of the Lindell Pavilion, luncheon at the Cottage, a drive through the park including much of the western "wilderness," and numerous conferences with the Forest Park site advocates accompanying the group.

The newspapers reported the arguments for and against all the sites in some detail. One of the drawbacks of Forest Park was that, unlike four of the sites, it was not on the Mississippi River, which had been so important to the Louisiana Purchase. Some of the other disadvantages of the Forest Park site were: the 650-acre site was too small and the surrounding property too expensive; there were legal problems both with the use of park land and with the refreshment concession for the park, which had been granted to Charles Schweickardt several years before; and, the major argument,

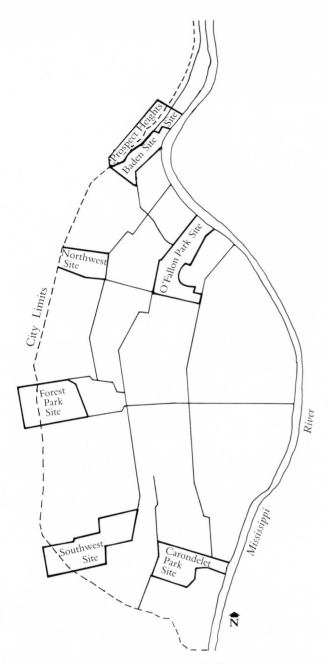

4-4. The seven sites considered for the World's Fair.

of-town visitors to the fair would visit Forest Park anyway. "If Forest Park were selected . . . there would be no other place for visitors to go, when they were tired of seeing the Fair. They would see the chief attractions of the city all in one place."

But the arguments in favor of the Forest Park site were strong. Irvine argued that transportation to the site was good, the streets to Forest Park were already in place, and the water pressure was good. He said the city would have enough to do building the fair without having to build a new boulevard system as well. Judge Terry pointed out that "the recent census showed that the center of population in St. Louis was from the foot of Washington avenue, running in a westerly direction, and terminating a few blocks beyond Forest Park" and said the city should continue to concentrate its development along this line. He also remarked that most of the $5 million raised for the fair had come from Forest Park neighbors, so they should have the fair. The trees of Forest Park would give shade from the heat, Norman J. Colman and Terry argued, and those that would have to be removed were not good park trees anyway since they were short lived and shallow rooted.

The Forest Park World's Fair Free Site Association argued that it would be better for the fair not to be located on the river, since even the Mississippi River couldn't compete with the Lake Michigan site of the Chicago fair. And the expense of the surrounding land was, they said, an advantage since it would prevent use for undesirable temporary developments. Besides, at Forest Park the first impressions of visitors to the city would be of the nicest sections of St. Louis. St. Louisans always took out-of-town visitors to Forest Park because they were proud of the park and its neighbors. Finally, they argued, the fair would improve the park, especially by the drainage that would be installed. The association's written argument concluded, "This is our end and aim; not Forest Park for the World's Fair, not a sacrifice, but the World's Fair for Forest Park; for its perfection, its monuments, its permanent results in giv-

there would be damage to "that glorious gift of nature," Forest Park.

Proponents of other sites conceded the attractiveness of Forest Park. They argued that out-

4-5. LPEC Treasurer William H. Thompson drove the first stake for the World's Fair in Forest Park on September 3, 1901.

ing St. Louis a finished and central garden fully a generation ahead of its time."

The LPEC directors announced their unanimous selection of the Forest Park site on June 25, 1901, one day after the twenty-fifth anniversary of the park's opening day. The choice was received enthusiastically by the newspapers. The *Post-Dispatch* said, "All things are possible for the World's Fair with the Forest Park site." The *Globe-Democrat* called the site "unquestionably the best" and remarked that "no one need fear for the safety of the park. . . . The ax will be applied as the skilled surgeon does the knife." The *Republic* reported that the selection was "widely discussed and universally approved in St. Louis yesterday. 'Just what I expected. Forest Park was really the only site available,' was the usual remark."[6]

Forest Park Keeper William S. Lamar assured St. Louisans the next day that even without its western half the park was more than big enough for St. Louis. Even on a hot Sunday when the eastern half of the park was crowded, he said,

very few people used the western wilderness. In the heavily used eastern half, parkgoers could admire a new floral design celebrating the coming World's Fair.

Approval of the decision was not quite as unanimous as the newspaper coverage implied. A month after the decision to use Forest Park was announced, Harry H. Werdes and John F. Bergherm, officers of the St. Louis Workingmen's Protective Association, filed suit to prevent the use of park land. The organization, probably one of the small, radical workingmen's associations active in the United States at that time, opposed the use of any park for the fair, especially Forest Park, "the only natural park and great common recreation grounds for all the people of St. Louis." They opposed fencing off a portion of the park temporarily, denying admission to those unable to pay the fair's fee. In the long run, too, the park seemed a bad location for the fair, which would cause "the destruction of the grand old forest now occupying that portion of the park."[7]

4-6. The fence that Mesker Brothers built to divide the fair site from the rest of Forest Park had an open design so parkgoers could see into the fair site even if they didn't pay to enter.

4-7. A steam shovel removed a park hill at the corner of Skinker and Lindell Boulevards to make room for World's Fair construction.

The *Republic* called the association "unknown," though Werdes claimed it had three thousand members. Bergherm charged that at least 10,000 labor union members opposed the use of the park, but the Building Trades Council, which had been involved in the fair planning since the beginning, took pains to dissociate itself from the suit, announcing a "monster parade and meeting" on Labor Day in honor of the World's Fair. The Building Trades Council was interested in the fair as a source of jobs for its members, which didn't interest Werdes, a tailor, or Bergherm, a cigar maker.

Francis called the suit "exceedingly annoying" and publicly worried about delays it might cause. Less than three weeks after the suit was filed, however, on August 12, 1901, Judge William Zachritz announced his decision for the LPEC and against Werdes and Bergherm. Fair officials were, the *Globe-Democrat* reported, "greatly elated over the outcome of the suit." The *Post-Dispatch* said editorially that "St. Louis breathed easier" at the decision. Charles H. Krum, representing Werdes and Bergherm, announced that they would appeal to the Missouri Supreme Court, but work on the fair continued as if the suit had ended, and there is no evidence it was pursued further. On August 21, 1901, President William McKinley issued a proclamation inviting "all the nations of the earth" to participate in the Exposition that would begin no later than May 1, 1903.

Francis and his staff were planning an elaborate fair. The U.S. government would have a pavilion. Most of the states and many countries wanted to be represented. Except for the Palace of Fine Arts, all of the structures to be built in the park would be temporary. Each state or country was responsible for building and removing its own pavilion. The LPEC would build and remove the fifteen main palaces, all but one of which would be made of "staff" (plaster of Paris mixed with fibers) on a wooden framework.

The fair's Palace of Fine Arts had to be fire-

4-8. Workmen transplanted some of the trees removed for the World's Fair, but cut down most of them.

proof, so it couldn't be built of wood and staff like the other palaces. That was good news for the School and Museum of Fine Arts, a branch of Washington University, which had been completing its plan for building a museum in the park when the city lent the park land for the fair. The fair's money could be used to build an art building that could become a permanent home for the museum. Ellis Wainwright, president of the museum board, was still in Europe, so board member William K. Bixby took a position as a member of the Committee on Art of the LPEC to help plan the fair's art building. Museum director Halsey Ives became director of art for the fair.[8]

The site the board had chosen for its museum, at the summit of the hill in the main "picture" of the fair, caused serious design problems for the LPEC and for the art palace's architect, Cass Gilbert. The plans included an exterior of gray limestone, which would not harmonize with the staff to be used for the temporary buildings of the Ivory City. At one point, fair officials considered putting the building on the campus of Washington University. The final decision was to build it atop the hill with temporary staff buildings, also designed by Gilbert, in front of it so that the view would be of the temporary buildings, Festival Hall and the Colonnade of States,

4-9. In 1902, the *Globe-Democrat* called the fair site inside Forest Park barren and unsightly. The River des Peres is visible in the foreground and the buildings of the new Washington University campus in the background.

and not of the permanent art building. To complete the picture, the lake extension built in the 1890s would be reshaped along more formal lines into a Grand Basin.[9]

On September 3, 1901, LPEC Treasurer William H. Thompson drove the first stake for the fair, though the LPEC did not yet have legal title to the site (Fig. 4-5). The ordinance granting use of the park required that the company file a bond of $100,000 (which could be increased by the board of public improvements) to assure restoration of the park at the conclusion of the fair. Although Francis and his associates were eager to begin work, Mayor Wells and Park Commissioner Ridgely decided in late September that LPEC workmen could continue surveying and engineering work, but that the cutting of trees must stop until the company had legal possession

of the land. The bond was signed on September 30, 1901, by all the members of the LPEC executive committee and many of the directors, including Nicholas M. Bell, who had been a state legislator when Forest Park was established in 1874.

On October 9, 1901, more than a month after the driving of the first stake, the company took formal possession of the park land without ceremony. By then a growing force of LPEC workmen was living and working in the park, supervised by Chief Civil Engineer Richard H. Phillips, whose brother Hiram was president of the board of public improvements. As soon as they had legal possession of the site, LPEC officials turned their attention to fencing it. Mesker Brothers built an iron fence separating the fair from the remainder of the park in an open style preferred by the park commissioner (Fig. 4-6).

4-10. A *Post-Dispatch* cartoon in 1903.

By the middle of October, workmen were draining the extended lake to reshape it, and clearing trees from the wilderness. One of the men told the *Globe-Democrat* that most of the trees were more than seventy-five years old and some were three hundred years old. As in the 1870s, columns of smoke marked the park's location, as trees were again burned and stumps blasted out with dynamite and gunpowder. A steam shovel leveled Wilderness Hill, near the intersection of Skinker and Lindell (Fig. 4-7). Elsewhere, men carefully dug some trees for replanting elsewhere on the fairgrounds or in the park (Fig. 4-8).

For months curious St. Louisans traveled to the park, the *Globe-Democrat* reported, "in auto, in [horse-drawn] landau, on horse, on [street] car and even afoot." In late November the number of visitors to the site in one day was estimated at 100,000 people. Many climbed the newly cleared

hill where the art palace would soon stand, to gain a panoramic view of the fair site. In April 1902, after the fence was in place, the *Globe-Democrat* reported that "half St. Louis" stood on the World's Fair site while the other half peered through the iron fence without realizing they were free to enter.

The western half of the park, the paper noted, was "temporarily . . . a barren, unsightly spot" (Fig. 4-9). Reaction to the scene was mixed. One day a *Globe-Democrat* reporter found that rich and poor, old and young felt "deepest regret" at the cutting of the trees "like the death of friends of former days" (Fig. 4-10). Two weeks later the paper reported that people were waiting to see what took the place of the lake and trees and "were content to await developments before passing judgment."[10]

As the ground was being cleared, the LPEC directors and the city considered the disposition of the River des Peres. The ordinance granting the fair site provided that the board of public improvements must approve plans and specifications for "all sewers, drains and conduits of any kind, and the laying of water pipes and fixtures" since after the fair all would become the property of the city. Repeatedly the LPEC submitted revised plans for the river and for water and sewer pipes to the board, where Commissioner Ridgely represented the park department. The river, particularly, was a matter of serious concern to the board for two reasons: changes made to the river channel inside the fairgrounds would affect the flow in the rest of the river, and the board was concerned about restoration of the river after the fair.[11]

Since the river ran through the sites of all but two of the exhibit buildings, fair officials wanted to cover the river within the fairgrounds and shorten its course. The board agreed to the rerouting and a temporary wooden channel for the river, provided the river would be restored after the fair "in accordance with landscape gardening ideas,"[12] and the LPEC would agree in writing to assume responsibility for any accidents or injuries caused by faulty construction of the channel (Fig.

4-11. Because the River des Peres crossed the sites of most of the planned World's Fair palaces, the LPEC placed it in a wooden underground channel for the duration of the fair.

4-11). After rerouting, the length of the river through the grounds was reduced by almost half.

Francis and his associates also had to settle with the individuals and groups occupying the western half of the park. Only two had a legal contract with the city granted by ordinance—the refreshment concession and the boat concession. Fair officials had taken the precaution of settling the refreshment concession with Charles Schweickardt before choosing the Forest Park site. Since Schweickardt had the exclusive right to sell refreshments in the entire park through March 1904, he could have thwarted LPEC plans to grant refreshment concessions for a fair scheduled for 1903. In early June 1901 Schweickardt waived his refreshment privilege in the part of the park to be used for the fair, asking only "that an

entrance to the World's Fair be placed . . . within a reasonable distance from the Cottage."[13]

The boating concession was not due to expire until April 1902. John H. Gundlach, one of the concessionaires, was already angry. He had advocated an O'Fallon Park site for the fair. In August he complained to Hiram Phillips that "it is well nigh impossible to row a boat in the lake" because Ridgely was not putting in enough water and had allowed the lake to become overgrown. Phillips refused to get involved, saying the LPEC had the right to break Gundlach's lease; the only question remaining was the price.[14] The LPEC executive committee minutes didn't record any claim from the boat concessionaires or approval of any payment to them. Gundlach and his partner settled for being released from their obligation to pay the

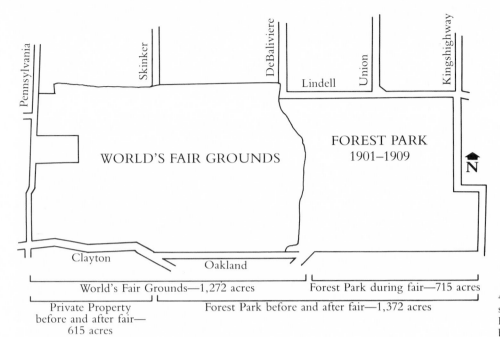

4-12. Map showing World's Fair site, the remainder of Forest Park, and some of the neighborhood in 1904.

city for the privilege of renting boats on a lake that no longer existed.

Other groups occupying the fairgrounds had less legal claim to settlement. The Gentlemen's Driving Club and the St. Louis Amateur Athletic Association (Triple A) were in the park only, the *Globe-Democrat* explained, under a permit of the park department that could be withdrawn at any time.

Triple A settled with the fair officials on a price of $2,000 for its clubhouse. The club asked city officials for permission to move to another location in Forest Park, and by early October the club had chosen a new location near the mounted police station. Triple A member G. F. A. Brueggeman designed, without fee, a new clubhouse, "twice as large as the old one and easier to keep in order." Under his direction the clubhouse was finished in sixty days and opened January 1, 1902. The club began work on two baseball diamonds, a quarter-mile cinder running track, a nine-hole golf course, and ten tennis courts.[15]

The Gentlemen's Driving Club was unable to relocate within the park. Its campaign for a new

speedway in the park proved unsuccessful, so the club moved to Waterworks Park in north St. Louis and became the North St. Louis Gentlemen's Driving Club. The St. Louis Cricket Club remained just outside the fairgrounds.

As the work of building the fair progressed, it became obvious that the project was much larger than anyone had realized. The fair eventually covered much more ground than the Forest Park site loaned by the city. Through deals of varying complexity, some extending into 1903, the LPEC leased land adjacent to the park on the north and west, almost doubling the grounds to more than 1,270 acres (Fig. 4-12). The area included the entire new campus of Washington University, which delayed its move west until after the fair (Fig. 4-13). The university buildings became headquarters and display units for the fair. The LPEC leased vacant land north of the park for the Pike, the fair's amusement area. In the spring of 1902 the fair directors realized they couldn't open in 1903, after the U.S. government and other exhibitors said they wouldn't be ready.

4-13. A portion of the World's Fair grounds during the fair. The building at the right was the administration building for the fair. After the fair, it was Brookings Hall, part of Washington University. The building to the left, the Italian Pavilion, was removed after the fair.

They postponed the fair's opening from April 1903 to April 1904, so the St. Louis fair, like the Chicago fair, was a year late.

As city officials became aware of the magnitude of this undertaking, they worried about the restoration of Forest Park. The ordinance granting the use of half of the park for the fair authorized the board of public improvements to increase the LPEC's bond "if it deem it necessary in the interest of the city." In January 1903 the board of public improvements authorized the park commissioner to hire a landscape architect to examine the fair site and estimate the cost of restoration. Ridgely hired Samuel Parsons, Jr., engineer and landscape architect of the Park System of Greater New York, who reported that the land would need regrading, top soil, and grass seed. Trees would need to be planted, the River des Peres would have to be rerouted, and the fair's artificial

waterways reworked (Figs. 4-14 to 4-16). He concluded that "it would not be at all extravagant to say that $1,000,000 would be needed." [16]

The board of public improvements voted unanimously to require an additional bond of $550,000. After a month with no response from the LPEC, the board asked the mayor to intervene. In February 1904, almost a year later, Mayor Wells reminded Francis that the fair could not open until the bond was posted. Francis indignantly denied that the LPEC would permit the "desecration of Forest Park." Finally, in August 1904, after the fair was half over, eight of the LPEC directors, including Francis, signed an additional bond pledging an amount not to exceed $100,000, with the permanent art building as additional security.

This argument between the fair directors and city authorities, including Ridgely and his suc-

4-14, 4-15, 4-16. A section of Forest Park as it appeared in July 1901 before World's Fair construction, in August 1902 during the construction, and in 1904 after the construction was complete, taken from the tower of the Lindell Pavilion.

cessor and close friend Robert Aull, revealed a serious difference of opinion about "satisfactory
park conditions."[17] The differences would reappear after the fair when park restoration began
(Fig. 4-17).

St. Louisans continued to enjoy the eastern
half of the park as they had in the 1890s. The zoo
was still popular. The newspapers often carried
illustrated stories about the animals, particularly
the birth of baby animals (Fig. 4-18). The *Post-
Dispatch* detailed the capture of Jack, the "lady
grizzly bear," who was "one of the star attractions at Forest Park."[18] The story that Little Nick,
the first son of Scrappin' Jennie the elk, could
walk at the age of one week rated front-page coverage. The Missouri Fish Commission continued
to use the fish hatchery lakes. The papers reported on cleaning out the spawning pond and
Superintendent Philip Kopplin, Jr., hand-feeding
Betty, the blind bass of Forest Park.

Sports organized by the clubs in Forest Park
continued during the fair. The St. Louis Cricket
Club played on the Forest Park Crease, near the
Lindell Pavilion. The new Triple A tennis courts
were in use by late May 1902, and the baseball
diamonds by June. The golf course took longer
than expected to complete and didn't host tournaments until May 1903.

Horseback riding continued to be popular in
the park. The *Post-Dispatch* commented that some
of the riders were "young ladies" who rode "in
truly independent fashion . . . . astride, and most
of the time sans hats."

Bicycling continued, though less popular
than it had been before the turn of the century. A
1902 St. Louis guidebook remarked, "Even now-
adays, when this sport has given way to others to
a great extent, there can always be seen scores of
wheels flashing through the trees" of Forest Park.
In June 1902 bikers revived the Forest Park Bicycle Race after an absence of about five years.
The *Post-Dispatch* announced the race in doggerel:

Get out the old bicycle
That grimy, ancient wheel,
That used to give us such a thrill
And make our senses reel. . . .
The auto-be-mo bubble
Is now the reigning fad,
Yet the old bicycle days
Made many thousands glad. . . .
Oh, we will give the autos
One long and merry chase,
For, hip, hooray, we're going to have
Another big road race.[19]

As this ditty implied, automobile use was
growing in St. Louis just after the turn of the century, though carriages still predominated. The
Post-Dispatch remarked in May 1902 that the
number of automobiles in St. Louis had increased
from thirty-five to two hundred in less than two
years.

Some of these automobiles were causing
problems in Forest Park. As early as 1901 a letter
to an editor urged the park commissioner to bar
automobiles from the park, since they often
frightened the horses and would surely cause an
accident with their great speed.

The commissioner didn't bar automobiles,
but "scorchers" who exceeded the park's eight-
mile-an-hour speed limit were arrested and fined.
Enforcement became easier in July 1904, when
the mounted police bought two "high-speed automobiles" equipped with "speed gauges" to en-
able the police to verify the automobile's speed
(Fig. 4-19).[20]

Although park employees built about a mile
of new road after the fairgrounds were fenced off
from the park, the roads were still inadequate.
The new road segments outside the fairgrounds
only replaced sections of road inside the grounds
and linked the remaining park roads. Traffic
increased greatly because vehicles needed for
fair construction entered the grounds through
the park.

Dusty roads were still a problem. As one
letter writer complained, "Forest Park is so thick
with dust out there that it is difficult to see a horse
you are driving; besides, the park is being ruined
out there on account of the dust; they never sprin-
kle the road at all."[21]

4-17. Many St. Louisans went to watch construction of the fair's palaces.

4-18. Visiting the Forest Park zoo, about 1903.

With the approach of the World's Fair, St. Louisans worked to beautify their city for visitors. As Mayor Wells wrote in 1901, "St. Louis . . . should put herself in order. She should prepare her gala attire, and wear it from the day the gates of the Fair are first open." Park Commissioner Ridgely explained, in words any gardener would appreciate, that he needed more time than some of the other departments. "A park is not like a house on which you can place the painters and decorators, and in short notice have a clean and rejuvenated structure, but in your park improvements everything has to have time, nature must be given a chance."

So that Forest Park would provide a suitable entrance to the fair, the park department used its own budget and solicited donations. Adolphus Busch donated a steel flag pole for Forest Park, and William C. Uhri gave a set of flags. Commissioner Ridgely welcomed the gifts, since the previous flagpole had been destroyed by the tornado of 1896. The city owned the streetcar pavilions, but the St. Louis Transit Company, which had taken over the operation of all the streetcar lines

to Forest Park, agreed to renovate them at its own expense.

As the exposition opening neared, park employees worked feverishly. They traced the Forest Park spring to its source, then piped it to a new site and built a shelter house. The city chemist tested the water from the spring, newly named Wells Spring, and found it to be "perfectly safe drinking water, free from any sewage contamination." They repaired the wooden bandstand on the island in Pagoda Lake, almost thirty years old and badly decayed, and replaced most of the foundation. The Lindell streetcar track loop, no longer in use since the streetcars didn't enter the park, was, an employee reported to Commissioner Aull, "transformed into a large carriage corral, to accommodate those visitors who drive to the fair."

Before the fair opened, men pruned the shrubs, removed all of the dead wood from the trees, and fertilized and raked the lawns. They resurfaced many of the drives, built new walkways, and placed a new large fountain jet in Sylvan Lake. New flower beds, with fleur de lis designs

4-19. Policemen and their driver in the "high-speed automobile" with a "speed gauge" tried to apprehend "scorchers" who exceeded the park's eight-mile-an-hour speed limit.

to honor the fair, graced the old police substation and the music pagoda.

The bridge that carried the Wabash railroad tracks over a park drive near the Lindell-Kingshighway entrance was enlarged so the road could be widened to accommodate increased traffic. Park commissioners had complained since 1897 that the bridge was inadequate. The railroad paid part of the cost, and the city approved its share of the expenditure after the fair had begun. According to Park Commissioner Aull, "The work was done under somewhat trying conditions. The Louisiana Purchase Exposition was open and trains running every fifteen minutes to and fro, besides the regular and through trains of the system."

During the fair, park employees exerted themselves to keep the park looking its best. As Aull explained, "All the vehicle traffic [to the fair] passed through the park, and all the supplies of

ice, food, etc., entered the grounds through Forest Park at night. In the evening when the crowds were leaving, thousands and thousands made their exit through the park, over the lawns and through the shrubbery."[22]

The extra effort in Forest Park showed clearly in its expenditures. For the fiscal year that included the World's Fair, total city expenditures increased, total park expenditures grew even faster, and expenditures for Forest Park climbed faster still. The Forest Park expenditure (which included the city's share of the expense for the Wabash bridge) almost doubled from the previous year and represented almost half of the total spent on parks. The Forest Park workforce had shrunk from its high of 106 in 1899 to 79 in 1902, but had to care for only half as much land. These numbers illustrate the city administration's determination to have the city look its best for the fair and to make sure Forest Park lived up to its bill-ing in a guidebook of the period as "second to none in points of utility and beauty."[23]

Around the park, too, vast changes took place as the city prepared for the fair. The city struggled to clean its air and water. The paving of streets leading to the park benefited fairgoers, parkgoers, and, not incidentally, West End residents. Construction accelerated in the private places north of the park, as the neighborhood became ever more fashionable. Some of the houses were rushed to completion to accommodate World's Fair guests. By 1901 there were enough families living nearby to attract Mary Institute, a private girls' school affiliated with Washington University, from its previous location on formerly fashionable Lucas Place downtown. In June 1901 school officials laid the cornerstone for a new building about four blocks north of the park.

East of the park on Kingshighway, former mayor Cyrus Walbridge was part of a group that erected the Buckingham Club, advertised as "a permanent brick and stone structure" with "a good view of the main buildings of the Exposition." It would be "run as a club hotel during the fair, entertaining none but members and their friends. Only a limited number of memberships will be sold, and everything will be first class."[24] After the fair it would become a hotel. Forest Park University erected a new building on its campus south of the park to serve as a hotel during the fair and a university building afterward. Profits from hotel guests, the school hoped, would help pay for the new building.

The Forest Park Highlands continued its previous activities and added new ones. The St. Louis Police Relief Association Benefit and various school picnics often filled the grounds. The Highlands' owner, Anton Steuver, added a new ride, the Loop the Loop, for the summer of 1902 at a cost of $15,000. A St. Louis doctor told the *Post-Dispatch* that the ride would "stop weak hearts."[25] "The Big Place on the Hill," as Steuver called it, opened at the same time as the fair, a full month earlier than usual.

From April 30, 1904, through December 1, 1904, St. Louisans and visitors who had the time and could afford the fifty-cent single-day admission charge (or could find a way to get into the fair without paying) enjoyed the fair. More than twenty million people went to the fair, an average of more than 100,000 for each day the fair was open. The fifteen exhibit palaces, all outlined with electric lights, covered 128 acres of the 1,272-acre fairgrounds, the largest fair site ever. More than nine hundred buildings, including refreshment stands, dotted the grounds. Twenty-two countries were represented, including Ceylon, Japan, and China. Forty-four United States cities, states, and territories had built buildings. The U.S. government had built a bird cage big enough for the birds to fly freely. A working coal mine was unusually realistic, since workmen preparing the site struck coal under the park. Hopes of displaying artifacts from several small Omaha Indian mounds on the site had died when ethnologist David I. Bushnell opened a mound and discovered its poor state of preservation. A Ferris wheel, moved from the Chicago fair, could carry 1,440 people (40 in each of its 36 cars) up 250 feet over the grounds. Balloons ascended from an Aeronautic Concourse close to the Athletic Field where the 1904 Olympics were being held, the third modern Olympiad and the first in the United States. Fairgoers marveled at the exhibits, from the new automobiles, to the floral clock 112 feet in diameter, to the cow made of butter. They ate ice cream cones and hot dogs, drank iced tea, and sang "Meet Me in St. Louis."[26]

In late November 1904 President Theodore Roosevelt, who had opened the fair by pressing a telegraph key in the East Room of the White House, arrived in St. Louis to visit the World's Fair. President and Mrs. Roosevelt took a carriage ride in Forest Park. A front-page headline called it, "A Quiet Drive Which Was Greatly Enjoyed." By that time, Francis and his associates had already begun to consider their next project—dismantling the fair and returning the land to its owners.

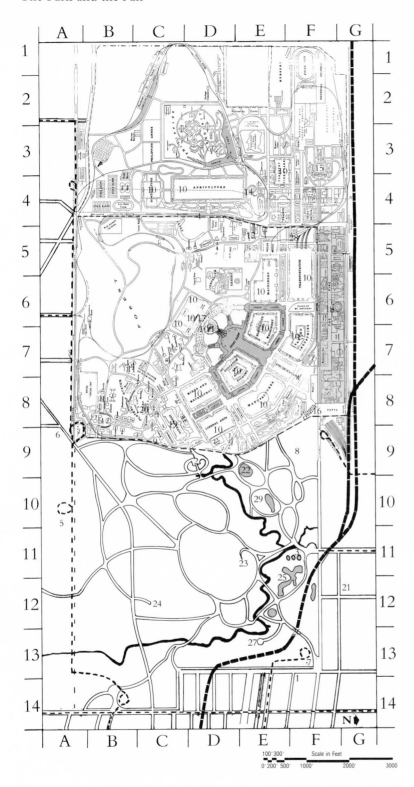

PARK LOCATOR MAP
(1901–1904)

1. Buckingham Club, F-13
2. Cottage restaurant (second location), D-9
3. Fish hatchery lakes, F-11
4. Forest Park, western boundary, A-4 to F-4
5. Forest Park Highlands, A-10
6. Forest Park University, A-9
7. Laclede Pavilion, F-13
8. Lindell Pavilion, F-9
9. Louisiana Purchase Exposition (1904 World's Fair) grounds, eastern boundary, A-9 to G-9
10. Exhibit palaces, various locations
11. Coal mine, B-7
12. Ferris Wheel (Observation Wheel), E-5
13. Festival Hall, D-6
14. Floral clock, E-4
15. Louisiana Purchase Exposition Company Administration Building (later Brookings Hall, Washington University), F-3
16. Main entrance (Lindell entrance), F-8
17. Palace of Fine Arts (later City Art Museum), D-6
18. Pike, F-5 to F-8
19. U.S. Government Building, C-8
20. U.S. Government Bird Cage (Smithsonian exhibit), C-8
21. Mary Institute, G-12
22. Music pagoda, E-9
23. Police Substation, E-11
24. St. Louis Amateur Athletic Association (Triple A) Clubhouse (second location), C-12
25. Sylvan Lake, E-12 and F-11
26. Wabash Railroad bridge, F-13
27. Wells Spring, E-13
28. Wilderness Hill (probable location before fair), F-5
29. Zoo cages (probable location), E-10

5

PUTTING THE PARK BACK TOGETHER (1904–1911)

Within six months after the close of [the World's Fair], the [Louisiana Purchase Exposition Co.] shall clear the park . . . of all tramways and railway tracks, rubbish and debris, and of all buildings . . . and other structures of every kind, and shall within twelve months after the close of [the] Fair . . ., fully restore the park . . . in accordance with plans to be approved by the Board of Public Improvements, and . . . subject to the inspection of the Park Commissioner and to his entire satisfaction and approval.—St. Louis Ordinance 20412, 1901

The directors of the Exposition . . . believe that this new park will be better than the old. The forest has gone—but in its place let us hope to see happy throngs of children browning in the sun.—Louisiana Purchase Exposition Company General Counsel Franklin Ferriss, 1905.

Like building the fair, removing it and returning the park land to the city took much longer than expected. The Louisiana Purchase Exposition Company (LPEC) had agreed to "fully restore the park" within one year after the close of the fair (Fig. 5-1). In fact, the work continued until April 30, 1913, exactly nine years after the fair opened, nine years of continuing conflict between city officials and fair officials.

Mayor Rolla Wells was near the end of his second term and Philip C. Scanlan had succeeded Robert Aull as park commissioner before city and fair officials could agree. The disagreements were sharp, even though Wells, Aull, and Scanlan were sympathetic to David R. Francis and his World's Fair associates. Wells had been one of the organizers of the fair in 1899 and instrumental in the city's decision to lend park land for the fair. He was a neighbor, political associate, and friend of "Dave" Francis. Yet, as he later explained, he believed it was his duty as mayor to insist that the LPEC restore the park (Fig. 5-2). Aull and Scanlan were Wells's appointees and moved in his social circle. Aull was a horse fancier, called "Colonel Bob" by hundreds of prominent St. Louisans. Scanlan was a member of an old St. Louis family,

the Christys. Like Wells and Francis, he lived in the fashionable West End a few blocks east of the park.

Actually, the park land was not restored but reshaped. Large open spaces and new buildings replaced the "magnificent forest" that had covered much of the western section of the park before the fair. Around the fair's Grand Basin, a new formal center emerged, with its axis from Art Hill to the Jefferson Memorial, built after the fair. The cleared slope of Art Hill revealed a new vista, and became a winter toboggan run and an amphitheater that accommodated thousands of people for civic celebrations after the fair. New paved roads and new underground water and sewer systems crisscrossed the western half of the park. Before these changes could take place, however, the LPEC and the city had to agree on a restoration plan.[1]

About six weeks before the fair closed, the LPEC appointed a restoration committee, chaired by David R. Francis, to draw a plan for restoring the park land. One of the members of the committee, William K. Bixby, was also a director of the School and Museum of Fine Arts, which

82

5-1. A view along the Grand Basin during the fair. After the fair, all of the buildings had to be removed and the land returned to park conditions.

planned to move into the fair's art building as soon as possible. Francis and his committee retained landscape architect George E. Kessler of Kansas City, who had been chief landscape architect of the fair (Fig. 5-3). Like the men who had drawn the plan for the park almost thirty years before, Kessler was trained in Germany. He had studied engineering, forestry, and botany and had been a practicing landscape architect since 1882. Beginning in 1892 he had designed the Kansas City park system.

Kessler's plans for the western half of Forest Park reflected his belief that the function of large urban parks was to allow "rich and poor alike" to enjoy "the quiet repose of the country and . . . freedom from the City cares and annoyances." If Kessler was aware of the rapid growth of active

recreation in the park, he either didn't approve of it or didn't think it was the LPEC's responsibility to provide for it. The western half of Forest Park, he wrote, should "be restored on the simplest possible lines and in complete harmony with its eastern portion" to retain "the sylvan beauties of Forest Park, its restfulness and opportunity for quiet enjoyment." The restoration plan should emphasize "the careful preservation of natural scenery . . . and constant [protection] against permanent encroachment of any structures, except those essential to public comfort."[2]

Public opinion was divided. Some people thought the company should leave some or even all of the fair structures in the park. Others believed that the company should remove everything from the park. Kessler advised Francis and

St. Louis Globe-Democrat.
MAGAZINE SECTION.

THE FAIR IS OVER.
NOW TO WORK.

5-2. The *Globe-Democrat* used the popular World's Fair statue of St. Louis to illustrate the job to be done.

his committee that they should leave the art building in the park and remove the other fair buildings (Fig. 5-4). The small railroad that climbed the hill to the art building should be removed, Kessler said. The River des Peres, he reported, "is now nothing more than a great sewer and should be permanently treated as such . . . throughout the entire length of the Park." The forest that had covered much of the land could be replaced with new sweeping lawns.[3]

At first, relations with the city were amicable. Kessler and the restoration committee met on the fairgrounds with the board of public improvements, which, by ordinance, had to approve the restoration. The board approved Kessler's concepts and asked for detailed plans, especially for the River des Peres. In January 1905 the LPEC hired Kessler as director of restoration to oversee

implementation of his ideas. Kessler presented the detailed plans to the board of public improvements. LPEC General Counsel Franklin Ferriss told the board that the directors "believe that this new park will be better than the old. . . . The forest has gone—but in its place let us hope to see happy throngs of children browning in the sun."[4]

The *Globe-Democrat* and others agreed that the restoration of the park land to prefair conditions was both impossible and undesirable. The park should be rebuilt, the paper said, according to a plan that should respond to public suggestions and be based on "study and deliberate judgment."[5]

In May 1905, after the board of public improvements had been considering the plan for almost four months, Francis and his associates, perhaps tired of waiting for the board to make up its mind, offered to give the city the park land and enough money to cover the cost of restoration, which they estimated at $100,000. The *Globe-Democrat* advised the city to accept the offer and to take its time in rebuilding the park. But the city would have none of that. Park Commissioner Aull estimated the restoration cost to be nearer $300,000 than $100,000. The ordinance required the LPEC, not the city, to restore the park land. In June 1905 the board of public improvements approved Kessler's plans with only minor modifications, and the LPEC agreed to do the work.

In early July 1905 the LPEC offered, and the city accepted, a bronze statue of the city's patron saint, the *Apotheosis of St. Louis*, to be made at the LPEC's expense from the temporary statue displayed at the fair (Fig. 5-5). The statue had been popular from the start, and editorial cartoonists and others had quickly adopted it as a symbol of the city. The company's offer, W. R. Hodges wrote the *Globe-Democrat*, should "silence carping criticism" of the LPEC.[6]

While the officials wrangled, the work of removing the fair buildings from the park began. The Chicago House Wrecking Company paid $450,000 for the privilege of wrecking the tem-

5-3. George E. Kessler, the fair's chief landscape architect, advised the Louisiana Purchase Exposition Company (LPEC) committee on rebuilding Forest Park from 1904 to 1909.

porary fair palaces, containing an estimated 100 million feet of lumber, 2 million square feet of window sashes, and copper wire worth $630,000. Much of the staff that covered the building exteriors was shipped to Venice, Illinois, to be reduced to plaster, though some remained in the park to be used as landfill. Many of the plants that had beautified the fairgrounds were stored at a temporary nursery to await replanting on the restored grounds. Others were sold.

It was also at this time, after a snow in January 1905, that LPEC employees discovered a natural toboggan slope down Art Hill, cleared of trees for the fair. Invited to try the slope for the photographer, Francis "reluctantly declined," the *Globe-Democrat* reported (Fig. 5-6).[7]

As spring arrived, St. Louisans went to the park to inspect the work in progress. In March 1905 an estimated 1,000 people paid twenty-five cents to enter the fairgrounds. Among the visitors were amateur photographers who took pictures of the ruins. The numbers of people and the new open spaces caused problems with the park's oak trees. The trees' shallow roots, Aull explained, couldn't stand the hot sun and the "tramping of the multitudes" of spectators. To try to save the trees, Aull decided, the fallen leaves would be left in place to protect the roots.[8]

Most people in the western half of the park were there to work. As the wrecking company fell behind schedule, LPEC crews did some of the removal work, then smoothed and graded the land and planted grass, shrubs, and trees. Near the Grand Basin, the fair's sunken garden again became a lake, later called Post-Dispatch Lake. Between the two large bodies of water ran a new lagoon. The crews left the fair's water and sewer systems for park use, though some of the fire hydrants seemed oddly located after the fair buildings were removed.

The company crews left many of the fair's paved roads and added new ones, for a total of about seven miles of paved roads and more than five miles of dirt roads. Some of the roads were given names connected with the fair: Government Drive ran below Government Hill, the site of the Missouri and U.S. government pavilions; Fine Arts Drive climbed Art Hill, site of the Fine Arts Palace; Lagoon Drive ran near the new lagoon. While Washington Drive was not maintained after the fair, a new strip of road was given that name; and Commissioner Scanlan named Wells Drive for the mayor.

The River des Peres became an open stream again after workmen removed its cover. Since the LPEC had not corrected the problem of the River des Peres, the city was forced to deal with it. A park department employee reported in 1905, "The River des Peres, which was formerly one of the principal landscape features of the park, has now become a public nuisance. . . . The stench

5-4. The World's Fair Palace of Fine Arts remained in the park after the fair was removed and later housed the City Art Museum. The wing visible at the right of the picture and a similar one out of the picture to the left were demolished after the fair.

arising from this stream at times when the water is low is stifling." The city's sewer commissioner considered the necessary work on the fifteen miles of the river within the city limits the most important problem facing his department.[9]

In June 1906 city voters approved a bond issue, and in 1911 the city began construction of the Forest Park Foul Water Sewer, a pipe under the river through the park. Built in three sections following the course of the river, it cost more than $70,000, including necessary pumping machinery, but soon proved inadequate.[10]

When LPEC officials considered a section of the fairgrounds finished, they opened it to the public. The new smooth, empty roads soon attracted motorists. In April 1907 twelve prospective automobile customers arranged with the LPEC for a race up Fine Arts Drive, which, the *Republic* explained, "gives practically a quarter of a mile climb, with a 30 percent grade, and is considered sufficient to test the cars to the utmost." The smooth new roads were also a temptation for unauthorized (and illegal) racing. In 1909 a patrolman of the mounted district, on a motorcycle,

watched the entrances to Forest Park from the county in the early morning hours and arrested several "auto racers and speeders who have been in the habit of hitting only the bumps when they come in from the rural roads," the *Post-Dispatch* reported.[11] Bicyclists, too, enjoyed the new roads. In 1908 the St. Louis Cycling Club arranged with the LPEC to use the new roads for a revival of the old Forest Park Road Race.

In 1906 the LPEC turned the art building over to the Washington University School and Museum of Fine Arts, as the two organizations had previously agreed. The art museum in Forest Park opened in late August 1906. Hours were nine to five every day for museum members and their families, only Saturday and Sunday for nonmembers.

On October 4, 1906, city and fair officials joined in unveiling the bronze statue of St. Louis in front of the museum. The *Globe-Democrat* reported, "The staff statue which had been admired by millions" became "the largest and most picturesque bronze statue in America."[12] As the mayor's daughter unveiled the statue, more than

5-5. The staff statue of St. Louis awaiting shipment to St. Louis for the World's Fair. Sculptor Charles H. Niehaus created the small version visible in the foreground; artisans then made the large scale version for the fair.

25,000 people cheered, thousands of them city employees who had paraded to the park (Fig. 5-7).

The statue quickly attracted visitors to the museum in the park. On the first Sunday after the unveiling of the statue, the park was thronged with pedestrians, carriages, and automobiles, and a record crowd of more than 6,000 went to the new museum. For about four months the art museum operated at two locations—the new one in Forest Park and the old one downtown. Attendance at the Forest Park museum was almost ten times the attendance downtown, and on January 1, 1907, the downtown location closed.

In March 1907 the Missouri legislature authorized the voters of St. Louis to approve a yearly real estate tax of two cents per hundred dollars valuation "for the establishment, maintenance or extension of a museum of art." The act provided that the museum "shall be forever free" to the residents of the city as long as the art museum tax was collected, but the museum could charge "for admission to the galleries and classes upon certain days other than public holidays" and

5-6. After the trees were removed for the fair, St. Louisans
discovered the fun of sledding
down Art Hill in 1905. Festival
Hall and the Colonnade of
States are visible in the background, hiding the art building.

could charge for admission of nonresidents (Fig. 5-8).[13]

St. Louis officials moved quickly to get the proposed tax on the city ballot for April 2, 1907, less than a month after the state law passed. The Central Trades and Labor Union endorsed the proposed tax after museum director Halsey C. Ives told union delegates that "the working classes . . . made up the majority of visitors, and were at the museum in Forest Park by thousands every Sunday." The tax passed easily. The *Post-Dispatch* remarked, "the popularity of the Museum with the Sunday afternoon visitors to Forest Park was largely responsible for the ample majority of votes in its favor."[14]

In November 1907 cooperation between city and fair officials disintegrated. The LPEC informed the board of public improvements that the park land was ready for return to the city, but the city refused to accept it. Park Commissioner Scanlan sent the company an official list of the

work that remained. Scanlan deplored the company's "ruthless destruction of majestic forest trees" and said the land still bore "many scars" from the fair.

Francis replied angrily, "The removal of such trees as were necessary to permit the construction of World's Fair buildings . . . cannot justly be called ruthless destruction." Francis pointed out that many of the conditions Scanlan complained of arose from the city's failure to approve plans submitted by the LPEC, or to protect the land already returned to the city.[15]

Francis had a bargaining point—money. As the LPEC settled its affairs, it appeared that the company would have a surplus. A sum of $15 million had been subscribed to build the fair by the U.S. government, by the city government, and by individuals called "stockholders" who had paid $100 a share. All the money, and more, had been spent building the fair, but the fair had collected money from such things as admissions,

5-7. A view in the 1950s of the bronze statue of the *Apotheosis of St. Louis*, unveiled October 4, 1906, as part of the reshaping of the park after the fair.

5-8. Visiting the art museum. Following the removal of the miniature railroad that climbed the hill during the fair, most mu-
seum-goers had to use muscle power to go up the hill—their own
or a horse's.

concessions, and salvage. According to the original agreements, any surplus would be divided
among the governments and the stockholders in
proportion to their original contributions. The
amount that a holder of a $100 share could expect
to receive would be small. Even if the fair had a
surplus of $400,000, each share would be worth
only about 27 cents.

In April 1908 Francis notified the city that
the company would comply with the city's requests for extra work in the park, even though
the company believed that it had "done more
than the ordinance required." Kessler's crews built
four new road bridges that, with the city's permission, the company named for the palaces that

had stood nearby: Liberal Arts Bridge, Manufactures Bridge, Education Bridge, and Transportation Bridge.

The LPEC also offered to build a monumen-
tal entrance to the park at DeBaliviere. Instead,
however, the city requested a shelter pavilion
where it could sell refreshments (Fig. 5-9). The
Cottage had closed when Schweickardt's lease expired in 1904 and remained closed amid objections to the sale of liquor in the park, which were
raised by such citizens as Anna Sneed Cairns of
Forest Park University. During the winter of
1907–8 the park department had demolished the
Cottage, then less than fifteen years old but considered beyond repair. So the city gladly accepted
the LPEC's offer for a $40,000 shelter atop Gov-
ernment Hill.[16]

Without explanation, in May 1908 the city
suddenly challenged the art museum's claim to
the Forest Park building. Scanlan wrote that the
art building was "the absolute property of the
city, to be dealt with as to the city seems best."
The city collected the new art museum tax, but
when the museum board of control tried to use
the money, the city refused to release any, on the
grounds that the museum, a department of Washington University, could not legally be tax supported. The museum board sued for the funds. In
October 1908, while the suit was still pending,
Scanlan insisted that the museum vacate the Forest Park building or restructure itself with a board
appointed by the mayor. The *Globe-Democrat* suggested sarcastically that the city could use the art
museum building as "the most magnificent shelter
and amusement palace in the United States."[17]

In 1909 the outlines of a settlement emerged.
The Missouri Supreme Court had ruled that the
school of fine arts could not receive the museum
tax. So by ordinance the city created the City Art
Museum, housed in the Forest Park building,
supported by city appropriations, and governed
by a board of control appointed by the mayor.
Director Ives resigned from the St. Louis School
of Fine Arts, which moved to the Washington
University campus.[18]

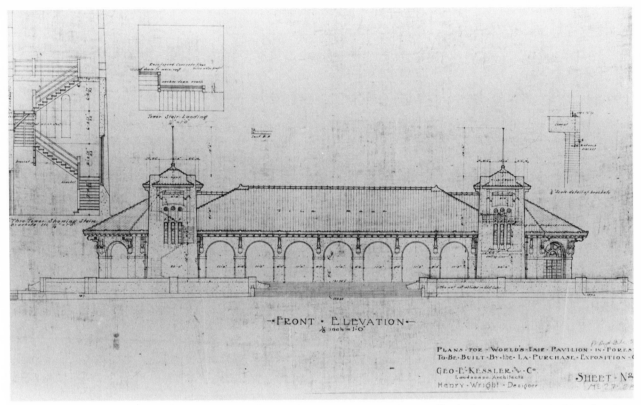

·FRONT·ELEVATION·

PLANS·FOR·WORLD'S·FAIR·PAVILION·IN·FORES
TO·BE·BUILT·BY·THE·LA·PURCHASE·EXPOSITION·C
GEO·E·KESSLER·&·C°
Landscape·Architects
Henry·Wright·Designer
SHEET·N°

5-9. In 1908, after demolition of the Cottage restaurant, city officials again wanted a place to sell refreshments in Forest Park, so they were delighted to accept the LPEC's offer to build this structure, the World's Fair Pavilion.

This arrangement lasted just over three years. In 1912 the Missouri Supreme Court ruled that the state law authorizing the art museum tax was constitutional except for the section that gave the tax money to a branch of Washington University. The city then abolished the Art Museum Board of Control and established a self-perpetuating Administrative Board of the Art Museum, funded by the tax approved in 1907 and containing no city officials.[19]

Francis, meanwhile, struggled to provide Forest Park with a statue of Thomas Jefferson to commemorate his role as purchaser of the Louisiana Territory. To finance the monument, he asked Congress to release the U.S. government's share of the fair surplus. In March 1909 Congress authorized the LPEC to spend up to $150,000 of the U.S. government's share, provided that the city and the LPEC would "jointly contribute an amount at least equal to" the amount contributed by the United States and the total cost of the memorial be at least $200,000.[20] This money made it possible to expand the plans to include a building as well as a statue.

On April 7, 1909, the board of public improvements and the LPEC reached a final agreement about the fair site. The LPEC had already begun construction of the Government Hill refreshment pavilion. If the company would finish the pavilion and would spend at least $200,000 on a monument to Thomas Jefferson, the city would consider the land restored. On the same day, Scanlan hired Kessler as the park department's landscape architect, to oversee the completion of restoration and to lay out the city's new small parks. While the LPEC's work was not yet complete, at least Francis knew what the city expected.[21]

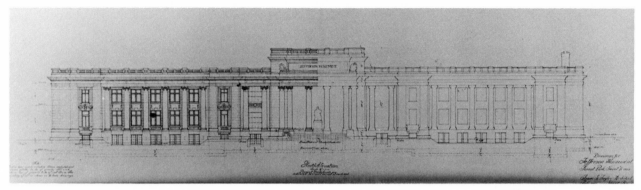

5-10. The Jefferson Memorial building commemorated President Thomas Jefferson's role in the Louisiana Purchase.

Still the controversy was not quite over. The plans for the Jefferson Memorial building had to be drawn and approved by the LPEC and the city (Fig. 5-10). The LPEC executive committee considered at least two sites: on Government Hill, near the pavilion, and on the site of the main entrance to the fair, near DeBaliviere. In March 1910, the committee chose the DeBaliviere site and unanimously agreed to expand the purpose of the building.

Francis disclosed the plans at a dinner in April 1910 marking the sixth anniversary of the opening of the fair. The building, he announced, would provide an entrance to the park, through an arch housing the statue of Thomas Jefferson. In addition the building would contain a meeting room and exhibit space for "the archives of the Exposition, historical data of the Louisiana Purchase territory and the collection of the Missouri Historical Society," which had long maintained offices, a library, and a museum downtown.

The LPEC and the Missouri Historical Society (MHS) had maintained a close relationship for a number of years. Pierre Chouteau's suggestion for a commemoration of the hundredth anniversary of the Louisiana Purchase had included a plan to provide a secure permanent space for the MHS, and the society had been instrumental in forming the LPEC. Francis had suggested to the Louisiana Purchase Convention in 1899 that Thomas Jefferson should be commemorated by "a structure, monument or museum or library."

By 1901 some were suggesting that the LPEC should build for the fair a permanent building that could continue to be used for "the libraries and collections of the Missouri Historical Society, The Academy of Science of St. Louis, and other organizations."

By 1906 the MHS building downtown and its surrounding neighborhood had deteriorated, and the MHS planned to follow the art museum to Forest Park. An October 1906 ordinance authorized the society to erect a building in Forest Park, but the campaign for funds was not very successful. During the period that the LPEC was debating the design and use of the Jefferson Memorial, the MHS was looking for a new building, so the two projects merged.

A group of architects said the design for the multipurpose building was unsatisfactory as a monument, while others defended the design. The LPEC directors didn't have time to argue. The company's ten-year charter would expire on April 20, 1911. After the corporate charter expired, General Counsel Ferriss advised, the last board of directors would become trustees with authority to settle the affairs of the corporation but not to "engage in a new business, or use the [corporate] funds for new enterprises."[22]

In January 1911 the city approved slightly revised plans for the building. In March an ordinance provided for the management and upkeep of the building and gave the park commissioner authority to designate space in the building for

5-11. Dedication of the Jefferson Memorial building on April 30, 1913, showing the marchers from Christian Brothers College in the foreground. The building was completed twenty-five years before construction began on the Jefferson Memorial in Washington, D.C.

the historical society. The MHS would put its materials on display to the public free of charge at least five days a week, including Sunday, and would pay the city $300 a year for heat, light, and water. The city would pay for building repairs. The 1906 ordinance allowing the MHS to build in the park was repealed, and the city reserved the right "to, at any time, revoke or modify" the society's license to occupy the Jefferson Memorial.

On April 1, 1911, less than three weeks before the LPEC charter expired, the company contracted for construction of the Jefferson Memorial, which began immediately with a ground-breaking ceremony on April 8, 1911, and cornerstone laying on May 1, 1911. Construction took two years and cost about $450,000. The building was dedicated on April 30, 1913, the ninth anniversary of the opening of the fair, and twenty-five years before construction began on the Jefferson Memorial in Washington, D.C. (Fig. 5-11). The arch at the center of the St. Louis building framed a statue of Thomas Jefferson by Karl Bitter, who had been chief of sculpture for the fair.

With the dedication of the Jefferson Memorial building, the LPEC's work was complete. The fair had brought great changes to Forest Park. Kessler said the park had received "improvements and betterments which fairly represent $500,000 of cost." This estimate didn't include the art museum, the statue of St. Louis, the World's Fair Pavilion, or the Jefferson Memorial, only landscaping, roads and bridges, sewers and water systems. The restoration, he said, "gives to Forest Park an impression of distances and magnitude that the old park did not possess. . . . Certainly there are no more impressive park views in the country than those afforded from Art Hill . . . and from Government Hill . . . across the broad meadows, the lakes and lagoons. . ., to the encircling sky line of the city."

The *Globe-Democrat* agreed that the work was a success. "Whether one looks up from the Memorial Building to the Art Museum, crowning Art Hill not far away, or down from Art Hill to the Memorial Building, . . . all regret for the primeval forest vanishes."[23]

Even after the dedication of the Jefferson

5-12, 5-13. Two views of the bird cage, showing the original wooden base and the walk-through tunnel for people.

5-14. Park department employees built a new monkey house in 1905 near the bird cage.

Memorial, the story of the World's Fair was not quite over. After having settled all outstanding obligations, the trustees of the former LPEC still had about $100,000. In 1916, following the advice of their lawyer, they formed a corporation called the Louisiana Purchase Historical Association to hold the remaining money "as an endowment fund . . . for the benefit of an historical museum and library . . . to consist of the archives of the Louisiana Purchase Exposition Company."[24] The corporation was merged into the Missouri Historical Society in 1925, as Francis had long intended.

During the wrangling over restoration, St. Louisans continued to visit the park, and park authorities provided a few new attractions, especially at the zoo. The small collection of mostly native American animals that the park department had maintained before the fair grew suddenly larger and more exotic as the fair closed. Many of the animals brought to St. Louis for display in various exhibits were left behind.

The zoo also acquired a spectacular new structure—the giant bird cage from the federal government exhibit. The cage was 228 feet long, 84 feet wide, and 50 feet high. During the fair

about a thousand birds flew freely inside the structure while visitors walked through an arched cage within the cage. In the spring of 1905 the city paid $3,500 to buy the cage, which had cost the federal government between $15,000 and $17,500. The purchase didn't include the birds, many of which U.S. authorities removed from St. Louis. Birds from other zoos as well as donations from private citizens restocked the exhibit (Figs. 5-12, 5-13).

The herds of deer, elk, and buffalo, which President Theodore Roosevelt had admired, were moved to new quarters near the bird cage. Park department employees built a new bear cage and a new monkey house (Fig. 5-14). Commissioner Aull told a *Globe-Democrat* reporter in August 1905, "The astonishing attendance this summer, both on week days and on Sunday, leaves no doubt that the bird cage, with a zoo around it, will become the chief feature of the park." One Sunday about twelve thousand people visited the bird cage and a special detachment of police was called out to keep things running smoothly.[25]

Over the next few years the city added birds to the collection, rebuilt the bird cage foundation, and installed an ice water fountain near the

5-15. The Forest Park greenhouses in about 1905, shortly before more were built. The Forest Park greenhouse complex supplied flowers for all the city's parks and public buildings.

bird cage, but major improvements were postponed while the city worked on more pressing needs. Some private citizens gave the zoo a higher priority than city officials did. Shirt manufacturer Cortlandt Harris enlisted C. F. Blanke, president of the Million Population Club (an organization working to raise the city's population above one million), in his campaign for a larger zoo, either in Forest Park or at the new Fairground Park on the site of the old Fair Grounds zoo. The zoo would attract people to St. Louis, Harris and Blanke said, and would be of educational value to school children. Scanlan was interested, but said his budget only allowed him to "barely maintain" the current zoo.[26]

Harris recruited other supporters. Taxidermist Frank Schwarz said he had long supported an expanded zoo. Harris, Schwarz, J. F. Abbott of Washington University, herpetologist Julius Herter, and ornithologist Otto Widman organized the St. Louis Zoological Society, which replaced the inactive Forest Park Zoological Association. At its first meeting the society elected Abbott president, Schwarz vice-president, and Harris secretary, and authorized an executive committee of fifteen people, including the mayor and the park commissioner. At first the new society was able to accomplish very little. By 1911, probably because of the lack of new exhibits, the zoo's popularity had begun to decline.

Besides the zoo, there was plenty to see and

do in the park. Visitors admired the flower beds, regularly replanted from the city greenhouses inside Forest Park, where a 1906 inventory counted more than 170,000 plants. These greenhouses also supplied flowers for other city parks and for park department exhibits outside the parks. Because of the demand for more plants throughout the park system, the city built more greenhouses in Forest Park and installed a new greenhouse heating system in 1906 and 1907. But by 1911 the park department again considered the greenhouses "taxed to the utmost" (Fig. 5-15).

By 1905 the Forest Park tree nursery contained 15,000 native seedlings from one to three years old and supplied young trees for the entire park system. By then the tree nursery was no longer near the center of the park but occupied six acres west of the greenhouses. Windstorms in May 1908 and July 1910 damaged trees and shrubs in Forest Park, some of which were replaced from the nursery. The spring and summer of 1911 brought particularly severe weather. In an April storm, the Post-Dispatch reported, "a mass of hail and ice fell from the clouds and covered the ground to a depth of two inches in less than two minutes."[27] Then in May, just as repairs were being completed, another hail storm caused serious damage, especially to the greenhouses.

Each year thousands of people attended Forest Park band concerts provided by the city. Others could admire the park's new statues, as well as the older statues of Bates and Blair. The

5-16. A photograph from the 1970s of the statue, dedicated on June 23, 1906, of Franz Sigel, a German-American Civil War general.

first new monument in Forest Park following the fair honored Franz Sigel, a German-American who had served during the Civil War as a Union general (Fig. 5-16). The statue, by German sculptor Robert Cauer, was paid for by donations from German-Americans throughout the country. About 1,000 people attended the unveiling ceremonies on June 23, 1906, which included two speeches in German.

In addition to the Sigel statue, the *Apotheosis of St. Louis* on Art Hill, and the new statue of Thomas Jefferson, parkgoers enjoyed the O'Neil Fountain or *Fountain Angel*, which stood near the Laclede Pavilion until it was moved near the Lindell Pavilion in 1916. David N. O'Neil donated the angel, a popular feature of the fair, to the park in 1907 to honor his father, Joseph O'Neil, who had been a member of the board of Forest Park commissioners in 1874.

A visitor could participate in or watch a variety of sports. Skating on the Forest Park lakes continued to be popular when weather permitted. In January 1905, with half the park closed to visitors because of the restoration, the thousands of skaters on the available lakes in the eastern section of the park threatened to break the ice. The *Globe-Democrat* reported, "Danger signals have been posted at Forest park, but . . . school children can not be kept away from the ice."

For cyclists, Forest Park became, instead of the destination for riders who started downtown, the starting point for bicycle tours into the country. A handbook published by the St. Louis Cycling Club in 1910 described a variety of recommended bicycle tours. The Clayton Road tour, for example, went through Forest Park and ended at Gumbo, Missouri, twenty-four miles away.

Spectators could go to the St. Louis Amateur Athletic Association (Triple A) to see tennis tournaments of state and regional interest. In 1904 and 1905, for example, the state tennis championships for singles and doubles used the Triple A

5-17. Missouri Fish Commission employees netted the fish from the Forest Park lakes, then stocked them in waters around the state, though none in Forest Park, to provide inexpensive nourishment for Missourians.

courts. Women's competitions, too, took place at Triple A. The *Post-Dispatch* said in 1907, "The A. A. A. deserves praise for the manner in which it supports tennis and the privileges it extends to the women of St. Louis." Triple A also sponsored golf matches on its nine-hole golf links, both among club members and against other clubs.

Triple A maintained track facilities and sponsored meets and races, although the club dropped its track team after 1905. In 1905, "a dual cross-country run between the M.A.C. [Missouri Athletic Club] and Triple-A runners" began at the Triple A clubhouse. A meet in 1907 attracted teams from the M.A.C. and the Central YMCA. "A few of the old Triple A veterans were lured by the sight of the knee pants and spiked shoes and before noon had resurrected their old duds and were out 'limbering up,'" the *Post-Dispatch* reported. In 1911 the M.A.C. sponsored a race described as a "modified marathon" over a course that included Forest Park roads.

The St. Louis Cricket Club continued to offer occasional games. The *Republic* reported in the spring of 1907 that the St. Louis Cricket Club would "again offer amusement for strollers at Forest Park each Saturday afternoon," an attraction that had been "missed for the last year or two."[28]

A stroller could visit the park lakes where the Missouri Fish Commission was raising native American fish such as bass, crappie, and perch (Fig. 5-17). Ordinances extended the fish commission's rights in the park through 1920 on about the same terms as originally granted in 1883.[29] Suggestions that the commission might stock some lakes for park fishing or operate an aquarium in Forest Park brought no results.

In addition, there were some new facilities for park visitors. By April 1910 the pavilion on Government Hill offered rest rooms and shelter from sun and rain. The building, sometimes called the Jefferson Pavilion at that time but later only the World's Fair Pavilion, had, Commissioner Scanlan reported, "proven popular from the start." By 1911 Forest Park again offered pic-nic grounds, absent during the fair, with five new toilets nearby. Parkgoers could buy refreshments at the new pavilion, at the Laclede Pavilion, or at the Lindell Pavilion,[30] no longer used as a streetcar stop since the line no longer entered the park. The Jefferson Memorial also offered public rest rooms when it was completed.

Picnickers drank the water of Wells Spring. So did "knowing German families on the North Side" and wealthy residents of the nearby private places, the *Post-Dispatch* reported, advised by their doctors to take the waters for their health. A line of carriages, automobiles, bicycles, and saddle horses formed as the health seekers waited their turn to drink the spring water and fill bottles and jugs for their households.[31]

Thousands of St. Louisans walked or rode through the park after church on Easter, to see and be seen as part of the unorganized gathering called the Easter parade, which grew as new churches opened nearby on Kingshighway. In 1907 people "devoted the afternoon to the display of their new spring plumes," the *Post-Dispatch* reported. "From early in the afternoon until sunset the stream of humanity in its best bib and tucker . . . flowed . . . along the winding walks of the park. . . . The automobile and the carriage were there, too." By 1911 few carriages were in evidence "in the lines of slowly moving automobiles and of sidewalk strollers. . . . Those [horses] whose owners had ventured into the company of limousines, touring cars and taxis seemed to realize that they were out of place."[32]

That summer a brave eighty-three-year-old man who had never seen Forest Park agreed to ride through the park in an automobile because, he said:

> I knew . . . that my family was fixed for life, and that when I die I want to die quickly. . . . I saw some deer, but you never have time to stop and get a good look at anything when you are in one of those automobiles. We went around in circles, and I spoke to the motorman [automobile driver] and asked him if he would know his way out again. . . . [When he said he would,] I was glad he was there.[33]

5-18. Glenn H. Curtiss made several flights over Forest Park in 1909. Most of the spectators missed the flights, however, since Curtiss flew in the early morning and late evening, when weather conditions were most favorable.

On occasion large crowds gathered to see the latest rage—aeronautics. In October 1907 more than 100,000 saw nine gas balloons take off from the grounds of the new Aero Club to begin the second international race for the James Gordon Bennett Cup. St. Louis was chosen as the starting point for the race because of its central location, far from large bodies of water and mountain ranges. The Laclede Gas Company manufactured a special light grade of coal gas and special pipes carried the gas to the park.

"The eyes of all the world are on St. Louis now," the *Post-Dispatch* said, as the nine balloons gathered from the United States, France, the German Empire, and Great Britain. The spectators began to gather hours before the start of the race. All the balloons ascended safely, and St. Louis waited for news of the balloonists. The winner, Oscar Erbsloeh, piloting the German entry *Pommern*, remained aloft forty hours and traveled to Asbury Park, New Jersey, landing only because

he had reached the Atlantic Ocean. He traveled a distance of 873.4 miles, more than twice the winning distance of 402 miles for the previous race in Paris. Indeed, all but one of the balloons in the race exceeded the winning distance in the Paris race.

About 40,000 people came to see a sideline to the balloon race, a competition for airships (later called dirigibles) over a triangular course in Forest Park, "a test," the *Post-Dispatch* said, "of the speed and dirigibility [steerability] of the airships."[34] The winner of the $1,500 first prize averaged better than twenty-five miles an hour, covering the two-mile course in four minutes and forty seconds.

During the next two years, the aeroplane, or airplane, replaced lighter-than-air craft in the popular fancy. To commemorate the one hundredth anniversary of its incorporation, St. Louis staged a massive Centennial Week celebration all over town from October 3 to 9, 1909. Forest Park

5-19. The Forest Park Highlands after the World's Fair. As he had in the 1890s, Highlands owner and operator Anton Steuver added new attractions almost every year.

provided open spaces for balloon ascensions from the Aero Club grounds and dirigible flights over Art Hill, but, as the *Post-Dispatch* reported, St. Louisans particularly wanted to see the airplane flights of Glenn H. Curtiss, winner of the recent international speed trials.

Curtiss's flights scheduled for Wednesday had to be postponed because police protection would be inadequate due to the number of men assigned to other centennial events. Early Thursday morning October 7, 1909, Curtiss made two successful test flights (Fig. 5-18). Walter B. Stevens's official account of Centennial Week said, "The first aeroplane flight seen west of the Mississippi took place at 6:21 Thursday morning." Curtiss flew

forty seconds, landed near the DeBaliviere entrance, took off again and flew another thirty-five seconds.

As news of the flights, witnessed by only a few early risers, spread, the *Post-Dispatch* reported, a crowd estimated at 300,000, "the greatest assemblage of people ever seen in St. Louis at one time and place gathered on the vast natural amphitheatre formed by the northern slope of Art Hill in Forest Park, and stood for hours." But the breeze was too strong for Curtiss to fly. Many of the spectators had left when, at dusk, Curtiss made a brief flight through the gathering shadows. In all, Curtiss made seven flights in Forest Park, averaging about one minute each, and

5-20. The extension of Lindell Boulevard westward to Skinker Boulevard made Washington University easier to reach from the east.

reached a maximum altitude of about sixty feet.[35]

Park finances were not a major issue in the period following the fair. The amount spent on maintenance of the eastern half of the park, while the western half was still controlled by the LPEC, averaged about $100,000 a year. Because of the purchase of new parks in 1908–9, the portion of the city's total park budget devoted to Forest Park declined from almost half in 1904–5 (an unusual year because of the fair) to between one-fourth and one-fifth in the fiscal years following 1911–12. The total dollars spent for Forest Park did not, however, decline, as total park expenses increased both in absolute amounts and as a percentage of total city expenditures.

Concession revenues were small. Because the main boating lakes were inside the fairgrounds, no revenue was recorded from the boating concession until 1910–11. Following the end of the Cottage lease, refreshments provided no income until fiscal year 1910–11, when refreshment concessions in the various pavilions began to pay the city a share of their receipts.

Fiscal year 1904–5 contained one financial transaction that could be viewed as a footnote to the finances of an earlier period. The city retired the thirty-year Forest Park bonds, issued in 1875 by St. Louis County and assumed by the City of St. Louis at the time of the separation of city and county.

Like the park, the land around it changed as the temporary fair structures were dismantled. During the fair, the Pike amusement area had occupied much of the land north of the park and west of Union. A scheme to make the Pike amusements permanent was abandoned after Washington University officials objected. Then developers tried to attract buyers for lots in the area where the Pike had been. In 1909 they dedicated a fifty-foot wide strip of land next to the park, from Union to Skinker, to the city for use as park land and as a road and sidewalk extension of Lindell. But development lagged, probably because the River des Peres crossed the area and the tracks of the Wabash Railroad and the Rock Island Railroad ran close to the park, crossing both Union and DeBaliviere at street level. East of Union, the private places north of the park continued to develop. Around the corner, along Kingshighway, developers built apartments and hotels. The Buckingham became a "strictly high-class hotel."[36] The Aberdeen, Bellevue, Colchester, and Devonshire apartments, or ABCDs, opened soon after the fair. In 1910 St. Louis University began to use playing fields and a wooden stadium outside the southeastern corner of the park. Brickyards dominated the nearby industrial district along the Missouri Pacific railroad tracks.

The Forest Park Highlands regularly added new attractions (Fig. 5-19). Some, like the miniature train, moved from the fair. In the theater, vaudeville shows featured such performers as Will Rogers, "Oklahoma cowboy, in difficult lariat feats and ranchman comedy"[37] and the annual Bastille Day show.

Forest Park University moved into its new building, which had housed visitors to the fair. To the south, people moved into cheaply constructed houses in about the area where former park squatters had erected shacks in the 1870s.

Improved access to the area west of the park, particularly by automobile, brought changes. Washington University moved into its new buildings in January 1905, after the LPEC moved out (Fig. 5-20). Skinker Road was widened from Forsyth south to Oakland in 1910.[38] Then new subdivisions began to open on the land used for the fair.

By 1911, although the park and the surrounding area had begun to fill, there was still much open land. Around the park, the increasing numbers of automobiles made development possible during the next few years. Inside Forest Park, many new facilities arose, encouraged by a new park commissioner, Dwight F. Davis.

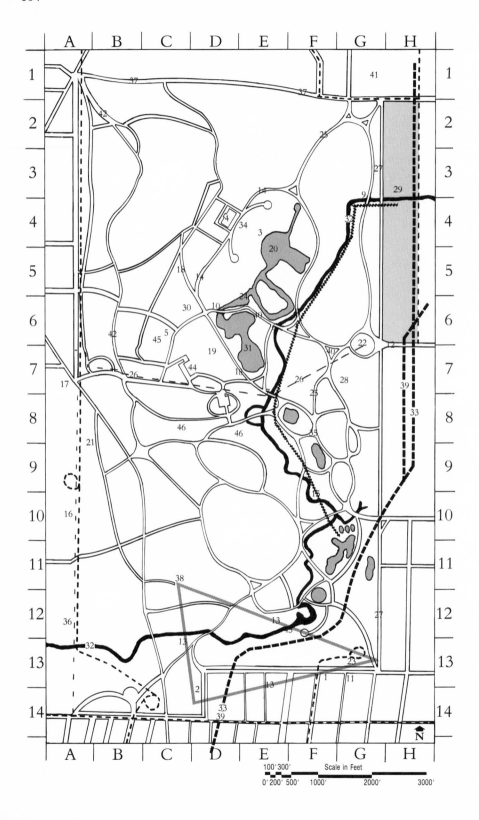

PARK AND NEIGHBORHOOD
LOCATOR MAP (1904–1911)

1. ABCD Apartments, F-13
2. Aero Club grounds, C-14 and D-13
3. Art Hill, E-4
4. Art Museum, City (St. Louis School and Museum of Fine Arts), D-4
5. Bird cage, C-6

Bridges

6. Education, E-6
7. Liberal Arts, E-7
8. Manufactures, F-6
9. Transportation, G-3
10. Washington, D-6

11. Buckingham Club, G-13
12. DeBaliviere Avenue, H-6
13. Dirigible race course, D-14 to C-11 to G-13
14. Fine Arts Drive, D-5 to E-3
15. Forest Park Foul Water Sewer, G-10 to H-4 (course farther east unknown)
16. Forest Park Highlands, A-10
17. Forest Park University, A-7
18. Government Drive (probable location), C-4 to F-7
19. Government Hill, D-6 and 7
20. Grand Basin, E-4 to F-5
21. Greenhouses and nursery, A-8 to B-9
22. Jefferson Memorial building, G-6
    Jefferson, Thomas, statue (see 22, G-6)
23. Laclede Pavilion, G-13
24. Lagoon, E-5 and 6

25. Lagoon Drive, F-8 to G-2
26. Louisiana Purchase Exposition Company (LPEC) restoration area, east boundary, A-7 to G-6
27. Lindell Avenue (later Lindell Boulevard), G-2 to G-13
28. Lindell Pavilion, G-7
Missouri Historical Society (eastern half of Jefferson Memorial Building, 22, G-6)
O'Neil Fountain (*Fountain Angel*, first location, see 23, G-13)
29. Pike (amusement area during fair), H-2 to H-6
30. Portland Cement Building, C-6
31. Post-Dispatch Lake, D-6 to E-7
32. River des Peres (western section relocated by LPEC), A-13 to H-3
33. Rock Island Railroad, D-14 to H-1
34. *St. Louis, Apotheosis of*, statue, E-4
35. Sigel, Franz, statue, F-8
36. St. Louis University playing fields, A-12
37. Skinker Road (later Skinker Boulevard) south of Forsyth Boulevard, A-1 to G-1
38. St. Louis Amateur Athletic Association (Triple A) Clubhouse (second location), C-11
39. Wabash (later Norfolk and Western) Railroad, D-14 to H-6
40. Washington Drive (probable location), D-6 to G-6
41. Washington University, G and H-1
42. Wells Drive (probable location), A-1 to B-7
43. Wells Spring, F-12
44. World's Fair Pavilion (Government Hill shelter, originally also Jefferson Pavilion), D-7

Zoo

45. Bear and monkey cages (approximate location), C-6
46. Deer, elk, and buffalo enclosures, C and E-8

6

DWIGHT DAVIS AND HIS LEGACY (1911–1930)

If we can't have the grass and the people in our parks, let's sacrifice the grass.—Dwight F. Davis, 1911

Between 1911 and 1930 Park Commissioner Dwight F. Davis and his successors filled Forest Park with expanded activities and new single-purpose facilities. Like Hiram Leffingwell, Davis had a vision of the park. Believing that the parks should be used for regularly scheduled recreation and for special civic events, Davis worked to attract visitors. The primary purpose of the park system, he said, should be "the raising of men and women rather than grass or trees." His policy was, "If we can't have the grass and the people in our parks, let's sacrifice the grass."[1]

Dwight Davis, a wealthy grandson of a major dry goods wholesaler in St. Louis, became park commissioner in 1911 when he was in his early thirties (Fig. 6-1). He was an enthusiastic amateur athlete who was the national outdoor men's tennis doubles champion from 1899 to 1901. In 1900 he donated a trophy for a new tennis championship, later known as the Davis Cup.

Davis's interest in athletics was a reflection of his position as a "progressive," part of an unorganized national movement of both Democrats and Republicans. In St. Louis, the progressives advocated reforms in city government (including ending the boodling system) and improvements in housing, sanitation, and education for the poor. The changes, progressives believed, were part of the country's democratic heritage and might be necessary to prevent class warfare, as the dispossessed asserted their rights.

Davis promoted organized recreation, particularly in the poorest areas of the city, as part of progressivism. Such recreation, he believed, would promote health and build character through teaching children to play by the rules. In June 1903 Davis announced his retirement from tennis competition in order to devote himself to a private St. Louis organization working to provide playgrounds for the city's children. There he worked with Charlotte Rumbold, a progressive and a member of the fashionable women's organization, the Wednesday Club. Rumbold, like Jane Addams in Chicago, was working to improve living conditions in the city's slums. The playground association disbanded in 1907 when the city's park department took over the work. Rumbold then went to work for the city as secretary of the recreation commission. Davis turned to elective office to advance his ideas, serving as a Republican member of the city's house of delegates from 1907 to 1909.

In 1911 Republican Mayor Frederick H. Kreismann, whom Davis supported, appointed Davis park commissioner, a position that would allow him to further the cause of public recreation. Although the newspapers endorsed the appointment, the city council at first refused to confirm him. Some councilmen had another candidate for the job. Others considered Davis too friendly to the Terminal Railroad Association, the owner of the Eads Bridge and opponent of a proposed city-owned "free bridge," an issue that dominated St. Louis politics for years.

It is difficult to imagine what the city's parks might have been like had the council not reversed itself a few days later, allowing Davis to take office. His political strength enabled Davis to put

6-1. Dwight F. Davis changed many of Forest Park's open lawns into golf courses, tennis courts, and other athletic facilities while he was St. Louis Commissioner of Parks.

his ideas into practice. One of his first official acts was to have the "Keep Off the Grass" signs taken down from city parks. Forest Park had had no such signs when it opened in 1876, but they had crept in over the years, probably in the 1880s and 1890s after the streetcars brought more people to the park.

After his four-year term as park commissioner ended in 1915, Davis chose to pursue his ideals in other ways, turning the park commissioner job over to his trusted subordinate, Nelson Cunliff, an engineer who had joined the park department in 1907, after working on Forest Park restoration for the Louisiana Purchase Exposition Company. By 1915 Cunliff was park department superintendent of construction, reporting directly to Davis. Cunliff continued Davis's policies, serving until 1920, when he resigned to accept a higher-paying job.

Cunliff's successor, Fred W. Pape, served until 1933 and continued Davis's and Cunliff's policies. Like Davis, Pape had both political and professional qualifications for the office. He remained a Republican city committeeman while he served as park commissioner under Republican Mayors Henry W. Kiel and Victor J. Miller. He had served as general superintendent of parks in the early 1900s, succeeding his father, William Pape. In the period immediately preceding his appointment as commissioner, Fred Pape had served in the forestry division of the park department for seven years, first as assistant superintendent and then as superintendent.

As Davis's successors continued to welcome new Forest Park users, and as St. Louis's growth westward and the increasing accessibility of the park by automobile brought increasing numbers of park visitors, conflicts arose. Before 1911 major park uses had coexisted peaceably, since Forest Park was big enough to hold them all with

6-2. The water hazard on the second hole helped make the Forest Park golf course one of the most difficult in the area.

6-3. Gaslights extended the hours at the Forest Park tennis courts until 9:30 P.M. Only those unable to play during the day were allowed to play after dark.

room left over. Different activities could use the same space on different days. The same stretch of lawn could hold a picnic one day, a baseball game the next, and a tennis game the day after. By 1930 it seemed that only the cricket lawn near the Jefferson Memorial remained to show how the open spaces had once been used. By the 1920s some St. Louisans had begun to call for a halt to additions to the park after the construction of various structures, including permanent athletic facilities and the expansion of the zoo, made such multiple uses difficult.

Davis saw the parks as ideal locations for playgrounds and athletic fields for young and old. A strong believer in the value of amateur athletics, Davis was the driving force behind the installation of athletic facilities and the organization of athletic leagues in all the city parks, including Forest Park, reportedly using his own money to help pay for new facilities. Athletic facilities were needed, the *Post-Dispatch* said, because of the dwindling supply of vacant lots in the city. The nationwide growth in recreation and Davis's preference for supervised recreation added to the

pressure for city-owned facilities. The city built many new athletic facilities, especially in the new Fairground Park and in Forest Park. As early as 1905 the *Post-Dispatch* had called for football, baseball, tennis, and golf facilities in Forest Park on the new open areas being cleared after the World's Fair. The city's fourteen baseball fields (nine in Forest Park) were proving insufficient for the demand, especially on Saturday afternoons, Sundays, and holidays, and there were no public golf or tennis facilities in Forest Park.[2]

Soon after he took office in 1911, Davis met with representatives of the private golf clubs in St. Louis, including C. Norman Jones, one of the founders of the Log Cabin Club, and Jesse L. Carleton, president of Glen Echo Country Club, to plan a public golf course in Forest Park as "a means of healthful exercise and amusement for thousands of persons who are unable to pay membership fees in clubs." The group rejected a suggestion by Henry W. Allen, secretary of the Bellerive Country Club, that it should hire a professional to lay out the course. Instead, Arthur Stickney, representing the St. Louis Country

What the New Fees for Forest Park Golf May Help.

6-4. Apparently, the *Globe-Democrat* favored fees for use of the Forest Park golf courses.

Club, inspected the public courses in New York; Samuel Rosenfeld of Westwood Country Club went to Chicago; Clark McAdams of Normandie Golf Club went to Boston; and Bart S. Adams, one of the organizers of Algonquin Golf Club, inspected the public course in Kansas City. Based on their reports, the group planned a nine-hole course that opened in early July 1912 with an exhibition game that included Commissioner Davis. "Mrs. E. H. Farrar, an athletic young woman, bareheaded and dressed in white, walked to a tee. . . , whirled a golf stick through the air and sent a ball soaring," the *Post-Dispatch* reported.[3]

The course was open all day every day. Golfers had to have a permit, which was free, and furnish their own equipment. Within a year, the course had been extended to eighteen holes. Soon a new nine-hole course joined the eighteen-hole course, and suspension foot bridges were installed across the park's lagoon.

Play began as early as 5 A.M. Davis, who had long contended that golf was not just a rich man's game, reported, "Every walk of life was represented on the links, from the barefooted boy to the member of an exclusive club." The *Globe-Democrat* reported in 1915 that golfers often had to wait their turn to play the eighteen-hole course, which was "regarded as the best—meaning the most difficult—in the St. Louis district" (Fig. 6-2).[4]

Davis also built tennis courts; in 1912 he added thirty-two to Forest Park. Like golf, tennis required a permit, which was free. The demand for tennis was almost insatiable. Tennis players arrived as early as 4:30 in the morning on hot summer days or played until the light faded at night.

Gaslights, installed in 1917, extended play until 9:30 P.M., which lessened the crowding, as did park department rules prohibiting night-time play by those who could play during the day. Night tennis attracted spectators who sat in their automobiles around the courts, requiring policemen to direct park traffic (Fig. 6-3).

In 1924, of the 140 municipal golf courses in the country, only ten were still free, including the two in Forest Park. In 1925 the city imposed the first charge for the use of permanent Forest Park facilities—$10 for an annual golf permit and $1 for an annual tennis permit—despite protests that the players had already paid for the facilities through their taxes. Single-game golf permits cost fifty cents for the eighteen-hole course and twenty-five cents for the nine-hole course. The city used the money from the permits to maintain the facilities. In general, the golf fees covered the cost of maintenance but the tennis fees did not (Fig. 6-4). The number of golf and tennis games dropped after fees were instituted but regained their pre-1925 levels by the spring of 1931.

Racial barriers were already restricting use of the Forest Park golf course, as the department

6-5. The caption of this drawing from the *Globe-Democrat* pointed out that by 1919 horses were seldom seen outside of the Forest Park bridle path.

kept the races apart in recreation facilities. Davis's racial policy is nowhere clearly stated, but he probably provided separate facilities, following the "separate but equal" doctrine upheld by the U.S. Supreme Court in 1896. An official report of the St. Louis City Plan Commission, which Davis chaired, remarked in May 1917 on "the necessity for providing separate [recreation] facilities for colored people and the failure of certain races to mingle harmoniously."

At the time, segregation in St. Louis was rather patchwork. Schools were segregated by law, though some other public facilities, such as libraries, were not. In 1916 St. Louis had overwhelmingly adopted a segregated housing ordinance. Although never enforced because of its unconstitutionality, the ordinance's housing patterns were continued for decades by informal practice and restrictive deed covenants.[5] In 1918, probably in response to the plan commission re-

port, the city bought Tandy Playground, which offered some athletic facilities, but no golf, for blacks.

In late 1917, following release of the plan commission report, the *Post-Dispatch* reported, "Three negroes . . . asked that one day a week, or certain hours on some days, be set aside for negroes to play golf on the Forest Park municipal links." Commissioner Cunliff refused the golfers' request, saying they would have to wait until a separate course could be built. This response stood until May 1922 when Albert H. Howard asked the St. Louis circuit court to compel Commissioner Pape to issue golf permits to him and other black golfers. The following year, in 1923, the court accepted Pape's solution of reserving the golf courses on Mondays from 6 A.M. until noon "for the exclusive use and enjoyment of colored persons." Following the ruling, the *Post-Dispatch* reported, "On occasions the 27 holes . . . have been given over to a solitary negro golfer." When white golfers protested that they would be unable to play on Labor Day morning, Pape refused to change the rules. The question of access by blacks to the Forest Park athletic facilities would, however, reappear.[6]

While he was building the Forest Park golf courses and tennis courts, Davis didn't neglect other sports. He resurfaced and lengthened the park's five-mile bridle path (a conversion of the seldom-used bicycle path) until it encircled the park (Fig. 6-5). "Soccer fields and baseball fields have been located in every available space," a department employee reported proudly in 1913.[7] By 1929, under Pape, Forest Park contained thirty-eight tennis courts, twenty baseball diamonds, two soccer fields, two handball courts, a croquet course, a cricket lawn, an archery range, and the two public golf courses.

Davis and his successors encouraged winter sports as well. When there was snow, department employees tended two toboggan slopes: a gentle slope on Bird Cage Drive, closed to automobile traffic to allow sledding, and nearby Art Hill

6-6. Both participants and spectators enjoyed the sledding on Art Hill.

where coasters could reach speeds of about 35 miles an hour after park department employees packed the hill with snow, then poured water over it (Fig. 6-6). Gasoline lights showed the path for night sledders. Employees also smoothed Grand Basin ice for skaters and tended bonfires at the top and bottom of Art Hill. Many St. Louisans sat in their automobiles to watch the fun.

In 1914 Davis remodeled the old Lindell Streetcar Pavilion, installing men's and women's lockers, toilets, showers, a refreshment stand, and a pro shop for the sale of golf and tennis equipment. The building was destroyed by fire in October 1925. The replacement building, the Field House and Restaurant, kept the pavilion's foundation and the lower portion of its tower (Fig. 6-7). The new building, which took more than a year and $150,000 to build, offered expanded locker facilities and a restaurant. Refreshments, rental of towels and lockers, and sale of golf and tennis supplies all produced revenue.

To promote use of the new athletic facilities citywide in the spirit of progressivism and to further "the elimination of semi-professionalism, gambling, abusive or profane language and foul or unfair tactics,"[8] Davis organized municipal amateur athletic leagues, beginning with soccer in 1912 and 1913. The leagues brought together existing teams from schools, neighborhoods, and businesses to compete for city championships.

The city's general director of athletics, Rudowe Abeken, who reported to Davis, organized and ran the municipal athletic leagues. Abeken added baseball, tennis, and golf competitions in 1913. The public school baseball league, formerly sponsored by the *Post-Dispatch* newspaper, soon joined the municipal baseball league. Some St. Louisans complained about the leagues' reservation of Forest Park baseball diamonds, but the city defended the practice, pointing out that some fields were always available for general use.

Spectators enjoyed the games from the start. In 1915 the three interdivisional soccer play-off games, one of which was in Forest Park, attracted

6-7. The Forest Park field house, built to replace the Lindell Pavilion, which burned in 1925. Only the clock tower of the old pavilion remained, without its top, which was damaged in the fire.

fifteen thousand spectators, the *Post-Dispatch* said, ten times the number that attended the professional soccer game the same day.[9]

In 1916, after several years of work, Davis succeeded in organizing the National Municipal Recreation Federation to sponsor intercity competitions. Although no longer park commissioner, Davis was president of the new federation, while Cunliff served as secretary-treasurer. The National Lawn Tennis Association donated a tennis trophy for the federation champion, doubtless at Davis's urging, and Walter D. Thompson, a St. Louis insurance agent and park neighbor, gave a golf trophy (Fig. 6-8).

St. Louis swept the first national municipal tennis tournament, defeating the New York entries in September 1916 on the courts near the Jefferson Memorial. Ted Drewes, who later delighted St. Louisans with his frozen custard, teamed with Fred Josties to win the doubles title. Drewes and Taylor Ward won singles titles. St. Louis golfers Jimmy Manion, Frank Pep, and Clarence Wolff didn't fare as well. The Chicago

team defeated them as well as golfers from Des Moines and Hartford, Connecticut, on the Forest Park course a few days later.

The federation suspended championship play during World War I but resumed in 1923 with a tennis tournament on the Jefferson Memorial courts. The golf tournament returned to Forest Park in 1929, with entrants from thirty-seven cities. Despite bad weather, five thousand spectators watched the final holes of play.

Other organizations also used Forest Park for championship events. In 1925 a national championship bicycle race on the Forest Park roads near the Jefferson Memorial attracted entrants from most states. In January 1926 the Western District Amateur Athletic Union (AAU) sponsored the first Silver Skates Carnival on the Grand Basin. Joseph Forshaw, president of the western district, said there were almost 100,000 spectators who stood six to eight deep around the Grand Basin and crowded Art Hill. The racers ranged from girls under twelve to men over sixty, with a silver skate trophy awarded to the leading

6-8. The caddies gather for the municipal championship tournament in Forest Park in 1919.

point scorer. The carnival also featured exhibitions of fancy skating.

The St. Louis Cricket Club still played in the park. Other groups organized games of polo, or fly and bait casting competitions. Davis and his successors welcomed them all.

While encouraging athletic competitions, Davis remembered his commitment to progressivism and to the playground movement, which served those not old enough or skilled enough to play competitive sports. As park commissioner, Davis was chairman of the city's Public Recreation Commission where he again worked closely with Charlotte Rumbold, who was secretary of the commission and general superintendent of recreation.

For a few years Forest Park was the site of a city-run playground, the World's Fair Model Playground, which reopened in July 1906 as one of the first municipal playgrounds. Attendance lagged, and by the time Davis became park commissioner in 1911 the Forest Park playground was gone.

Forest Park's main role in the playground movement was as a large open space for special events. In 1901 the *Globe-Democrat* pointed out that trips to Forest Park were one way organizers gave the children from the playgrounds "a taste of the fresh, pure air of the country."[10] Rumbold had to discontinue these outings in 1909 because of the expense of carfare. Beginning in the summer of 1907, the first full summer of municipally operated playgrounds, children from all over the

6-9. Children from playgrounds all over the city gathered in Forest Park for the playground festival. Here they are probably in line to receive the refreshments donated by civic organizations.

city gathered at the end of the summer on the lawn near the Lindell Pavilion for the first playground festival. The festival continued into the 1930s, with displays of the children's summer craft projects and simple athletic contests. The athletic competitions "for colored participants" were held at a different time from the "white events," but all the children were encouraged to participate and to display their handicrafts (Fig. 6-9).[11]

In 1913 Secretary Rumbold added a playground pageant—"Pantomime of the Sleeping Beauty." Each playground, including those for blacks, was assigned a section of the pageant, which the children enacted in homemade costumes. Rumbold used the pantomime as part of

the preparations for a much larger and more elaborate production that would include the entire city: the Pageant and Masque of St. Louis. Rumbold initiated the idea as a way of spreading the benefits of the recreation concepts of progressivism to the entire city, adults as well as children. To do this, she needed adult cast members, a script, publicity, and money. The Pageant Drama Association soon formed to produce the show.

The members of the association supported the pageant for a variety of reasons. For Rumbold, a member of the Executive Committee, the pageant was an example of her motto, which may have been somewhat naive, "If we play together, we will work together." Davis, also a member of

6-10. Cover of program for the Pageant and Masque of St. Louis shows some of the historical and symbolic characters from the production. The show continued through June 1, since rain forced the cancellation of one of the scheduled performances.

the executive committee, said, "The real purpose of the pageant . . . is to develop . . . community spirit." Some businessmen promoted the pageant to attract visitors and investments to the city. Civic leaders saw the show as a chance to unite a city still divided by ethnic and racial differences and by the lingering resentments from defeat of a proposed 1911 city charter. Some of them hoped a revised charter could be approved after the production.[12]

The pageant and masque commemorated the one hundred fiftieth anniversary of the founding of St. Louis (Fig. 6-10). For each of four nights in the summer of 1914, an estimated 100,000 people filled temporary seats on Art Hill. On a stage over part of the Grand Basin, and in canoes in the Grand Basin, a cast of more than 7,000 St. Louisans presented a pageant in which they enacted the history of the city and a masque in which Love, encouraged by St. Louis, subdued Gold and his assistants, War and Poverty (Fig. 6-11).

Despite different motivations, almost everybody considered the show a success. Receipts, including gifts, exceeded the $125,000 cost of the production by $17,000. One spokesman said the pageant had been one of the greatest advertisements ever created. Rumbold said it had accomplished everything she had hoped.

After the pageant, voters did approve the new city charter, under which parks had a less important place than before in the city administration. The park department became the Division of Parks and Recreation of the new Department of Public Welfare, instead of being a separate department as it had been and would become again in 1958. The mayor appointed the Director of Public Welfare, who, in turn, appointed the Commissioner of Parks and Recreation, still usually called the park commissioner.[13] Approval of the charter did not, however, bring about the new community spirit Davis and Rumbold had hoped to foster, since segregationists used its initiative provision to pass the segregated housing ordinance of 1916.

Clinging to the belief that if St. Louisans played together they would get along better together, the city government in 1915 decided to promote increased use of recreation facilities with a Municipal Play Day in several parks. Thousands of people went to Forest Park for activities, including a kite-flying contest, golf competitions, picnics, concerts, and games of handball, tennis, baseball, cricket, and polo. That night, new gasoline lights illuminated the Horseshoe of Light that included the art museum, the World's Fair Pavilion, the Jefferson Memorial, and the clock on the

6-11. View of production of pageant and masque, showing spectators on Art Hill, stage and scenery over Grand Basin. An estimated 100,000 people attended each of the four performances.

Lindell Pavilion. Mandolin clubs from Soldan High School and Washington University accompanied singers who serenaded from boats on the lagoon.

In 1916 the Pageant Drama Association used its surplus funds from the pageant and masque for performances of *As You Like It* in celebration of the three hundredth anniversary of the death of William Shakespeare. The site for the performance was a natural amphitheater near Art Hill, soon known as the Municipal Open Air Theatre, or Municipal Theatre. The amphitheater held chairs for ten thousand, one tenth of the Art Hill capacity (Fig. 6-12).

The cast of the production, like the site, while smaller than the pageant's, was by no means small. The cast of one thousand actors included out-of-town professionals plus St. Louis amateur folk dancers and folksingers who presented May Day revels of Shakespeare's time. Attendance averaged eight thousand a night for the week-long show, despite some rainy nights.

Municipal Play Day in 1916 was the second and last; the celebration was discontinued during World War I and not resumed. The 1916 Play Day used the new municipal theatre for a minstrel show, starring Mayor Henry W. Kiel as interlocutor. Since Kiel probably appeared in blackface, the minstrel show surely didn't help ease racial tensions.

Cunliff and Mayor Kiel wanted to build a permanent theater, and in 1917 they got their chance. A coalition like the one that had produced the pageant and masque, between city officials who believed in progressivism and businessmen who wanted to promote the city's economy, built the permanent theater. The Advertising Club of St. Louis wanted to produce a show for the June 1917 convention in St. Louis of the Associated Advertising Clubs of the World. The club decided on an outdoor production of *Aida*. Club members met with city officials and agreed to contribute part of the cost of making the municipal theater into a permanent open-air theater. Another private organization, the St. Louis Fashion Show, also agreed to contribute. The park department would pay the rest of the cost of what Cunliff saw as a "people's theatre . . . that will tend towards bringing all parts of our City together . . . for knowing one another they will like one another."

6-12. The Pageant Drama Association opened the Municipal Open Air Theatre, shown here, in 1916 with *As You Like It*. The man shows the size of the stage area and the two oak trees that framed it. Behind him, the small bridge spanning the River des Peres is visible.

6-13. The Municipal Theatre became a fixture in Forest Park in 1917 after construction of permanent facilities, including 10,000 seats.

Cunliff already had plans, drawn in part by Tom P. Barnett, who had designed the downtown Hotel Jefferson, used by many World's Fair visitors (Fig. 6-13). For *Aida*, as for *As You Like It*, the principal performers were out-of-town professionals. St. Louis volunteers made up the chorus.[14]

The *Post-Dispatch* called the theater "an exceptionally good place for the two things most important in any theatre—seeing and hearing," but reported annoyances that would continue. One was the weather. The *Post-Dispatch* review of the opening-night performance, halted after two acts by thunderstorms, was headlined "'Aida' Fine As Far As It Went; It Went Half-Way." Another was a lack of audience etiquette—some people came late and others left early to catch streetcars home.[15]

The following month the St. Louis Grand Opera Company produced *I Pagliacci* in the new theater. Again, St. Louis volunteers formed the chorus. Ticket prices ranged from twenty-five cents to two dollars, compared to five dollars at private indoor theaters. The company also offered twelve hundred free seats and free standing room for twenty-five hundred.[16]

Beginning in August 1917, the St. Louis Fashion Show used the theater to display the latest in women's wear, to promote St. Louis garment manufacturers, and to attract store buyers to St. Louis instead of Chicago or New York. By 1919 the show was called the St. Louis Fashion Pageant, an elaborate production with a script, models, dancers, and singers, all supervised by the businessmen of the St. Louis Style Show Committee, who donated their time. The *Globe-Democrat* said the pageant showed "100 garments with the accompanying chic hats, smart footwear and accessories displayed on living models."[17] Footwear was always featured in the show, the paper explained, because St. Louis led other shoe producing centers in style and in volume.

The city allowed these groups to use the theater rent-free with the understanding that they would keep ticket prices low and contribute any profits for theater upkeep and improvement. That way, Cunliff explained, the theater promoted the uplift envisioned by progressivism as "workmen and their families" could enjoy "artists whom they otherwise could not afford to hear."[18]

Beginning in the summer of 1919, a new organization, the Municipal Theatre Association of

St. Louis (MTA), produced musical entertainment in the theater. The MTA was a private organization, with committees of volunteer businessmen like those of the Style Show Committee. The MTA scheduled six weeks of musical theater for the summer of 1919. The St. Louis Symphony Orchestra provided instrumental music. A local volunteer chorus of 160, many from local high schools and universities, joined 40 professional opera singers. Ticket prices ranged from twenty-five cents to a dollar, with more than a thousand free seats.

The season was underwritten by private citizen guarantors, who agreed to provide funds if box-office receipts failed to cover costs. By the middle of July that prospect appeared quite real, partly because of bad weather. Lighter, more popular shows replaced planned productions of *Fra Diavolo* and *Carmen*, and Mayor Kiel urged St. Louisans to fill the theater.

By the end of the season the deficit had been reduced from $57,000 to less than $4,700, the amount to be divided among sixty-one guarantors. Mayor Kiel said, "We have established a new form of entertainment . . .—municipal opera." But it wasn't really municipal; every year the MTA needed a city permit to use the theater. Although the organization had no formal connection with the city government, Mayor Kiel was president and Commissioner Cunliff was a director, so the lines between the city government and the MTA were blurred. And it usually wasn't opera, but operetta and other popular fare, which audiences had indicated they preferred. Nevertheless, soon St. Louisans called the MTA productions the municipal opera, the Muny opera, or just the Muny.

Other groups also used the theater. The playground festival pageant played in the theater, beginning in 1916, every year until the 1930s, with hundreds of children, black and white, participating every year.

In the early 1920s the theater housed in one year a Memorial Day service and concert, a Flag Day Celebration, a Monster Band Concert given by the Musicians' Mutual Benefit Association,

6-14. The students of Mary Institute, a girls' school then located near Forest Park, presented *The Rose Maiden* in the Municipal Theatre in May 1923. The covered walkway visible in the background offered audiences some shelter from sudden showers.

6-15. Thousands of St. Louisans demonstrated their patriotism by marching two and a half miles to Forest Park in the 1918 Liberty Loan Parade, which took more than two hours to pass any point. Thousands more met them in the park for a program that included an invocation by Archbishop John J. Glennon and a band concert by about 3,000 musicians led by Lieutenant John Philip Sousa.

and a demonstration of a sound amplifier given by the Bell Telephone Company, in addition to the MTA, the playground pageant, and the style show. Grand opera returned with productions by impresario Guy Golterman in 1924, 1925, and 1926 (Fig. 6-14).

The MTA used some of its excess funds to give free voice lessons to St. Louisans who wanted to be members of its chorus. Both the MTA and the style show used excess funds for theater improvements, including sounding boards, sound amplifiers, development of acoustics, comfort stations, and new chairs.

In 1925 the municipal opera season expanded, and the organization asked for and received city permission to use the theater on the dates in August already granted to the St. Louis Style Show Committee. The fashion pageant moved to an open-air theater outside Forest Park and never returned to the park, though other groups still used the theater.[19]

The new theater and the newly discovered amphitheater on Art Hill were put to work during World War I for patriotic gatherings, much as another part of the park had been in the 1890s for Dewey Day, but on a much larger scale. One of the largest crowds ever in Forest Park went for a Liberty Loan rally in 1918 to raise money for the war effort. A 350-piece band under the leadership of Lieutenant John Philip Sousa paraded to the park, as did veterans of the Spanish-American War and the Civil War. Other groups joined the parade, many with their own bands. The postal employees, the Boy Scouts, and a group from St. Louis University all marched. The *Post-Dispatch* noted "the local recruits for the British army in Palestine" and "the Polish volunteers for service in France." The Catholic Women's League, the Navy League, the Junior League of St. Louis, the YMCA, YWCA, YMHA, the Red Cross, the Knights of Columbus, the Elks, the Shriners, Moolah Temple and Alhambra Grotto, the Knights Templar, the Moose, the Red Men, and the Modern Woodmen all sent marchers. Women employees of local stores and other businesses were evident, especially the Famous & Barr drum corps. The unions marched: the photoengravers and other printing trades, the building trades, the carpenters, the metal trades, the bricklayers, and the teamsters. The City Club, the Advertising Club, and the Chamber of Commerce sent delegations. The "negro societies," the *Post-Dispatch* reported, marched last. The marchers joined a crowd of two hundred thousand people on and near Art Hill, many of whom had walked long distances when even the extra streetcars assigned

6-16. The crowd in Forest Park on June 19, 1927, cheered Charles A. Lindbergh for his flight from New York to Paris. In this picture, twenty-one U.S. Army pursuit planes are entertaining the crowd.

6-17. Lindbergh decorated the statue of St. Louis with a wreath.

to the Forest Park route proved inadequate. Sousa reportedly said that it was "not only the largest crowd I ever saw, but the greatest I ever heard of in the world" (Fig. 6-15).[20]

Fourth of July celebrations during the war also provided a chance for St. Louisans to demonstrate their patriotism in Forest Park. In 1917, the first Independence Day after U.S. entry into the war, the Forest Park Golf Club, a new organization for park golfers, sponsored a Fourth of July tournament in which each golfer paid the Red Cross a penny a stroke. The next year a Fourth of July parade to Art Hill featured foreign-born St. Louisans including, the *Star* reported, Czechs, Slovaks, Ukrainians, Lithuanians, Greeks, and about two hundred Chinese. In the face of sometimes violent anti-German feeling, groups that identified with German culture were noticeably absent. Other St. Louisans went to the municipal theater in 1918 for an Independence Pageant in

which the Allied nations told of the wrongs done them by the Central Powers, and the Courts of Justice, Truth, and Liberty summoned the United States to enter the war and help the Allies to victory.

A program in the theater in May 1919 celebrating the Allied victory featured the St. Louis Symphony Orchestra and the Pageant Choral Club, the *Globe-Democrat* reported, as well as "local club and society women" and "scores of young girls of prominent St. Louis families, supported by uniformed soldiers, sailors and marines, and the uniformed girls' drum corps of a local downtown store" in patriotic tableaux.[21] In June a memorial service on Art Hill honored those from St. Louis and St. Louis County who had been killed in the war. An elaborate Fourth of July celebration to honor returned servicemen was canceled at the men's request. Instead, the Mayor's Welcome Home Committee offered all returning servicemen free reserved seats at the municipal opera performance on July 4.

The period following the war saw a noticeable decline in mass gatherings in Forest Park, perhaps because of postwar disillusionment. But the large crowds returned to Forest Park on Sunday, June 19, 1927, when St. Louisans again had something to cheer. More than 100,000 people jammed Art Hill to welcome Charles A. Lindbergh back to St. Louis after his nonstop flight from New York to Paris had won the $25,000 Orteig prize and made the young pilot an international hero. Lindbergh had lived in St. Louis less than two years, but he made the city world famous. His plane, named *The Spirit of St. Louis* at the request of the group of St. Louis businessmen who helped finance the flight, carried the city's name across the ocean (Fig. 6-16).

Lindbergh's welcome in Forest Park was tumultuous, as his receptions in Paris, New York, and Washington had been. Lindbergh flew *The Spirit of St. Louis* from Lambert-St. Louis Flying Field toward the park, where, the *Globe-Democrat* said, a "roaring, teeming multitude" awaited him

6-18. The trophies, medals, and gifts presented to Lindbergh went on display in the west wing of the Jefferson Memorial, as seen here, after continuing donations made the collection too large for the Missouri Historical Society's display space in the east wing.

while "invisible myriads of people . . . listened to the . . . broadcast by KMOX [radio], 'The Voice of St. Louis.'" The crowd cheered each time Lindbergh flew low over the park. While Army aviators thrilled the crowd, Lindbergh landed *The Spirit of St. Louis* at Lambert Field and returned in another plane that landed in the park.

When Lindbergh mounted the Art Hill speakers' platform he was greeted by another ovation. The crowd cheered again when Dwight Davis, then serving as Secretary of War, presented Lindbergh with a commission as colonel in the Air Corps Reserve. Lindbergh spoke briefly, then concluded the ceremonies by hanging a wreath on the statue of St. Louis (Fig. 6-17). That evening when Lindbergh attended the municipal opera, a record twelve thousand people crowded into the theater and many others waited outside hoping to see him.[22]

The following week the Missouri Historical Society (MHS) displayed the Lindbergh collection of more than a thousand medals, scrolls, and gifts in thirteen large cases at its museum in the east wing of the Jefferson Memorial. Two city de-

6-19. An early zoo building. The sign says, "Do not feed or tease the animals." Visitors enjoyed the Forest Park zoo, but Park Commissioner Davis opposed setting park land aside for it.

tectives guarded the collection. The first Sunday the display was open, more than fifteen thousand people saw it between 10 A.M. and 5 P.M., and several hundred more were still waiting when the doors closed. Lindbergh agreed to leave the collection on display more than the few weeks he had originally intended.

The exhibit remained popular. The historical society later estimated that in the first year 1,495,000 people from all over the world saw it. In March 1928, after the exhibit had been open more than nine months, the People's Motorbus Company announced that a special bus line would run to the Jefferson Memorial on Sunday afternoons.

New trophies and gifts were added as they arrived. Soon the exhibit had outgrown the space and was moved to the west wing of the Memorial, previously used as a meeting room and municipal opera rehearsal hall (Fig. 6-18). In addition to the eighteen cases full of trophies, the MHS said it had many other items as well as "tons of mail" not on display. In 1933 Lindbergh and his wife Anne gave the trophies to the historical society, where some of them were still on display more than fifty years later.

After the welcoming celebrations had ended,

St. Louisans continued to look for ways to honor Lindbergh. Suggestions included renaming various places to honor him, such as Lindell Boulevard, next to the park, and the park itself. A statue in heroic size near the statue of St. Louis appealed to some. In the end, a road in St. Louis County, Denny Road, became Lindbergh Boulevard, despite a protest that Lindbergh had lived in St. Louis "only a short time and never owned a foot of ground in the county."[23]

Although most visitors to the MHS went to see the Lindbergh collection, the society also maintained other displays. Its library and archives were of particular interest to scholars and to MHS members, but the society was handicapped by limited funds and a small staff. Revenues came from the excess World's Fair funds and from member's dues and donations, which remained at the same level from 1913 into the 1940s.[24]

But the years of Davis and his successors didn't represent a complete break with Forest Park's past. While St. Louisans enjoyed the new athletic facilities and attended events at the new theater and the Art Hill amphitheater, traditional attractions continued to delight parkgoers. Some

NOTICE

Pupils of the St. Louis Schools

Do you love animals? Do you like to go to Forest Park to see them?

If so, you can do something to make the Zoo larger and better by taking this pamphlet home. **Show it to your father, uncle, older brother, or whoever votes.**

Make them promise to

VOTE—FOR a One-fifth of a Mill.

SCRATCH ~~AGAINST a One-fifth of a Mill.~~

at bottom of ballot with candidates, for the Zoo Amendment. Election, November 7th. One-fifth of a mill (only **two cents on $100**). This will give St. Louis the finest Zoo west of New York City.

You bought elephant "Jim" for the Zoo, now urge the voters to do their duty by voting **"FOR."**

A Zoo is educational.
A Zoo advertises our city.
A Zoo brings visitors here.
A Zoo is the biggest attraction we can have.

We request every pupil to get the promise of at least **one voter**, and if you do we will win.

We thank you for your support.

The Zoological Society of St. Louis

6-20. This Zoological Society flyer helped the zoo tax pass easily in 1916.

attractions, like the landscape, developed according to plans Davis made for them. Others, including band concerts, continued but declined during Davis's administration. Still others, such as the zoo, grew despite his opposition. The expansion of the zoo soon resulted in a clash between Davis and area businessmen.

After he became park commissioner, Davis considered what to do about the zoo near the World's Fair bird cage. Since Dwight Davis's progressivism emphasized structured, supervised recreation, the zoo was not a high priority for him (Fig. 6-19). In a statement with which many would later agree, Davis said he preferred a "glimpse of a herd of animals roaming apparently at will through natural surroundings" to "the sight of the same animals closely confined in a super-heated and super-odoriferous building." If the zoo were going to acquire a large number of tropical animals needing heated buildings, Davis believed the city should buy land for the zoo "rather than destroy a portion of our existing park properties, in order to provide a site which would in a short time be too small for the purpose."[25]

But the St. Louis Zoological Society began a campaign to build a major zoo in Forest Park that would entertain and educate St. Louisans and, not incidentally, attract out-of-town visitors. The Forest Park location was best, many believed, because it could be reached by anyone for five cents carfare. The society encouraged people to donate animals to the zoo, partly to revive the zoo's flagging popularity and partly to force the city to increase its financial support of the zoo. Broker George Dieckman and society officers, including Cortlandt Harris, gave some of the animals themselves and persuaded friends to donate others. But Davis still considered the collection "inadequate in size and wretchedly housed."

St. Louisans living south of the park wavered on the zoo question. The South Forest Park Residents' Association at first said it was "heartily in favor of the zoo." Later, a leading member of the residents' association, Anna Sneed Cairns of Forest Park University, complained that the "roar

6-22. Zoo Director George P. Vierheller watches a chimpanzee with his snack at one of the zoo's refreshment stands in about 1950. Vierheller developed the animal performances that brought the zoo nationwide publicity in newspapers, magazines, and newsreels.

6-21. The naturalistic bear pits, built using molds of bluffs near Herculaneum, Missouri, attracted visitors in the 1920s.

6-23. Zoogoers gather around Miss Jim, the elephant that school children bought with their pennies in 1916.

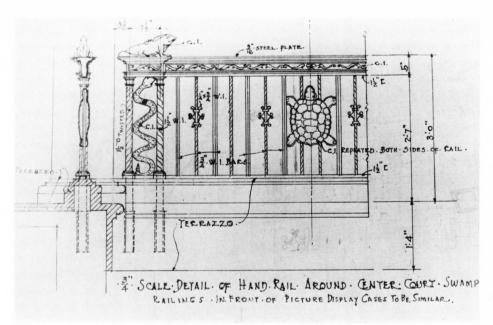

· ¾" · SCALE · DETAIL · OF · HAND · RAIL · AROUND · CENTER · COURT · SWAMP
RAILINGS · IN · FRONT · OF · PICTURE · DISPLAY · CASES · TO · BE · SIMILAR ·

6-24. Drawing for detail in the reptile house. Appropriate architectural decorations were also used inside and outside of the primate house and the bird house.

of lions and the growl of bears" frightened the young women students in the dormitories.[26] The residents' association and others opposed the use of tax funds for the zoo, funds they said should be used for more pressing civic needs.

Despite this opposition, the city considered an ordinance to set aside approximately 70 of Forest Park's about 1,370 acres as the St. Louis Zoological Park. Davis contended that the ordinance was illegal since it gave the zoo board of control complete authority over a section of park land. City Comptroller James Y. Player, however, supported the bill, noting that there would be plenty of park land outside the zoo. The ordinance passed despite Davis's objections. Mayor Kiel signed it in early December 1913, telling Davis, "The people of St. Louis want a zoo awfully bad . . . a lot of elephants, lions, tigers, and monkeys."[27] Despite his opposition to the zoo, Davis took his place on the board of control and was elected president, a position succeeding park commissioners would hold until 1960. Zoo Keeper Martin Angermeyer continued to care for the animals, as he and his father before him had done before the ordinance passed.

The zoo's problems were far from over, since the ordinance gave land to the zoo, but no money. Animals continued to pour in. Conditions that "very much shocked" a visitor in July 1914 had deteriorated so far by April 1915, as Cunliff prepared to take office, that some members of the zoo board considered giving the entire collection to the Kansas City Zoo. In July 1915 the city made a special emergency appropriation for a zoo building, which became the lion house.[28]

As the city was taking emergency measures, a new state law promised a permanent solution. The March 1915 law permitted St. Louis to adopt a special zoo tax like the art museum tax. If the tax passed, the zoo would have its own funds, and park commissioners would no longer have to use Forest Park appropriations for the zoo. Unlike the law authorizing the art museum tax, the zoo act made no provision for admission charges on special days or for nonresidents, saying only that the "zoo shall be forever free to the use of the inhabitants of the city wherein it shall be located" as long as the zoo tax was collected. Also unlike the art museum, a majority of the members of the zoo board of control were city officials.[29]

6-25. The *Post-Dispatch* took a pessimistic view of the climb to the art museum in 1915. The cartoon's caption included revised nursery rhymes: Jack and Jill went up the Hill/To use the Art Museum./And after they'd walked down again/A doctor came to see 'em.//Little Jack Horner sat in a corner,/'Way out in Forest Park./"I started to see the pictures," he said,/"But I won't get there till dark."//Rub-a-dub, dub, three men in a tub,/They rocked it and got a bad spill./But they said: "O, dear,/We'd rather be here/Than climbing that Forest Park Hill."//Little Bo Peep, lost her sheep,/And didn't know where to find it./As little sheep will, it climbed Art Hill, And she said, "O, well, never mind it."

As part of the campaign for approval of the tax, the zoo board encouraged a drive among the city's school children to raise money for a new elephant (Fig. 6-20). On April 5, 1916, the children paraded to welcome Miss Jim, the elephant bought with the pennies they had contributed. So many people went to see Miss Jim in the next few weeks that the city installed semaphores in two locations near the zoo to signal whether automobiles or pedestrians had the right of way.

The *Post-Dispatch* supported the zoo tax. So did the *Star* and the *Globe-Democrat*, which said, "Everybody is for it."[30] The tax passed easily.

After the tax passed, the board changed Angermeyer's title from keeper to superintendent and commissioned an elephant house for Miss Jim.

The next structures, perhaps because of Davis's earlier arguments, were either low and inconspicuous or natural looking. An artificial chain of lakes flowed into a new seal basin. The bear pits, opened in 1921, 1922, and 1923, appeared to be natural formations but were concrete, cast using molds of limestone bluffs above the Mississippi River near Herculaneum, Missouri (Fig. 6-21). The bear pits received national recognition; the superintendent of the National Zoo in Washington came to St. Louis specifically to see them and praised them highly.[31]

From 1922 to 1962 the zoo was largely shaped by its chief administrator, George P. Vierheller. Vierheller began to work at the zoo in 1918 as secretary to the board of control (Fig. 6-22). After Superintendent Angermeyer died in 1922, the board made Vierheller, then forty years old, superintendent as well as secretary. In 1928 he became Director of the St. Louis Zoological Park, a new position that he held until he retired in 1962. Under Vierheller the zoo attracted visitors with its new buildings, new animals, and performing animal shows. While Vierheller and his staff promoted the educational and scientific value of the zoo, most zoogoers came for entertainment.

New structures opened quickly: the primate house in 1925; the reptile house in 1927 (Fig. 6-24); then the small mammal pits, similar to the nearby bear pits, but smaller; then the bird house in 1930. Vierheller also encouraged attendance with special attractions, like rides on Miss Jim (Fig. 6-23).

Each year, zoo attendance seemed to grow, though an accurate attendance count was impossible since the zoo was not fenced off from the park. Still it was clear the zoo was popular with St. Louisans and with tourists who came to St. Louis to inspect the zoo they had seen in newspapers, magazines, and newsreels.

Unlike the zoo, the art museum was not a major concern for Davis or his successors. The

6-26. The park department double-deck bus carried parkgoers from the streetcar stops to park attractions such as the zoo. A semaphore to control pedestrian traffic is visible on the left side of the photograph.

museum already had a suitable physical plant and a designated tax when Davis took office. The park commissioner didn't sit on the art museum board, which included no city officials. Davis and his successors worked to landscape the art museum grounds as part of a comprehensive park landscape plan, and Davis's successors worked to provide transportation to the museum.

Like the zoo, the art museum developed ways to encourage attendance, including scheduled special exhibits and programs for children and adults by the museum's Educational Depart-

ment. Annual museum attendance grew gradually from fewer than 15,000 people in 1911 to more than 30,000 in 1930, but museum officials thought more people might visit the museum if it were more accessible. Citizens pointed out that the "shoe-destroying and skirt-defiling" pedestrian cinder paths to the museum from the two nearest streetcar stops lacked adequate shade and benches (Fig. 6-25).[32]

Davis did nothing to provide transportation up the hill, so the museum underwrote Sunday bus service by a private bus company in 1912, but

6-27. Children learn about the collection from the City Art Museum's Educational Department, established in 1923 to provide programs for adults and children.

usage was disappointing, and the service didn't last long. For some night-time events the St. Louis Art League, a private group, provided automobile transportation between the museum and the streetcar lines.

After a brief trial in 1915, Cunliff began a daytime municipal bus service in Forest Park in August 1916. Some people thought the bus line should be an interim measure until a trolley line in the park, planned by city officials after extensive research in other cities, could be constructed.

Cunliff, however, considered the trolley line too expensive to be practical, and it was never built; the bus line operated into the 1930s.

For a five-cent fare parkgoers could ride part or all of a loop from several of the park entrances to the Jefferson Memorial, the art museum, and the zoo. A single-deck bus for twenty-five passengers operated on weekdays and a double-deck bus for fifty-four people ran on Sundays and holidays (Fig. 6-26). Although one of the major reasons for beginning the bus service was to supply

6-28. In about 1916 Cass Gilbert drew this plan to enlarge the art museum (making it eight times the size of the building he had designed for the World's Fair) and to provide formal landscaping on Art Hill and around the Grand Basin. Only the retaining wall and balustrade around the Grand Basin were built.

service to the art museum, only about ten percent of the passengers went there, the *Star* reported.[33] Art museum attendance continued its steady growth, but didn't jump dramatically (Fig. 6-27).

Both art museum and park department workers landscaped the outside of the museum building. In a burst of enthusiasm at about the time the park bus service began, William K. Bixby, president of the museum board of control, asked Cass Gilbert to draw a plan for museum expansion and for landscaping Art Hill (Fig. 6-28).[34]

The museum never implemented Gilbert's expansion plans, but the park department adopted some of the landscaping plans as part of a formal treatment of land in the park's center, around the Grand Basin and on Government Hill, which the national *Journal of the American Institute of Architects* called "the most ambitious scheme for the improvement of a section of a municipal park on formal lines ever attempted in America." The ambitious plan was not completed. But, beginning in late 1917 when the city hired Gilbert to oversee the work, the basin gradually acquired a retaining wall and a formal balustrade.[35]

That landscaping fit into a larger landscape scheme that Davis had commissioned for the entire park. When he took office, Davis had discovered that Forest Park had no landscaping plan. Planting, he found, was done "in a rather haphazard manner, depending largely upon the whims of whoever happened to be in charge of the parks at the time." So Davis and City Landscape Architect

George E. Kessler developed a plan in 1911–1912. Davis began a "policy of bringing together isolated flower beds into one comprehensive floral scheme . . . leaving the rest of the park for lawns, trees or shrubbery" or, perhaps, athletic fields. Under the plan, Davis returned the southwestern corner of the park to wilderness, planting hundreds of thousands of tree seedlings and wildflower seeds. Also under Kessler's plan, Government Hill received a formal "floral scheme," and two flights of steps up the hill for those who wished to climb and enjoy the breeze and the view (Fig. 6-29).[36]

Davis worked to get a fountain for Government Hill in 1912, by trying to persuade the Ladies' Confederate Monument Association to substitute a fountain on Government Hill for its planned statue. The proposed memorial's design by George Julian Zolnay had won the association's design competition, which specified that the monument could show "no figure of a Confederate soldier, or object of modern warfare." But the idea of commemorating Confederate soldiers was distasteful to some. After a stormy session, the city council approved an ordinance accepting the monument and requiring the Confederate Monument Association of St. Louis to maintain it (Fig. 6-30).[37] The monument was the only one in the park that had required an ordinance. One councilman said he was in favor of the ordinance because the Civil War was over. Another said that St. Louis might injure its trade with the South by

6-29. Government Hill some time between 1914 (when the steps were built) and 1930. Davis's policy concentrated formal landscaping in a few locations, such as this one.

rejecting the monument. The monument was un-veiled on December 15, 1914, but near Lindell Boulevard, not on Government Hill.

As with other park facilities, Davis's successors followed his lead in landscaping the hill. When former St. Louisan Samuel Moffitt donated one thousand cherry trees to Forest Park in 1928, most of them went to Government Hill. And in 1930 the city provided a Government Hill fountain, which the *Star* said provided "a new note in the evening symphony of beauty in Forest Park" (Fig. 6-31). The varying shapes of the sprayed water and the gradually changing shades of light on the water, from green through blue to red, brought "audible sighs of satisfaction and exclamations" from spectators standing on the hill or seated in their automobiles.[38]

Davis proposed another floral facility for Government Hill, a palm house and conservatory to be formed by glassing in and heating the World's Fair Pavilion. Although a conservatory had been repeatedly recommended as both in-structive and attractive, beginning with the 1876 plan for the park, it was one of the few improvements Davis proposed for the park but failed to get funded. His successors found another way to provide the floral display house, though not on Government Hill. During the winter of 1916–17 Head Gardener John Moritz turned a section of one of the park greenhouses into a display featuring water, flowers, and benches for relaxation and escape from wintry weather. Moritz and his staff used the display to teach visitors about the kinds of plants that would grow well in various sections of the city, especially those areas veiled in smoke and gas (Fig. 6-32). During the 1920s the display gradually became a floral show that changed monthly. The show was popular and "received favorable comment from many out-of-town horticulturists and botanists," Pape said.[39] By 1926 the floral display section of the greenhouses had become known as the "Jewel Box," after a visitor's remark to Moritz that the flower patterns resembled a jewel box.

6-30. Photograph taken in the 1970s shows a detail of the Confederate Memorial, unveiled December 15, 1914. The bronze relief shows a young man leaving home to fight for the Confederacy, a controversial subject even though the Civil War had ended almost fifty years before.

the French and Spanish Colonies in Missouri stood near the Jefferson Memorial, but construction work around the River des Peres prevented its becoming a drinking fountain until 1941.

As he had with the new athletic facilities, Davis put the park's green spaces to work to further the ideals of progressivism by providing supervised activities for the young to teach them the value of abiding by rules. From 1909 to 1917 the city recreation commission located some of its children's gardens on the south side of the park near the Forest Park greenhouses. Any boy in St. Louis between eight and sixteen could have seeds, instruction, and land for a garden, if he would work in it twice a week for two hours a visit. The gardens also served Davis's and Rumbold's progressivism by supplementing the diets of the boys' families with the vegetables the boys grew and took home.

Since Davis was one of the organizers of the St. Louis Boy Scouts, it is not surprising that one of the first Boy Scout Camporalls held in the United States was on Forest Park's Art Hill in 1911 (Fig. 6-34). Three hundred boys from fifteen St. Louis troops camped in the park overnight and thousands of spectators watched them demonstrate their new skills.

Not only Boy Scouts slept in the park that year. During a 1911 heat wave Davis invited St. Louisans to escape the baking city by spending the night in the park. He asked the police to suspend enforcement of the park curfew. His successors continued the practice. Cunliff waived the curfew in 1916 on the condition that children sleeping in a park must be accompanied by at least one parent. No "objectionable dress" was permitted, but pajamas were considered proper. In 1927, the *Star* reported, between 500 and 700 "inhabitants from the congested districts" slept in Forest Park on newspapers, blankets, or automobile cushions. Sometimes the night's sleep was interrupted by a rain shower or by armed robbers. Pape told the *Star* after a 1927 incident that robberies were unusual "and the nights usually pass peaceably for the sleepers."[41]

As Davis and his successors landscaped the park, they accepted new statues for it, including the Jahn Memorial, donated by the St. Louis Turnverein in 1913 to honor the founder of the international gymnastic and fraternal society. Though Davis failed to persuade the Confederate Monument Association to donate a fountain, other organizations and individuals donated fountains and drinking fountains. Near the park's western border, the Musicians' Memorial Fountain offered cooling drinks to passersby (Fig. 6-33). The Bertha Guggenheim Memorial Fountain, also called the Pan Fountain, splashed near the municipal theater. After the fountain's design was criticized as unartistic and tasteless, the city required design changes before allowing the monument to be installed in the lily pond next to Pagoda Lake.[40] The Memorial to the Frontier Women of

6-31. Government Hill after installation of the fountain in 1930. The changing shape of the fountain's spray and the changing color of its lights at night fascinated St. Louisans.

However, Davis invoked the curfew when he believed it necessary to promote order and proper behavior in the park. When he announced in July 1912 that he would enforce it, the *Star* responded, "Lovers who seek a place in the park where spooning is allowed because of the dark, will find themselves hunted by cops in plain clothes, for loving's illegal as everyone knows. . . . Commissioner Davis says it must stop, and if you make love he may call a cop. . . ."[42] The young couples were sometimes disturbed by the police and sometimes by robbers, but despite the interruptions and despite public disapproval, they continued to park automobiles in Forest Park at night.

Band concerts, which had been a great attraction in the 1890s, were much less frequent under Davis and his successors. One reason was the lack of a bandstand after 1911, when Davis abandoned as unsafe the wooden music pagoda, which had been in the park since opening day. Before crews had time to work on the pagoda, it blew down in a storm and was damaged beyond repair. The city sponsored occasional band concerts at several other Forest Park locations, including the World's Fair Pavilion, but such recreation was not a high priority with Davis and his successors. In 1925 St. Louis lawyer Nathan Frank donated funds for a new bandstand on the site of the old music pagoda, at the request of city officials (Fig. 6-35). He urged them to make their needs known to other wealthy St. Louisans so they, too, could make contributions to the city.

Unlike the concerts, holiday celebrations continued to grow. The Fourth of July continued to attract people to the park after World War I. In 1921 the *Globe-Democrat* said that Forest Park was "literally swamped with picnickers . . . wherever big trees furnished cooling shade." Many brought phonographs and musical instruments with them. The boat concessionaire was kept busy all day. At the zoo, picnickers admired the new bear pits.[43]

The Easter crowds were bigger than ever. For Easter 1915, the first after the opening of the new Roman Catholic cathedral on Lindell, the *Globe-Democrat* said that rising hemlines allowed glimpses of "fascinating ankles." About 30,000 people entered the park through the Lindell-Kingshighway entrance alone, and "at one time more than 1000 automobiles were waiting to enter the park" (Fig. 6-36).[44] In 1927 more than 5,000 worshipers gathered near the Lindell-Kingshighway entrance to take part in St. Louis's first Easter sunrise service. The service, which became an annual event, featured an address by Edward S. Travers, rector of St. Peter's Episcopal Church, who had originated the idea (Fig. 6-37).

As the Easter traffic jams illustrated, St. Louisans were turning to the automobile in great numbers. The number of motor vehicle licenses issued in the city increased from 9,867 in 1914 to 60,473 in 1921 to 168,703 in 1930. The park's road system and entrances, designed for small numbers of carriages, were overwhelmed by these automobiles, especially the Lindell-Kingshighway en-

6-32. Head Gardener John Moritz supervised these displays inside one of the Forest Park greenhouses. The shows provided an attractive escape from winter weather as well as instruction about the types of plants that could be grown in different parts of the city, all in half a greenhouse less than one hundred feet long.

trance. The city street department reported in 1916 that the adjacent street corner was probably the busiest corner in the city on Sundays, with as many as 2,400 vehicles an hour, almost fifteen percent of the licensed automobiles in the city of St. Louis. Davis's response was to reshape the road system to accommodate the traffic, rather than to try to limit the number of automobiles. After several experiments Davis installed a traffic circle inside the entrance, but the problems continued.[45]

Cunliff proposed a new entrance in 1915, but Samuel B. McPheeters, president of the police board, attacked the plans as "impractical and inartistic." Instead, the park department constructed an alternate entrance at West Pine to divert traffic from the Lindell-Kingshighway entrance, but the congestion remained as the number of automobiles grew. The city also worked on the park's other entrances, including the DeBaliviere entrance, which was enlarged by the city's purchase of small amounts of private property.[46]

The park's winding roads, too, caused problems in an automobile age. As Davis pointed out in 1912, "roads which were entirely adequate for horse-drawn traffic are often dangerous for the swift-moving automobile."[47] In Davis's mind, it was the park, not the traffic, that must change. He eliminated a sharp curve known as Dead Man's Curve; in six and a half years it had caused eighteen accidents and two deaths.

As they would for years, drivers often lost their way in the confusing road system. In 1928 the *Post-Dispatch* told of a truck driver with a load of bricks who was confused by "the labyrinth of circling ways. . . . Directions to the nearest exit didn't help much. He was always lost after the second fork in the road. Finally by accident" he found his way out of the park.[48] A park department employee had suggested as early as 1915 that the department should issue a booklet with a map to help motorists who were having trouble finding their way around the park, but no action was taken.

Despite the increasing number of facilities in

6-33. The Musicians' Memorial Fountain, dedicated in 1925 with a concert by a 150-piece band, commemorated the services of two officers of the American Federation of Musicians. A photograph from the 1970s.

Forest Park and despite Dwight Davis's interest in planning, Davis didn't see a need for a comprehensive plan for the park. In 1917 the City Plan Commission, chaired by Davis, issued planner Harland Bartholomew's reports on the city's problems and the city's recreation system. The commission called Forest Park "one of the largest and best equipped parks in existence," suggesting only improvements to the Lindell-Kingshighway entrance. Instead of a plan for Forest Park, the commission recommended the purchase of more park land east of Grand Avenue for neighborhood parks and of large "public reservations . . . well outside the city limits" to serve as "outing places," much as Forest Park had in the 1870s.[49]

Perhaps Davis saw no need for a park plan because of the relative abundance of resources available for Forest Park. The vast new spaces cleared for the World's Fair, and then left as open lawn when the fair was removed, seemed ample for every imaginable new use. And funding was relatively plentiful both for maintenance and for new facilities.

But in the 1920s conditions began to change. A major increase in the number of parks and the addition of numerous neighborhood playgrounds, encouraged by Davis, meant that the park commissioner was supervising almost one third more land than he had in 1903 and almost three times as many separate locations. The park budget had to stretch to cover them all at a time when the city's financial situation was deteriorating. By 1927 the city had a deficit of almost $1 million, while the art museum, zoo, and public library had reserves totaling about $500,000. City officials tried to turn the taxes designated for those institutions into general revenue, but the Missouri Supreme Court ruled against the city.[50]

As in the 1880s, because of financial hard times in the city, park maintenance budgets were meager. In the fiscal year 1916–17 Forest Park had received more than $190,000. During the 1920s the park's allocation was usually lower, dipping below $150,000 in 1927–28. Perhaps because of the needs of the new parks, Forest Park, which contained more than fifty-six percent of the city's park acreage in 1922, received less than thirty-two percent of the funds from a citywide park maintenance budget that Pape considered inadequate. Forest Park's budget was further strained by rising wage rates in the 1920s.

The park still produced small amounts of revenue from the boating and refreshment concessions and from letting the privilege of retrieving lost golf balls (which were resold). Beginning in 1920 the refreshment stands, or refectories, were operated by the park department, rather than a concessionaire, and produced a small profit for the city. But the small amounts of revenue were inadequate to supplement maintenance appropriations. As a result, necessary maintenance was deferred, and the department had to lay off many longtime employees. Pape and his subordinates commented often on the folly of postponing maintenance, saying it was difficult to predict how much repairs would cost in the future "but it stands to reason that it will be more."[51] Some maintenance was paid for with funds appropriated for hiring the unemployed, or was performed by prisoners from the city workhouse.

Because of the quirks of municipal finance, while there was little money for maintenance of existing facilities, there were funds for construction of new ones. In 1923, businessmen and progressives again united to support an $87.4 million bond issue for projects all over the city, including $1.3 million for improvement of existing parks and playgrounds. Voters approved the bonds, which financed work in Forest Park, including the Government Hill fountain and the field house built after the Lindell Pavilion burned.

The bond issue also financed a project park commissioners had requested for years—work on the River des Peres (Fig. 6-38). Despite construction of the Forest Park Foul Water Sewer and then

a Forest Park Storm Water Sewer, the river had continued to invade the park with its smells and floods. At least three children had drowned in the river, which led the Missouri Supreme Court to write in a 1913 opinion that the city was creating and maintaining an "inexcusable nuisance." Just before the 1923 election to approve bonds for the River des Peres sewer, a billboard in Forest Park said, "Think this over. What other Big City would have an open sewer running through a fine big Park? Henry W. Kiel, Mayor."[52] The River des Peres proposal passed by more than 3 to 1.

The bond issue provided funds for turning the river into a sewer for its entire course through the city. In the park, the river was rerouted so that it roughly followed the park's northern and eastern boundaries, then put into horseshoe shaped concrete sewer pipes tall enough to hold a two-story house easily. Spectators went to the park to watch a 300-ton shovel scoop up six cubic yards of dirt at a time (Figs. 6-39, 6-40). Department employees built a new lake, later called Jefferson Lake and a series of lagoons over parts of the sewer.[53]

In 1930, after the sewer was complete, a park

6-34. Boy Scouts began camping in Forest Park in 1911 for one of the first Camporalls held in the United States.

department employee wrote, "Behold, the day has arrived and . . . joy is in the hearts of the employees of Forest Park, who have fought this treacherous river." The massive new sewer didn't solve all the Forest Park drainage problems; heavy rains still brought flooding, especially at the municipal theater and the golf course. Some St. Louisans mourned the loss of the River des Peres, recalling when they could see "the fresh footprint of a raccoon in the soft mud of the . . . bank."[54]

As the River des Peres sewer was being completed, another section of Forest Park was torn up to replace the elevated railroad tracks through the park. The project was also paid for by the 1923 bond issue as part of a citywide reduction of railroad grade crossings (places where railroad tracks and streets crossed at the same level). The tracks through the park were depressed and the route altered slightly, to allow a bridge to be built outside the park. As a result, the bridge carrying the railroad tracks over Grand Drive, built with such effort in 1904 during the World's Fair, was no longer needed and was removed.

The bond issue also included $400,000 for construction of an aquarium in Forest Park. At first the zoo board of control made plans to build and operate the aquarium, but Zoo Director Vierheller believed that $400,000 was inadequate for construction of a first-rate facility and that operating the aquarium would strain the zoo's budget. In 1945, more than twenty years after voters had approved the aquarium bonds, the city renounced its rights to issue them, though some St. Louisans continued to favor the project.

Like the park, the land around it filled up during the teens and twenties as the city continued to grow west, bringing conflicts between park administrators and neighbors, especially along the southern border. In general, land use around the park continued much as it had in the nineteenth century. Until it was found unconstitutional in 1924, a 1918 zoning ordinance gave the force of law to the different uses that already existed around the park. Custom, and the factors that had been in effect before zoning, retained the differences after that.

The private places that extended north and east from the park corner at Kingshighway and Lindell continued to fill with what the *Post-Dispatch* called "beautiful and costly" residences, like the "marble palace" of Mr. and Mrs. Edward A. Faust at 1 Portland Place.[55] Lindell Boulevard, bordering the park on the north, contained similar residences as far west as Union. While some moved into the area, others moved farther west. Mary Institute, after less than thirty years, left its Lake Avenue buildings in 1929 and moved to a new campus in St. Louis County.

Washington University remained and grew. Its medical school campus, designed by Theodore C. Link, who had helped draw the 1876 Forest Park plan, was located diagonally across the park from its main campus. The large green spaces on the campuses of both the medical school and the main university extended the park's serenity into the surrounding city (Fig. 6-41). Both Barnes Hospital and nearby Children's Hospital were associated with the medical school. Other hospitals nearby included Jewish Hospital, Shriner's Hospital for Crippled Children, and St. John's Hospital. Central Institute for the Deaf built a school near the park in 1928.

Other developments around the park were also similar along the diagonals, in part because the River des Peres flowed from the northwest to the southeast corners of the park. North of Forest Park and west of Union, near where the river entered the park, residential development continued to lag, slowed by the unsewered river and the Rock Island railroad tracks. Beginning in the late teens and early twenties, there were some single-family homes in the area, but apartment houses and hotels were the rule north of the Rock Island railroad tracks, a long block away from the park, with restaurants, theaters, and other businesses along DeBaliviere.[56] Downstream, diagonally across the park, the river and the Missouri Pacific tracks slowed residential development. St. Louis

6-35. St. Louis lawyer Nathan Frank donated the money for this bandstand, which could hold seventy musicians, in 1925, saying, "All that I have, all that I have acquired, I owe to St. Louis."

6-36. By 1924, the date of this Easter traffic jam, horses and buggies no longer paraded in the park. The Chase Hotel, visible in the background, opened in 1922. In 1929, the Park Plaza Hotel would open next door.

University High School moved next to the St. Louis University stadium in the middle 1920s. The high school and the university shared the playing fields. By 1930 the city had improved access to the school by opening the section of Oakland Avenue where formerly there had been only streetcar tracks, from Kingshighway west to Forest Park University, thus completing the frame of roads around the park.

On another diagonal, the southern section of the west side and the northern section of the east side contained apartment buildings, mixed on the east side with hotels, including the Buckingham Hotel and the Forest Park Hotel. The Chase Hotel opened in 1922 and the Park Plaza Hotel in 1929, both on the site of the Kauffman (then Bixby) house, which was torn down in the early 1920s. Like New York's Plaza Hotel, which overlooked Central Park, the Park Plaza was easily visible from inside the park.[57]

By 1926 the Hi-Pointe corner, southwest of the park, already contained a movie theater and two gas stations. One of the stations stood on a triangle of land that had been offered to the city as an entrance to Forest Park. In 1922, after the city had ignored the offered sale for eighteen months, the owners withdrew the offer and sold the land to the Pierce Oil Company.[58]

6-37. Beginning in 1927, worshipers stood near the eastern edge of Forest Park for the Easter sunrise service. This picture is from 1929.

The Wiltshire and Versailles apartments looked east across Skinker into Forest Park by the late 1920s. Nearby, new subdivisions opened rapidly. Even those that did not touch the park, such as Skinker Heights on Ellenwood Avenue, and Hampton Park (more than a mile west of the park) advertised their locations as near the park. Soon there were churches for the people in the new houses west of the park, beginning with the Episcopal church of St. Michael and All Angels (later St. Michael and St. George) in 1913, then United Hebrew Temple, Memorial Presbyterian Church, and the Eighth Church of Christ, Scientist.

Growing development meant increased automobile traffic around and through Forest Park. Many St. Louis County residents used the Clayton Road route through Forest Park, as county farmers had done in the 1870s. In 1915 the resi-

dents of Hillcrest (just across Skinker Road from the park) asked for, but didn't get, a new entrance to Forest Park opposite their subdivision. Instead the park department widened Government Drive as part of a diagonal connection through the park, and, in 1915, the city used Forest Park land to widen Skinker.

The greatest conflict between park administrators and park neighbors occurred along the park's southern border. The park land near the southern border had long housed various dirty, ugly, or noisy support services, such as the greenhouses and the mounted police station. It was surely not a coincidence that these facilities began to cluster along the southern border as the city's wealthiest and most influential citizens began to move into the private places north of the park. The trend continued into the twentieth century, despite efforts by the South Forest Park Residents' Improvement Association, organized in 1912 by Anna Sneed Cairns and others. The association immediately pushed for a north-south road through the middle of Forest Park, but without success. In 1914 the group succeeded in persuading the city to improve Oakland Avenue from Forest Park University west to Skinker, but they couldn't get improvements to the park land that they faced across Oakland.

From 1909 to 1917 the southern neighbors looked at the greenhouses and the children's vegetable gardens run by the recreation division. After the children's gardens closed, the city built a group of workshops for carpenters, painters, plumbers, blacksmiths, and auto mechanics, which centralized park department craftsmen near the greenhouses, while department offices remained downtown. The tree nursery moved out of Forest Park in the early teens, but the number of greenhouses continued to grow, producing coal smoke when they were heated.

In December 1918 Forest Park again became a focus for those trying to foster growth of the city's economy. The city set aside land near the mounted police station for a landing field for aerial mail, or airmail, despite objections to such

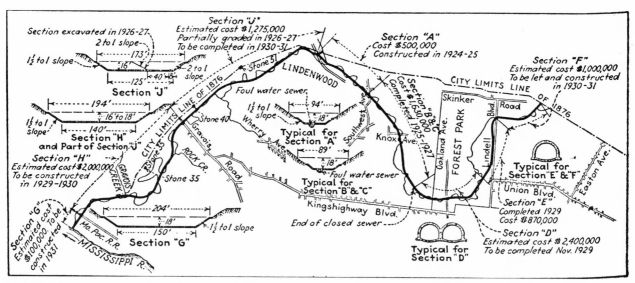

6-38. Map shows course of the River des Peres and of the River des Peres sewer through the city of St. Louis, including Forest Park.

a use of park land. The business community, represented by the Chamber of Commerce, supported an airmail field as important for the city's development. City officials believed, according to the *Globe-Democrat*, that any other site would be "so far from the main Post Office that it would take longer to get mail to the landing field than for it to come from Chicago."

The Chamber of Commerce donated half the $25,000 needed for grading the field and erecting a surplus Army hangar. The city paid the other half from funds appropriated for advertising purposes. Major Albert Bond Lambert, on behalf of the Missouri Aeronautical Society, agreed to contribute $3,000 for material needed to complete the hangar.

Airmail service between St. Louis and Chicago began in Forest Park on August 16, 1920. Pilots made one flight each way daily, except Sunday, year-round, circling the field until they reached their flight altitude of 1,000 feet, then crossing the park diagonally to the Lindell-Kingshighway entrance (Fig. 6-42).

The Forest Park airmail service lasted less than a year, ending June 30, 1921, after Congress, bent on saving money, refused to underwrite air-

mail service deficits for another year. The U.S. government took back its movable equipment, but the airfield and the hangar remained in the park.[59] Despite what St. Louisans would later say, Charles Lindbergh never flew the mail out of Forest Park.

After airmail service ended, private pilots, including William B. Robertson, Charles R. Wassall, and H. H. Hunter, used the Forest Park airfield for exhibition flights that attracted so many people, especially on Sundays, that it was hard for the flyers to land. After the city prohibited the pilots from charging for rides in July 1921, Forest Park flights were no longer profitable. The pilots moved to a larger St. Louis County field, which later became Lambert-St. Louis Municipal Airport, but the Forest Park field remained as an emergency landing field.[60]

Nearby, the park was again serving the city's poor. In 1919 the park department and the Red Cross opened a vacation village on the park's southern edge for families who otherwise couldn't afford to take vacations. The village included a hospital with a nurse, a mess tent where the average cost of a meal was ten cents, four showers, a children's playground, and easy access to the zoo.

6-39, 6-40. The River des Peres Sewer pipes, financed by a 1923 bond issue, ran near the park's boundary north of the Jefferson Memorial. Downstream, along Forest Park's eastern border, the size of the river required two pipes, each 29 feet wide and 23 feet high.

6-41. A drawing of Barnes Hospital and the Washington University Medical Schools, designed by Theodore C. Link and dedicated in 1915. Because of the dogleg in Kingshighway, visible here, most of the buildings faced into Forest Park. The trees and the playing field in the foreground of this picture are part of Forest Park.

"Fathers and other working vacationists," the *Post-Dispatch* explained, could continue to go to work using the nearby streetcar lines.[61]

That same summer the Automobile Club of St. Louis opened an automobile tourist camp in the park near the vacation village. The camp contained some tents and hammocks, although most of the tourists carried camping equipment with them (Fig. 6-43).

Things could have been worse for the park's southern neighbors if the city had not rejected Anton Steuver's 1918 plan to mine fire clay under Forest Park's southern edge. Steuver's Highlands Fire Clay Company, south of the park, offered to pay the city for the privilege of following a vein of clay under the park, saying it would otherwise have to move out of the city. Mayor Kiel supported the plan because it would produce revenue for the city without any damage to the park, while continuing to employ a hundred workers.

But a former professor of mining engineering said the mining might change the land into "a series of sinks and shell holes." Neighborhood groups opposed the bill. The Central Trades and Labor Union was against it. The *Globe-Democrat* called the clay mining "a dangerous experiment" that "might work all right, but it might not."[62] The board of aldermen approved the plan, then a week later unanimously reversed itself because of public opposition.

By late 1919 lawyer Taylor R. Young had had enough of these developments, which he said decreased the value of his house on Oakland. He sued Commissioner Cunliff, challenging the use of land along the park's southern boundary for Triple A, the mounted police station, the aviation field, the greenhouse complex, and the tourist camp and vacation village. He also called the court's attention to "unsightly and unsanitary piles of rocks and stones . . . along the south line of Forest Park, near Skinker Road" and, for good measure, challenged the practice of charging admission at the municipal theater, and the contracts for refreshment sales. Oddly, Young, while

6-42. An airmail pilot rests on a plane he used to fly the mail from Forest Park to Chicago in late 1920 and early 1921. The pilots averaged about 77 miles an hour, reaching Chicago in about three and a half hours.

objecting to these nonmunicipal uses of the park land, didn't object to the state of Missouri's continued use of the Forest Park lakes as a fish hatchery, perhaps because the state's activities were concentrated near the northern edge of the park.

Young's case dragged through the courts for more than three years before a judge dismissed it in 1922. In the meantime, the aviation field had closed and the tourist camp would soon follow. By 1925 the park department considered the camp "an eyesore and a detriment to the beauty of the well-kept park," the *Globe-Democrat* said.[63] Tourists, too, were unhappy with the inadequate facilities, which couldn't be expanded without encroaching on the adjacent wilderness area. The camp was removed in 1925.

The question of the use of Forest Park land by Triple A was not so easily resolved. As early as 1907 there had been suggestions that the use of

park land by a private club was inappropriate. Some golfers suggested that the easiest way to build a public golf course would be to take over Triple A's nine-hole course and enlarge it. Instead Davis built the public course.

In response to Young's suit, the club vigorously defended its record. It had sponsored tennis tournaments in which many nonmembers competed and benefit matches, such as those in 1903 by Dwight Davis to raise money for the playgrounds. It had spent about $100,000 in the park, planting five hundred trees, and building the golf course, clubhouse, and tennis and handball courts. Club officials pointed out that, while the clubhouse was limited to members, anyone could use the athletic facilities. City officials agreed that they had never heard of anyone being denied a chance to play there. Young's position was that club members made it unpleasant for nonmembers to use the facilities. A club member probably didn't help Triple A's case when he said the golf course "was quite overrun [by nonmembers] when, in wet weather, the municipal course was closed."[64]

Triple A stayed, but in 1925 the city altered the agreement with the club. When the city imposed fees for the use of the public golf and tennis facilities, Triple A agreed to pay the city about $12,000 annually, $10 for each club member, the amount of an annual golf permit for the public course. The city then issued each member a golf permit, valid only on the Triple A course. Permits for the municipal courses were not valid at Triple A, ending regular use of the course by nonmembers. The city used the money from both types of permits to maintain the municipal courses, while Triple A continued to maintain its own. But the agreement did not end the Triple A controversy, which would erupt again.

In the meantime the Triple A tennis courts continued to host a variety of tournaments, some of national or international interest. The 1925 National Clay Court tournament, the 1927 Davis Cup zone matches between Japan and Mexico, and the 1928 U.S. Davis Cup team trials all used the Triple A courts. Spectators, members and nonmembers alike, could see, admire, and learn from the championship grade of tennis.

In the 1920s the South Forest Park Residents' Association lost one of its organizers. In 1925 Mrs. Cairns closed Forest Park University after poor health prevented her from running it. In 1926 she sold the university buildings, which were then torn down.

The next few years brought new construction to the land along Oakland west of the Forest Park University campus. The Pom Oak Apartments, with four- to six-room apartments for forty-two families opened in 1927 with moderate rentals of $60 to $80 a month. Nearby, ground was broken in 1928 for the new Evangelical Dea-

coness Hospital. The new Jewish Orphans' Home was built in the late 1920s on vacant land a few blocks west of Deaconess Hospital. Much of the land in the area was subdivided, and houses built, with much smaller lots and more modest houses than the fashionable areas north and west of the park. Filling stations and small apartments, too, entered the neighborhood around George Dewey Public School, built in 1917.

In September 1926, after Mrs. Cairns had sold her school, the Chamber of Commerce sponsored another activity in southern Forest Park intended to bolster the city's economy. More than 300,000 people went to the St. Louis Exposition on forty-five acres along the park's southern edge. The chamber advertised the exposition,

6-43. A 1920 view of the automobile tourist camp, which the Automobile Club of St. Louis opened in 1919 so travelers could spend the night in the open instead of "going to hotels in hot and dusty cities."

6-44. The southern edge of Forest Park and the Forest Park Highlands in the late 1920s, showing a streetcar near the Highlands entrance. The vacant land at the lower right became the site for the Arena in 1930. Smoke marks the location of the Highlands Fire Clay Company near the top left corner of the picture.

which took more than three months to build, as the "biggest event since the St. Louis World's Fair." Like the fair, the exposition fenced off part of the public park, then charged St. Louisans to enter. The *Post-Dispatch* reported that the exposition provided six hundred booths displaying St. Louis's "industrial products and its chief commercial wares," an automobile show "in three very large tents," and an "entertainment program—bands, vaudeville, and a large spectacle."[65]

Bad weather plagued the exposition from the beginning. To prevent a deficit, the exposition, scheduled for two weeks, was extended for a third. The third week was also rainy, so the extension only increased the deficit to an estimated $30,000. The plan of Carl F. G. Meyer, President of the Chamber of Commerce, to make the exposition an annual event with a permanent Forest Park building was discarded. That was probably a relief to nearby residents and to the hospitals along Kingshighway whose patients had been disturbed by the "French 75" cannons, fired as part of the entertainment.

Among the sponsors of the exposition were Ben G. Brinkman and his associates who had bought the Forest Park Highlands from Anton Steuver in the early 1920s when his health began to fail. The group continued to operate the Highlands rides, including the roller coaster, and the other attractions.

On October 12, 1929, as the U.S. financial and industrial sectors began to follow the farmers into depression, Brinkman and his associates opened a new building, called simply the Arena, on previously vacant land just west of the Highlands (Fig. 6-44). The building's lamella roof covered, without a post or column, more than three acres, an area that could seat 21,000 people. The *Post-Dispatch* said the building was the "largest of its kind in the world, having more floor space than [New York's] Madison Square Garden."[66]

The Arena's massive display space decreased the use of park land for events like the exposition. When the Arena opened, it held, simultaneously, the National Dairy Show, the St. Louis National Horse Show, and the Better Foods Show. Four-H Club members who came to St. Louis for the shows were guests of the Chamber of Commerce

6-45. The Arena was large enough to house the National Dairy Show, the St. Louis National Horse Show, and the Better Foods Show simultaneously in 1929. The Arena outbuildings housed some of the cattle entered in the National Dairy Show. The Forest Park greenhouses and plant propagating grounds are visible at the bottom of the picture, separated from the Arena by Oakland Avenue and the streetcar tracks.

on trips to Forest Park to see the Lindbergh trophies at the Jefferson Memorial and to visit the zoo. The annual Boy Scout Circus and Merit Badge Show moved to the Arena in 1930 and broke all attendance records, and the National Dairy Show returned in October 1930 (Fig. 6-45).

A group of stables outside the park's southern border attracted horseback riders to Forest Park. The Missouri Stables and the J. E. Van Eppes Stables boarded and rented horses. Both stables offered lessons for individuals and for groups. The private Riding and Hunt Club served members only. Almost all riders arrived by car, then mounted and rode along the Forest Park bridle path. Early morning was the popular time, especially Saturday for children and Sunday for adults. In 1929 the city installed a stoplight to halt automobile traffic on Oakland. From horseback, riders could control the light, which they had

helped pay for. Riders pressured the city to keep the Forest Park bridle path well maintained and well marked.

Again in the 1920s, aroused public opinion prevented proposed construction along the park's southern border. Unlike Steuver's mining plans, these proposals eyed land in the park's southeastern corner, made available by the removal of the River des Peres. When School Board President Arthur A. Blumeyer proposed construction of a new Central High School in Forest Park in 1929, the *Post-Dispatch* said, "There are already too many invasions upon the purely park uses of this great tract."[67]

Commissioner Pape had another plan for the site—a stadium. The *Star* pointed out that a 50,000-seat stadium would increase traffic congestion in the park: "It would mean noise and confusion where there should be quiet and rest-

6-46. These men are sailing model boats, probably in Pagoda Lake, around the bandstand. Automobile drivers caused traffic jams when they slowed down to look.

fulness, bird songs and the color and perfume of flowers." It urged St. Louisans to preserve Forest Park "as a forest of trees rather than a forest of buildings."[68]

The *Post-Dispatch* said the stadium was a step in the wrong direction. The Cottage had been torn down; the tourist camp was gone; the mounted police and the streetcar lines had both reduced their use of park land. This reclamation of park land should continue, not reverse. The proposal was dropped, then briefly revived in 1935. Again press reaction was unfavorable, and the stadium was not built.

The stadium plan, however, caused St. Louisans to consider what had been happening to the park. The *Post-Dispatch* calculated that forty percent of the park was devoted to special uses, including 210 acres of public golf courses, 80 acres of park drives, 75 acres of Triple A, and 72 acres of zoo. Other special uses, including the bridle path, baseball and tennis facilities, emergency air field (surrounded by baseball playing fields), municipal theater, mounted police station, and greenhouses, brought the special use total to more than 550 of the park's 1,371 acres. The paper said that birds had been driven from the park and that it was almost impossible for people in the park to escape the sound of automobiles and the smell of exhaust.

By then no one seemed to have a clear and convincing vision of what the park should be. Neither Dwight Davis nor Charlotte Rumbold, who had shared such a vision, was in St. Louis. Rumbold had endured years of conflict with the board of aldermen over, among other things, her insistence on hiring only on merit, deliberately ignoring political considerations. The board repeatedly refused her salary requests, though she had won a national reputation in the playground movement and served as an officer of the Playground Association of America. In 1915 Cunliff persuaded her not to resign in a salary dispute, but the next year, after a salary showdown, she left St. Louis to work for a private foundation in Cleveland. She retired in 1933 and died there in 1960 at the age of ninety. Davis had chaired the City Plan Commission, then served overseas during World War I. After the war, he had lived in St. Louis for a few years before leaving to hold several appointive federal positions, including Governor General of the Philippines and Secretary of War, returning to St. Louis only for occasional visits. He died in his home in Washington, D.C., in 1945.

Some St. Louisans thought the park should be "a natural forest or wilderness." Others agreed with the letter writer who wrote the *Post-Dispatch* that such a retreat would not attract "one-quarter of the people" who were using the park. Anyone who wanted "solitude and forests" had only to drive out of the city.[69] The progressives' notion of improvement through recreation lingered along-side the business notion of the park as an economic asset and tourist attraction. No longer did competing interests try to find a use they could all agree upon, like the pageant and masque. It seemed that almost everything someone wanted and could finance found its share of park space.

In 1930, perhaps in response to criticisms about park overcrowding, Commissioner Pape tried to evict the men who sailed their model boats in Pagoda Lake on weekends. The boats, models of real sailing ships, were as big as three feet long and seven and a half feet tall. The men used long bamboo poles to guide the boats and sometimes raced them (Fig. 6-46). The *Post-Dispatch* commented, "A more innocuous sport it would be difficult to find." The problem, Pape said, was not with the sport but with the automobile congestion caused when drivers slowed down to look.[70] Defenders of the model boats pointed out that kite flying near the lake was another likely cause of the congestion and that golf, tennis, and baseball probably caused much more. The model boats stayed, but a few weeks later Pape removed the archers from their range near the mounted police station.

Despite such minor changes, Forest Park in 1930 was busy and crowded. Although the park still contained statues, trees, and flowers, most of it was not a quiet refuge from the sights, sounds, and pressures of the city, but a recreation center, educational resource, and civic gathering place, with sports, sights, museums, shows, and amusements for almost every taste. These diversions would be valuable to St. Louisans and visitors during the hard times of the 1930s and early 1940s.

NEIGHBORHOOD LOCATOR MAP (1911–1930)

1. Arena, G-7
2. Buckingham Hotel, C-10
3. Central Institute for the Deaf, F-11
4. Chase Hotel, C-10

Churches

5. Eighth Church of Christ, Scientist, D-2
6. Memorial Presbyterian Church, D-2
7. St. Louis Cathedral (Roman Catholic), C-11

8. St. Michael and All Angels (later St. Michael and St. George) Episcopal Church, D-1
United Hebrew Temple, see 6, D-2

9. Clayton Avenue, F-1 to F-11
10. DeBaliviere Avenue, A-5 to C-5
11. Dewey, George, Public School, G-3
12. Forest Park Highlands, G-7 and 8
13. Forest Park Hotel, D-10
14. Forest Park University, G-6
15. Highlands Fire Clay Company, G-8
16. Hillcrest subdivision, E-1
17. Hi-Pointe corner, G-2

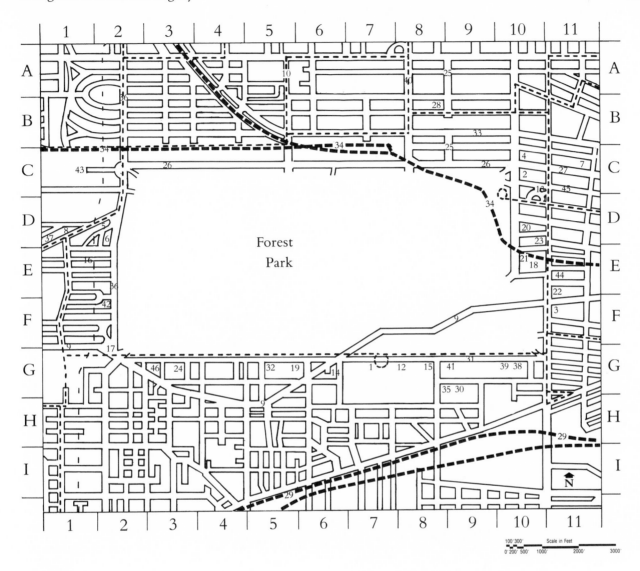

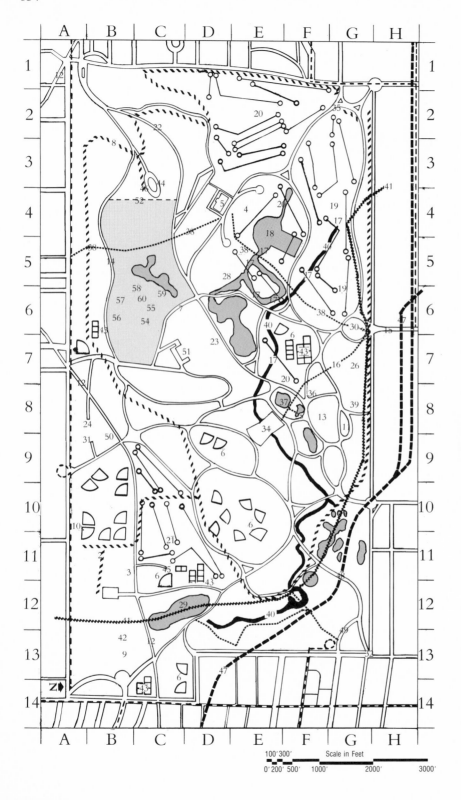

Scale in Feet
100′ 300′
0′ 200′ 500′   1000′   2000′   3000′

PARK LOCATOR MAP (1911–1930)

1. Airfield (later athletic field called Aviation Field), B-10 and 11
2. Airmail hangar, B-11
3. Archery range, B-11
4. Art Hill, E-4
5. Art Museum, City, D-4
6. Athletic fields, A-7, C-13 and 14; central fields, D-9, D-11 to E-10, F-6; Triple A, F-12 (see 1, B-10 and 11)
7. Bird Cage Drive (later part of Washington Drive), C-6 and 7
8. Bridle path, B-3 and throughout park
9. Central High School (approximate proposed location), B-13
10. Clay mining (approximate proposed location), A-10
11. Confederate Memorial, G-8
12. Clayton Avenue, A-1 to C-14
13. Cricket field, F-8
14. Dead Man's Curve, B-5
15. DeBaliviere Avenue, H-6
16. Field house and restaurant (former Lindell Pavilion location), G-7
17. Footbridges: suspension, E-5 and E-6; regular, E-5, E-6, E-7, F-5, G-4
Frank, Nathan, Bandstand (see 37, F-8)
Frontier Women of the French and Spanish Colonies in Missouri, Memorial to the (see 30, G-6)
18. Grand Basin, E-4 and F-5
19. Golf course, 9-hole municipal, G-2 to G-6
20. Golf course, 18-hole municipal, D-1 to G-7
21. Golf course, Triple A, C-9 to D-11
22. Government Drive (widened and probable diagonal connection through park), B-2 to E-7
23. Government Hill and illuminated fountain, D-6 and 7
24. Greenhouses and children's garden, A-8 to B-9
25. Guggenheim, Bertha, Memorial (Pan) Fountain, F-8
26. Handball courts, G-7
27. Incinerator, B-8
28. Jahn, Friederich Ludwig, Memorial, D-5
29. Jefferson Lake, C and D-12
30. Jefferson Memorial building, G-6
31. Jewel Box (first location), B-9
32. Lindell-Kingshighway entrance, G-13
Lindell Pavilion (see 16, G-7)
Missouri Historical Society (see 30, G-6)
33. Mounted Police Station, B-12
34. Municipal Open Air Theatre (Municipal Theatre), E-8 and 9
35. Musicians' Memorial Fountain, G-2
36. O'Neil Fountain (Fountain Angel, second location), F-8
37. Pagoda Lake, F-8
38. Pedestrian paths to art museum, A-5 to E-4 to G-6
39. Playground pageant (probable first location), G-8
40. River des Peres Lagoon (later shortened), D-12 to G-4
41. River des Peres sewer, A-12 to H-4
St. Louis Exposition (temporary; see 1, B-10 and 11)
Shields, Mary Leighton, memorial, sundial (first location; see 51, D-7)
42. Stadium (proposed location), B-13
43. Tennis courts: Hampton Avenue, B-6; Jefferson Memorial, F-7; Kingshighway, C-14; Triple A, D-11 and 12
44. Tourist camp, automobile, C-3
45. Triple A Clubhouse (second location), C-11
46. Vacation village (approximate location), C-3
47. Wabash (later Norfolk and Western) Railroad, D-14 to H-6
48. Wabash Railroad Bridge (removed), G-12
49. West Pine Drive, G-12 and 13
50. Workshops and stables, B-9
51. World's Fair Pavilion, D-7
52. Zoo (St. Louis Zoological Park), approximate western boundary, B and C-4
53. Bear Pits, C-5
54. Bird House, C-6
55. Elephant House, C-6
56. Lion House, B-6
57. Primate House, B-6
58. Reptile House, B-6
59. Small Mammal Pits, C-6
60. Seal Basin, C-6

7

FEW RESOURCES, MANY PEOPLE (1930–1945)

I regret very much indeed, that due to the curtailment of finances, it will be impossible for this department to issue the customary printed report. . . . The parks and playgrounds in the city of Saint Louis show an ever increasing attendance.—Fred W. Pape, Commissioner of Parks and Recreation, 1932

No doubt the restricted use of gasoline and tires was in a large measure responsible for the added use of the parks and recreational facilities.—Palmer B. Baumes, Commissioner of Parks and Recreation, 1943

Owing to the war emergency, we are greatly handicapped by man-power shortage, priorities, and our inability to promptly obtain necessary materials, supplies and equipment.—Arthur R. Brunk, Superintendent of Construction, Division of Parks and Recreation, 1943

Between 1930 and 1945 shortages of money, manpower, and materials, caused by the Great Depression and World War II, made park maintenance increasingly difficult. At the same time, increasing use, combined with vandalism, made such maintenance increasingly important. As in the late 1920s, new construction could sometimes be financed when maintenance of existing facilities could not (Fig. 7-1).

Four park commissioners wrestled with the problems. Republican Fred W. Pape served until a new mayor, Democrat Bernard F. Dickmann, took office in 1933. In 1933 the new appointee was Dickmann's next-door neighbor, William A. Miller, a retired grain dealer who had worked in the mayor's campaign. Miller ran the department along patronage lines. Miller's term as commissioner was brief; he died in office May 13, 1936.

Miller was succeeded by Joseph J. Mestres, whose political qualifications were more evident than his professional ones. The *Post-Dispatch* called Mestres "one of the few remaining Democratic politicians of the old school" and said he had "held the Seventh Ward 'in Line' for the Mayor." Mestres said his job would be to see that every employee was "absolutely loyal to the Mayor."[1]

After the election of Republican Mayor William Dee Becker in 1941, Mestres was replaced by Palmer B. Baumes of Baumes Engineering Company, who quickly moved to replace Mestres's Democratic employees with Republicans (Fig. 7-2). The only major department head he retained was City Forester and Landscape Architect Ludwig Baumann, who had been in office before Mestres, serving as acting park commissioner after Miller's death and before Mestres's appointment. Baumann continued to serve as landscape architect until a reorganization in the early 1940s abolished the position. He remained the city forester until his death in February 1944.

Baumes's attempts to clear out all the Democratic employees failed after the city agreed they were protected under the merit system. But Baumes was able to work with members of both parties and served as park commissioner for almost twenty years, under Republican Mayor Aloys P. Kaufmann from 1943 to 1949, Democrat Joseph M. Darst from 1949 to 1953, and Democrat Raymond R. Tucker from 1953 until Baumes's retirement in 1960 at the age of seventy-seven.

The city's financial condition, bad in the 1920s, grew worse during the depression of the

7-1. Federal funds financed several new facilities in Forest Park in the 1930s, including this waterfall, called the Cascades.

7-2. Palmer B. Baumes, in a photograph taken at about the time he became Commissioner of Parks and Recreation in 1942. He served until 1960.

1930s. Park administrators had to face increased usage with inadequate budgets, a situation similar to that at the end of the nineteenth century. The assessed valuation of city property decreased by almost 20 percent between 1929 and 1940, resulting in lower tax receipts. All departments, including the park department, made adjustments. A short work week allowed the park department to spread the work among a larger number of men, most of whom worked part time. By 1937 most department employees were working only fourteen days a month at three dollars a day.

During the 1940s World War II caused shortages of materials and men, especially young men (Fig. 7-3). By the end of the war, 30 percent of park department employees were older than sixty-five and 6 percent were older than seventy-five and physically unable to trim trees.

With gradually returning prosperity during the 1940s, some services cut during the 1930s could be restored. In 1941, for instance, the direc-

tor of public utilities announced that all of the one thousand electric lights in Forest Park would again burn all night. The lights had been turned off at midnight (1 A.M. during the municipal opera season) during the 1930s to save money. But Forest Park, which from 1930 to 1945 contained more than 43 percent of city park acreage, only received 30 to 35 percent of total park maintenance funds, and less than 16 percent of total park expenditures.

As in the nineteenth century, destruction and theft of property plagued park administrators. So the city hired park guards, similar to the park police of the 1890s and coping with the same kinds of problems. Despite the guards' efforts, people destroyed trees, shrubs, and flowers, stole plumbing fixtures and door locks, defaced the statues, and burned benches in the barbecue pits. The guards also worked to protect parkgoers from danger or annoyance. The sergeant of the park guards reported in 1938 that his men had been able to improve the reputation of the Laclede Pavilion, formerly "internationally known as a rendezvous for degenerates" (probably the homeless unemployed).[2]

In the 1930s and 1940s maintenance funds also had to cover damage caused by increasing park usage. Travel restrictions, first financial and then wartime regulations, caused many who had previously sought recreation outside the city to stay home and crowd the parks. During the 1940s new people moved into the city to take wartime factory jobs. Many of them went to the park often, as did servicemen stationed at bases near St. Louis.

As in the past, funds for park work were drawn from a variety of sources. Private money provided some services, but Forest Park would have suffered even more than it did in the 1930s without the various federal relief programs. The Civil Works Administration (CWA), the Federal Emergency Relief Administration (FERA), the National Youth Administration (NYA), and the Works Progress Administration (WPA) supplied workers. The Public Works Administration (PWA)

7-3. A Fourth of July picnic in Forest Park during World War II illustrates the absence of young men.

helped finance construction projects to boost employment, much as the locally financed Forest Park lake extension project had done in the 1890s.

A federal PWA grant, for example, finally allowed the city to build a floral display house for the Jewel Box exhibits that Head Gardener John Moritz had begun in one of the greenhouses. After Moritz died in 1931 his successor, Henry Ochs, continued the displays, sometimes using the Jewel Box displays to reproduce a painting. In February 1932 the design reproduced *Blossom Time* by Wallace Nutting, the *Post-Dispatch* said, with "a weather-beaten old house, . . . a birch-

bark water wheel," and "a tiny rustic bridge" nestled among masses of flowers. The paper said, "The illusion of solitude is remarkable in a garden that occupies only half a greenhouse less than 100 feet long."[3]

Beginning in the winter of 1933–34 the greenhouse remained open during the evenings so more people could see the display. Easter Sunday was the most popular day at the Jewel Box. In 1934, 25,752 people entered the greenhouse between 5 A.M. and 9:20 P.M., often waiting in long lines.

Park officials considered a new Jewel Box im-

7-4. The new Jewel Box, officially named the St. Louis Floral Conservatory, opened November 14, 1936. Commissioner Fred W. Pape and City Engineer William C. E. Becker took about 4,000 comparative light-intensity readings in existing greenhouses and in experimental models while designing the new building.

7-5. View inside the new Jewel Box shows flat roof. Tropical and subtropical plants planted near the walls formed a backdrop for changing displays in the center.

portant enough to merit the allocation of $75,000 from the 1923 bond issue for the city's share of the cost, despite the city's financial difficulties. In early 1935 the park department announced plans for what the *Post-Dispatch* called a "new Jewel Box of unique, modernistic design." The design was the result of a year of testing by the park commissioner and City Engineer William C. E. Becker, using several miniature models (Fig. 7-4). The design was intended to admit the greatest amount of light in the winter, to reduce damage from hail, and to reduce maintenance costs. Only the walls were glass; all of the horizontal surfaces were metal. Rolled awnings regulated the amount of light, replacing the usual lime and cement mixture painted on greenhouse glass.[4]

The *Post-Dispatch* called the design "the last word in display greenhouses," though some called it a "forbidding block of ice." Despite the criticism, the board of public service approved the plans and called for bids. Becker recalled much later that one of the country's largest greenhouse builders refused to bid, saying the design wouldn't

work. But seven companies did bid for the job, with the Robert Paulus Construction Company, a St. Louis firm, winning the job.[5]

The new Jewel Box, officially named the St. Louis Floral Conservatory, opened on November 14, 1936. Palms, ferns, and other tropical and subtropical plants grew along the inside walls, leaving the center free for changing displays. The first show contained more than three thousand chrysanthemum plants in a formal Chinese garden design. Despite the department's tight budget, there was no admission charge for any of the Jewel Box displays (Fig. 7-5).

The building's design worked as Becker had intended and received national recognition. An article in *Architectural Forum* on the use of glass in construction included the Jewel Box as a successful example.[6] When hail storms in the spring of 1938 broke more than a thousand panes of glass in the park greenhouses, the Jewel Box was undamaged.

The building was an immediate popular success as well. After it had been open less than three

7-6. The Seven Pools waterfall, built in the late 1930s, in an area of Forest Park called the bowl. Barnes Hospital is visible in the background.

months, electric lights were added so it could stay open from 9 A.M. to 9 P.M. to accommodate the crowds. An attendance count in 1938–39 showed almost 416,000 visitors in a year when the art museum set a new record at just over 390,000.

Federal funds also supplied part of the cost of two new waterfalls for the park. One, the Seven Pools, was in the section called the bowl, near the southeastern corner of the park (Fig. 7-6). The other, a seventy-five-foot waterfall later called the Cascades after the World's Fair Cascades down Art Hill, was on a steep slope west of the art museum. Like much of the park, this waterfall was not as natural as it looked. An underground circulating pump forced the water up the hill so it could fall down the rocks to the pool below.

The city added two rose gardens near the Jewel Box in the late 1930s, containing more than thirteen thousand plants. One, in front of the Jewel Box, was lighted at night with mushroom lights, forming a path into the building. Ochs's workers also built a rose garden next to Barnes Hospital, following complaints from hospital patients about the noise from the athletic fields that had been there (Fig. 7-8).

St. Louisans still retreated to the park in hot weather. In the early 1930s park gardeners added two new canna beds in the circles at the top of Art Hill, where hundreds of motorists parked during the hot summer nights. Some may have been there simply to enjoy the cool breezes. Others used it as a "lovers' lane." "Just why is it," one wrote the *Star*, "that you can't park your car in Forest Park . . . without having to contend with a policeman shining a big spot light in your face? I can't see what business it is of theirs if you have your arm around your friend's neck, or if you are holding her hand."[7] As in the 1920s, neither the curfew nor occasional attempted robberies deterred the parkers.

For picnickers, the department used some of its limited funds to provide new cooking facilities and to match PWA funds for comfort stations in the late 1930s. The demand for permits for large

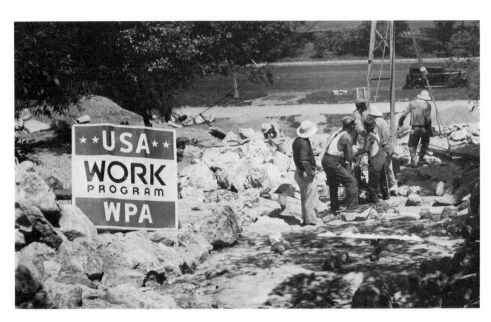

7-7. WPA employees at work on a Forest Park waterfall.

picnics was so great that organizations had to make reservations months in advance.

While the financial situation was difficult everywhere during the 1930s, the zoo did not suffer as badly as the rest of the park. Of course tax collections had decreased, but available figures indicate that tax support for the 70-acre zoo regularly exceeded appropriations for the remaining 1,300 acres of Forest Park. The zoo's refreshment stands also provided revenue for the zoo.

Still, the expense of caring for the new exhibits opened in the 1920s, combined with the drop in revenue, left the zoo without money for building projects. Like the park department, the zoo used federal funds to help finance new facilities. The zoo had managed to save enough money for a new antelope house, which opened in April 1935, almost five years after the bird house. The next two units, the hoofed animal yards and the great ape house, were possible only because 45 percent of the construction cost was paid with federal funds. Both the antelope house and the shelters in the yards were covered with imitation boulders modeled after rock outcroppings found at Graniteville, Missouri. Although the zoo was financed and administered separately from the

park, there was no physical separation of the zoo grounds. Even the sidewalk around the zoo, visually separating the zoo from the rest of the park, was not complete until 1934.

The zoo administration still worked to attract St. Louisans and tourists. A show by performing chimpanzees was enormously popular (Fig. 7-9). In the early 1940s it moved to a new arena with seats for about 3,500 spectators. In the 1930s the zoo added a performance by the big cats, and then an elephant show (Figs. 7-10, 7-11). New exotic animals, like the two giant pandas, were immediately popular (Fig. 7-12). In the bird house, daily feeding of the two hornbills was a popular attraction. Outside the reptile house, crowds gathered to watch the force-feeding of Blondie, a python (Fig. 7-13).

At the art museum, regular special exhibits attracted thousands to study artworks not in the museum's collection. In 1932–33 the museum held twenty-two special exhibits, ending with a display of James McNeill Whistler's portrait of his mother, which was shown for a month. In 1940 more than 47,000 visitors came to the museum to see a comprehensive exhibition of the works of Pablo Picasso.

The museum also enlarged its own collec-

7-8. The southeastern corner of Forest Park, showing the hospital buildings along the jog in Kingshighway and the rose garden that replaced athletic fields after the noise disturbed hospital patients. At the bottom of the picture Clayton Avenue leaves the park going east, dividing the rose gardens from additional park land to the south.

tion, using about half of its tax funds (which it defended against renewed city attacks) for maintenance and half for acquisitions to supplement the Washington University collection still on loan. Other items were purchased with the income from special endowment funds or acquired by gift. In late 1938 the *Post-Dispatch* reported, "The museum now has an impressive collection of its own," including Egyptian objects, medieval arms and armor, and Renaissance paintings, sculpture, furniture, and ceramics.[8] By 1939 the museum was open until 9 P.M. one night a week from late July to early November, with members of the educational department giving talks. By that time, it was also operating a restaurant.

Museum attendance held its own despite the lack of park bus service. In 1925 the city had permitted a private company, the St. Louis Bus Company, to run a bus line to performances at the municipal theater. After the new service began, there was an abrupt decline in passengers and revenue for the park department buses, a decline that continued into the early thirties, despite new park department buses. In the summer of 1933 the city discontinued the bus service to save money. The People's Motorbus Company briefly operated a weekend service in the park, but receipts were disappointing, and the company ended the service. Private bus companies continued to run buses to municipal theater performances.

Daytime park users, however, again complained about the lack of bus service, particularly to the art museum. One St. Louisan remarked that the city should be willing to take a loss on service to the museum: "Ye gods, who ever heard of a profit in connection with art museums, sym-

7-9. Preparing to transport the zoo's performing chimpanzees.

phony orchestras and like civic enterprises!" The Public Service Company, then in receivership, wouldn't operate the line unless it received a subsidy from the city. The city, with a deficit of more than $2 million, wouldn't pay. A 1939 plan to have the art museum and the zoo each pay a third of the cost fell through, and there was no daytime park bus service until August 1945.[9]

The Municipal Theatre Association also struggled through the Depression. The 1930 season represented a turning point. The 1929 season had ended in a deficit, despite a benefit concert by the U.S. Marine Band. So the association allied itself with the New York theater Shuberts. They planned to offer more expensive productions at the same ticket prices, in the hope that increased attendance would raise total receipts. Grand opera, which had returned to the schedule in prosperous years and had been included in the season as late as 1928, again gave way to more popular shows. The association also spent $25,000 that year for improvements to the theater, including work on the lighting system and installation of a revolving stage. The strategy was only partially successful. As the 1930 season came to an end, the deficit was almost $10,000, though receipts were higher than before. The guarantors were called upon to supply $30,000 to cover the two years' deficits.

Over the next few years the association was once again profitable, against a national backdrop of closing outdoor summer operas. Guarantors were repaid out of the profits. By January 1937 the association was financially stable enough to announce an architectural competition for an expected $100,000 improvement to the theater, which, like the Jewel Box and the zoo construction, would be partly paid for with PWA funds (Fig. 7-14). Joseph D. Murphy and Kenneth E. Wischmeyer won the competition, and the PWA supplied almost $90,000 for work at the theater between 1938 and 1941. By May 1940 the new semicircular entrance and box office was in place.

Use of the facility by groups other than the Municipal Theatre Association declined during the 1930s (Fig. 7-15). When the Young Negro Democratic Club requested permission to use the theater in September 1936, which would not have interfered with the Municipal Theatre Association schedule, the city made no response for over a month and then refused the application without explanation.[10] In 1936, however, the Easter sunrise service moved there.

The annual playground pageant in the theater and the nearby playground festival continued to bring children from all over the city to Forest Park from 1907 until 1938. The children participated in athletic contests, displayed their handi-

7-10. The zoo big cat show began in the 1930s.

crafts, and received refreshments, sometimes from the St. Louis *Times* newspaper.

In 1938 the pageant left the municipal theater. Instead of a daytime activity in Forest Park, the pageant became ten nighttime pageants, with athletic contests and craft displays at neighborhood playgrounds around the city. The park administration explained the change as a convenience for the families and friends of the participants, and in fact total attendance more than doubled. Under the new arrangement, however, black and white families ended the summer playground season separately instead of together in Forest Park.

Because the theater was city property, park

department employees, paid from the department's limited budget, provided flowering plants for it and maintained the grounds, as they did at the zoo, the art museum, and the Jefferson Memorial. They worked particularly to maintain the two large oak trees that framed the stage of the municipal theater, hiring tree surgeons to test and X-ray the oaks. City Forester Ludwig Baumann also consulted experts who were in St. Louis to attend the 1938 meeting of the National Shade Tree Conference. The *Post-Dispatch* reported, 'A few of the arboriculturists thought that . . . the trees would not live much longer.'[11] The trees, however, were still growing in the 1980s.

The Missouri Historical Society continued to display the Lindbergh trophies and to maintain its other collections, though it was short of funds and without a director until 1946. The society preserved old city records and reorganized exhibits to tell a historical story. On the occasion of the society's seventy-fifth anniversary in 1941, the *Globe-Democrat* noted that the archaeological collection and the library were consulted by scholars from Europe and from institutions around the United States, including the Smithsonian Institution.

Some people might have thought that the park had enough visitors without inviting more. Others believed that the park should be used to attract tourists to St. Louis. A "Visit St. Louis" campaign, begun in 1936 by the city government and the Chamber of Commerce, prominently featured the zoo, the art museum, the municipal opera, and the Lindbergh trophies. Zoo Director George P. Vierheller attributed an increase in zoo visitors to the campaign, which may also have had a role in the opera's return to profitability. A 1942 article in the national *Collier's Weekly* magazine, reprinted in a St. Louis newspaper, said of the opera, "It is estimated that a quarter of each night's audience comes from out of town. In the parking lot that handles 5000 cars a night, licenses from all 48 states have been seen at one performance." Other national magazines joined *Collier's* in lauding the Muny. In 1943 *Newsweek* took no-

7-11. The arena for the big cat show offered seats for 1,200 people. An enclosed runway connected the arena cage with the lion house.

7-12. The two giant pandas, Happy and Pao Pei, attracted crowds of visitors to the zoo. After they died, the zoo tried unsuccessfully to obtain another pair.

7-13. In 1936, Reptile Curator Marlin Perkins, far left, operating the pump, began to force-feed Blondie the python in public, in response to numerous requests to see how it was done.

tice of the theater's twenty-fifth anniversary. *Fortune* said the municipal opera "probably has no counterpart anywhere; it seems to appeal to almost everybody."[12]

The city and the Chamber of Commerce continued the Visit St. Louis campaign into the 1940s, even when the war made travel difficult. In 1943 moviemaker James A. FitzPatrick spent five days in St. Louis making a Technicolor movie travelogue, including scenes at the zoo. In 1944 the Visit St. Louis Committee published *Forest Park and Its History*, a seventy-two-page book about the park, calling it the "crowning glory of the City of St. Louis."[13]

During World War II the park also attracted military personnel. The city offered them golf permits at a discount, the Municipal Theatre Association gave a thousand free tickets a night, and the art museum provided a lounge with reading matter and letter-writing materials. Beginning in the summer of 1941 the park housed servicemen, after the War Department took over 17 acres in the southeastern corner of the park as a recreation camp for soldiers on weekend leave (Fig. 7-16). Small tented huts called "hutments" could accommodate a total of 1,500 white ser-

vicemen; the Army Recreation Camp for Negroes was more than a mile east of the park at Spring and Chouteau. The Forest Park camp was very popular with servicemen because of the convenience of the golf courses, the tennis courts, the zoo, the art museum, the historical society, and the municipal opera.

The park also welcomed conventioneers. The zoo prepared special animal shows and erected temporary seats for delegates and visitors to the national American Legion convention in St. Louis in 1935. The American Legion emblem, displayed on Government Hill in flowers and colored foliage, honored them (Fig. 7-17). Park department employees replanted the emblem each spring for more than ten years.

In 1940 the Improved Benevolent and Protective Order of the Elks of the World, which the *Post-Dispatch* called the "largest Negro lodge in the United States," held a Forest Park golf tournament as part of its convention in St. Louis. About one thousand men entered the tournament over the eighteen-hole course in Forest Park, beginning at noon on a Monday, indicating that the Monday-morning-only rule was sometimes waived. In 1942 the St. Louis Paramount Golf

7-14. The new entrance for the Municipal Theatre, financed in part with PWA funds, was its third. The two previous ones were wooden, but this one was built of concrete.

Club held its "fall golf tournament for Negroes" on the Forest Park eighteen-hole course over a weekend without noticeable protests.[14] But the general Monday-morning rule remained and was not loudly questioned.

Another group of golfers, those with physical disabilities, asked for but didn't get improved access to the golf course. In 1939 J. T. Willey, a tool and die maker with a heart condition, asked for an ordinance permitting "golfers with physical handicaps or more than 50 years old" to use motor scooters on the golf courses if they paid an extra one-dollar fee. The aldermen told Willey politely that the idea had merit, but didn't pass the ordinance.[15]

Golf remained very popular with St. Louisans as well as visitors who were legally, physically, and financially able to use the course. The Forest Park golf courses remained the only municipal golf courses in the city, and park department employees maintained them as best they could despite damage from heavy use and beginning players. As similar concessionaires had done since the late 1880s, Ed Duwe offered sports equipment for rent. Duwe was well known to golfers, and an open tournament in Forest Park bore his name, beginning in the middle 1930s.

In 1941 Baumes lowered the cost of play with an offer to rent five golf clubs, a bag, and three used balls for fifteen cents a day. Ed Duwe offered free group lessons. Since a weekday permit to play eighteen holes of golf cost fifty cents, a beginning golfer could try the sport for sixty-five cents.

For tennis players, the park department managed to allocate funds for the construction in 1936 of an all-weather surface on tennis courts near the Hampton Avenue entrance. The new courts were open for more playing days than clay courts elsewhere in the park and were much cheaper to maintain, but most of the courts remained clay.

The national municipal tennis tournament returned to Forest Park in 1936. A tally of the championships between 1923 and 1936 showed that St. Louis players had won eleven of the forty-two titles awarded, including Ted Drewes's four men's singles victories.

The park department encouraged tennis players by offering free lessons. In 1941 championship players Bill Tilden and Fred Perry were in town for exhibition matches at Triple A and offered a few hours of instruction on the Forest Park courts.

During the 1930s and 1940s, in addition to being invited to witness tennis exhibition matches and tournaments at Triple A (the St. Louis Amateur Athletic Association), nonmembers were sometimes invited to participate in Triple A

7-15. By the 1930s the Boy Scouts were one of the few organizations that shared the theatre with the Municipal Theatre Association.

events. The club hosted a hole-in-one tournament sponsored by the *Globe-Democrat* during the 1930s and 1940s. Anybody who was interested could watch the golfers try to sink one (or more) of three shots, and anyone who wished to enter was welcome to participate.

In 1942 the city raised the fees for the use of the public tennis and golf facilities. However, the amount Triple A paid remained the same.[16] Since the park department stopped reporting the numbers of golf and tennis games played in the park, it wasn't possible to know whether the increased fees kept players away from the public facilities. Any golfers deterred by the higher fees were probably replaced by those prevented from playing at the suburban country clubs and pay courses by the rationing of gasoline and tires. With the new fee structure, the tennis fees usually covered related expenses while the golf fees did not. The difference was due to a number of factors, including the failure to raise Triple A's contribution and

the number of low-cost golf permits issued to military personnel.

Besides Triple A, other private groups offered sports shows for spectators in the park. Beginning in the 1930s fly and bait casters held state and national competitions for accuracy and distance in Forest Park. In 1944 competitors included St. Louisan Robert Piros, Sr., who, according to the *Post-Dispatch*, "set world and national records with his long salmon fly casts . . . [using] a bamboo pole." During the meet, open to spectators free of charge, competitors broke five records and tied another five. Between tournaments, casters went to the park to practice. In the late 1930s the casters were numerous enough for the park department to find the funds for a "new log cabin of rustic design . . . treated against fire and termites," built on the edge of Post-Dispatch Lake as headquarters for the Forest Park Baitcasting Club (Fig. 7-18).[17]

The privately sponsored Silver Skates car-

7-16. Part of the U.S. Army recreation camp in Forest Park, with hospital buildings along Kingshighway visible in the background. Commissioner Baumes reported that the camp, which housed servicemen on leave from Fort Leonard Wood, Scott Field, and other nearby bases, was the finest anywhere in the country.

nival used the Forest Park ice into the early 1930s, before moving to indoor facilities such as the Arena. The Arena Figure Skating Club presented an occasional show in Forest Park such as the 1945 "St. Louis on Ice," given despite uncertainty about the weather. Unorganized ice-skating and sledding continued to be popular in Forest Park, weather permitting (Fig. 7-19). Skaters used the Grand Basin, Jefferson Lake, and Post-Dispatch Lake, despite the fact that the Winter Garden indoor skating rink was a few blocks north of the park. Skating in the park, however, was free.

The Municipal Athletic Association continued to sponsor baseball and soccer games in Forest Park, but the championship games, and most of the spectators, were elsewhere. Softball and gridball, a type of touch football, used the Forest Park playing fields in the 1930s and early 1940s, with wartime disruptions when many of the athletes left for military service.

These sports, too, found a place in the limited park department budget. In 1937 and 1938 the department graded 34 acres, formerly the air-mail field, installed sewer and water systems, and built baseball and softball diamonds to replace the fields removed from the vicinity of Barnes Hospital. Around the new playing fields employees built a new horse exercise track, while continuing to maintain the park's bridle path (Fig. 7-20).

Reports of the death of bicycle riding proved premature. Bicycle riding for recreation was popular in the park through the 1940s. Bicycle races returned to the park in the 1930s and 1940s, especially after the city built a Forest Park bicycle racing track in the late 1930s. Like much of the construction in the park in the 1930s, the track, an oval one quarter of a mile around and designed to accommodate eight riders abreast, was partly financed with federal funds. The Missouri division of the Century Road Club used the track in the southeastern corner of the park for races in 1941.

For those who preferred their exercise afoot, there was a new path in 1936, the Nicholas M. Bell Hiking Trail. Bell, who died in 1931, had been a state legislator during the establishment of the park. He often told the story of the controversy in the 1870s, giving credit for the original idea to Hiram Leffingwell. He had, in fact, recommended a memorial in the park to Leffingwell, but none was erected.

Handball continued, as did boating. The rental boats belonged to a concessionaire, continuing a practice begun in the 1880s. As in the 1890s, the demand for boats sometimes exceeded the concessionaire's supply. In 1931 Pape reported that would-be renters were sometimes waiting for boats as late as midnight (Fig. 7-21). In an arrangement similar to the 1891 lease requiring Charles Schweickardt to build a new restaurant, the 1943 boat concession contract with the K-

7-17. Government Hill some time after 1935, with the American Legion emblem visible to the right of center.

Line Company required the company to build new concrete docks in return for a five-year contract.

Model boats and archery, which had been controversial in the 1920s, seemed to cause few problems in the 1930s and 1940s. Model boating became a children's competition, as the public elementary school manual arts classes conducted races on the Forest Park lakes of model boats made at school. In 1938 Mestres quietly allowed the St. Louis Archery Club to return to the range from which Pape had evicted it in 1930. The club held occasional tournaments, including the St. Louis Prep School Archery Tournament, cosponsored by the Stix, Baer and Fuller department store in 1941. The tournament attracted seventy-five archers, ranging in age from eight to eighteen, and representing thirty-two schools.

Private groups sponsored games of cricket and even marbles in Forest Park. In 1941 the finals of the *Star-Times* marbles tournament used the tennis courts near the Jefferson Memorial.

Large numbers of people went to Forest Park for holidays and special events, especially during World War II when people wanted to demonstrate their patriotism and to be together, as they had during earlier wars. In 1940 after war began in Europe, the city again sponsored a Fourth of July celebration on Art Hill in Forest Park, as it had

during World War I. The patriotic parade included veterans of both the Union and Confederate armies. Although there were several other celebrations, more than 100,000 people went to Forest Park for the speeches, patriotic music, and fireworks display. The rally, Mayor Dickmann said, should be "a warning to any Nazis and other subversive elements groups that may be in the city." The next year the new mayor, William Dee Becker, announced that he wouldn't sponsor a municipal show because the celebration had "resulted in severe traffic congestion and was a potential hazard to children and grownups."[18]

On July 4, 1942, the United States was at war, and more than 5,000 troops came to St. Louis from Fort Leonard Wood to participate in the Fourth of July parade and a rally in Forest Park. Many of the men camped in or near Forest Park.[19] Unlike the World War I parades, in the World War II parades European ethnic groups were not in evidence, probably in deference to the ideal of the melting pot.

Not every special event in the 1940s was war related. The 1941 General Motors Parade of Progress showed, the *Star-Times* said, "what is going on behind the scenes in industrial research laboratories of the world to improve modern life" and "our ways of living twenty years hence." More than 9,000 people went the first day to see such wonders as "a mercury vapor lamp no larger than

7-18. Practicing casting from the park dock in Post-Dispatch Lake.

a cigarette . . . , a television–telephone . . . , the cold stove of tomorrow on which the cooking is accomplished without heat. . . , the facsimile newspaper which is printed on an ordinary appearing radio receiver in the living room . . . [and] the microfilm library which projects a favorite volume on a screen in half-inch high letters." The show, at about the site of the 1926 Greater St. Louis Exposition, was on a much smaller scale and, unlike the Exposition, was free of charge.[20]

Easter continued to be an important event in Forest Park through the 1930s and 1940s. The Metropolitan Church Federation sponsored the Forest Park Easter sunrise service, beginning in 1932. In 1936 the service moved to the municipal theater. Special streetcars and buses began to run to the theater before 5:00 A.M. After the service, children had time to go to Sunday school before returning to the park for an Easter egg hunt. By 1937 part of the service was broadcast "by KSD [radio] and the WEAF network from 6:30 to 7

o'clock."[21] Thousands came to the park that year to see the first Easter display in the new Jewel Box.

In 1942 the Easter sunrise service was, as the *Post-Dispatch* pointed out, part of "America's first wartime Easter since 1918." The service started an hour later because of War Time, later resumed as Daylight Savings Time. Zoo Director Vierheller reported that the zoo hosted "probably one of the biggest crowds ever to visit there on a single day." The art museum and the Jewel Box, unlike the zoo, were able to count their attendance. The art museum drew almost 8,000 with an American Indian exhibit and a photographic show. More than twice as many, almost 17,000, went to the Jewel Box.[22]

As in the 1920s, crowds in the park meant automobile traffic (Fig. 7-22). Forest Park had always been a driving park, and administrators had worked since the 1870s to provide the necessary roads in and around it. The city's response to the

7-19. Sledding on Art Hill in 1937.

7-20. Many of the horses on the bridle path lived in stables just south of the park. Some of the Forest Park tennis courts are visible behind the riders in this photograph from the 1940s. Deaconess Hospital is visible to the right, just outside the park's southern border.

7-21. The electric boats, introduced in 1930, were so popular that people sometimes waited until midnight for a chance to rent one.

growing traffic problem there in the 1930s was, like everything else, shaped by budget considerations that forced the city to accept changes it might otherwise have rejected.

First, officials considered traffic congestion on Kingshighway, along the eastern edge of the park. Plans to use private property east of Kingshighway for widening the street were quickly dropped, probably because of the expense. Instead the city turned a strip of park land into part of Kingshighway. For years, this strip had contained a park drive called Kingshighway Drive, which paralleled Kingshighway Boulevard, the city street. Under the new arrangement, the city street became one way northbound and the park drive one way southbound, in effect widening

Kingshighway into the park with a boulevard strip in the middle.[23]

East-west traffic became heavier as more and more people moved west into St. Louis County. During the 1930s, while city population declined, county population increased 12 percent. Between 1935 and 1940, 80 percent of new construction in the metropolitan area was outside the city limits. City attempts to save money while dealing with the traffic took even more park land than the Kingshighway changes. In 1929 Park Commissioner Pape had recommended a road inside Forest Park parallel to Oakland (similar to the Kingshighway Drive arrangement) as "the means of relieving a serious traffic condition along Oakland Avenue," a condition made worse by the opening

7-22. Even in the winter, large numbers of people went to the zoo. Visitors especially enjoyed feeding times for the animals, such as these sea lions.

of the Arena, on Oakland, the following year. At the same time, Missouri Highway Department engineers were planning for a "proposed traffic relief superhighway" for traffic from the west, which would bring traffic into the city near Clayton Road. The engineers had rejected proposed alternate routes, such as Delmar and Page, as too far north, and their decision was final since the state was paying to build the road.[24]

Since Oakland was already overloaded, another road was needed to carry the superhighway traffic east into the city. When the state engineers chose a route through the park, the city agreed to it in 1934. The state selected the route and paid for road construction, but the city had to pay for all the land needed for the new road, the Oakland Express Highway. City officials estimated that, even using Forest Park land, the city would need to spend $735,000 for the rest of the land for the highway. Like the zoo twenty years before, the

highway entered the park largely because the city already owned the land.[25]

The new road was a fifty-foot wide concrete roadway with fences along both sides and grade separations from intersecting roads (Fig. 7-23). The route of the highway through the park roughly paralleled Oakland, cutting off a park strip of varying width, and forcing the city to rebuild some of its plant-propagating facilities and to reroute part of the bridle path. Two pedestrian bridges and three tunnels, one large enough for horseback riders, joined park sections divided by the road.

The curve of the new highway through the southeastern corner of the park, known as the bowl, required the city to find a new location for the statue of Edward Bates. The statue went to a less important location northwest of the art museum, and the park's southeastern entrance virtually disappeared.[26]

7-23. A curve in the Oakland Expressway in the 1940s, looking east past the army recreation camp to the gas storage tank outside the park. The fenced highway divided the park land from additional park land out of the picture to the left.

As the highway neared completion, an article in *Scientific American* said the road, "the only one of its kind outside the New York City area," was being "watched with interest by other cities" to see if it could fulfill the promise that "motor travel can be made safe as well as rapid" by separating highway traffic from that on city streets.[27] It didn't live up to the planners' hopes, and engineers were soon working to redesign it.

From the time it opened in mid-July 1936, the highway was clearly considered no longer park land. The city counselor ruled that the city's thirty-mile-an-hour speed limit would apply, rather than the park's limit of twenty.

The twenty-mile-an-hour speed limit for the park roads had been set in 1935, an increase from the previous eight miles an hour, but, like earlier park speed limits, the twenty-mile-an-hour limit was often ignored. A letter writer complained to the *Post-Dispatch* in 1936, "Several times in the last month, I have driven through the park at the legal speed. I have passed no moving automobiles . . . [but] hundreds of cars have passed me . . . traveling at speeds up to 40 miles or more an hour." During an enforcement campaign in 1936, police arrested 61 Forest Park drivers on speeding charges, though some complained about "a system of enforcement that resembles the methods of the German Schutzstaffel or the Russian Cheka."[28]

Drivers in the park, even taxi drivers, still got lost. The *Post-Dispatch* commented in 1943, "Getting lost in Forest Park is a long-standing affliction of life in St. Louis. . . . Those winding drives are a trap for the motorist, unless he has the forethought to take a compass and map along when he enters the park."[29] To help drivers find park attractions, the park department erected directional signs in the early 1940s. The signs helped, but didn't end the problem. For those who had found where they were going, the park

7-24. The Laclede Pavilion as it appeared in 1938 during demolition. The towers stood until 1942.

provided a growing number of parking lots and parking spaces along the roads, but these parking spaces would soon prove inadequate.

As park officials had done in the 1880s and 1890s with the police department, Commissioner Baumes managed in the 1940s to have another city department provide for park needs, when the city's department of streets and sewers took responsibility for the maintenance of all park drives from the park department. Baumes was pleased with the new arrangement, though it was the opposite of Park Commissioner Richard Klemm's recommendation in 1887 that Clayton Road should be moved outside the park "so as to have all the [park] roads and drives under the supervision of the Park Commissioner."[30]

Shortly after workmen moved the Bates statue from the park's southeastern entrance, another entrance landmark disappeared, this one from the park's northeastern entrance. In 1938 a portion of the floor of the Laclede Pavilion, near the Lindell-Kingshighway entrance, collapsed (Fig. 7-24). The city closed the building, and then, after much discussion, tore it down, leaving

only the towers, which housed public comfort stations and an electric substation for the park lights. George F. Hellmuth, an architect for the board of public service (and later a principal in Hellmuth, Obata, and Kassabaum, Inc.), drew plans for a decorative pergola to connect the towers, with flowers, a tree-lined sidewalk, and a fountain with colored lights. Mayor Dickmann liked the design, but others weren't so sure, and the pergola and fountain were never built. Instead, the transformers were moved underground, the towers were torn down, and nothing remained of the pavilion. Since only the tower of the Lindell Pavilion remained, tearing down the Laclede Pavilion removed the last of the streetcar pavilions that had been the entrances to the park for millions of St. Louisans since the 1890s (Fig. 7-25).

With all the development in the park, it might seem that no natural areas remained, but that wasn't true. The growth of the road system in Forest Park was only part of a continuing tension between the natural and the artificial in Forest Park. Tree cultivation was another. The park still

7-25. The Laclede Pavilion in its heyday. The lamppost at the corner of Kingshighway and Lindell, visible at lower left, later stood in the garden near the Jewel Box.

had "45,450 trees and varieties too numerous to mention," City Forester Baumann reported in 1934 after CWA men had surveyed the trees in various city parks.[31] Forest Park had so many trees that Baumann transplanted some elms and sweet gums to other city parks.

But the trees were not just a natural occurrence. They needed care and, in some cases, replacement. Trees died in dry weather because the watering system was inadequate. In 1942 alone, Baumann wrote, Forest Park lost eight hundred trees to "age, storms and lightning." The Superintendent of the Forest Park Golf Courses removed several "objectionable trees, which obstructed the play and especially vision" on the golf courses in the early 1940s.[32] Trees removed in the

1930s were cut in stove-wood lengths and distributed to needy people. By the 1940s, presumably because of returning prosperity, the dead wood became fuel for park barbecue pits around the city.

While city employees were removing park trees, some groups followed the example set by Samuel Moffitt in 1928 and donated trees to Forest Park. St. Louis club women of the Missouri Federation planted forty-five trees near the art museum in 1932 for the bicentennial of the birth of George Washington. Camp St. Louis of the United Confederate Veterans planted five trees. The United States women's relay team, coached by St. Louisan Dolores (Dee) Boeckmann, planted the Olympic oak tree awarded for its victory at

7-26. The United Sons and Daughters of the World War held this ceremony April 11, 1933, to dedicate a grove of trees in remembrance of veterans of World War I.

the 1936 Olympic Games in Berlin. The Women's Chamber of Commerce dedicated a tree with a marker to former St. Louis Mayor Henry W. Kiel, and New York Mayor Fiorello H. Laguardia brought a dogwood tree from the site of the 1939–1940 New York World's Fair (Fig. 7-26). In the early 1940s Forest Park was one of the locations for Arbor Day tree-planting ceremonies by St. Louis school children.

Flowers, too, were either donated or supplied by the city. The Holland Bulb Company of Haarlem, Holland, donated 10,000 hyacinth bulbs, which soon bloomed on Government Hill. For the year 1938–39 the department estimated that 110,000 plants a year were necessary for Forest

Park and 220,000 for other parks and park strips, plus more to be displayed in local flower shows.

The plants came from the city greenhouses, consolidated in Forest Park in the 1890s. The greenhouse complex near the park's southern border clearly had a high priority with administrators. Greenhouse space was repeatedly added during the 1930s, and the heating system revamped, despite financial difficulties and earlier objections by park neighbors such as Taylor Young. By the early 1940s greenhouse space totaled 30,000 square feet, and the number of plants raised had increased from an estimated 266,000 in 1935–36 to more than one million a year.

The lawns, too, required care from a tight budget. During the hot, dry summer of 1930, for instance, a crew of men was on duty for weeks in Forest Park to put out fires started by careless motorists throwing lighted matches from automobile windows. In 1937, on the other hand, the grass grew so well that the park department couldn't keep it mowed. Someone suggested 100 sheep plus a shepherd to keep the animals in the park and out of traffic. Apparently the suggestion was not adopted, but it is surprising that the park plantings received as much care as they did when it seemed that everything else in the park depended on either federal or private funds. Clearly, such plantings had a high priority with park officials.

Proposals for Forest Park continued to reflect the tension between nature and development. A letter to the editor of the *Post-Dispatch* in 1935 said St. Louis should remove both the Triple A club and the municipal golf courses, "banish golf from Forest Park at once and forever, and then try to restore the park to its former sylvan charm and beauty" (Fig. 7-27).[33] Others wanted new buildings, often in the southeastern corner of the park, which had been the focus of suggestions in the 1920s. Proposals for a new city psychopathic hospital and a state cancer hospital were made, then discarded following loud opposition. Then the army recreation camp prevented building in the corner until after the war.

7-27. Painting a Forest Park scene in 1940. Some parkgoers still sought the quiet, scenic areas.

7-28. A scene at one of the Boy Scout Camporalls in southern Forest Park.

The city did accept one small addition to the park, a thirty-five-foot Alaskan Indian totem pole erected on the site of the old tourist camp. The totem pole, earlier refused by the zoo, was accepted, probably by Mestres, as a gift to "the children of St. Louis by Ben Weisman, treasurer of Union-May-Stern Co.," department store operators.[34]

Some land came back to park department control. The mounted police vacated their station, the building Commissioner Jonathan P. Fechter had opposed so strenuously in 1890. First the police returned about twenty acres of pasture land, no longer needed as the department was steadily motorized. Then they moved out of Forest Park entirely.[35] The park department took over the old station and used it as an extension of the maintenance shops. In the early 1940s it became a stable for park department horses and mules, and the former stables became additional shop and storage facilities.

In 1944 and 1945 the National Aviation Trades Association attempted to revive the Forest Park airfield near the mounted police station for busi-

nessmen traveling in private planes. But the plan fell through, either because of public opposition or the shortage of private planes after the war. Instead the old hangar building became a park department storage facility, and the field remained what it had been since the late 1920s—a group of playing fields along the southern edge of the park, called Aviation Field, where the boy scouts camped every year. For the 1934 Camporall, a combination camp and rally, more than a thousand Boy Scouts from St. Louis and St. Louis County pitched their tents for two days (Fig. 7-28).

With budgets tight, the city worked to increase revenue produced by the park. Besides raising fees for tennis and golf, city officials changed E. H. Duwe's contract for collecting lost golf balls from a flat fee to a certain amount for each ball with a minimum guarantee, thus increasing revenue. Duwe also operated the golf shop in the field house under a contract with the city that called for a flat fee.

Revenues from the refreshment stands were low, probably from a deliberate policy of keeping

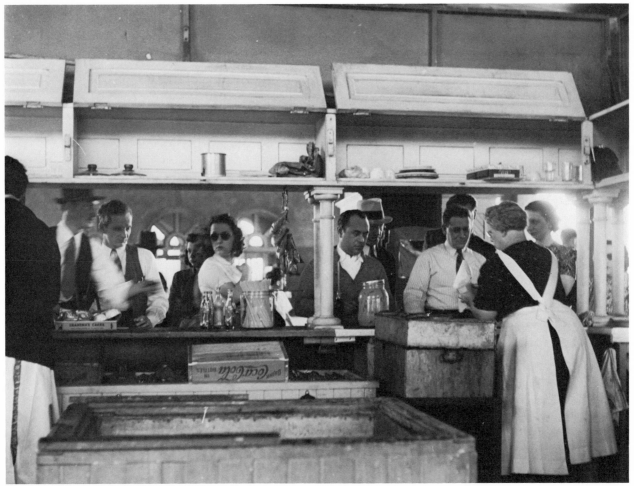

7-29. Park Department employees sold refreshments in Forest Park at stands in the field house, the World's Fair Pavilion, the Jefferson Memorial and near Art Hill in 1940. The small reported profits from the operation probably didn't cover the overhead costs.

prices down and perhaps also because of poor management. During the 1930s the department didn't report the Forest Park refreshment net revenue separately, only combined with revenue from Fairground and Carondelet parks. The net from the three parks combined averaged about $8,000, less than the almost $12,000 the zoo derived from the stands on its grounds, though the parks' gross was almost $54,000 compared to the zoo's average gross of about $46,500. Net revenue from the park stands probably didn't cover overhead (Fig. 7-29). Boating usually operated as a concession with the city receiving 10 percent of the gross.

With budgets so tight, the city was not happy when the director of the new Missouri Conservation Commission (which had replaced the Fish Commission) notified city authorities in early 1938 that the state would abandon the Forest Park hatchery to save money (Fig. 7-30). The city, through Congressman John J. Cochran, got the United States Bureau of Fisheries to take over the work and to build a rubble stone building in which the hatchery manager could live and work (Fig. 7-31). No one could be found to take over the city-sponsored band concerts, however, which were discontinued in 1931 until after World War II.

7-30. The federal government took over the operation of the Forest Park hatcheries in 1938 after the state cut them from its budget.

Around the park, the 1930s and 1940s were mostly years of consolidation rather than new building. In 1944 Sam Koplar linked the Park Plaza Hotel with the Chase Hotel, operating them as the Chase-Park Plaza. Koplar and his associates already controlled the Forest Park Hotel. The Washington University Medical Center included, by 1945, Barnes, St. Louis Children's, and St. Louis Maternity hospitals. Nearby were other hospitals, including Jewish, Shriners', Frisco, and St. John's hospitals.

South of the park, the Highlands and the Arena were sold in foreclosure proceedings to the Reorganization Investment Company, which operated them until 1947. The Highlands continued to add new rides and to attract families and school picnic groups. For a while during the

1930s, the Highlands attracted customers with Dollar Days, when a dollar bought an entire afternoon or evening at the park, including all rides. By 1945 returning prosperity had made such low prices unnecessary.

Residential development around and beyond the park slowed, but didn't stop, during the 1930s. The greatest development was in the section north of the park and west of Union. The depression of the Wabash tracks, abandonment of the Rock Island right-of-way, and sewering of the River des Peres opened the way for the development of large single-family houses on the long lots bordering the park, and by 1940 houses had been built on about half of them.

So the park and the neighborhood, like the rest of the country, struggled through the 1930s

7-31. As part of the hatchery operation, the federal government paid for the construction of this headquarters building. The design of the hatchery building is similar to that of the new comfort stations elsewhere in the park, partially funded by the federal government in the late 1930s.

and early 1940s. For some, the park had provided a job during the hard times of the 1930s. For many, the park had provided welcome free relaxation and a chance to escape their troubles temporarily. As 1945 ended, people looked forward to peace and prosperity. Forest Park officials entered the postwar years confidently, overlooking the warning signs from the 1920s.

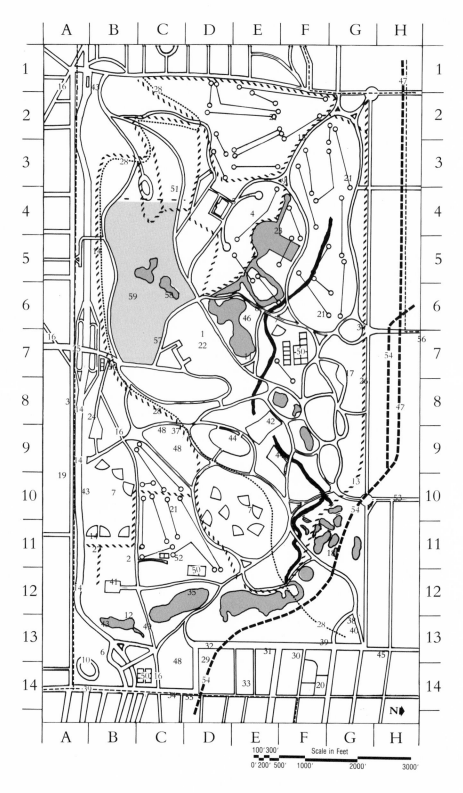

PARK AND NEIGHBORHOOD LOCATOR MAP (1930–1945)

1. American Legion flower emblem, D-7
2. Archery range (resumed), B-11
3. Arena, A-8
4. Art Hill, E-4
5. Art Museum, City, D-4
6. Army Recreation Camp, B-13 and 14
7. Athletic fields, F-6; Aviation Field, B-9 to 11; central fields, D-11 to E-10
8. Baitcasting clubhouse and docks, E-6
9. Bates, Edward, statue (second location), F-3
10. Bicycle track, A-13 and B-14
11. Boat docks, E-7
12. Bowl Lake, B-13
13. Bridle path (rerouted), G-10 and throughout park
14. Bridges and tunnels across highway, A-5, A-8, A-9, A-11, A-12
    Camporall site (temporary; see 7, B-10 and 11)
15. Cascades waterfall, F-2
16. Clayton Avenue, A-1 to C-14
17. Field house, G-7
18. Fish hatchery building, G-11
19. Forest Park Highlands, A-10
20. Forest Park Hotel, F-14
21. Golf courses: municipal 9-hole and 18-hole, D-1 to G-7; Triple A 9-hole, C-9 to D-11
22. Government Hill, D-6 and 7
23. Grand Basin, E-4 and F-5
24. Greenhouses, A-8 to B-9
25. Hampton Avenue entrance, A-7
26. Handball courts, G-7
27. Hangar (formerly airmail hangar), B-11
28. Hiking Trail, Nicholas M. Bell, G-13 to C-1
    Horse exercise track (see 7, B-9 to 11)

Hospitals

29. Barnes, D-14
30. Frisco Railroad, F-13

31. Jewish, E-13
32. St. Louis Children's, D-13
    St. Louis Maternity (see 29, D-14)
33. St. John's, E-14
34. Shriner's, for Crippled Children, C-14

35. Jefferson Lake, C and D-12
36. Jefferson Memorial building, G-6
37. Jewel Box (second location and St. Louis Floral Conservatory), C-9
38. Kiel, Henry W., memorial marker, G-12
39. Kingshighway Drive (probable length, widened to become part of Kingshighway Boulevard), A-14 to G-13
40. Laclede Pavilion (removed), G-13
    Missouri Historical Society (see 36, G-6)
41. Mounted Police Station, B-12
42. Municipal Theatre, E-8 and 9
43. Oakland Express Highway, A-1 to B-14
    Parade of Progress, General Motors Exposition (temporary, see Athletic fields: Aviation Field, 7, B-10 and 11)
44. Parking lots, D-9 and E-9
45. Park Plaza Hotel, H-13
46. Post-Dispatch Lake, D-6 to E-7
    Psychopathic hospital (proposed, 6, B-14)
47. Rock Island Railroad right-of-way (abandoned), H-1 to H-9
48. Rose gardens, C-14, C-9 (Jewel Box)
49. Seven Pools waterfall, C-13
    State cancer hospital (proposed, 6, B-14)
50. Tennis courts, A-7 (relocated, Hampton Avenue); Jefferson Memorial, F-7; Kingshighway, C-14; Triple A, D-11 and 12
51. Totem pole, Alaskan, C-3
52. Triple A Clubhouse (second location), C-11
53. Union Boulevard, H-10
54. Wabash (later Norfolk and Western) Railroad, D-14 to H-6
55. Washington University Medical School, D-14
56. Winter Garden skating rink, H-7

Zoo (St. Louis Zoological Park)

57. Antelope House and Hoofed Animal Yards, C-7
58. Great Ape House and chimpanzee arena, C-6
59. Primate House, B-6

8

WHOSE PARK IS IT ANYWAY? (1945–1976)

Every citizen of this city and everybody who lives within a hundred miles who ever uses [Forest Park] thinks this is his park.—St. Louis Alderman Daniel McGuire, 1984[1]

Park administrators who believed that the end of the Depression and the war would solve Forest Park's problems were mistaken. As the park and its surrounding neighborhood filled with specialized uses, the "turf" of different groups, the areas they wished to control, conflicted and overlapped, resulting in repeated major disagreements and questions of priority. In some cases, as with the zoo and the art museum, the city had taken from the park department the authority to control a section of the park. In other cases, as with the municipal theater, longtime arrangements under city permits lulled a group into thinking it had legal control.

In some ways, the park was a victim of administrators' success in providing a variety of facilities to attract a variety of interests, as Andrew McKinley and M. G. Kern had planned. By 1976 Forest Park had the driving roads and "resting places," including those where people parked at the top of Art Hill. The floral conservatory, the bandstand, the free zoo, the "elegant museum"—Forest Park had them all. The park's neighborhood had filled, in part with the residences of the wealthy St. Louisans early park proponents had hoped to attract. On top of McKinley and Kern's driving park, George Kessler's landscape design, and David Francis's World's Fair reminders, Dwight Davis had placed facilities for organized, structured recreation.

Many people in the St. Louis area felt they had a stake in the park. The growing political power of a variety of groups and their assertion of their rights, all part of national trends, meant that a variety of people expected to be consulted. Environmentalists, zoogoers, picnickers, golf and tennis players, landscape architects, birders, architects and planners, people who lived or worked near the park, all these and more wanted to have a say in decisions about the park. So the park was the subject of various trade-offs and compromises.

The city's serious financial problems often turned the question of who would control into a question of who would pay. Migration of individuals and businesses to St. Louis County accelerated in the postwar years, undermining the city's tax base and dramatically altering the relationship between the city and the county. The city's population shrank and by 1970 was smaller than it had been in 1920. Meanwhile the county population, less than half the city's in 1950, was almost twice the city's by 1976.

The decrease in the city's tax base resulted in severe financial problems for Forest Park. At first, capital improvement funds were available from bond issues approved by voters in 1944 and 1955. But a small 1962 bond issue provided no money for Forest Park, and in 1966, as some voters resisted bond issues and tax increases, bonds for the parks fell short of the required two-thirds vote, as did bonds for the zoo and art museum. The next ten years were a period of cuts in services, delays in maintenance, little or no construction, and a scramble for funds. As in the 1930s and 1940s, vandalism stretched the park department's already tight budget. Federal funds helped some in the late 1960s and the 1970s but were never enough. Private funds and county tax funds helped to finance park facilities like the zoo and the art museum, so the city no longer had complete control.

Four park department heads confronted these problems between 1945 and 1976. Palmer B. Baumes, appointed in 1941, served until he retired in 1960. The next head of the department, Virginia O'C. Brungard, entered political life through membership in two nonpartisan women's groups—the League of Women Voters and the Wednesday Club. At the request of the Wednesday Club, which had encouraged Charlotte Rumbold's work in the playground and recreation movement, Brungard ran for and won a seat on a board of freeholders elected in 1949 to write a new city charter. Although voters defeated the group's proposed charter, the president of the board of freeholders, Raymond Tucker, ran successfully for mayor in 1953, with Brungard as organizer of Women for Tucker. Tucker appointed Brungard Director of Public Welfare, making her, reportedly, the first woman in St. Louis history to serve in a mayor's cabinet. Baumes was one of her subordinates until his retirement.

Brungard soon said the department of public welfare had "just too much for one department

8-1. Since the 1890s St. Louis doctors had been advising mothers to take their babies to Forest Park for the fresh air.

8-2. Louis W. Buckowitz, Director of Parks, Recreation and Forestry from 1965 to 1973, points to the results of park vandalism.

8-3. Richard A. Hudlin sued in 1945 to be allowed to compete in the municipal tennis championship. This picture was taken in the late 1960s or early 1970s.

to handle." She and Mayor Tucker supported charter amendments that voters approved in November 1958 dividing the Department of Public Welfare into three departments, one of which was the Department of Parks, Recreation and Forestry, usually called the park department. Thus the park department was again, as it had been before 1915, a separate city department. Under the amended charter, the park department had, for the first time, a six-member advisory board, appointed by the mayor. The head of the department was the Director of Parks, Recreation and Forestry (usually called the parks director), who was appointed by the mayor.[2]

After Baumes retired in 1960, Mayor Tucker appointed Brungard as parks director. She served until 1965, resigning after Alfonso J. Cervantes defeated Tucker. Cervantes appointed lifelong

politician Louis W. Buckowitz, who liked to be called "Uncle Louie," a Democratic committeeman who had supported Cervantes against Tucker (Fig. 8-2). In the 1973 election Buckowitz supported John H. Poelker in his successful campaign to unseat Cervantes. Following Poelker's election, Buckowitz left the park department and later reentered politics, becoming committeeman again in 1975 and then alderman in 1977. Poelker appointed Buckowitz's wife, Georgia L. Buckowitz, parks director, an appointment that City License Collector Benjamin L. Goins and others saw as a payoff for the Buckowitzes' support. Georgia Buckowitz served until 1981 when she was succeeded by George M. Kinsey, who had been supervisor of parks since 1967, reporting to the parks director.

Blacks were the first St. Louisans to challenge park turf arrangements after World War II. In the postwar period, blacks began to move into the residential areas north of Forest Park Boulevard as landlords divided and subdivided apartments. Many of the new residents moved into the area from outside the city; others had been displaced by urban renewal downtown.[3]

As the war ended, the St. Louis park department continued to follow a policy of supplying "separate but equal" facilities for blacks and whites. Free band concerts were informally segregated. The black newspaper *Argus* reported in 1945 that the park department had hired William Rollins's band as "the first Negro band to play concerts for park and playground entertainment in the history of the city." The band played at the black playgrounds and community centers, though black St. Louisans could also attend the band concerts in Forest Park.[4]

The policy of racial segregation was more definite at the playgrounds, which continued to have separate pageants and athletic competitions. A playground official told the *Argus*, "There can be only a white champion and a Negro champion and no city champion."[5]

The city also provided separate athletic facilities. The four baseball teams of the Municipal Athletic Association's "Colored League" played only against each other and in Tandy Park, not Forest Park. In tennis, the Tandy Park courts were for black players and the Forest Park courts were for whites. The Municipal Tennis Association, a division of the Municipal Athletic Association (MAA), excluded blacks from its championships.

But as World War II ended, blacks across the United States, including St. Louis, claimed their civil rights. St. Louisan Richard A. Hudlin, a black tennis player and executive secretary of the Tandy Park Tennis Club, used a lawsuit in his attempt to enter the city's tennis championship.[6] Hudlin had been captain of the University of Chicago tennis team and was social studies teacher and tennis coach at the city's Sumner High School for blacks (Fig. 8-3). (He later coached Arthur Ashe and Althea Gibson.)

To compete for the St. Louis championship, a player had to be a member of a tennis club affiliated with the Municipal Tennis Association. Hudlin charged in 1945 that he had been prevented from joining such a club, although he was a city taxpayer, and that the tennis association and its president, Martin J. Kennedy, had refused to recognize the Tandy Park Tennis Club solely on racial grounds.

Circuit Court Judge Waldo C. Mayfield refused to interfere. He ruled, as judges often did at the time, that because the tournament was run by the MAA, a private organization, his court had no power to intervene. The *Argus* pointed out that some of the MAA officials were city employees and said the decision "bore all the earmarks of the ante-bellum thinking on the part of those who claim that no basic rights of the Negroes are violated when we are denied the free use of the park facilities."[7]

The color line separated golfers as well. The city had never built a golf course for blacks. Black golfers still used the Forest Park courses on Monday mornings, as they had since 1923. A black golfer recalled years later that a whistle blew at the end of the allotted time, and the black players had to leave the course whether or not they had finished their games. The city relaxed the rule only for golf tournaments conducted by black associations such as the Paramount Golf Club.

In the late 1940s blacks and some whites worked to end such separation. In 1947 the *Argus* sponsored a tennis clinic at the Tandy courts featuring white players such as Earl Buchholz and his son as well as blacks such as Richard Hudlin. Black golfers convinced the park department to remove the time restrictions, which was done without fanfare and without incident.

Seating at the municipal opera, formerly conducted under what the *Argus* called "a sinister system of manipulation," was quietly opened to all in 1948. The *Argus* credited the change to the Mayor's Commission on Race Relations and Jacob M. Lashly, president of the Municipal Theatre Association.[8]

8-4. George Stewart, the St. Louis municipal champion, in the finals of the National Public Parks Tennis Tournament in August 1951.

A study conducted for the Urban League in 1948 concluded that blacks could use most of the city's outdoor recreation facilities for baseball, softball, tennis, and archery and that they encountered no restrictions at the zoo, art museum, or municipal opera. Black organizations and schools used the Forest Park picnic grounds in the late 1940s, as they had for years, although there is evidence that the park department assigned the picnics of black groups to O'Fallon Park in north St. Louis unless the group specifically requested Forest Park. A survey conducted for the Urban League in 1948 found that fewer than 5 percent of St. Louis blacks reported "any embarrassing or unpleasant experiences with white people" while attending the municipal opera or while visiting Forest Park or other public parks. By contrast, 36 percent reported unpleasant experiences on streetcars or buses, and 25 percent while shopping in department stores.[9]

In the summer of 1949 attention focused on the city's racial policy in all the parks, after whites physically abused blacks following desegregation of the swimming pool in Fairground Park. Mayor Joseph M. Darst's new Council on Human Relations, which had replaced the Commission on Race Relations, asked for a report. It said:

The Division of Parks and Recreation has no clear-cut statement of policy on the use of facilities. . . . The administration seemingly has sought to meet the problem of racial relations by sidestepping, expediency and balancing of pressures. . . . It is clear that throughout [Baumes's] administration, the Division

8-5. The 1968 march to honor Dr. Martin Luther King, Jr., ended with a memorial service in Forest Park.

of Parks and Recreation was bolstering and encouraging the practices of segregation and, in fact, discouraging the tendencies toward intergroup participation.[10]

By 1951 the policy of the Municipal Tennis Association had changed; the city's municipal champion that year was the "Negro southpaw" George Stewart (Fig. 8-4).[11] There were changes at the municipal theater too. In 1959 the city permitted the National Association of Negro Musicians to hold "a mass musical festival" there.[12]

In 1968 Forest Park was the site for racial cooperation. The *Post-Dispatch* said that "tens of thousands of Negro and white St. Louisans" at-

tended a memorial service in the park after the assassination of civil rights leader Dr. Martin Luther King, Jr. The service concluded a march across the city beginning at the riverfront Gateway Arch (Fig. 8-5). Blacks moved from their traditional place at the foot of the parade to lead the marchers, including white community leaders such as St. Louis Mayor Alfonso J. Cervantes, St. Louis County Supervisor Lawrence K. Roos, and Harold J. Gibbons, president of the Teamsters Joint Council. The marchers entered the park at Union Avenue and gathered on the cricket field for a short program. As march organizers had requested, the mayor's office, the Human Development Corporation (the city's antipoverty agency), and the steamfitters' local union paid for buses to take the marchers out of the park as soon as the program was over, thus preventing possible violence. Later observers cited the memorial, and the participation by white St. Louisans, as one of the reasons that St. Louis escaped the violence that erupted in many U.S. cities after King's death.[13]

In late 1976, following Richard Hudlin's death, the city dedicated six lighted Forest Park tennis courts near Barnes Hospital as the Richard Hudlin Memorial Tennis Courts. By the time of his death, Hudlin had not only been allowed to join the Municipal Tennis Association, he had served as its president.

By 1976 laws requiring segregation had been replaced by laws prohibiting discrimination across the United States. Yet some people saw evidence of continued discrimination in the park facilities. Although blacks made up more than 40 percent of the city's population by 1976, and many lived a few blocks north of the park, less than 35 percent of park users were black.[14] Blacks and whites played golf in mixed foursomes, but other park users often divided along racial lines. Many observers saw the separation as a matter of personal choice but urged the administration to provide for the interests of all racial groups in park facilities.

Meanwhile, in the early 1960s, the city had moved to end discrimination at the privately operated Triple A (St. Louis Amateur Athletic Association) facilities in Forest Park. In 1962 the associate city counselor ruled that the club was not subject to the city's ordinance prohibiting racial discrimination in public accommodations because it was a private club, even though it occupied city-owned land. Although Richard Hudlin had accepted a similar ruling in 1945, conditions had changed by the 1960s. The city's black population had grown from less than 13 percent in 1950 to more than 28 percent in 1960, enough to elect black aldermen.

When Brungard questioned the club's right to use park land, no one seemed to remember what the agreement between the city and the club had been. A simple notice from the city that the club could no longer use the land would have been sufficient. Instead, in November 1962 a city ordinance aimed at Triple A covered all possibilities when it terminated any "agreement, contract, lease or permit" for the use of park land by any private club for the exclusive use of its membership and forbade any future permit or license to such a club.[15] Club members voted overwhelmingly to give up the park site and move to a new location in St. Louis County instead of opening club facilities to nonmembers.

Following a club election in September 1963, new Triple A officers, elected on a platform "To Keep Triple A in Forest Park," tried again to reach a satisfactory settlement with city officials. As part of its drive to stay in the park, the club's new board of directors emphasized that the club would not discriminate against proposed members on racial grounds. All who did not wish to join the club could use the facilities by paying a fee. A group of club members met unofficially with "members of the city's Negro community and pulpit" to discuss plans to open the club to all. Triple A invited some blacks to join, and the city moved to give Triple A more time to work things out.[16]

In late October 1965, after more than three years of controversy, the city and the club reached an agreement. The club agreed to accept anyone who applied for membership, to allow nonmembers to use its athletic facilities on a fee basis, to pay the city half of the fees received, and to increase its payment to the city for each member from $10 to $15. The city then issued a one-year permit for the club to use park land.[17]

Although the segregation issue had been settled, Triple A remained a private club using public land. After the clubhouse burned down in November 1976, the *Post-Dispatch* called on the city to evict the club from Forest Park (Fig. 8-6). However, less than two weeks after the fire, and more than four months before Triple A's permit was due to expire, the city issued a new five-year permit to the club, and the club rebuilt in the park.

As the battle over Triple A illustrated, groups other than the park department governed large

8-6. The ruins of the Triple A clubhouse after the 1976 fire.

sections of Forest Park, some under renewable permits and others under more permanent arrangements. One of the more permanent arrangements was with the zoo board. The loss of park department control over Forest Park land had been, in fact, the basis for Dwight Davis's objection to establishing the zoo as a separate agency in 1913.

But the zoo had been a popular idea with St. Louisans at the time, and zoo officials exerted themselves through the years to maintain that popularity with all segments of the population, an effort that was largely successful. The leader in this effort was Zoo Director George P. Vierheller, the chief staff member of the zoo since 1922. By 1962, he was nationally known and *Life* magazine reported the retirement that year of St. Louis's "Mr. Zoo." His successor was R. Marlin Perkins, a former St. Louis zoo curator, internationally known for his "Wild Kingdom" television program (Fig. 8-7).

More than a million people every year enjoyed the zoo, which couldn't count its attendance until the 1980s, but took seriously its charge to be "free to all." A study in the mid-1970s concluded that from 30 to 45 percent of Forest Park visitors

8-7. Marlin Perkins, who became Director of the St. Louis Zoo in 1962, displays a monkey. After becoming zoo director, Perkins continued to appear on national television in "Wild Kingdom."

8-8. The Kiener Gate entrance to the zoo and the adjacent serpentine brick wall, both built in the 1960s as part of the first fence to divide the zoo from the rest of the park.

8-9. Phil the gorilla was so popular that after he died in 1958 the zoo had him mounted and put back on display.

8-10, 8-11. A baby tapir and a zebra at the zoo in the 1970s.

the zoo a series of five-year permits to use the land. Parking fees from the lots went to the zoo, while the city continued to maintain free parking spaces on nearby park streets, for those who could find a space.

During the 1960s the zoo board increased its control of the zoo land by dividing the zoo from the rest of the park with a fence. Zoo Director Perkins explained that the fence was necessary for security reasons, to protect the zoo from vandalism, to prevent "injury to intoxicated persons who have wandered in convinced they could wrestle an alligator and win," and to prevent people from "finarking" the bird cage—running around the cage yelling "Finark! Finark!" to get the birds to "call back, run around and get all excited."[19] Whatever the reason, the fence emphasized the boundary between the zoo and the rest of the park. Kiener Gate, near the bird cage, connected sections of serpentine brick wall modeled after Thomas Jefferson's walls at the University of Virginia (Fig. 8-8). Much of the rest of the fence was chain link, not as decorative, but allowing glimpses of the zoo to drivers and pedestrians on nearby park roads.

The city's declining tax base during the postwar period made the zoo tax inadequate to maintain and expand the zoo as the board wished, even though the rate was raised during these years. Following the defeat of a zoo bond issue proposition in 1966 (it received a majority but not the necessary two-thirds), donations from individuals and corporations supplemented tax funds and revenue from zoo operations and concessions. Periodically, the idea of charging admission was considered, but always discarded (Fig. 8-9).[20]

In 1971 voters in both St. Louis and St. Louis County prevented such an admission charge and surprised many observers by voting to form a Metropolitan Zoological Park and Museum District (usually called the zoo-museum district), which established a tax to support the zoo, the art museum, and the Museum of Science and Natural History, located in St. Louis County. Because

went to the zoo.[18] Most of the visitors arrived in automobiles, and parking space was soon at a premium. So the zoo built two parking lots in the early 1950s, following complaints from drivers that they had to park a mile away or give up after looking an hour for a space. Because the southern lot was outside the zoo boundary, the city gave

of the larger tax base in the combined area, a lower tax rate produced about twice as much revenue as the previous collections in the city alone.[21]

Changing finances meant changing control. The new law replaced the zoo board of control with a zoological subdistrict commission of five county residents and five city residents, elected by the commission with the approval of the mayor and county executive. City officials, who had previously been a majority of the board, held no seats on the commission. The St. Louis Zoological Society was gone too. After years of conflict, the zoo commission replaced it with the St. Louis Zoo Association (later the St. Louis Zoo Friends Association), which helped supply funds and volunteers (Figs. 8-10, 8-11).[22]

Despite financial problems, the zoo administration had managed to add new facilities between 1945 and 1976. By 1976 zoogoers could visit the new elephant house built around an arena for the summertime elephant show, or enjoy the penguins inside and Siegfried the walrus outside the nearby aquatic house. They could walk through the renovated World's Fair bird cage or look for the cheetahs and cubs in the cheetah survival center. They could watch the cats running, playing, or lounging at Big Cat Country, which replaced the old lion house with a naturalistic setting that Dwight Davis might have approved as being in the spirit of the bear pits. Those who could pay could ride the zoo train around the grounds, watch the mice burrowing through their breadloaf home in the children's zoo, or enjoy the zoo's animal shows (Fig. 8-12).[23]

The zoo brought the city national recognition in magazines from *Coronet* to *Saturday Review* (Fig. 8-13). The American Association of Zoological Parks and Aquariums (AAZPA), the national professional group, awarded its prize for

8-12. Beginning in 1963, the zoo train offered visitors an enjoyable ride and an aid to tired feet. It also provided revenue for the zoo.

8-13. Zoo officials took advantage of various opportunities to publicize the zoo and its animal shows.

the best new exhibit to the St. Louis Zoo in 1976 for Big Cat Country. Other AAZPA awards in the 1970s indicated that the zoo had become what it had failed to be in the 1890s, "a first class zoological garden."

The art museum board was another of the groups that legally controlled a major park facility, a control that changed, reflecting the shifting balance in city-county influence. Like the zoo, the art museum expanded into the park in the postwar period. The museum had contemplated expansion as early as 1916, but built its first addition in the 1950s, adding, with approval from the board of public service, a new restaurant, a gallery, and a long-needed auditorium. Behind the museum, a new parking lot carefully avoided a seventy-five foot, two-hundred-year-old oak tree.[24]

The next expansion didn't require more park land. Renovation of the museum's west wing, completed in September 1962, added a nine-thousand-square-foot mezzanine. Then work slowed because costs ran above estimates, fund-raising lagged, and a bond issue to finance construction failed. The museum stretched its budget by using volunteers, beginning in the 1950s with formation of Friends of the City Art Museum. As it had in the past, the museum also relied on donations to supplement its tax revenues. Individuals continued to donate objects for the museum's collection. Corporations often paid the costs of special exhibits and fund-raising events.

But the museum's budget was still inadequate to support its program. In 1959 the museum's board voted to close the museum one day a week as an economy measure, and in 1967 the board imposed the first admission charge in the museum's history during a special exhibition, the "Drawings of Degas." After that, special exhibits had an admission charge or a "suggested donation."[25]

8-14. Construction of the new wing of the art museum in the 1970s behind the museum. The location of the addition preserved the view across the Grand Basin and up Art Hill.

After creation of the zoo–museum district in 1971, the museum could again add new facilities. At that time, the museum name changed from City Art Museum of St. Louis to The St. Louis Art Museum, reflecting support and control by both St. Louis and St. Louis County. The art museum's board turned authority for the museum to a new art museum subdistrict commission, chosen in the same way as the zoo's. Since the art museum board had not included city officials since 1912, no city officials were removed from the board in the reorganization.[26]

By 1976 the museum had begun renovation of the east wing and had announced plans for a new wing surrounding the earlier auditorium addition (Fig. 8-14). The renovated east wing re-

opened in December 1977 to general critical acclaim, including an article in *Architectural Record*.

The new tax did not solve all the museum's budget problems. In 1976 the museum used, besides tax revenue from the zoo–museum district and revenue from operations, private and corporate funds, and federal, state, and private foundation grants. The museum continued to be closed on Mondays and on Tuesday mornings.

The lack of public transportation to the museum did not seem to affect attendance, which hit a postwar low of about 276,000 for the year 1951–52 and a high of over 700,000 in 1970, depending to a large extent on the year's special exhibits. Buses ran directly to the museum only from 1945 to 1948, with generally low usage. The bus loop was revived periodically, always with the same results—low usage and deficits. More than 40 percent of the 1948–49 attendees, a record of almost 516,000, came for the nineteen-day showing of the Berlin Masterpieces, paintings taken from two German museums and hidden in salt mines during World War II. The Public Service Company ran special buses to the exhibit, and the opening-day crowd set a one-day attendance record of 13,117, despite traffic tie-ups and waits of about an hour to enter the galleries (Fig. 8-15). People bound for the exhibit had to compete for road and parking space with spectators on their way to the Silver Skates ice-skating program, held at the Grand Basin on the same day. This scheduling problem showed a lack of coordination between museum and park officials.

But such lapses were rare, and the museum retained its popularity and its national recognition into the 1970s. In the mid-1970s, the museum attracted from 8 to 25 percent of parkgoers, depending on the season, more visitors than any other facility except the zoo. A representative of the American Association of Museums who had last visited the museum in 1971 commented in the early 1980s on the museum's improved financial condition, praised its building improvements and additions, and called its educational programs "models of good utilization of great resources."[27]

8-15. Part of the crowd that came to see the Berlin Master-pieces at the art museum in 1949. The sign reminds visitors that the show is free only in St. Louis and asks for a donation to be used for the relief of destitute German children.

The Missouri Historical Society (MHS) was, like Triple A, a private group that used a section of Forest Park with the city's permission. The society's use of park land was not as controversial as Triple A's, since entrance to the society's museum was free to all St. Louisans.[28] The society had been located in the park since 1913. It occupied a growing portion of the Jefferson Memorial building until, by 1976, it used the entire building as well as an underground addition.

Charles van Ravenswaay became the society's first full-time director in 1946. He and his successors tackled its financial problems. The historical society had never received tax revenue, so the directors collected funds by raising membership fees, attracting more members, and encouraging donations. The photographic archive became a source of revenue in the 1960s, after the society raised the formerly nominal copying fees. The Women's Association, a volunteer group organized the year after the Friends of the City Art Museum, instituted two major fund-raising operations, the Country Store at the Jefferson Memorial, and the annual Flea Market sale of donated furniture, clothing, toys, and other items, conducted in cooperation with Stix, Baer & Fuller department store. MHS income doubled from 1946 to 1951 and then doubled again in the next five years, keeping ahead of postwar inflation.[29]

As more funds became available, the society increased its holdings and began new programs. Groups of school children were able to "hold history in their hands" as Daniel Boone's flintlock and Auguste Chouteau's coat came out of the glass cases. *Time* magazine reported that "Harvard Historian Arthur Schlessinger, Jr., had been so impressed that he promised to 'tell the Massachusetts Historical Society all about it.'"[30]

After the society decided it needed more space than the Jefferson Memorial building could provide, it asked for and got a 1970 ordinance that gave the MHS permission to build (at its own ex-

8-16. The Missouri Historical Society reported that it decided to build this addition to the Jefferson Memorial underground because of the "prohibitive cost of reproducing" the existing building and from "a very sincere desire to disrupt as little park land as necessary."

pense) and occupy an underground addition on the site of a parking lot south of the Jefferson Memorial. The addition, designed by Sverdrup and Parcel and Associates became city property as soon as it was completed, as the memorial had, but the historical society controlled activities inside both the memorial and the addition (Fig. 8-16).[31]

The new addition stretched the MHS's financial capacity, made parking more difficult, and failed to attract large numbers of visitors. A study of park users in the mid-1970s estimated that the MHS averaged about 500 visitors a day, half of the Jewel Box average. Despite these difficulties, the society continued to operate its museum and to make its library and archives available to re-

searchers, including the growing numbers of people doing genealogical research in the 1970s.

The story of the municipal theater in the years following 1945 also illustrates the division of control of Forest Park. Occasionally, the theater still held events other than the shows of the municipal opera. The Easter sunrise service continued to use the theater until the late 1960s before falling victim to poor attendance.[32] A Jewish religious service was held there in the spring of 1947. On November 22, 1964, a memorial service marked the frst anniversary of the death of President John F. Kennedy.

But the story of the theater after World War

8-17. The rotunda at the Municipal Theatre, overlooked by most theater-goers in their hurry to take their seats.

II was almost entirely the story of the private not-for-profit Municipal Theatre Association, called the municipal opera, the Muny opera, or just the Muny. So completely had the Muny taken over the theater by 1968 that the city changed the name of the street in front of the theater from Theatre Drive to Municipal Opera Drive in honor of the association's fiftieth season. The MTA continued to obtain city permits to use the theater, but on a five-year basis rather than the previous one-year permits. By the 1970s the MTA considered the theater its property and opposed any use of it by others.

Perhaps most noticeable about the municipal opera operation was how little it changed in the years following 1945. A volunteer board of direc-tors set policy. The board traditionally included the mayor, the parks director, and one other city official, which gave the city some say in the orga-nization into the 1980s, but as a small minority on a board of more than forty people. Private guarantors, more than a thousand businesses and individuals, continued to pledge underwriting funds each year (or, in later years, lend the organi-zation $50 for return at the end of the season), but their money was always safe after 1930. Ticket prices rose, but the Muny offered almost fifteen hundred free seats for each performance on a first-come-first-served basis. The usual Muny production was Broadway musical comedy, with out-of-town stars, backed by a singing chorus and a separate dancing chorus, both chosen through St. Louis auditions. Traditionally, one production each summer was a children's show, featuring a local children's chorus. In 1948 *Time* magazine at-tributed the Muny's continuing popularity and fi-nancial success to "the quality of its performances. Even a foreign critic from Dallas recently admit-ted that St. Louis's Municipal Opera is to summer operetta companies 'what the Metropolitan is to grand opera.' Unlike the Met, however, the Muny has no deficit."[33]

As it had since the 1920s, the MTA paid for new theater facilities, including large cooling fans, which ran during intermission. A fountain commissioned by the association board and de-signed by Robert Charles Smith of the Washing-ton University School of Fine Arts sparkled in the park near the theater. A detailed report on city government issued in 1941 recommended that the Municipal Theatre Association and the Missouri Historical Society should pay some of the cost of the landscaping and guard services that the city provided for them. No action was taken at the time, but later, when park budgets shrank, the institutions took over some of these functions.

The Muny made some other changes over the years. The headliners changed from Broad-way stage stars to Hollywood movie stars to tele-vision stars. Sometimes a grand opera was one of

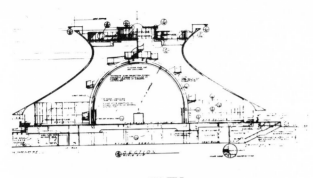

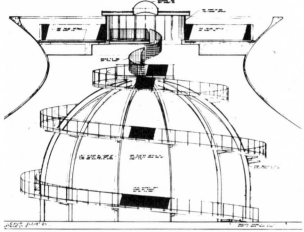

8-18 a, b. Drawings show the interior construction of the planetarium, including the spiral stairway to the roof-top telescopes
and the domed ceiling of the star chamber.

the shows, like *Madame Butterfly* in 1960. The 1967
season included something new—ballet with
Dame Margot Fonteyn and Rudolph Nureyev.
The 1968 season featured two innovations: *Hello,
Dolly!* closed on Broadway for a week to play the
Muny; and Herb Alpert and his Tiajuana Brass
gave a one-night show. Orchestral concerts began
in 1976. The shows that summer ranged from
concerts by the New York Philharmonic, and a
Russian Festival of Music and Dance, to a show
by Dixieland trumpeter Al Hirt and another by
country-western singer Roy Clark. But the Muny
didn't forget the old shows. Another of the attractions in 1976 was the Muny's tenth performance
of *Show Boat*, first performed on the Forest Park
stage in 1930.[34]

Almost all of the audience arrived by private

car, although it was possible to reach the performances by bus into the 1970s, and the Cheshire
Inn, near Hi-Pointe, carried its dinner patrons to
Muny opera performances in a double-deck bus.
By the mid-1970s there were two large parking
lots near the theater. Some people expressed fears
for the future of the Muny opera, but the outdoor
summer operetta season survived, despite the
old problem of St. Louis's summer weather, and
new challenges from the introduction of air-
conditioning (first in movie theaters and then in
homes), the rise and fall of the drive-in movie
theater, and the arrival of television (Fig. 8-17).
By 1976 most people had forgotten that the MTA
had once shared the theater with numerous other
groups, and most St. Louisans seemed willing to
let the MTA continue to occupy the theater.

Of course, the city still controlled many of
the Forest Park activities in the postwar period.
Several of them expanded and built new facilities,
often using a combination of public and private
funding. One such new building was the McDonnell Planetarium.

The 1955 city bond issue of more than $110
million included $1 million for construction of
a planetarium at an unspecified location. Following almost two years of study, the City Plan
Commission recommended a site at Lindell and
DeBaliviere, adjacent to Forest Park, rejecting
various locations inside the park. The Lindell-
DeBaliviere site was close to the Jefferson Memorial and could accommodate such facilities as a
science center, museum of natural history, or
aquarium. The plan commission soon reversed
itself, however, because an attempt by the city
to break subdivision restrictions on the site
would probably mean an expensive legal battle
with neighbors. Instead, the commission recommended that the city build the planetarium in the
southern part of the park, on the site of the old
mounted police station. Since the building was
scheduled for demolition, the commission said,
construction of the planetarium building would
not be a further encroachment on the park. The

8-19. Waiting in line to see inside the full-scale model of the Apollo 8 capsule at the McDonnell Planetarium in the late 1960s.

new site, the commission pointed out, was also big enough for a science museum and a museum of natural history.

The city approved the site, the St. Louis architectural firm of Hellmuth, Obata, and Kassabaum drew plans, and construction began after demolition of the mounted police station in 1960. *Architectural Forum* commended the unusual building, clearly visible from the nearby highway, "Looking like some strange craft spun down to earth from outer space, . . . St. Louis's new planetarium perches gracefully on a rise in . . . Forest Park" (Fig. 8-18).[35]

Although city officials expected it to be self-supporting, the planetarium was in financial trouble even before it opened. When bond issue funds proved inadequate, James S. McDonnell, founder of McDonnell Aircraft Corporation in St. Louis County, gave $200,000 from two foundations, covering the cost of the star projector. At first, attendance, spurred by the U.S.-Soviet race to the moon, justified officials' expectations that revenue would cover operating costs. For the first star show, in April 1963, more than four hundred visitors filled the star chamber to capacity, while others were turned away. The 100,000th visitor passed through the turnstile after the building had been open less than four months, and during the first year the planetarium broke even.

Because admission to the planetarium was

8-20. The McDonnell Planetarium at night in the 1970s. The lights in the windows indicate the building was open for a *Laserium* show.

8-21. Steinberg Rink in late 1957. The building visible behind the skaters housed lockers and changing rooms as well as space to sell refreshments and to sell and rent skates. The building was one of three cited when the American Institute of Architects elected its designer, Frederick Dunn, a fellow in 1962.

free, with a charge only for the sky show, high attendance did not necessarily produce revenue. The planetarium operated at a deficit every year except the first year it was open, a deficit the city had to cover. Average attendance continued at about 300,000 a year through the 1960s, at a time when art museum attendance, in a much larger building, averaged slightly more than 480,000 a year, but annual deficits ranged from almost $30,000 to more than $50,000.

McDonnell continued to provide major funding for the facility, especially for the educa-

tion program, and in 1964 the city named the facility the McDonnell Planetarium.[36] Many of the planetarium displays related to the U.S. space program, for which the McDonnell company was a major contractor. In 1965, for example, visitors could see the scorched heat shield of the McDonnell-manufactured Gemini capsule used in the country's first two-man space flight. A full-scale model of the three-man Apollo capsule that made the journey to the moon attracted 3,000 people in one day, and a lunar rock from the Apollo 12 mission was displayed in 1972 (Fig.

8-22. Roller skating at Steinberg Rink in the early 1970s.

8-19). In 1973, the planetarium's tenth anniversary, an eighty-seven-foot tall Thor rocket went on permanent display outside the building.

Unusual astronomical events also sparked special programs. For a partial solar eclipse in 1970 members of the Astronomical Society of St. Louis and the McDonnell Astronomical Club projected an image of the eclipse onto a bedsheet for a crowd of a thousand.

But none of these activities attracted enough revenue to prevent serious financial problems. In March 1971 city officials, trying to deal with city budget problems and facing a projected planetarium deficit of $150,000, considered closing the building. Instead, the city increased the size of the planetarium commission, its governing body.[37] Volunteers worked to increase attendance and revenue. New revenue-producing programs began, including science shows and telescope tours to the roof of the planetarium.

In June 1975 *Laserium*, an entertainment show, opened in the star chamber. A taped program of music by composers ranging from Corelli to the Rolling Stones accompanied light effects from a laser projection system. *Laserium*, which was a psychedelic experience for young St. Louisans, generated more revenue than the sky show. By 1976 total annual attendance at the planetarium was again over 300,000, more than a third at *Laserium*. But the deficits continued, and city officials continued to search for ways to reduce or eliminate the drain on the city's resources (Fig. 8-20).

The city also added new buildings to the administrative complex along the southern border of the park, despite earlier objections from neighbors to the south. Funds from the 1955 bond issue financed several buildings, including a building to house department offices, which had been downtown. While the office building took park land, it also made it likely that department officials would be aware of the park's condition.

The city built new facilities for athletes, too, again using a combination of city and private funds. The largest single donation made to the park in its first hundred years was for construction of the Mark C. Steinberg Memorial Skating Rink. Mrs. Steinberg, widow of a St. Louis investment broker, admired a rink in New York's Central Park and decided to make a donation to Forest Park, as Nathan Frank had in 1925.

In early 1955 Mrs. Steinberg said that the

8-23. James Franciscus, left, and Earl (Butch) Buchholz, Jr., in the opening day exhibition match at the Dwight F. Davis Tennis Tournament Center.

Mark C. Steinberg Charitable Trust would pay two-thirds of the construction cost of a rink costing up to a million dollars if the city would pay the remaining third. The rink would make ice-skating in the park possible all winter, without regard to St. Louis's changeable weather, and would be used for roller skating in the summer. The city quickly decided to accept the gift, to provide its share of the cost from 1944 bond issue funds, and to name the rink the Mark C. Steinberg Memorial.[38] The plan commission chose a site near Kingshighway, partly because of its convenience to public transportation.

The idea of the skating rink was generally applauded, but St. Louis Children's Hospital objected to the location because noise from the rink would disturb patients. Perhaps remembering the cost of removing the playing fields next to Barnes Hospital, the city shifted the site several hundred

yards away from the hospitals and also from the bus stop.

The rink opened on November 11, 1957, to an opening-day crowd of more than 2,600, mostly children on their Armistice Day holiday (Fig. 8-21). Attendance continued strong, especially during the school Christmas vacation. By the end of December more than 100,000 skaters had used the facility.

But, like the planetarium, the rink soon ran into problems. The refrigeration unit necessary for ice-skating had repeated mechanical problems. Attendance began to drop as other rinks, both public and private, opened in the metropolitan area. Average monthly attendance fell from 50,000 in 1958 to less than 35,000 in 1959 to less than 8,000 by 1976. Some skaters avoided the rink's admission charge by skating on the Forest Park lakes when the ice was thick enough.

The park administration sponsored a variety of programs at the rink to attract skaters. In 1976 there were skating lessons, family hours, and moonlight sessions both winter and summer. In the winter there was also a hockey instruction program, which was open to girls beginning in 1974. While both sexes participated, skating was one of the activities that voluntarily divided along racial lines. Almost all of the ice skaters were white, while almost all of the roller skaters were black (Fig. 8-22).

Like Steinberg Rink, the major new tennis facility was possible largely because of private funds. During the 1950s the city had gradually paid to hard-surface the park's clay tennis courts, as an efficiency study had recommended, but couldn't find the funds for a championship facility that many wanted. In 1965 a city ordinance approved a proposed Dwight F. Davis Tennis Tournament Center and authorized the mayor and the comptroller to work with a private group on the design and construction of the center and to receive donations for the center.[39] Plans for the facility near the Jefferson Memorial, where the city's championship courts were already located, included one court reserved for tournament play

8-24. The Laclede Gas Company paid $80,000 for repairs to the Forest Park field house after accepting responsibility for this damage from a 1949 explosion and fire.

and a small stadium. The city made three appropriations for the center, totaling $75,000. By 1968 donations had made it possible for the city to spend more than $200,000 on the center.

The city-owned center opened in June 1966 with the U.S. hard-court championship tournament of professional tennis, preceded by an exhibition doubles match won by tennis professional Earl (Butch) Buchholz, Jr., a St. Louisan, and actor James Franciscus, a former St. Louisan (Fig. 8-23). Admission charges for the tournament ranged from 50 cents to $4.50 for a single event. Total attendance for the six–day match was estimated at more than 12,000, almost 2,000 more than had attended the matches the previous year when they were held at Triple A. The Dwight Davis Tennis Tournament for public parks players, named for Davis in 1958, followed the professionals into the center. The winners of the Davis Tournament would represent St. Louis in the National Public Parks Tennis Tournament, which Davis had begun in 1916 and which continued past 1976. Improvements to the center continued.

By the mid-1970s the center included eighteen lighted championship courts and a stadium with seats for 15,000. Other planned facilities, including five indoor courts, weren't built for financial reasons.

As they had since the 1870s, other private groups also helped maintain sports facilities or supply programs, and some, the concessionaires, paid the city for the privilege. For several years the Red Cross helped the park department offer free classes in canoeing. Laclede Gas Company paid the city $80,000 for field house repairs and renovation after the company accepted full responsibility for an explosion and fire in late 1949 (Fig. 8-24). By the time a grand jury reported that it was unable to determine the cause of the explosion, the repairs had been completed. In 1955 golf professionals from clubs in the area donated their time for free golf lessons for high school students.

The archery club maintained the Forest Park range for members and nonmembers to use for practice and for tournaments. In 1967 the Na-

8-25. Children fishing in Bowl Lake for the first fishing derby in June 1949. Although various groups had raised fish in the Forest Park lakes since the 1880s, fishing was not permitted until 1945.

tional Archery Association held its championship tournament in Forest Park. The fly and bait casting club held various demonstrations and schools on the park's lighted docks to teach the sport to newcomers.

Private groups helped support fishing in Forest Park after the city began, in 1945, to permit summertime fishing in certain park lakes by children under sixteen years old. (The city later extended the age limits, then removed them entirely in 1972.) Two private groups, the St. Louis Sports Council and the Greater St. Louis Lions Clubs, sponsored children's fishing derbies in the park, beginning in 1949, offering free "hook, line, sinker and bamboo pole" for each child (Fig. 8-25). Citywide, the *Globe-Democrat* reported, 15,000 children competed, 3,500 of them in Forest Park, "many of them less than 8 years old and a surprising number of them girls."[40]

In the 1950s the clubs took over the work of

raising fish in the Forest Park lakes from the federal government, which closed its Forest Park fish hatchery as an economy measure in June 1947. Volunteers from the clubs, assisted by staff from the Wildlife Conservation Federation of Missouri, "planted" over 100,000 fingerlings from the Missouri Conservation Commission in park lakes in the spring, then captured some in the fall and "transplanted" them to other Forest Park lakes as well as to lakes in other city parks (Fig. 8-26). By the 1970s the clubs were no longer active in the park, so park department employees stocked the lakes, usually every ten days during the summer, with catfish and carp, probably the only fish that could live in the lakes' dirty waters.

Sometimes people criticized the park department's relationship with these outside groups. A 1941 study of city government found that the park department had too close a relationship with the Municipal Athletic Association, which was pri-

8-26. Seining the fish from the Forest Park rearing ponds in 1955. Volunteers took over the operation after the federal government ended its operation in 1947.

8-27. Mayor John H. Poelker and Director of Parks, Recreation and Forestry Georgia L. Buckowitz open a new section of the bicycle path for riders in the American Cancer Society's fund-raising Bike-A-Thon.

vately controlled, though it used city employees.[41] The report also criticized the department's emphasis on competitive sports. After that, the park department worked with more athletic associations and organized some noncompetitive programs in Forest Park, such as a children's day camp. The Municipal Athletic Association, organized by Dwight Davis to include all amateur teams in the city, became simply one among many organizations getting permits for scheduled games on the park fields, including the Catholic Youth Council (CYC), Federal Employees' Association, De-Molay, the YMCA, the Khoury League, and the American Legion.

Another focus of criticism, as it had been in the 1890s, was the letting of concessions. In 1967 the unsuccessful bidder for the boat concession charged that Director Louis Buckowitz had improperly revealed information about his bid to the other bidder, the son of a close friend of the mayor. At the same time there were charges of favoritism in Buckowitz's decision to allow another company to operate the refreshment concession in the Forest Park field house rent-free. In the end, the boat contract went to the mayor's friend, the field house contract was awarded with rent retroactive to the end of the previous contract (although there was another bid that might have yielded more revenue for the city), and the mayor reprimanded Buckowitz for "poor judgment" in the two matters.[42]

There was no noticeable complaint, however, when charitable groups used Forest Park for fund-raising sporting events, often long-distance walks, runs, and bicycle rides, like the Heart Association "Heart Pump" bicycle ride and the March of Dimes "Stroll-a-Thon." Each participant found contributors who would agree to give a certain amount to the charity for each mile he or she covered.

When park administrators couldn't find a donor to fund facilities for a popular activity like biking, they provided the money from the department budget. The park had no bicycle racing facility after highway construction destroyed the track in the early 1960s, but park employees built a recreational bicycle path in 1968 by paving a portion of the bridle path, reconverting the bridle

8-28. Playing handball in Forest Park in the 1970s. The sport had attracted players to Forest Park since Dwight Davis's time.

path to the bicycle path it had been in the 1890s (Fig. 8-27). Horseback riding had declined gradually over the years and then dropped off abruptly when the Missouri Stables closed in late 1968. The new bicycle path, like the old one, prevented possible accidents by getting bikers off the park roads.

By the mid-1970s the path had grown to 7.5 miles, and more than 500 bikers used it on a single August weekday. For a brief period in the late 1960s bicycles and tricycles were available for rent in the park. Mostly, though, bikers rode into the park from adjacent neighborhoods or brought their bikes into the park by car. Runners also came from the neighborhood or arrived by car to use the bicycle path, sometimes conflicting with bikes. Roller skaters, too, competed for use of the path.

Other sports also conflicted sometimes. In 1972 the board of aldermen considered, but rejected, a resolution that would have permitted sledding on various golf course hills. The sleds could damage the greens, several aldermen

pointed out, and children could sled elsewhere in the park.

The golf courses could make other park activities hazardous. In 1948 Baumes closed a portion of the bridle path because of the danger of its location near a fairway. The eighteen-hole course's design, across the Grand Basin and the bottom slopes of Art Hill, threatened boaters on the lake and strollers in the area. The summertime conflict continued to be a source of concern past 1976.[43]

In the mid-1970s some planners questioned the allocation of 20 percent of the park's acreage for golf courses used by 7 percent of park visitors on a typical summer day. But the courses had their defenders, despite repeated complaints over the years that they were poorly maintained. One golfer remarked that many of the golfers "can't afford to belong to a country club, so this is their country club."[44] Despite the conflicts and the criticisms, the athletic facilities and programs stayed, mostly under park department control.

8-29. Active and passive recreation share the park peacefully.

8-30. Harriet Bakewell, who selected the stones, and Director of Parks, Recreation and Forestry Virginia Brungard inspect a marker for the John F. Kennedy Memorial Forest in 1964. A *Post-Dispatch* fund-raising campaign that year paid for new trees in the forest, as well as elsewhere around the city.

In the 1970s more than 700,000 people a year used the park's athletic facilities for a bewildering variety of activities. By 1976 the park contained the city's only public skating rink, golf courses, cricket, rugby, and archery fields, two-thirds of the public handball courts, more than a third of the tennis courts, as well as softball, baseball, and soccer fields, and fishing lakes (Fig. 8-28). Bicyclists, joggers, boaters, and many others used the park. These athletes represented less than 35 percent of park visitors, while the sports facilities occupied about 50 percent of the park's space and consumed an unknown percentage of the park's limited budget. City financial reports were not detailed enough to provide such information.

Park administrators also tried to find room and funds for passive recreation, a new term in the 1950s for activities that had been in the park since the 1870s (see Fig. 8-1). Baumes explained that passive recreation included

resting momentarily in . . . some shady spot enjoying an informal communion with nature. . . , soak-

ing up the rays of the sun, or seeking refuge from the sun under the leafy trees, watching the shifting cloud formations in the sky overhead, or being fascinated by the play of water at the fountains, waterfalls, or lakes.

"Unfortunately," Baumes wrote in 1955, "the many varying phases of active recreation, have, in a large measure, usurped a major portion of our present park area" (Fig. 8-29).[45] In the late 1950s Baumes tried to reverse the trend by creating an area for passive recreation near the Lindell-Kingshighway entrance with new shade trees and shrubs, flower beds, walkways, benches, and a new triangular fountain.

Donations financed reforestation of the southwestern section of Forest Park. In 1964 the city named the area the John F. Kennedy Memorial Forest (Fig. 8-30). At the same time, the *Post-Dispatch* ran a fund-raising campaign, similar to its call for donations for a lake extension in the 1890s, and printed the names of all who contributed. The funds paid for trees to be planted all over St. Louis, especially in the newly named forest, where they joined trees that Davis had planted and some from the time before the land was a park.

By 1976 new facilities, most of them donations, welcomed quieter park visitors. The Jewish Tercentenary Flagpole and the Rosenbaum memorial trees beckoned near the Lindell-Kingshighway entrance. New fountains and statues decorated the area around the Jewel Box: the Colonial Daughters Fountain, the Lander Fountain, a lamppost from Kingshighway, the Vandeventer Place gates, the floral clock honoring St. Louisans who had served in the Korean War, and the statue of St. Francis of Assisi were all new to the park (Fig. 8-31). The Mary Leighton Shields Sundial was in the Jewel Box gardens rather than on Government Hill, where it had been erected in 1915. Outside Steinberg Rink an abstract casting by Jacques Lipchitz entitled *Joie de Vivre* puzzled skaters (Fig. 8-32). The Frankenthal Memorial Drinking Fountain had attracted thirsty people at the World's Fair Pavilion for a few years in the

8-31. The floral clock in the Jewel Box gardens. Below the clock, flowers formed the inscription, "Hours and flowers soon fade away." The Vandeventer Place gates are visible in the right rear.

1960s, but was gone by 1976. A short distance from the Bates statue, dedicated when the park opened in 1876, a small marker commemorated the park's hundredth birthday. Near the bottom of Government Hill, below the pavilion, the White Pine Statue stood surrounded by a grove of living pine trees that honored winners of the St. Louis Award, an annual award to the person who had made the greatest contribution to the metropolitan St. Louis area.[46]

As with other park attractions people were more willing to donate statues and trees than to help maintain them. To decrease maintenance costs, plantings in Forest Park gradually became smaller and more concentrated. Beginning in the late 1940s, for example, gardeners were more likely to plant flowering trees adapted to the St. Louis climate and, Baumes said, "hardy enough to withstand the constant wear and tear to which all our facilities are subject." Most of the "wear and tear" in the 1970s was not from parkgoers but from the park department's motorized lawn mowing equipment.[47]

When city budgets grew increasingly tight in the 1960s and 1970s, the number of plantings fell sharply. By 1976 the Forest Park greenhouses

held only 100,000 plants at a time, compared to 3 million in the early 1950s. The Government Hill gardens had disappeared, replaced by lawns surrounding a fountain in need of repair. In the early 1970s vandals smashed the fountain's lights, which went unrepaired until 1980 when federal funds became available. The fountain Baumes had installed near the Lindell-Kingshighway entrance was out of service, but no repairs were made because, as Parks Superintendent George M. Kinsey pointed out, "that's not as high a priority [for the city] as the operating lights at City Hospital or power problems at a fire house."[48]

In 1969 the St. Louis Beautification Commission hired Washington University architecture student Dennis Bolazina to survey all public art in St. Louis, including Forest Park. He reported unrepaired damage to the Jahn Memorial, the Angel Fountain, the St. Francis of Assisi statue, and the statue of Pan in the Guggenheim Fountain. Bolazina's recommendation for a commission with its own director and budget for art maintenance city-wide went nowhere, though the publicity given his report brought offers of help from private groups, and park department employees did what they could to repair the effects of the

8-32. The Steinberg Memorial Trust, which had helped pay for the skating rink, donated *Joie de Vivre* for placement near the rink entrance.

years and vandals. The Fountain Angel statue went into storage for safekeeping before moving in 1975 to the Missouri Botanical Garden. The Guggenheim Fountain moved temporarily to the Missouri Botanical Garden, then to a new home in Columbus Square Park.

But the problems of vandalism and aging facilities continued. The Frankenthal Fountain was stolen, replaced, then stolen again and not replaced. Someone knocked the nose off the Thomas Jefferson statue at the Jefferson Memorial (Fig. 8-33). Vandals repeatedly took or broke St. Louis's sword, and the city repeatedly replaced it. The field house tower clocks, which had stopped in the late 1950s, weren't repaired.

The Jewel Box, too, felt the pinch. The only major addition inside, between 1945 and 1976, was the Magna-harp and chimes donated by Harry J. Kiener as a memorial to his mother, fa-

ther, and brother. A waterfall, planned for years, was finally built in 1978 with federal funds. The floral displays changed only three times a year instead of every month. Nighttime hours disappeared as the Jewel Box went to a 9 to 5 schedule. To help support the Jewel Box, in 1970 the city began charging twenty-five cents for admission, except on Monday and Tuesday mornings when admission was free. To encourage use of the facility when it would otherwise be closed and to produce additional revenue, in the 1970s the city opened the Jewel Box and the adjacent gardens for weddings and parties to those willing to pay the fee.

In the mid-1970s an average of almost 1,000 people a day visited the Jewel Box, including students from schools in St. Louis and St. Louis County who attended the nature study and horticultural education programs. This number was slightly more than half the annual attendance reported in 1951–52.

Like athletes, those interested in the park's plants and wildlife contributed facilities and sometimes protested park department maintenance. The St. Louis Bird Club, later the St. Louis Audubon Society, had been promoting Forest Park as a bird haven as early as 1919 (Fig. 8-34). The club conducted regular bird walks in Forest Park into the 1980s, finding it one of the finest places in the St. Louis area to see birds, especially warblers. The Audubon Society and other bird lovers repeatedly protested park department clearing of brush because it removed bird habitat.

In the late 1960s the Audubon Society teamed with the city beautification commission, whose offices were in the old Forest Park keeper's house, to provide a new facility for those enjoying wildlife in the park—a combination bird sanctuary and nature trail. The trail wound through the Kennedy Forest with plants tagged for identification and rest areas with benches for those studying wildlife. A few years later seventeen-year-old Peter Wolff and others worked with a Boy Scout troop to turn a portion of the nature trail into a trail for the blind, though none of the workers

8-33. In the 1970s the statue of Thomas Jefferson stood in an open loggia at the Jefferson Memorial. In the 1980s, the Missouri Historical Society glassed in the area.

was blind. The Missouri School for the Blind made Braille signs to highlight "animal sounds, flowing water, fungus and foliage . . . [and] a tree stump, on which the years of growth can be felt in the rings," the *Post-Dispatch* reported. A cable connected the signposts, allowing the blind to follow the path unaided.[49] Unfortunately, few

blind visitors used the trail, which soon fell into disrepair. The nature trail was not much used by sighted people either because of a growing fear of crime in the secluded portion of the park.

A tamer way to see birds was to feed the domestic ducks in Pagoda Lake around the bandstand (Fig. 8-35). Many of them were donations,

8-34. These walkers in the 1950s watched birds in Forest Park, as similar groups had done at least since 1919. In 1945 the St. Louis Bird Club counted 105 species of birds in Forest Park in one day.

Easter gifts that parents furtively left in the lake after the children tired of them.

Picnics, too, presented financial problems and questions of turf. The park department issued permits for large picnics; small picnics were permitted at any time or place in the park in the 1940s. Baumes remarked in 1950, "There seems to be no limit to the number of benches and picnic tables as well as camp stoves that should be provided."[50] All these picnickers left litter for park employees to clean up (Fig. 8-36).

During the summer of 1954 Baumes ex-panded the picnic area by clearing woods in the eastern and southwestern sections of the park, despite a protest from the *Post-Dispatch*. The southwestern section of the park was where Commissioner Pape had refused to clear trees to enlarge the automobile tourist camp; Baumes evidently considered picnics a more appropriate park activity. Department employees installed tables, benches, camp stoves, and trash containers in the newly cleared picnic areas. New regulations, which prohibited picnics outside the designated areas, together with appeals for picnickers to use

8-35. Feeding the ducks in Pagoda Lake delighted several generations of St. Louis children and their parents.

8-36. Cleaning up the litter left by picnickers strained limited park budgets.

the trash containers, reduced but didn't eliminate the litter problem (Fig. 8-37).

Picnics continued to be popular through the 1970s, but with some changes. In the 1970s carry-out food from restaurants near the park often replaced the traditional picnic basket. With more St. Louisans working a five-day week, Saturday replaced Sunday as the favorite picnic day (Fig. 8-38). Most groups requesting permits came from the area immediately around the park. Family gatherings outnumbered school picnics three to two, with churches, clubs, and companies also represented.

Band concerts were also subject to budget cuts and controversies. City-financed band concerts resumed after World War II, then ended in 1950, following budget cuts. So private groups sponsored concerts, beginning in the late 1950s. Laclede Gas Company and the Recording Industry Trust Fund cosponsored a series of concerts in the city's parks, including some in Forest Park under the baton of Laurent Torno. KMOX radio broadcast several. The St. Louis Symphony Or-

chestra presented free concerts in the park in the late 1960s and early 1970s. The *Globe-Democrat* estimated that 20,000 people went to Art Hill for a concert in June 1968. The following year the concert closed with Tchaikovsky's 1812 Overture, complete with cannons firing at the base of the hill.

Rebellious young people used concerts to try to stake out their own area on nearby Government Hill in the late 1960s and early 1970s. During Earth Week in April 1970 the hill held an Eco-fair planned as "an environmental teach-in" but dominated by a rock group called Rush.[51] In May a group of young people met with Parks Director Louis Buckowitz to ask for a permit for regular Sunday rock concerts, a meeting that failed to bridge the generation gap. The bearded, long-haired young people arrived at Buckowitz's office wearing ragged clothes. Buckowitz refused their request, saying the city did not issue any Sunday permits. The amplified music had disturbed park visitors and zoo animals, park officials said, though there was no mention of complaints about

8-37. Signs such as this one erected in 1954 restricted picnicking to designated areas in the park.

the symphony's cannon. In addition, previous concerts had caused traffic problems, illegal beer sales, heavy littering, and the illegal use of drugs.

By early July the Sunday rock concerts had resumed, without a permit, and the Yippies (Youth International Party) announced plans for a week-long "Festival of Life," with music and discussion sessions (Fig. 8-39). When the festival opened on Sunday, July 12, local bands entertained 2,000 to 4,000 people with hard rock music. Nearby 10,000 Boy Scouts were leaving the park following their Camporee, which had featured a visit by Lady Baden-Powell and a Saturday night campfire at Art Hill. Boy Scout board member Robert Hyland, General Manager of KMOX Radio, had arranged for television stars Sid Caesar and Mike Connors to appear at the campfire.

At the Yippie festival, police were out in force. They arrested three people they suspected of possessing marijuana. Although the festival was scheduled to continue through Saturday,

most of the festival-goers left early Wednesday morning, following bad weather and reported crimes.

Soon, however, tensions between city officials and young people who liked rock music eased. Rock concerts became an accepted park event, as users of different ages and tastes in music shared the park amicably. During the summer of 1972 thirty rock and jazz concerts were presented at various parks and recreation centers in St. Louis, including one at Steinberg Rink. In 1974 KSHE, a rock FM radio station, sponsored a combination rock music concert and kite-flying contest. A policeman reported that there were few problems with an estimated 21,000 young people who came to the aviation field on a warm, sunny day when a fuel shortage might have prevented them from going farther away. Beginning in 1975, those who liked rock could enjoy it inside the planetarium at the *Laserium* shows.

Besides the Eco-fair, Forest Park was the site for a few other protests. In 1964, when the observance of Armed Forces Day (formerly Army Day) moved to Forest Park, about twenty-five demonstrators, black and white, had protested United States participation in the war in Vietnam. They attracted little attention from the people who had come to see a Gemini spacecraft made by McDonnell Aircraft Corporation, and Little John and Honest John rockets from St. Louis's Emerson Electric Corporation. People also gathered for two nights in late August 1968 to protest police actions at the 1968 Democratic National Convention in Chicago at rallies sponsored by the *St. Louis Free Press*, a newspaper that appeared sporadically.

But most St. Louisans who went to Forest Park, even during the turbulent 1960s, went not to protest but simply to enjoy themselves. One event popular with parkgoers, beginning in the late 1960s, was the folklore federation's festival, which celebrated the variety of cultures in the United States with songs, dances, puppet shows, and foods native to a variety of European, Asian, African, and Latin American countries.

8-38. Picnickers in Forest Park often strayed outside the designated areas.

Beginning in 1972 the ethnic displays were part of a larger Forest Park festival called Fair St. Louis, planned as "a miniversion of the 1904 St. Louis World's Fair." Like the World's Fair organizers, sponsors of Fair St. Louis hoped to attract tourists to St. Louis; unlike the 1904 promoters, they didn't charge admission (Fig 8-40). The St. Louis Visitors' Center, sponsor of the fair, announced that an international village at the Grand Basin would contain eighteen local ethnic groups, including African, German, Czechoslovakian, Mexican, Greek, Israeli, Scottish, Scandinavian, Latin American, Hungarian, and Serbian representatives. The U.S. Army's Golden Knights team parachuted onto the old aviation field. By the end of the weekend, the *Post-Dispatch* said, beer and food "were completely sold out. . .—but with a Sunday crowd estimated by police at 80,000, what could one expect?" In 1976 the fair included shows in honor of the American Bicentennial as well as "its usual mixture of foreign food, music and crafts."[52]

St. Louis families had celebrated holidays in Forest Park since the 1880s, and many continued to celebrate Memorial Day, Labor Day, and the Fourth of July in Forest Park, even when there were no formal programs planned. On July 4, 1968, despite a "Water and Sky Spectacle" on the downtown riverfront near the Gateway Arch, Forest Park was crowded. The *Post-Dispatch* reported that "the pedestrian equivalent of traffic jams" developed on the zoo paths and hundreds stood in line to ride the zoo trains.[53]

Although the Easter parade and then the Easter sunrise service disappeared from Forest Park, thousands of St. Louisans continued to visit Forest Park on Easter to admire the Jewel Box display and to visit the zoo and the art museum. On Easter in the 1960s and 1970s the Horseless Carriage Club of St. Louis gave free shows of antique

8-39. Young people danced to the rock music at the World's Fair Pavilion in the early 1970s, but park officials were less enthusiastic.

automobiles in Forest Park. In 1970 the club's "Concours d'Elégance" included a 1909 Hupmobile, a 1930 Chevrolet ambulance, and a 1948 Kaiser.

Although crowded on nice days in the spring and summer, especially on weekends and holidays, the park was practically empty in the winter and on most nights. In winter some school groups came for classes and tours at the zoo, art museum, historical society, planetarium, and Jewel Box. Municipal opera performances in the summer and nighttime art museum events brought people to the park after dark. After the *Laserium* shows began, planetarium attendance was the most evenly divided among the seasons and between day and night of any park attraction. Night-

time games on lighted athletic fields brought out players and spectators. Hot weather brought people to the park to sleep in the late 1940s, but the practice was obsolete by the 1970s (Fig. 8-41). By then, most St. Louisans had home air conditioning or at least an electric fan.

In 1974 the short-lived Forest Park Associates, a group of organizations and businesses located in and around the park (including the park department), tried to balance usage of the park among the seasons by publicizing special Christmas activities in the park. In the Jewel Box, Santa or Mrs. Santa visited on certain days for pictures with children while adults enjoyed the traditional poinsettia display. The group publicized the planetarium's sky show about the Star of Bethlehem,

8-40. The St. Louis Visitors' Center sponsored Fair St. Louis near the Grand Basin. The picture is from June 1975.

a Christmas concert at the art museum, and Christmas shopping at the zoo gift shop. Members of the St. Louis Blues hockey team greeted visitors at Steinberg Rink.

The Forest Park Associates also revived an activity that thousands of St. Louis spectators had enjoyed in the early twentieth century—ballooning. Following a brief ascent during the 1972 Fair St. Louis, several of the colorful balloons rose from the cricket field in 1973 as part of the Christmas activities of the Forest Park Associates (Fig. 8-42).

The next year the rally moved to September, probably for warmer weather. Thirty balloons assembled in the park from as far away as Texas and Canada. Harper Barnes reported for the *Post-Dispatch* that the balloons' propane heaters made "the approximate sound of a field full of drag-ons clearing their pipes."[54] The event continued after the Forest Park Associates disbanded and soon became so popular that would-be spectators jammed highway exits and park entrances.

Despite the varied attractions available in Forest Park, some St. Louisans didn't go there because they feared they would be crime victims. Park officials worked with the St. Louis police department to dispel such fears. Both park police (park department employees) and the St. Louis police department patrolled Forest Park. The park policemen lacked authority to make arrests and had to call a city policeman for major problems. Park officials repeatedly asked for funds for additional park police to fight rising crime in the park. Instead, the police department increased its patrols in Forest Park. St. Louis Police Chief

8-41. People spent hot summer nights in Forest Park in the late 1940s, as they had since 1911, despite occasional crimes against the sleepers.

Eugene Camp told a *Globe-Democrat* reporter in 1970 that "we want to make it perfectly clear to everyone that it is safe to come [to Forest Park]."[55]

Late in 1970 the police department accepted Mayor Cervantes's recommendation to revive the mounted police, which had been abolished in 1948. The mounted police would patrol in Forest Park, though Chief Camp preferred jeeps. The old airplane hangar became the mounted police headquarters and stable, since the 1894 mounted police station and stables had been demolished in 1960.

Mounted police began patrolling the park in April 1971. Like earlier park police, they protected parkgoers from themselves as well as from wrong-doers—their first official action was the rescue of a fourteen-year-old boy, knocked unconscious when his canoe capsized. Major crime in the park decreased, and people felt safer. A study conducted a few years later concluded that, in fact, the major decrease in crime in the park had occurred in 1969 and 1970, prior to creation of the mounted patrol. However, most St. Louisans credited the mounted police for their increased feeling of security in the park (Fig. 8-43). The *Globe-Democrat* said, "The mounties came to Forest Park . . .—and crime went."[56]

Of course, there were still crimes in the park. A major problem in 1974 was bicycle theft. By the fall of 1975 a plainclothes police "decoy squad" of bicycle riders had decreased the number of such thefts, but police advised parkgoers to observe certain precautions such as not riding (or walking) alone.

A study of crime in Forest Park, completed in 1977, concluded that St. Louisans were safer in the park than outside it, since the crime rate in Forest Park was less than one percent of the rate for the entire metropolitan area. In a telephone survey of city and county residents, fewer than 10 percent of respondents said that security in the park needed to be increased.

Policemen also worked to decrease use of Forest Park for homosexual activity, an illegal activity that offended many parkgoers. St. Louis police announced a drive in 1975 "to repress homosexual activities in Forest Park rest rooms near athletic fields where Little League teams play." While none of the men had approached any of them, boys complained about what they had seen. In two weeks mounted patrol officers arrested seventeen men on charges of lewd and lascivious conduct in the rest rooms. By 1976 gays had moved to the area near the Kennedy For-

8-42. The 1973 Forest Park balloon rally. Later rallies attracted many more balloons and many more spectators.

est. Their attitudes toward police were somewhat uneven. One man said,

> Some of us don't drink or are too young to go to the gay bars. . . . Non-gay persons would come here late at night and harass us. . . . When somebody comes through the area and starts to bother us . . . we chase them and make a lot of noise, hoping we'll attract the attention of the cops.[57]

At the same time, police were arresting homosexuals in Forest Park every day. The police department shifted responsibility for the operation from the mounted patrol to the Tactical Anti-Crime Team (TACT), following complaints that a police officer and a civilian were treated differently after being arrested for the same offense, and that police officers were recommending a particular bonding company. The captain of the Hampton Avenue District station later received a written reprimand for these irregularities.

Despite some problems, an estimated 4.5 million people visited Forest Park each year, almost all of them in cars, until it began to seem that the automobiles had taken over the park. While public transportation ran to and across the park during the 1970s, use of private automobiles was far more common. All of those automobiles required more roads and far more parking facilities. An even thornier question of land allocation was the use of park land for through roads, a question that dated back to the 1870s.

Roads continued to require constant maintenance. Drivers still complained about getting lost in the park, as city officials worked to improve the sign system (Fig. 8-44). City officials also regulated parking and revised the flow of traffic. A 1960 ordinance raised the park speed limit from twenty to twenty-five miles an hour, but drivers often ignored the new limit, as they had earlier ones, despite periodic enforcement campaigns. Traffic regulations also influenced who used the park: pickup trucks were prohibited from park roads, even when they weren't used for commercial purposes (Fig. 8-45).

Some St. Louisans suggested that motor vehicles should be banned in the park on certain days to encourage pedestrian traffic. However, the lack of public transportation to some facilities, especially the art museum, made such suggestions seem impractical, and none was implemented.

Roads designed to accommodate local traffic took small pieces from the edges and corners of the park. After enlargement of the intersection of Kingshighway and Lindell in 1958, Baumes claimed the ornate gaslight from the corner for the Jewel Box rose garden. Roads to and around the park were widened to carry more traffic. Often this widening was accomplished by removing the center boulevard strip, which had formerly carried the shade and quiet of the park into the city. The city paved the center strip of Kingshighway, treated as a boulevard strip since the 1930s, even though it was actually part of Forest Park.

Much more park land was paved, however,

8-43. The city police department revived mounted police patrols in Forest Park in 1971 to lessen people's fears of crime in the park.

8-44. Despite the presence of direction signs like this one in the 1970s, people still got lost in Forest Park.

for through highways. The period of the late 1950s and early 1960s was a time of major highway construction in St. Louis. Many city officials and residents considered such construction essential for the city's continued economic health. The major disagreements were over the roads' locations. Like the earlier Oakland Expressway, proposed roads often ran across park land. A letter writer pointed out in the *Post-Dispatch* in 1961,

> Forest Park is especially attractive to the [highway] planners because it has major arteries approaching it from all directions (originally provided for easy access to the park); it requires relatively little whittling here and there to fit this or that traffic need; it is already non-tax producing. . . ; and, best of all, . . . no homeowner's or business group will swing into action to defend the park area.

Highway planner Myer Abelman said, as a private citizen, that when "parks get in the way of highways, we have to go through them," but not everyone agreed. Gerhardt Kramer, president of the preservationist Landmarks Association, said, "Of course land next to the St. Louis parks is expensive . . . because parks create high land values. . . . The value of park land . . . is far greater than the value of most other land in the city."[58]

The Forest Park Expressway, sometimes referred to as the Rock Island Expressway because it used the abandoned Rock Island railroad right-of-way, was built beside the Wabash tracks through the park beginning in March 1959. A suit by park neighbors Joseph and Mary Kirkwood to prevent the use of about 6 acres of park land was unsuccessful, as the Missouri Supreme Court ruled that the highway would serve park purposes by removing traffic from its winding drives.[59]

While the city was planning the expressway, Missouri highway planners were at work on a much larger project—widening the Red Feather Highway, previously the Oakland Express Highway, and linking it to U.S. Highway 40 (the Daniel Boone Expressway). In 1958 highway department officials announced plans for expansion of the highway, which they considered substandard, from four to six lanes. The expansion would have to be made northward, into the park, they said, in order to make a proper connection with the Daniel Boone Expressway. The new highway included cloverleafs at both Hampton and Kingshighway as well as enough land for eight lanes, though only six were built at that time. The Kingshighway cloverleaf cut through the dogleg around the southeastern corner of the park, in existence when the park opened in 1876. Myer Abelman said that straightening the Kingshighway dogleg would "save four or five minutes of driving time," but it separated the children's playground and the rose garden from the rest of the park. The southeastern corner seemed even less a part of the park after the city changed the names of the streets along the dogleg.[60]

Although the city had asked the state high-

8-45. Traffic jams such as this one prompted zoo officials to build two parking lots in the 1950s.

way department to "make every effort to minimize the amount of park property taken, consistent with good, safe design,"[61] the highway took 44 acres of park land (almost 68 counting the land already paved for the Oakland Expressway), including tennis courts near Hampton and near Kingshighway, the bicycle track at the southeastern end of the park, a group of greenhouses, and the nearby head gardener's cottage. The highway cut through Clayton Avenue, which ceased to be a route through the park, as park authorities had been requesting since the 1870s. But the early

commissioners would probably not have considered the highway a good trade-off.

Many who deplored the loss of park acreage reluctantly accepted the plan. Parks Director Brungard said, "I want the city to hold onto every bit of the park it possibly can. . . . I know we have to have these improved highways, but we very much need parks and recreational space." The *Post-Dispatch* pointed out that the "highway certainly must be widened," and the use of park land became inevitable when the city used park land for the Oakland Expressway, "be-

8-46. The Veiled Prophet queen inaugurates a short-lived Forest Park carriage service in 1953.

fore anyone could foresee present traffic requirements." Others disagreed. Letters in the *Post-Dispatch* called the road "outlandish and destructive" or predicted that by the year 2019 Forest Park would be entirely concrete.[62]

To make matters worse, the state paid only $858,000 for the land. The city estimated that it would cost $500,000 to relocate the greenhouses, tennis courts, baseball fields, and comfort stations that had to be moved for the highway, leaving only $358,000 to be used to improve park and recreation facilities throughout the city. (A suggestion that the replacement greenhouses should be built outside the park, instead of using more Forest Park land, was not adopted, probably because the city wished to keep all the greenhouses together and did not want to pay to rebuild all of them elsewhere.) To avoid delay in the construction of the highway, the city accepted the price.

Motorists on the highway could see into the park as they drove. At Christmas they could enjoy a red plastic ribbon that made the planetarium look like a Christmas package. The ribbon and

bow began as a 1970 student prank. In later years the ribbon had official approval and a variety of private companies donated the ribbon or its installation.

After the highways were built, commuters continued to use park drives. In the 1970s as many as half of the automobiles on the park drives on a typical day were only passing through. Many were crossing the park from south to north. Residents south of the park often asked for, but didn't get, a direct north-south route through the center of Forest Park. Instead, drivers who didn't want to go around the park on Kingshighway or Skinker drove through on winding park roads.

By 1976 Forest Park was framed by major streets: Oakland and Highway 40 along the south, Kingshighway to the east, Skinker to the west, and Lindell and the Forest Park Expressway to the north. All were multilane streets with heavy traffic that could be heard inside the park and discouraged approach to the park on foot or bicycle. Because Highway 40 was fenced, those approaching from the south without a car had to use the

8-47. The Arena after a 1959 tornado blew down one of its towers. Rather than rebuild the tower, the owners had the undamaged tower removed.

pedestrian bridges or underpasses, as they had since construction of the Oakland Expressway.

Park land separated from the southern section of the park by the highway held an underground fire and police alarm headquarters, paid for with funds from the 1944 bond issue. Although it was completed in 1958, the alarm headquarters was not activated until 1964 because of the expense of connecting cables.

Although it might seem that every proposal that could be financed was carried out, that wasn't true. Amusement rides were not permitted in Forest Park, even on a temporary basis, although they were allowed in other St. Louis parks. The reason for this policy is not clear. Perhaps it was because of the proximity of the Forest Park Highlands, though the policy remained after the Highlands closed in 1963. Maybe residential neighbors used political pressure to keep the rides out, or perhaps the policy was simply a method of rationing park space. Because of the policy, the city rejected a proposed miniature railroad near the Grand Basin, though the zoo board later accepted one

inside the zoo grounds. Although Mayor Raymond R. Tucker permitted Alderman Alfonso J. Cervantes to run a carriage service in the park, he vetoed Cervantes's pony ride in 1954 because the rides "might in time lead to . . . ferris wheels, carousels and similar types of amusement devices" (Fig. 8-46).[63] In 1971, however, while Cervantes was mayor, the pony ride operated for a while. When Louis Buckowitz tried to accept the Forest Park Highlands carousel (which the zoo board had already turned down saying it wasn't running an amusement park), the usually agreeable parks board asserted itself. Five of the six members of the parks board resigned in protest. The five resigning members were quickly replaced with influential St. Louisans, but the carousel stayed out of the park.

A proposal to hold a 1953 World's Fair in the eastern section of the park promised to provide a much larger controversy than the one in the early 1900s between those who favored the fair and those who opposed such use of park land. However, United States entry into the Korean War in June 1950 ended the project.

The southeastern portion continued to be the target for almost endless suggestions, including a veteran's hospital in 1946. In 1947 the St. Louis Anti-Slum Commission rejected a proposal to use the area for low-rent housing. In 1969 the St. Louis Junior Chamber of Commerce proposed and the St. Louis Audubon Society opposed a recreation complex for the handicapped on the land. Judge David J. Murphy was less explicit about the part of Forest Park he had in mind for a juvenile detention center, but he didn't get park land either. In 1972, saying that the park "is hardly the sylvan glen that its originators and its supporters so extol," the Rev. Edward J. O'Donnell suggested that part of it could be sold for residential development and the money used to build parks in the city's slums, but that idea was never seriously considered.[64]

The city's financial problems, especially in the 1960s and 1970s were, to a certain extent, a blessing, though well disguised, since they decreased the number of proposals to use park land. As long as funds were available, the city could add facilities without having to make difficult decisions about priorities. Each proposed project seemed important enough to merit room. The zoo, the museums, the playing fields, the plantings, the administrative buildings, the roads and parking lots, the surrounding neighborhood—all grew until they began to collide. The park sometimes seemed a collection of different institutions, each with its own users, funds, priorities, and board of control.

The variety of organizations that controlled part of the park made it more likely that anyone in the city or county would be represented, but they made it difficult for anyone to consider the park as a single entity. There were some hard questions about the park that needed to be considered: Who should it serve? What standards should be set for parkgoers' behavior and how would the standards be enforced? How much land should be allocated for sports, for the institutions, for green space, for other uses? Should it be a central gathering place for massive numbers of people? Who should pay for what? What should be the relationship between the park and its neighbors?

By 1976 Forest Park had a variety of neighbors with an interest in what went on there. The land around the park was expensive and almost all occupied, causing noise and bustle, bringing new visitors into the vicinity, and tempting neighbors and others to try to expand onto park land.

West of the park, residential subdivisions and high-rise apartment houses continued to be well maintained. The Washington University campus, though it contained several postwar buildings, still had much open space and preserved the view from the park to Brookings Hall, which had been the administration building for the 1904 fair.

North of the park, residents of the private places fought to maintain their neighborhood, partly through the designation of the Central West End Historic District. Some houses were torn down and some new ones built, but the large, well-maintained single-family homes still lined Lindell and the private places.

Apartment buildings and hotels lined Kingshighway south of the Chase-Park Plaza Hotel. New buildings filled the hospital complex at the park's southeastern edge. The hospitals and nearby doctors' offices drew people from a large region for the latest medical treatments. Traffic and parking were continuing problems. East of the hospitals, Washington University Medical Center Redevelopment worked to revitalize an area the city had declared blighted.

The Arena remained south of Forest Park, but without its towers, removed after a 1959 tornado blew one off (Fig. 8-47). In 1976 the Arena was again in financial trouble after years of relative prosperity.[65] The rides of the Forest Park Highlands were gone, destroyed by a fire in 1963. The Highlands site held instead the Forest Park campus of the St. Louis Community College. Office buildings, a motel, and a restaurant replaced most of the St. Louis University playing fields on Oakland. The athletes of St. Louis University High School and Forest Park Community

8-48. Construction in the medical complex on Kingshighway in the 1970s made the city more visible from inside the park.

College practiced on the Forest Park playing fields, crossing Highway 40 through a tunnel.

In August 1968 the Junior College District (later St. Louis Community College) requested three acres of land near its Forest Park campus for the district's administration building. Mayor Cervantes and Comptroller John H. Poelker supported the proposal, saying the highway separated the land from the park and the purchase money could be used to buy park property elsewhere in the city. However, Donald Gunn, president of the board of aldermen, opposed the proposal. Both the *Globe-Democrat* and the *Post-Dispatch* supported Gunn, and Cervantes hastily dropped the proposal.

In November, after hockey fans looking for parking spaces near the Arena caused a memorable traffic jam, Sidney Salomon, Jr., and Sidney Salomon III, owners and operators of the Arena and of the St. Louis Blues hockey team, proposed a parking lot inside Forest Park. They would pay, they said, to tear down the obsolete incinerator on the proposed site. In its place they would build a parking lot (connected to the Arena by a covered walkway), useful to park visitors and junior

college students as well as to hockey fans. For events at the Arena, they would rent the lot from the city. Mayor Cervantes supported the plan, but opponents were vocal. The *Post-Dispatch* said the unused incinerator could be torn down and the land used to replace land lost to the highway and the Forest Park Expressway. Letter writers to both the *Post-Dispatch* and the *Globe-Democrat* objected to the use of the land for a private business. The City Plan Commission denied the proposal in May 1969 because it "conflicted with the policy of preserving park land for recreation."[66]

In late 1972 the question was again that of parking, this time for the hospital complex on Kingshighway. Park officials generally overlooked use of the park for overflow parking by hotels near the northeastern edge of the park, probably because it usually occurred at night when the park was not full. Parking by staff and visitors of the hospitals clustered near the southeastern corner was a different matter. Repeatedly in the 1950s and 1960s the city had taken action to prevent the use of Forest Park as an "all-day parking lot" for the hospitals, but the problem remained (Fig. 8-48). In 1972 Barnes Hospital proposed an underground parking garage in the section of Forest Park south of the hospitals. After the re-routing of Kingshighway separated the corner from the rest of the park, the park department had found its rose garden difficult to maintain. An architect's rendering showed the proposed garage covered with trees, paths, and a fountain. Response to the plan was generally favorable, and the city accepted it.[67]

After the garage was completed, however, the trees weren't planted and the fountain and paths weren't built. Instead, Barnes built six lighted tennis courts, which the hospital and the park department jointly decided to name for Richard Hudlin. After all the years of controversy about what the southeastern corner of the park would contain, the answer in 1976 was an underground alarm building, a highway cloverleaf, an underground garage, which Barnes Hospital maintained and from which it collected revenue, and tennis courts that the hospital also maintained—probably not the conclusion envisioned by those who had opposed earlier proposals for the corner as far back as the 1920s.

In 1975, perhaps encouraged by the hospital's success, the Salomons tried again for the Arena parking lot. Mayor John H. Poelker supported the proposal, but there was again immediate and vocal opposition. In a controversy that echoed the 1918 arguments over allowing clay mining in the same general area of the park, proponents, including the mayor, argued that the lot was necessary to retain the taxes and jobs provided by Arena operation. Verner I. Burks, chairman of the city's Landmarks Commission, opposed the plan, pointing to the land taken for the zoo's south parking lot and the Barnes Hospital garage. Both a *Globe-Democrat* editorial and a *Post-Dispatch* column suggested that the Democratic mayor and aldermen might be swayed by Salomon's past contributios to the party. A private environmentalist group, the Coalition for the Environment, offered to pay to convert the area to green space. After opponents jammed an aldermanic hearing, the Arena parking lot was not built. Instead the city itself cleaned up the proposed parking lot site. The Coalition for the Environment said the controversy showed the need for a park plan; and representatives of neighborhood groups called for a commission to supervise development of a citywide parks master plan.

The following year, St. Louis Children's Hospital proposed a hospital expansion over several lanes of Kingshighway, some of which were part of the park though they had been used as a city street since the 1930s. The battle resumed and continued after Mayor Poelker signed the ordinance permitting the construction.

This new proposal only strengthened the belief of some members of the St. Louis Chapter of the American Institute of Architects (AIA) that the park needed a comprehensive plan. Major decisions were being made on a case-by-case basis, often after considerable acrimony; no one knew in advance what was acceptable for the park. A plan such as the park had had in the 1870s could define what it should be and who should control it. The AIA chapter invited a team of experts to come to St. Louis in the fall of 1976 to study the park and make recommendations. The team, called a Regional/Urban Design Assistance Team (R/UDAT), included urban planners, a landscape architect, an urban economist, and a lawyer. The team toured the park and interviewed numerous people during its short stay in St. Louis—less than a week. It then issued a report containing its findings and recommendations, including regional control of the park, "getting as many automobiles as possible out of Forest Park," and having the state legislature reestablish the boundaries because of confusion over their location. As a first step, the team recommended collection of data about the park to be used in making a long-range plan.[68]

The report reignited controversy. KMOX-TV called the regional plan "unworkable and unrealistic," because "city voters aren't about to give up control of the park," and "voters of this region aren't going to levy a new tax for improving Forest Park—a facility they already accept as just

8-49. Placement of this wooden Indian head in Forest Park in May 1977 touched off a controversy.

EPILOGUE

While various R/UDAT suggestions were criticized, the idea of a plan for the park was not forgotten. In May 1977 Arthur H. Boundy announced that the Save Kingshighway Fund, a group of park neighbors, landscape architects, and others originally organized to stop the expansion of Children's Hospital, had reorganized as the Forest Park Preservation Fund Charitable Trust to support some of the R/UDAT recommendations.

When Parks Director Georgia Buckowitz accepted a wooden Indian Head for Forest Park that same month, Robert W. Duffy, *Post-Dispatch* arts editor, who found the sculpture "of questionable quality," said she should have asked the city's Landmarks and Urban Design Commission to review the decision. The episode, he said, illustrated the need for a park plan (Fig. 8-49).[70] But the ordinances governing placement of art in public parks were conflicting, the decision was made, and the statue stayed.

Then, the same month, it became apparent that the controversy over the hospital addition wasn't over. The new mayor, James F. Conway, refused to issue building permits for the addition, and the hospital filed a suit, which was later combined with a suit against the addition filed by park neighbor Joseph P. McKenna.[71]

While those cases made their way through the courts, another battle began. In December 1977 the Museum of Science and Natural History announced its plan to pay for, build, and operate an underground museum in the park next to the planetarium. In the early 1970s the science museum had made plans to leave its location in Clayton's Oak Knoll Park, about a mile west of Forest Park. A site selection study by Hellmuth, Obata & Kassabaum, Inc., in 1975 identified the Forest Park area as preferable to other locations such as downtown or west county.

Museum officials probably didn't expect a major outcry. There had been repeated suggestions since the beginning of the century that the science museum should be in Forest Park. The City Plan Commission had twice chosen a plane-

fine." A spokesman for Mayor Poelker called regional control unlikely. He said, "It seems the moment anything in the city becomes desirable or a treasure, there's a movement to extract it from city government." The *Post-Dispatch* commented editorially that the city "has funded and controlled the park with reasonable success since the last quarter of the nineteenth century."[69]

So the story of Forest Park's first century ended as the park had begun—in controversy. However, the terms of the argument had changed considerably. In the 1870s opponents had challenged the park's very existence saying that such a large, remote park was unwise and unnecessary for the city of St. Louis. In the 1970s Forest Park was nearly central in the St. Louis area, both in location and in importance. The discussion by then was how best to preserve this vital metropolitan resource for generations to follow.

8-50. The Forest Park Master Plan Advisory Task Force attempted to allocate park land among varied users, including the golfers, each reluctant to give up any of its territory.

tarium site big enough to hold the museum, and St. Louis County Supervisor Lawrence K. Roos had suggested merging the tax-supported museum and the money-losing planetarium in 1973. The museum had commissioned Hellmuth, Obata & Kassabaum, Inc., architects for the planetarium, to design the museum. Mayor Conway called the planned underground museum "good sense,"[72] and Parks Director Georgia Buckowitz didn't see any problems.

Others, including architects, urban planners, and environmental organizations such as the Coalition for the Environment, objected loudly. The underground building was bad enough, they said, but the planned parking would soon be inadequate, and the science museum would have to ask for more land. They said new development in the park should await completion of a park master plan.

Charles Kindleberger, chief planner for the Community Development Agency (CDA), successor to the City Plan Commission, pointed out that his agency had already begun the planning process. CDA, which had federal funds for planning, had contracted with a private research firm for a study of users and nonusers of the park. The report later circulated in draft form with more than a hundred pages of data from telephone interviews, interviews with people leaving the park, and from the files of the police department and of organizations within the park. That study, too, reflected St. Louisans' approval of the park. More than 90 percent of park users said they were satisfied with the park as it was. In a telephone survey in St. Louis and St. Louis County, more than 60 percent of the people questioned said they used Forest Park as much as or more than other parks, and almost 75 percent said they didn't want any changes in the park.

In September 1978 Mayor Conway did what officials often did with a controversial issue—he appointed a Forest Park Master Plan Advisory Task Force to consider a park plan. The task force included representatives of the groups that had recently been most vocal about the park—the Coalition for the Environment, the American Society of Landscape Architects, the AIA, and the Forest Park Preservation Fund Charitable Trust. Other task force members represented city government—the board of aldermen, the mayor, the park department, the street department, and the parks board. Still others represented those who lived near the park and, later, park users such as the Paramount Golf Club. The task force, along with CDA staff and paid planning consultants, reviewed the available data about the park, interviewed representatives of a variety of organizations within and around the park, and held public hearings and public workshops (Fig. 8-50). Participants in the hearings and workshops included young people, the elderly, residents of the Hi-Pointe area, and representatives of Paraquad, advocates for the disabled. The task force and consultants then tried to draw a plan that would deal successfully with the park's complexity, the numbers of people jockeying for control, and the various pressures on the park.

The task force proposed a plan, but many people strongly objected to parts of it. By the end of 1985 the plan had not been accepted by the city of St. Louis. In the meantime, two of the disputes that had energized the call for a park plan, those over the hospital and the museum of science, had ended. The Missouri Supreme Court had ruled in June 1979 that the method the city had used to transfer the land to St. Louis Children's Hospital was illegal. The hospital then decided to expand within the medical center rather than move or try again to extend over Kingshighway. In the early 1980s science museum officials abandoned their attempt to build in the park. Instead they announced that they would use an office building across Highway 40 from the park and build a link to the planetarium over the highway. Then, in April 1983, voters in city and county approved a tax increase for the science museum. The city sold the planetarium to the museum for one dollar and leased it the land under the building.

The controversy about the plan was only one in a long series of arguments about the park, stretching back more than a century. Like earlier arguments, the disagreement over the plan reflected different ideas of what the park should be and of the proper balance of political power in the St. Louis region. In some ways, the fight over the park plan was good news. It showed clearly that many St. Louisans cared what happened to Forest Park.

Through the years, many St. Louisans had cared about Forest Park, including Hiram Leffingwell, who possessed the two essentials—a vision of the park and the ability to get others to share his vision. It's not clear how much of the first plan for the park was Leffingwell's, how much McKinley's, and how much Kern's, but it is remarkable how much the park of the 1970s and 1980s reflected that 1875 plan. After a hundred years, Forest Park contained the museums, the floral conservatory, and the free zoo the planners had envisioned. One major facility the planners mentioned was missing a hundred years later—a supervised children's playground.

The park became, as the early planners had intended, easily accessible for St. Louisans from all parts of the metropolitan area, as well as large numbers of tourists. Although the city had decided to move large civic celebrations downtown, there were still large gatherings in Forest Park, and there was still plenty to do there. People went there to play or watch league games, to see birds, to sit on the grass, to have a picnic, to enjoy the water, to attend a performance, to see an exhibit, to watch zoo animals, to drive through to work, and for dozens of other reasons. Some observers deplored many of these activities, but all were in the spirit of the original plan, and all brought people to the park.

Of course, from the beginning different people had wanted the park to serve different purposes. Officials had dealt with competing demands by allocating space for various activities and by sometimes formally or informally giving authority to other organizations. In 1976 the park department continued to operate many of the major facilities, including Steinberg Rink, two golf courses, the tennis and handball courts, the field house, the lawns and flowerbeds, the fountains and waterfalls, and the Jewel Box. The zoo and the art museum were city-county governmental agencies, tapping the county's growing wealth and giving representation to county residents. The sports leagues, Triple A, the Missouri Historical Society, and the Municipal Theatre Association continued as private organizations using park facilities under different types of permits, drawing support from residents of the city, the county, and the surrounding region.

Through the years, Forest Park had reflected the city's life and growth. St. Louisans might have preferred to forget certain episodes, notably political payoffs, crime, racial segregation, and pollution of rivers. An accurate understanding of the past, however, could serve as a guide when considering the park's future.

Certainly, Forest Park, like many major public facilities in older cities all over the country, had serious problems in the 1970s and 1980s. Vandalism, aging, and steady use had taken their toll on park facilities, and the city couldn't find the funds for needed major repair or replacement. Even with the River des Peres underground, northern sections of the park often flooded after heavy rains. The park's boundaries were unclear, even to those who had tried to study the matter. Supplying adequate roads and parking spaces was a continuing problem.

Yet Forest Park's history could be reassuring to those considering these problems. Forest Park administrators had faced similar difficulties in the past, and the park had survived them all. Money for maintenance and improvements had almost always been inadequate for what administrators wanted to do. The behavior of some parkgoers had caused complaints since 1885, when the arrival of the streetcars meant more and different people could easily reach the park. Automobile traffic had been a concern since the auto came to St. Louis. Arguments about the appropriate use of park land dated back at least to the early 1890s when the police department took 20 acres for the mounted police over Park Commissioner Jonathan Fechter's strong objections.

Forest Park had always been politically controlled, which sometimes had unfortunate consequences. More often, however, as the 1918 clay mining proposal illustrated, the political process protected the park. Forest Park had a large constituency—all those who went to the park to visit or to drive through as well as many more who considered Forest Park a major asset and perhaps cherished memories of happy times there. Whenever they considered the park threatened, they informed their elected officials of their displeasure.

Forest Park began and survived because it filled the needs of a variety of groups and because it had leaders who perceived these needs. Young or old, wealthy or not, active or passive, all different kinds of people used the park. Hiram Leffingwell had an idea for a great park to serve all of them—an idea he was able to transmit to McKinley, Kern, and their successors. David R. Francis spent years bringing a World's Fair to Forest Park and convinced many of his contempo-

raries to join him. Dwight Davis's vision of a park and playground system brought new recreation facilities to Forest Park. Charlotte Rumbold's pageant led to the construction of an open-air municipal theater in Forest Park and to the use of Art Hill for mass civic celebrations. Davis's and Rumbold's visions, too, inspired their successors.

What Forest Park needed again in the 1970s and 1980s was some individual or group that could look at the facility as a whole, define and balance conflicting needs, make plans, and generate funds. Groups such as the Forest Park Associates, the R/UDAT, and the master planners had tried to do some of these things, but no one was doing them on a continuing basis. The city park department, overwhelmed with the day-to-day problems of keeping parks and playgrounds operating all over the city with an inadequate budget, probably had neither the time nor the energy to tackle such questions.

Forest Park visitors in the 1970s and 1980s enjoyed the many park attractions that past park departments had added over the years. Each year in the 1970s and 1980s more than four million visitors found Forest Park a place of entertainment, recreation, and relaxation. Uncounted thousands or millions drove through on the park's drives, on the Forest Park Expressway, or on Highway 40. The drivers could take pleasure from their view of the park's trees and flowers, or chuckle over the planetarium's Christmas ribbon, or remember trips to the zoo, or catch a glimpse of a game on one of the park's playing fields. All these people, and many others, considered Forest Park essential to St. Louis.

There was little doubt, given the variety of needs the park served, that the park would continue to be, with or without a plan, the focus of controversy for contending groups in the region. There was also little doubt, given St. Louisans' continuing concern and affection for the park, that those who cared about it would find a way to ensure that Forest Park would continue to be a major regional resource and recreation ground into the twenty-first century.

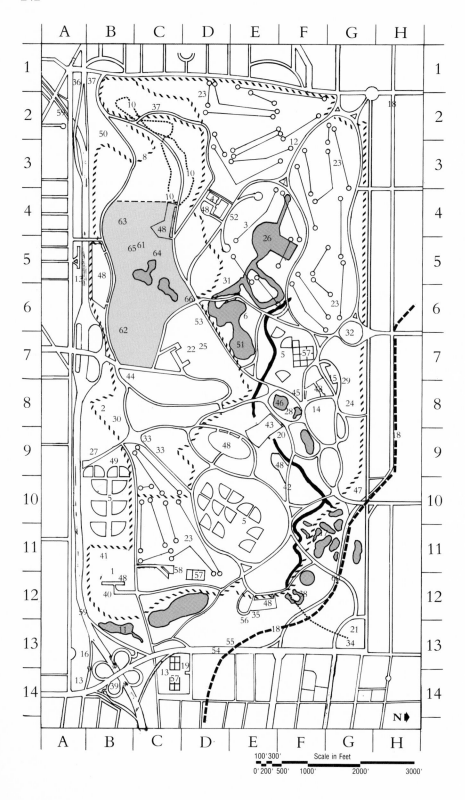

PARK LOCATOR MAP (1945–1976)

1. Archery range, B-11
2. Arena parking lot (proposed), B-8
3. Art Hill, E-4
4. Art Museum, St. Louis (formerly City Art Museum), expansion, D-4
5. Athletic fields: Aviation Field, B-9 to 11; central fields, D-11 to E-10; Langenberg Field, F-6 and 7
6. Baitcasting clubhouse and docks, E-6
7. Bates, Edward, statue, F-3
8. Bicycle path (formerly bridle path), C-3 and throughout park
9. Bicycle track (removed), A-13 and B-14
10. Bird sanctuary, B-2 to D-3
11. Bowl Lake, B-13
12. Cascades waterfall, F-2
13. Children's playgrounds, A-5, A-14, C-13
14. Cricket field, F-8
15. Field house, G-7
16. Fire and Police Alarm Center, A-13
17. Fish hatcheries (including parts of former Sylvan Lake; the hatcheries are now closed), F-11 to G-10
Forest Park centennial marker (see 7, F-3)
18. Forest Park Expressway, F-13 to H-1
19. Forest Park Parking Center, underground (Barnes Hospital Parking Garage), C-13
20. Fountain (near Municipal Theatre), F-8
21. Fountain, Triangular, G-13
Frank, Nathan, Bandstand (see 46, F-8)
22. Frankenthal Memorial Drinking Fountain (removed), D-7
23. Golf courses: Eisenhower Municipal, 18-hole, D-1 to G-6; 9-hole municipal, G-2 to G-6; Triple A, 9-hole, C-9 to D-11
24. Golf course driving range, G-8
25. Government Hill and illuminated fountain, D-6 and 7
26. Grand Basin, E-4 and F-5
27. Greenhouses (relocated), B-9
28. Guggenheim, Bertha, Memorial (Pan) Fountain (removed), F-8
29. Handball courts, G-7
Hudlin, Richard, Memorial Tennis Courts (see 57, C-14)
30. Incinerator, B-8
31. Jahn, Friedrich Ludwig, Memorial, D-5
32. Jefferson Memorial building and expansion, G-6
Jefferson, Thomas, statue (see 32, G-6)
33. Jewel Box Gardens, C-9
 Colonial Daughters Fountain
 Floral Clock
 Lamppost (moved from Lindell-Kingshighway intersection)
 Lander Drinking Fountain
 Rose gardens

 St. Francis of Assisi, statue
 Shields, Mary Leighton, Sundial (second location)
 Vandeventer Place gates
34. Jewish First American Settlement Commemorative Monument and Flagpole, G-13
35. *Joie de Vivre*, E-12
36. Junior College District administration building (approximate proposed location), A-1
37. Kennedy, John F., Memorial Forest, A-1 to C-2
38. Lake Louie, F-12
39. Low-rent housing (approximate proposed location), B-14
40. McDonnell Planetarium (later part of St. Louis Science Center), B-12
41. Mounted Police stable (formerly hangar), B-11
42. Municipal Opera Drive (formerly Theatre Drive), F-8 to F-10
43. Municipal Theatre, E-8 and 9
44. Native American (Indian head) statue, B-7
45. O'Neil Fountain (Fountain Angel, removed), F-8
46. Pagoda Lake, F-8
47. Park keeper's house, G-10
48. Parking lots: art museum, D-4; field house, F-7 and 8; municipal theatre, D, E, and F-9; Steinberg skating rink, E-12; McDonnell Planetarium, B-12; zoo, B-5, C-4
49. Parks, Recreation and Forestry, Department of, office building, B-9
50. Picnic grounds (expansion), B-2
51. Post-Dispatch Lake, D-6 and 7
52. *St. Louis, Apotheosis of*, statue, E-4
53. St. Louis Award (White Pine Statue), D-6
54. St. Louis Children's Hospital expansion (proposed), D-13
55. Steinberg, Mark C., Memorial Skating Rink (approximate proposed location), E-13
56. Steinberg, Mark C., Memorial Skating Rink, E-12
57. Tennis Courts: Davis Tennis Tournament Center, F-7; Hudlin Memorial, C-14; Triple A, D-11 and 12
58. Triple A Clubhouse (second location, third building), C-11
59. U.S. Highway 40 (Daniel Boone Expressway), A-1 to C-14
 Veterans' hospital (proposed; see 39, B-14)
60. Wabash Bridge, G-11

Zoo (St. Louis Zoological Park)

61. Aquatic House, C-4
62. Big Cat Country, B-6
63. Cheetah Survival Center, B-4
64. Children's Zoo, C-5
65. Elephant House (second location), B-5
66. Kiener Gate, D-6

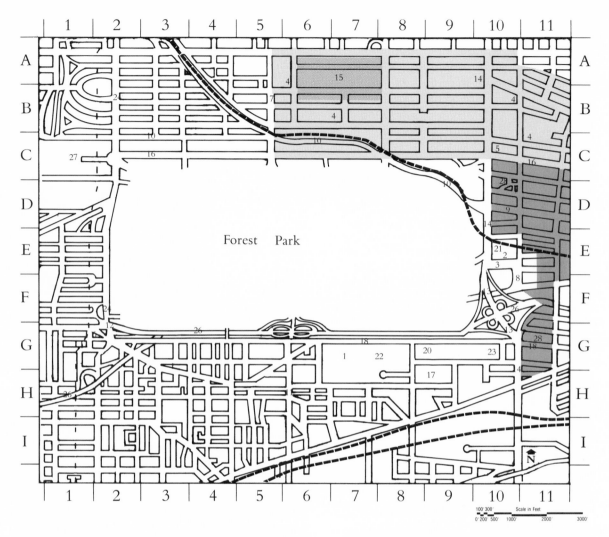

NEIGHBORHOOD LOCATOR MAP
(1945–1976)

1. Arena, G-7
2. Barnes Hospital, E-10
3. Barnes Hospital Plaza (formerly Kingshighway Boulevard), E-10
4. Central West End Historic District, A-5 to C-11
5. Chase-Park Plaza Hotel, C-10
6. Cheshire Inn, G-1
7. DeBaliviere Avenue, A-5 to C-5
8. Euclid Avenue (formerly Kingshighway Boulevard), E and F-11
9. Forest Park Avenue, D-10 and 11
10. Forest Park Expressway (Rock Island Expressway), C-2 to D-10
Forest Park Highlands, removed (see 22, G-7 and 8)
11. Hampton Avenue, G-6 to I-6
12. Hi-Pointe corner, G-2

13. Kingshighway Boulevard (new section), E-10 to G-10
14. Kingshighway Boulevard (existing section), A-10 to E-10; G-10 to I-10
15. Kingsbury-Washington Terrace Historic District, A-6 to B-7
16. Lindell Boulevard, C-2 to C-11
17. Missouri Stables (removed), H-9
18. Oakland Avenue, G-1 to G-11
19. Office building (later used by St. Louis Science Center), G-9
20. Restaurant and motel, G-9
21. St. Louis Children's Hospital, E-10
22. St. Louis Community College, Forest Park Campus, G-7 and 8
23. St. Louis University High School, G-10
24. Skinker Boulevard, A-2 to F-2
25. Union Boulevard, A-8 to C-8
26. U.S. Highway 40 (Daniel Boone Expressway), H-1 to F-11
27. Washington University, Brookings Hall, C-1
28. Washington University Medical Center Historic District and Redevelopment Area, C-10 to G-11

Appendix 1. BUILDINGS, STATUES, AND MONUMENTS*

BUILDINGS STANDING IN 1985
(not including the zoo)

Art Museum (1, D-4)

Built of Bedford gray limestone and Roman brick about 1904 for Louisiana Purchase Exposition (St. Louis World's Fair) by LPEC Architect Cass Gilbert. Cost more than $610,000. Used during fair, along with two temporary annexes, as Fine Arts Palace. Given to city by LPEC as part of World's Fair site restoration. Occupied in 1906 by School and Museum of Fine Arts, a department of Washington University, and opened to public August 1906. In February 1909 occupied by City Art Museum (later St. Louis Art Museum). After that, all additions and renovations paid for with art museum funds.

Restaurant addition built in 1954–55. Auditorium wing built in 1959 at cost of about $1 million, designed by Murphy and Mackey. Administration wing built in 1977–1980 at cost of about $7.5 million, designed by Howard Needles Tammen & Bergendoff. Renovation of west wing of Cass Gilbert structure in 1961–1962 cost $450,000. Major renovation of east wing in 1975–1977 cost $8,013,850, designed by Hardy Holzman Pfeiffer Associates. Underground addition to administrative wing, a basement extension for conservation labs and some service operations designed by Smith & Entzeroth, built in 1984–85 at a cost of $2.4 million. In September 1985, the west wing closed for renovation. Scheduled to reopen in August 1987 after work expected to cost $12.6 million.

Baitcasting Clubhouse (2, E-6)

Constructed late 1930s on edge of Post-Dispatch Lake. Used as headquarters for Forest Park Baitcasting Club.

Davis, Dwight F., Tennis Tournament Center (3, F-7)

Opened June 1966. Total cost more than $200,000. City appropriations totaled $75,000. Private contributions made up the rest. (Also on this site, Davis Center Plaques.)

*The numbers in parentheses following the name of each structure are the location number and coordinates on the map on p. 268. Some locations contain or have contained more than one structure. Costs were paid by the city unless otherwise noted.

Field House and Restaurant (4, G-7)

Built on foundation of Lindell Pavilion after pavilion destroyed by fire in 1925. Dedicated September 10, 1927. Cost $150,000. Contained athletic locker facilities, pro shop, restaurant, and refreshment stand. Financed by bond issue funds. Exploded and burned November 7, 1949. Laclede Gas Co. paid $80,000 for reconstruction and repair. (Previously on this site, Lindell Pavilion.)

Fire and Police Alarm Center (5, A-13)

Voters approved bonds in August 1944. Originally planned for site outside the park, but the cost of land later considered prohibitive. Completed in 1958, but not activated until March 1964, when availability of cable sheathed in polyvinyl chloride instead of lead brought costs to an affordable level.

Fish Hatchery Building (6, G-11)

Built in 1938–39 by the U.S. Bureau of Fisheries. In use by August 1939. Exterior of Missouri limestone. Topped by copper weather vane in the shape of a fish. Replaced earlier building whose dates are uncertain but which was considered dilapidated by 1938. In early 1980s used as residence for park keeper.

Forest Park Parking Center, underground (7, C-13)

Authorized in 1973. Constructed and operated by Barnes Hospital, contained 1,208 parking spaces underground, Hudlin Memorial Tennis Courts above. Extension authorized in 1983 to allow garage to occupy a total of 728,100 square feet and to contain 1,945 parking spaces. Cost of extension $9 million, including landscaping, exercise and fitness center, four racquetball courts, and children's playground above it, all to be dedicated to the city for public use. Barnes Hospital to maintain center and pay city $50,000 a year, amount to be increased if hospital increased parking fees. (Also on this site, Hudlin Memorial Tennis Court Marker previously on this site.)

Frank, Nathan, Bandstand (8, F-8)

Dedicated October 18, 1925. Donated by Nathan Frank. Designed by Heffensteller, Hirsch and Watson. Cost about $50,000. Renovated in June 1981 with $13,000 from Central West End Charitable Trust, raised by Central West End Association. Several firms and individuals also donated services for restoration. (Previously on this site, Music Pagoda and Spring, Summer, Fall, and Winter.)

Greenhouses, relocated (9, B-9)

First greenhouse in Forest Park built in 1892. All park department greenhouses consolidated into Forest Park in 1897. Gardener's lodge next to greenhouses was the gardener's residence at least 1897 to 1931, later removed. Additional greenhouses constructed at various times over the years. One of the greenhouses used as floral display house (or Jewel Box) from 1916 until 1936. Several greenhouses had to be relocated in 1962 for construction of Highway 40. A suggestion at that time that the replacement greenhouses should be built outside the park was not adopted.

9

Hangar Building (Mounted Police Stable) (10, B-11)

U.S. Army hangar donated by army and erected about 1919 for U.S. air mail service. Cost of erection paid half by city and half by St. Louis Chamber of Commerce. Left when air mail service discontinued in 1921. Used as storage building by park department. Then taken over by mounted police when they were reestablished in 1970.

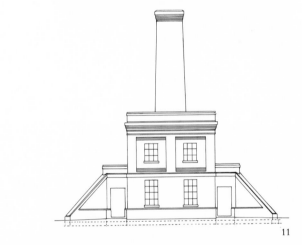
10

Incinerator (11, B-8)

Built in 1928 by E. A. Brunson Construction Co. Cost less than $15,000.

Jefferson Memorial (12, G-6)

Constructed and given to city by LPEC as part of rebuilding of fair site. Ground breaking April 8, 1911; cornerstone laying May 1, 1911; dedication April 30, 1913. Designed by Isaac S. Taylor and Oscar Enders. Cost $450,000 to $480,000. At first, Missouri Historical Society (MHS) used east wing. West wing used as meeting rooms for various civic groups and, later, as rehearsal hall for Municipal Theatre Association. Lindbergh trophies displayed in east wing beginning in June 1927. By 1947, MHS occupied entire building except furnace room, public rest rooms, and some small storerooms. Public rest rooms closed and removed about 1972, so that MHS occupied the entire building. Underground addition designed by Sverdrup and Parcel and Associates. Paid for by MHS, but became city property as soon as completed. Cost $807,557. Ground breaking May 1970; dedication April 29, 1972. In 1983–1984 central courtyard of addition roofed over as Isaac H. Lionberger Courtyard Gallery by MHS, financed by gift from Anne L. Lehmann in honor of her father. Designed by John Dean and Associates. Dedicated October 3, 1984. On April 30, 1985, MHS dedicated the cleaned and newly glass-enclosed loggia. The renovation was financed by the Whitaker Chari-

11

12

table Foundation and Mr. and Mrs. Edward Bakewell, Jr. Approximate cost $325,000; architect Heinz Zobel. (Also on this site, Thomas Jefferson statue, Stupp Memorial Fountain, and Memorial to the Frontier Women of the French and Spanish Colonies in Missouri.)

Jewel Box (St. Louis Floral Conservatory) (13, C–8)

Dedicated November 14, 1936. Design by City Engineer William C. E. Becker. Cost more than $100,000, paid in part (probably 45 percent) with Public Works Administration (PWA) funds. Contractor Robert Paulus Construction Company. Replaced earlier "Jewel Box" displays inside one of Forest Park greenhouses. Chimes donated in 1951 by Harry J. Kiener. Waterfall added in 1978; designed by Booker Associates; paid for out of federal block grant funds.

13

McDonnell Planetarium (part of St. Louis Science Center) (14, B–12)

Officially opened April 1, 1963. Built on the site of the Mounted Police Station. Dedicated May 30, 1963. Named for James S. McDonnell in 1964. Design by Hellmuth, Obata and Kassabaum. Cost $1.2 million; $850,000 from bond issue funds, $150,000 from other city funds, $200,000 from James S. McDonnell and McDonnell Aircraft Corporation Foundation. Closed October 1983. Sold to Museum of Science and Natural History January 1, 1984, for $1.00.

Reopened July 20, 1985, as the St. Louis Science Center following renovation costing $3 million and financed with science center funds, including large contributions from Emerson Electric Charitable Trust ($400,000). the McDonnell Douglas Foundation ($400,000), the Monsanto Fund ($600,000), and the James S. McDonnell Foundation (matching grant of $1.4 million). Renovation designed by Henderson Gantz Architects. (Previously on this site, Mounted Police Station.)

14

Municipal Theatre (15, E–8, E–9)

Site first used in June 1916 for performances of *As You Like It* and again in August 1916 for a minstrel show. Permanent theater, designed in part by Tom P. Barnett, built in 1917 at cost of about $20,000. Different accounts of how cost was distributed, but likeliest is Advertising Club of St. Louis, $4,000; St. Louis Fashion Show, $2,000; and the city, $14,000. Opened June 5, 1917, with performance of *Aida*. First Fashion Show held in August 1917. First performances by Municipal Theatre Association in 1919. Numerous additions over the years, paid for in part from revenues of various groups using theater.

15

Box office pavilion in 1939 designed by Murphy and Wischmeyer. Paid for in part by PWA funds.

Park Keeper's House (16, G-10)

Constructed by Forest Park commissioners as administration building. Designed by J. H. McNamara. Completed by June 1876. Used as offices by commissioners, then as residence by park keepers until early 1920s, then by parks superintendents or commissioner of parks and recreation until 1966. House was damaged by fire in 1966 and remained vacant until City Beautification Commission used as office in 1967. Then used by Bicentennial Commission. After 1976 used by Recreation Division under name of Cabanne House. In early 1980s vacant and unused.

16

Parks, Recreation and Forestry, Department of, Office Building (17, B-9)

Completed 1960. Designed by Rathman, Koelle, and Carroll. Paid from 1955 bond issue funds. Park department staff moved from Municipal Courts building downtown. At the same time the department built a new shop building, boiler house, underground steam system, soil shed, and a garage at the administrative area.

17

Steinberg, Mark C., Memorial Skating Rink (18, E-12)

Opened November 11, 1957. Designed by Frederick Dunn architect and Frank Hamig engineer. Design was one of three cited by American Institute of Architects when Dunn elected a fellow in 1962. Cost about $1 million paid one-third by city and two-thirds by Mark C. Steinberg Charitable Trust.

Triple A (Amateur Athletic Association) Clubhouse, Third (19, C-11)

Built with Triple A funds on same site in 1977 after previous clubhouse burned to the ground. (Previously on this site, Triple A Clubhouse, second.)

18

Workshops and Stable (20, B-9) (not shown)

Completed in 1918. Workshops housed park department carpenters, painters, plumbers, machinists, blacksmiths, and auto mechanics. Stables sheltered horses and mules that worked in parks. In early 1940s department horses and mules moved to Mounted Police Station, vacated by police department, and stables were converted to additional shop and storage facilities.

19

World's Fair Pavilion (21, D-7)

Designed by Henry Wright. Constructed by LPEC in 1909–1910 and given to city as part of World's Fair site reconstruction. Cost about $35,000. Also called Jefferson Pavilion at first, later only called World's Fair Pavilion. Exterior restored in 1980 at cost of $300,000 to $350,000, including cost of rehabilitating illuminated fountain on Government Hill. (Previously on this site, Frankenthal Fountain and Mary Leighton Shields Sundial.)

21

BUILDINGS REMOVED BY 1985**
(excluding the zoo)

Cabanne House (22, F-13)

Built with private funds before 1876 as private residence near eastern edge of land that became Forest Park. Used as offices by the park superintendent and the park engineer until headquarters building near Union was completed. Torn down, probably in early 1882.

22

Cottage Restaurant, First (Forsyth House) (23, G-8)

Built with private funds before 1876 as private residence. Used as Cottage Restaurant by Aimee Garnier until 1878, by George D. Rilling from 1880 to 1881, by C. W. Herbert from 1881 to 1884. Used as extension of picnic ground concession by E. R. James from 1884 to 1885. Reopened as restaurant in 1885 by Charles Schweickardt. Torn down by Schweickardt in 1893.

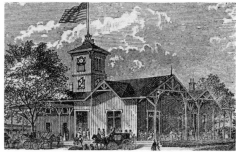

23

Cottage Restaurant, Second (24, D-7) (not shown)

Constructed in 1893 by Charles Schweickardt. Required by city to cost "not less than" $15,000 of Schweickardt's money and to become city property. Burned May 14, 1894.

Cottage Restaurant, Third (24, D-7)

Constructed in 1894 by Charles Schweickardt in same location as previous building and became city property. Operated by him as restaurant until end of March 1904, when his lease expired. Closed in April 1904 and not reopened. Demolished by city during winter of 1907–8.

***Construction costs were paid by the city unless otherwise noted.

24

Laclede Pavilion (33, G-13)

Built as streetcar pavilion by Forest Park, Laclede, and Fourth Street Railway Co. Designed by Eames and Young. Cost at least $25,000. Completed by 1893 and became city property. Closed in 1938 after a portion of floor collapsed. Building torn down in 1938, leaving only towers, which housed an electric substation and public rest rooms. Boys of NYA (National Youth Administration) cleared away bricks and debris. Towers torn down in 1942. (For additional items that are or were at this location, see Fountain, Triangular.)

33

Lindell Pavilion (4, G-7)

Completed in 1892 as streetcar pavilion by Lindell Railway Co., required by city as condition of being awarded route to spend at least $25,000 on shelter, which immediately became city property. Designed by firm of Eames and Young in Spanish style. Ceased to be streetcar shelter when Lindell tracks removed from park for 1904 World's Fair. Remodeled in 1914 as locker room and pro shop for golf and tennis players. Destroyed by fire October 16, 1925. Only a portion of the clock tower remained. Replaced by Field House and Restaurant.

4

Mounted Police Station (14, B-12)

Completed August 1894. Financed and owned by St. Louis Police Department. Architect W. J. Legg; contractor Kelly & Lawton; brickwork by W. J. Baker. Took a year to build and cost $46,570. Police Department moved out in middle 1930s. Park department took over and used for shops. In the early 1940s renovated as stable for park department horses and mules. Used during the 1950s as headquarters for the St. Louis Office of Civil Defense, which moved from City Hall in late 1952. Torn down in 1960.

14

Music Pagoda (Bandstand) (8, F-8)

Wooden. Of Syrian design. Architect James Stewart. Cost Forest Park Commissioners about $7,000. Completed by June 1876. Closed as unsafe by 1911. Damaged beyond repair by storm, wreckage burned, probably around 1912. (Replaced by Nathan Frank Bandstand.)

Police Substation (25, E-10)

Constructed 1890 and financed by St. Louis Police Department. Cost almost $5,500. Meteorological observatory established in tower by 1891. At that time a marker was installed with inscription on the main face: on the main face, "Above City Directorix 80.073 Ft. Forest Park Meteorological Station 1880"; then proceeding counterclockwise: "Above Mean Line Gulf of Mexico 492.783 Ft.

8

/ Latitude 38 [degree sign] 38' 24".03 / Longitude 90 [degree sign] 16' 28".32"

All police department activities moved to mounted police station in August 1894. Building then used as housing for park department employees. For example, zoo keeper Charles Angermeyer lived there with his family at the turn of the century. Weather observatory remained at least until 1896. Police substation torn down some time between 1958 and 1963.

Triple A (St. Louis Amateur Athletic Association) *Clubhouse, First* (26, F-5)

Built with St. Louis Amateur Athletic Association funds in 1897–98. Sold for $2,000 to Louisiana Purchase Exposition Co. in 1901.

Triple A Clubhouse, Second (19. Triple A Clubhouse, third, C-11)

Designed by G. F. A. Brueggeman. Built with Triple A funds in 1901 to replace previous clubhouse vacated to make way for 1904 World's Fair. Officially opened January 1, 1902. Wooden. Burned to ground in November 1976. (Replaced by third Triple A Clubhouse.)

STATUES AND MONUMENTS STANDING IN 1985
(excluding the zoo)

Bates, Edward, statue, second location (27, F-3)

Unveiled at first location, June 24, 1876 (see first location, 46, B-13). Sculptor J. Wilson McDonald. Bronze, on pedestal of red granite from quarries near Pilot Knob, Mo. Cost about $11,000. Pedestal by McBane & Lee, approximate cost $6,750. Inscription carved in pedestal: "Bates." On sides of the pedestal are portrait heads of Capt. James B. Eads, Gov. Hamilton R. Gamble, Charles Gibson, and Henry S. Geyer.

Statue originally intended for Lafayette Park. St. Louis County appropriated $5,000 for the Lafayette Park statue. The Bates Association, especially its president Charles Gibson and his supporter James B. Eads, raised about $3,000. The remaining $3,000 paid by the Forest Park Commissioners. Moved in 1934–1935 to make way for construction of the Oakland Express Highway (later Highway 40).

Bates helped frame Missouri's first state constitution. He became first U.S. cabinet member who lived west of the Mississippi River when appointed Secretary of War in 1850 by President Millard Fillmore. He never served in the position, however, resigning as soon as he heard of his appointment. Many Republicans supported Bates for

25

26

19

president in 1860, but the nomination went to Abraham Lincoln, who appointed Bates attorney general. (For additional item on this site see Forest Park Centennial Marker.)

Blair, Francis Preston, Jr., statue (28, G-13)

Unveiled May 21, 1885. Sculptor Wellington W. Gardner.

Bronze statue on granite pedestal. Cost about $10,000.

Statue donated by Blair Monument Association and presented to Mayor David R. Francis by Association president Peter L. Foy. Pedestal paid for by city.

Inscription on front (east) of pedestal: "Frank P. Blair, Jr., Born Feb'y 19, 1821—died July 8, 1875"; on back of pedestal: "This monument is raised to commemorate the indomitable free-soil leader of the west; the herald and standard bearer of freedom in Missouri; the creator of the first volunteer Union army in the South; the saviour of the state from secession; the patriotic citizen-soldier, who fought from the beginning to the end of the war; the magnanimous statesman, who, as soon as the war was over, breasted the torrent of proscription, to restore to citizenship the disfranchised southern people, and finally, the incorruptible public servant."

Blair lived as a child in Washington, D.C., where his father owned and edited the *Washington Globe*. After Blair settled in St. Louis in 1847, he served at various times as a member of the Missouri Legislature, a United States representative, and a United States Senator from Missouri. In the Union army he attained the rank of major-general. His brother, Montgomery Blair, was one of Dred Scott's lawyers and served in Lincoln's cabinet with Edward Bates. Although one of the organizers of the Republican party, Frank Blair left it because of his opposition to the reconstruction policies and was the Democratic candidate for vice president in 1868.

Colonial Daughters Fountain (29, C-9)

Built 1947 by park department employees. Concrete fountain and pool. Contribution of $350 from the Colonial Daughters of the 17th Century.

Inscription on small plaque in ground nearby: "Dedicated by Missouri Society Colonial Daughters Seventeenth Century 1947." (Also at this location, Floral Clock, Lamppost, Vandeventer Place Gates.)

Confederate Memorial (30, G-8)

Unveiled December 15, 1914. Sculptor George Julian Zolnay. Bronze high relief of southern family on granite shaft showing spirit of the south in low relief. Cost about $20,000. Donated by the Ladies' Confederate Monument Association.

27

28

29

Inscription on front (south side) of shaft: "Erected in memory of the soldiers and sailors of the Confederate States by the United Daughters of the Confederacy of St. Louis";
on back of shaft:

> To the memory of the soldiers and sailors of the Southern Confederacy, who fought to uphold the right declared by the pen of Jefferson and achieved by the sword of Washington. With sublime self sacrifice, they battled to preserve the independence of the states which was won from Great Britain, and to perpetuate the constitutional government which was established by the fathers. Actuated by the purest patriotism they performed deeds of prowess such as thrilled the heart of mankind with admiration. "Full in the front of war they stood," and displayed a courage so superb that it gave a new and brighter luster to the annals of valor. History contains no chronicle more illustrious than the story of their achievements; and although, worn out by ceaseless conflict and overwhelmed by numbers, they were finally forced to yield. Their glory, "on brightest pages penned by poets and by sages, shall go sounding down the ages." "We had sacred principles to maintain and rights to defend for which we were in duty bound to do our best, even if we perished in the endeavor." Robert E. Lee

on bottom of north of base:

> George Julian Zolnay, Sculptor/Wilbur Tyson Trueblood, Architect/Frederick Charles Bonsack, Consulting Architect/Charles Axtall Rosebrough, Builder

on east base of bronze:

> G. J. Zolnay 1914

Small bronze plaques with letters "U D C" on south side of base, space on north side where similar plaque had been.

Davis, Dwight F., Tennis Center and Stadium Plaques (3, F-7)

Installed about 1966 to acknowledge donations to the center.

Inscriptions: "In memory Rae Samuels Linden and Teddy R. Samuels from the Samuels Families"; "Howard V. Stephens, Jr. Memorial Court"; "Donated by Joseph Sunnen"; "Laura Sproule Love Court"; "In memory of David P. Wohl"; "Claude I. Bakewell, Jr. Memorial Court"; "Andrew W. Johnson Memorial Court Donated

30

3

by his friends"; "Joseph L. Werner Memorial Court"; "Louis D. Beaumont Stadium." (Also on this site, Davis Tennis Center.)

Floral Clock (29, C-9)

Dedicated July 2, 1951, to all St. Louisans who participated in the Korean War. Design by Henry Ochs, City Floriculturist. Underground mechanism constructed by Russell Vance. Electrically operated, 35 feet in diameter. (Much smaller than 112-foot diameter floral clock just outside the park as part of the 1904 World's Fair.) Aluminum hands. Face and three-foot wide numbers of flowers.

Floral inscription: "Hours and flowers soon fade away"; granite plaque at bottom of clock: "Korean War Memorial Dedicated by Mayor Joseph M. Darst July 2, 1951." Floral numbers and inscription later replaced by concrete. (For additional items on this site, see Colonial Daughters Fountain.)

29

Forest Park Centennial Marker (27, F-3)

Dedicated 1976. Bronze plaque on granite.

Inscription: "In commemoration of the foresight of dedicated St. Louisans in preserving park space and the Centennial of Forest Park June 25, 1976 This monument presented by the Bicentennial Committee of the Board of Aldermen of the City of St. Louis Paul J. Simon, President/Frank C. Boland, Chairman/Eugene O. Bradley, Vice Chairman/Delores Glover/Alfred Giuffrida/Albert Holst, Sr./Vincent C. Schoemehl, Jr./John H. Poelker/Mayor, City of St. Louis/Georgia L. Buckowitz/Director of Parks.

27

Fountain (31, F-8)

Installed 1972. Designed by Robert Charles Smith. Five concrete pillars, concrete pool. Commissioned by Municipal Theatre Association.

31

Fountain, Illuminated (32, D-7)

Oval concrete pool with large fountain and one hundred smaller jets; drains over brownstone cascades into rectangular brownstone pool. Illuminated by lights of changing colors. Constructed by city in 1930.

Construction complicated by discovery of cinders and plaster under site, probably debris from the World's Fair used as fill. Shut off for repairs in 1975, restarted briefly in 1980, after renovation of fountain and World's Fair Pavilion costing almost $400,000. In operation again in 1983 after repairs costing $3,000 to $4,000.

32

Fountain, Triangular (33, G-13)

Concrete. Constructed by city in 1958–59 to encourage passive recreation. Improvements, including fountain, cost $10,000.

Reported in 1979 to be out of service because of an electrical problem. Operating properly in 1985. (For additional items that are or were on this site, see Laclede Pavilion, *Waves, Memories, Reflections,* and O'Neil Fountain.)

33

Jahn, Friedrich Ludwig, Memorial (34, D-5)

Unveiled October 11, 1913. Sculptor Robert Cauer. Bronze with stone base, granite steps. Cost about $14,000. Donated by Jahn Monument Committee, Otto F. Stifel chairman.

Inscription on stone plaques with gilded letters. On left side of pedestal: "Dedicated by the Nord Americanischen Turnerbund Oct. 1913/ Rededicated August 15, 1972 American Turners Sound Mind Sound Body"; under statue: "Friedrich Ludwig Jahn The Father of Systematic Physical Culture"; on right end of pedestal: "Dedicated by the North American Gymnastic Union Oct. 1913"; space below where plaque removed. On plaques around semicircle, beginning at left: "Ohio/South Central," North Pacific/Southern California," "Kansas/Missouri New Orleans," "Up. Mississippi/Connecticut," "Indiana/Chicago," "New England/New Jersey"; to right of central plaque: "New York/St. Louis," "Wisconsin/ Philadelphia," "Pittsburg/Minnesota," "Rocky Mountain/Pacific," "Illinois/Middle Atlantic," "Western New York/Lake Erie." On lower right of rear of bust: "Robert Cauer/Darmstadt." On lower left of rear of bust: "geg Lauchhammer."

Jahn was the founder of the Turnverein, an international gymnastic and fraternal society. He was called the "father of gymnastics" and was often referred to as "Father Jahn" or "Vater Jahn." He lived and died in Germany. The small statues of athletes were often vandalized or removed.

34

Jefferson, Thomas, statue (12, G-6)

Unveiled April 30, 1913, as part of dedication of Jefferson Memorial building. Sculptor Karl Bitter, who had been Chief of Sculpture for the World's Fair. Marble on granite base. Given to city by LPEC as part of park reconstruction.

Inscription on front (north) of base: "Thomas Jefferson."

The statue weighed sixteen tons and was carved in place. Jefferson was the third president of the United States and was primarily responsible for the Louisiana Purchase, celebrated by the fair.

12

Jewish Tercentenary Flagpole/Jewish First American Settlement Commemorative Monument (35, G-13)

Dedicated Thanksgiving Day, November 22, 1956. Sculptor for limestone base, Carl Mose. Donor, The American Jewish Tercentenary Committee of St. Louis, chaired by Rabbi Ferdinand M. Isserman of Temple Israel.

Inscription on base west face: "Proclaim liberty throughout the land Who shall ascend into the mountain of the Lord"; on east face, "And none shall make them afraid For the widow for the stranger for the fatherless 1654 1954"; on concrete marker in ground to west: "Commemorating the establishment of the first Jewish settlement in America at New Amsterdam in 1654 Thanksgiving Day 1954"; on two bronze tablets: "American Jewish Tercentenary 1654–1954 Man's Opportunities and Responsibilities under freedom."

Symbol of religious and other United States freedoms and in commemoration of the first Jewish settlers in North America on September 7, 1654.

35

Joie de Vivre (36, E-12)

Unveiled November 9, 1962. A seven-foot bronze cast, one of seven, of a Jacques Lipchitz work completed in 1927. Cost $50,200. Total cost, including landscaping and installation, exceeded $63,500, all donated by Steinberg Memorial Trust.

Inscription on red granite stone: "'Joie de Vivre' Jacques Lipchitz Sculptor."

Frederick Dunn, the Steinberg Rink architect, worked with landscape architect Harriet Bakewell to design the setting. The sculpture was placed on a low cylindrical bronze pedestal in the center of a small square paved with glacial stones from the Minnesota-Wisconsin border, backed by a low limestone wall, with plantings of pyracantha, evergreen ground cover, and a sour gum tree. By 1985 sour gum tree was gone.

36

Kennedy, John F., Forest Markers (37, B-1, B-2, A-1)

Erected about 1964. Granite boulders with bronze plaques.

Paid for with funds donated to *Post-Dispatch* tree-planting campaign.

Inscription in boulders: "John F. Kennedy Memorial Forest"; on bronze plaque on boulder added after this photograph was taken: "Donated by readers of the *St. Louis Post-Dispatch*." Bronze plaque missing from some markers by 1985.

37

Kiel, Henry W., Memorial Tree Marker (33, G-13)

Erected sometime after 1925. Bronze plaque on concrete base.

Inscription: "This tree is dedicated to the Hon. Henry W. Kiel Mayor of St. Louis from 1918 to 1925 by the Womens' Chamber of Commerce."

33

Lamppost, Kingshighway (29, C-9)

Erected in park 1958.

Moved from location in center of intersection of Kingshighway and Lindell to make room for road widening in 1958. Had probably lighted that intersection since 1890s. By 1985 all arms were missing and post was somewhat rusty.

29

Lander Drinking Fountain (42, C-9)

Dedicated June 13, 1953. Designed by Joseph Murphy of Murphy and Mackey to be a comfortable drinking fountain for "even the tiniest tot." Cost $1,500. Financed by bequest from Morris Lander.

Two tall, joined Carnelian granite columns and a separate smaller one close by symbolize a family group.

Inscription on top of joined columns: "Lander Fountain In fond memory of our daughter Celia"; on base of single column: "Joseph D. Murphy and Eugene J. Mackey Architects." Memorial to Lander's daughter Celia, who was killed in an accident December 11, 1938, the first fatality on the Express Highway, and "a lasting symbol of the constant necessity for safety on the highways." Other sites considered—near the Triple A tennis courts or on Government Hill.

42

Langenberg, H. F., Field Markers (38, F-7)

Wood with carved and painted letters. Installed after ordinance named a rugby field for H. F. (Harry) Langenberg in 1983 to honor his commitment to sportsmanship and amateurism for fifty years and to commemorate the Quinquagenary (fiftieth anniversary) of the Missouri Rugby Football Union and the Rambler Rugby Club.

Meteorological Marker (see Police Substation, 25, E-10)

38

Musicians' Drinking Fountain (39, G-2)

Dedicated May 30, 1925. Sculptor Victor Holm; architectural setting by Gabriel Ferrand, both on faculty of Washington University. Panel and tablet of bronze on limestone stele with granite base and two drinking spouts. Separate concrete reflecting pool. Cost about $5,000. Donated by American Federation of Musicians.

Inscription on tablet: "The American Federation of Musicians presents to the City of St. Louis this memorial to Owen Miller and Otto Ostendorf secretary and treasurer, respectively, of the Federation for many years, in grateful appreciation of their devoted services. Anno Domini MCMXXV." Carved in granite base: "MCMXXV."

Native American/Indian Head statue (40, B-7)

Erected 1977. Sculptor Peter Toth. Wood on concrete base. Donated by sculptor, base constructed by park department.

Inscription on wooden plaque on base: "Donated by Peter Toth to symbolize plight of Native Americans 1976."

Toth intended to erect a similar statue in each of the fifty states as "a memorial to the native Americans to illuminate the stark tragedy unsurpassed in the annals of civilized nations." The Forest Park sculpture was the twenty-fourth.

Rosenbaum, Connie, Memorial Tree Marker (41, F-12)

Pink granite marker installed 1975. Inscription: "In Memoriam Connie Rosenbaum 1946–1974."

Connie Rosenbaum worked as a reporter for the *Post-Dispatch* and lived near Forest Park. She had worked for the extension of the bicycle path and used it often. Following her death in 1974 a group of her fellow employees at the *Post-Dispatch* planted a group of trees and installed this marker near the path as one of the memorials to their friend.

St. Francis of Assisi, statue (42, C-9)

Dedicated August 15, 1962. Sculptor Carl Mose. Bronze, 12-foot statue. Donated by Alice M. Turner. (For additional items on this site, see Lander Drinking Fountain, after item 37; and Shields Sundial, after item 44.)

Inscription on bronze plaque: "Presented to the city of St. Louis 1962 by Alice Martin Turner in memory of her husband Harry Turner / He kept Holy his highest hope / Carl C. Mose, Sculptor."

Turner drowned in the Mississippi River in December 1931 after he jumped from the deck of the harbor boat *Erastus Wells*. According to the *Post-Dispatch*, Turner was "known in St. Louis in the 1920s as the eccentric member of a socially prominent family. . . . [He] was the publisher and chief writer of an off-beat magazine called Much Ado, which was in frequent trouble with postal au-

39

40

41

thorities." He had also written articles for William Marion Reedy's magazine the *St. Louis Mirror*, had been one of St. Louis's first automobile salesmen, and driven in automobile races. Some people had objected to the erection of the statue in the park on the grounds that St. Francis specifically represented Roman Catholicism. The *Post-Dispatch* defended the statue on the grounds that St. Francis, famed for his love of nature, was more appropriate for the park than the warrior St. Louis whose statue had been in the park for more than fifty years.

42

St. Louis, Apotheosis of, statue (43, E-4)

Unveiled October 4, 1906. Sculptor Charles H. Niehaus.

Cast in bronze at Winslow Brothers Co. of Chicago, after popularity of temporary "staff" statue at World's Fair. Granite pedestal. Cost $42,285. Given to city by LPEC as part of restoration of Forest Park after 1904 World's Fair.

Inscription on front (north) of base: "Presented to the City of St. Louis by the Louisiana Purchase Exposition Company in commemoration of the Universal Exposition of 1904 held on this site"; on both sides of pedestal: "Saint Louis."

The St. Louis figure from the statue was used as a symbol for the city until replaced, almost entirely, by the Gateway Arch. Cleaned by Phoebe Dent Weil in 1977. Statue's sword broken or stolen and replaced in 1970, 1972, 1977, and 1981.

43

St. Louis Award (White Pine) Statue (44, D-6)

Dedicated September 9, 1965. Sculptor Kent Addison. Corten, 9-foot statue of pine tree on concrete pedestal with grove of living pine trees, one for each recipient of St. Louis Award.

Inscription on bronze plaque: "The St. Louis Award established in 1931 by David P. Wohl to honor annually those who had made the most outstanding contribution to the metropolitan St. Louis area"; near bottom of Corten: "K A 65."

Shields, Mary Leighton, Sundial (42, C-9)

Unveiled June 10, 1915, at 21. World's Fair Pavilion (21, E-7). Bronze sundial on granite base. Donated by Missouri Society of the Colonial Dames of America.

Inscription on sundial: "We live in deeds not years"; on granite around dial: "Mary Harrison Leighton Shields"; on bronze plaque at foot of base: "Erected by the Missouri Society Colonial Dames of America A tribute to the memory of Mary Harrison Leighton Shields who orga-

44

42

nized the society in 1896 and was for seventeen years its president 1913."

Located on terrace of World's Fair Pavilion. Later moved to this location in Jewel Box gardens.

Sigel, Franz, statue (45, F-8)

Unveiled June 23, 1906. Sculptor Robert Cauer.

Bronze on pedestal. Cast at Lauchhammer foundry in Saxony (later part of Germany). Cost about $10,000. Donated by Sigel Monument Association, Judge Leo Rassieur, president.

Inscription on front (north) of base: "To remind future generations of the heroism of the German-American patriots of St. Louis and vicinity in the Civil War of 1861 to 1865 General Franz Sigel"; on rear of base, upper right corner: "Executed by Robert Cauer Sculptor 1906."

Sigel was born in Germany and came to St. Louis in 1858 as teacher at the German Institute. He had military experience in Germany and at the beginning of the Civil War he organized a regiment of Union volunteers, mostly German-Americans, and became a major-general. He did not return to St. Louis after the war. Funds for the statue were raised from German-Americans throughout the country. President Theodore Roosevelt spoke at a benefit meeting when he went to St. Louis for the dedication of the World's Fair in 1903. Sigel was later the subject of a statue in New York by sculptor Karl Bitter, also financed by German-Americans.

45

Stupp Memorial Fountain (12, G-6)

Dedicated April 15, 1984. Built by Missouri Historical Society from $350,000 bequest by Louise M. Stupp. Designed by Mackey and Associates.

Inscription on south side of fountain rim: "This memorial fountain is dedicated to the history of Missouri and was erected by Louise M. Stupp in memory of her parents, George and Caroline Stupp, and her brother Oscar C. Stupp. 1983"; on side of fountain below inscription: "Mackey and Associates, Architects."

Between fountain and Jefferson Memorial, pavement contained large granite map of Lewis and Clark journey embellished with quotations from the diaries of the Lewis and Clark Expedition.

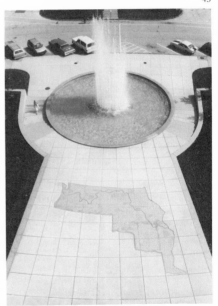

12

Vandeventer Place Gates (29, C-9)

Installed as a backdrop for the Jewel Box rose garden in 1950–51.

Granite with wrought iron gates. "Vandeventer Place" carved in top of each side. By 1985, center carriage gate was missing; only side pedestrian gates remained.

The Federal Government donated the gates to the city after it took a portion of Vandeventer Place for a veterans' hospital, later Cochran Hospital. Vandeventer Place, a

29

private place located several miles northeast of the park, had been a fashionable address in the late 1880s before the exodus to new locations like the private places north of Forest Park.

Waves, Memories, Reflections (33, G-13)

Installed April 4, 1985. Sculptor David King. Steel tubes, pipe, plate, and a ball of welded scraps. Commissioned by Vivace, an event in the St. Louis Arts Festival, as a temporary exhibit.

33

STATUES AND MONUMENTS REMOVED BY 1985 (not including the zoo)

Bates, Edward, (46, B-13) (not shown)

For details of statue, see Bates, Edward, statue second location.

Frankenthal Memorial Drinking Fountain (21, D-7)

21

Erected about 1963. Sculptor Carl Mose. Bronze figure on limestone pedestal. Cost about $3,000. Donated in memory of Alex Frankenthal by his sister.

Inscription: "Come be refreshed. In memory of Alex Frankenthal."

Located on terrace of the World's Fair Pavilion. Stolen and replaced once. After stolen again, not replaced.

Frontier Women of the French and Spanish Colonies in Missouri, Memorial to the, Pioneer Woman Drinking Fountain (12, G-6)

Dedicated October 5, 1929. Became drinking fountain 1941.

Sculptor Nancy Coonsman Hahn. Bronze figure on granite pedestal.

Cost about $5,000. Donated by the Daughters of the American Colonists. Dedicated to the Pioneer Women of Upper Louisiana.

Temporary location at southeastern corner of Jefferson Memorial because of work on River des Peres sewer. Moved in 1941 to a location directly north of the Memorial. Later removed to Missouri Historical Society offices.

12

Guggenheim, Bertha, Memorial (Pan) Fountain (47, F-8)

Unveiled sometime between August 1917 and May 1919. Sculptor Joseph A. Horchert. Limestone. Donated by her husband. Contained drinking fountain.

Located on south edge of lily pond. Removed following repeated vandalism, but pond, benches, and rocks remained.

Hudlin, Richard, Memorial Tennis Courts Marker (7, C-13)

Plaque on stone pedestal. Dedicated 1976 as part of dedication of Hudlin Tennis Courts.

Inscription: "These courts are dedicated to the memory of Richard Hudlin tennis coach 1898 to 1976 by the people of St. Louis, the Parks, Recreation and Forestry Department and Barnes Hospital, October 14, 1976."

Removed for construction of extension of parking center.

Mississippi River Marker (48, C-12) (not shown)

Erected November 3, 1983. Bronze plaque on stand. Donated by Museum of Science and Natural History using grant from Arts and Education Council of Greater St. Louis.

Inscription:
   The Mississippi River Once Flowed Here
   The Mississippi River once flowed here. You are standing, in fact, on the ancient bed of that river. The valley with two small lakes that stretches to the north and south of you is all that remains of the channel cut by the rushing waters of the Mississippi during the Illinoisan glacial stage more than three-hundred thousand years ago.
   Four times during the last two million years, glaciers spawned in eastern Canada spread slowly southward into what is now the United States. Twice these great masses of ice—in places, hundreds of feet thick—crunched into northern Missouri scouring the hills and filling the valleys with debris. The third ice advance, the Illinoisan, left Missouri relatively free of ice but covered most of Illinois. A small lobe of ice, however, did move westward from Illinois and into St. Louis as far as O'Fallon Park and Kingshighway. The ice dammed both the Mississippi and the Missouri rivers causing the waters to back up and form a large, temporary lake that covered much of the north St. Louis area. Unable to break through the dam, the Mississippi cut a new channel around the

47

7

ice lobe through the eastern edge of Forest Park. Once having skirted the ice, the river turned east and flowed down the valley of Mill Creek to regain its present channel. Evidence of the Mississippi's detour through Mill Creek may be seen in the unusually large valley through which the tiny Mill Creek flowed.

Map shows the portion of the Illinoisan glacier and the impounded water of the Mississippi River as they appeared about three-hundred thousand years ago. For reference, the lake and glacier are superimposed upon a modern street grid of St. Louis.

Marker made possible by a grant from the Special Projects Fund of the Arts and Education Council of Greater St. Louis St. Louis Museum of Science and Natural History

Vandalized and removed.

O'Neil Fountain/Fountain Angel (49, F-8)

Erected 1907. For first location, see Fountain, Triangular (33, B-13). Sculptor probably Rafaello Romanelli, not Romano Romanelli. Bronze with concrete basin on marble column, stone pedestal. Base designed by Marimer and Lebaume; cost about $1,000. Donated by David N. O'Neil to honor his father Joseph O'Neil, one of Forest Park Commissioners. Statue displayed at St. Louis World's Fair. After repeated damage by vandals in 1960s, removed from park and placed in storage. Restored by Phoebe Dent Weil and moved to Missouri Botanical Garden in 1975–1976.

Shields, Mary Leighton, Sundial (21, D-7) (not shown)

For details of sundial, see Shields, Mary Leighton, Sundial, pp. 260–61.

Spring, Summer, Fall, Winter (8. Frank Bandstand, F-8) (for picture, see Music Pagoda, p. 251)

Accepted June 8, 1886. Marble. Full-size statues of the four seasons. Donated by Mary J. Rankin, the widow of a marine lawyer. Removed, probably when wooden bandstand was demolished.

Totem Pole, Alaskan (50, C-3)

Presented July 3, 1936. Carved of single redwood and painted in various colors. Presented by Ben Weisman, treasurer of Union-May-Stern Co., to the children of St. Louis. Removed.

49

50

MAJOR ZOO BUILDINGS AND STATUES STANDING IN 1985

Antelope House and Hoofed Animal Yards (51, C-7)

Antelope House opened April 1935; nearby yards finished January 20, 1937. Cost $175,000. Designed by John E. Wallace. Both house and shelters in yards covered with imitation boulders modeled after rock outcroppings found at Graniteville, Mo. For yards, 45 percent of construction costs paid with federal funds.

Aquatic House (52, B-4)

Opened May 6, 1961. Architect John E. Wallace. Renovated 1976. Renovation won 1977 American Association of Zoological Parks and Aquariums award for best new exhibit. Living coral reef exhibit opened September 3, 1981, second in nation after Smithsonian Institution in Washington, D.C.

Baer, Isabel, Drinking Fountain (64, C-6)

Erected 1962. Designed by Gyo Obata. Donated by Howard F. Baer in honor of his wife's birthday. Inscription on side of top spiral: "For Isabel who loves children." The fountain replaced the Mark Twain drinking fountain. Similar fountain, without inscription, in plaza opposite Big Cat Country.

Bear Pits (53, C-5)

First unit opened June 13, 1921. Others opened in 1922. Used thirty-five molds of cliffs above Herculaneum, Mo., made by Victor Borcherdt who had built bear pits in Denver Zoo. Renovated in 1962, including addition of waterfalls and fountains. Cost of renovation paid out of bond issue funds.

Big Cat Country (54, B-6)

Construction began November 1974. Dedicated December 1975. Opened to public May 2, 1976. Designed by Peckham-Guyton, Inc. Cost about $1.5 million.

Bird Cage (55, C-6)

Built in about 1904 for Smithsonian Institution exhibit of birds, part of U.S. Government exhibit at World's Fair. Cost U.S. Government about $17,500 from appropriation for government buildings. Bought by city in

---

†All financed from city appropriations before 1916, from zoo funds afterward unless otherwise noted.

1905 for $3,500, cage's appraised value. Foundation reconstructed in 1909–10. Cage renovated 1967, cost $200,000, plans by Hellmuth, Obata & Kassabaum. Rededicated September 8, 1967. Dimensions: 228 feet long, 84 feet wide, 50 feet high.

Bird House (56, C-6)

Ground breaking November 6, 1929. Opened September 29, 1930, east of the Elephant House and connected to it. Total cost of building almost $240,000. Designed by John E. Wallace. Had glass fronts for the large cages with a screen wire grill on each side so visitors could hear bird songs. Renovated and reopened September 22, 1979. Renovation, designed by Peckham, Guyton, Albers, and Viets, Inc., cost $1.5 million and won American Association of Zoological Parks and Aquariums Significant Achievement Award in 1980.

Elephant House, First (57, C-6)

Built in 1916–17 at cost of $21,706. Designed by T. P. Barnett Co. Completed about May 1917. Remodeled into offices and gift shop for St. Louis Zoo Association after new elephant house opened in 1957. Vacant after Zoo Association moved to new administration building in 1969. Remodeled into Whittaker Room for porcelain birds as adjunct to Bird House in 1979.

Elephant House, Second (58, B-4)

Construction began January 1956. Opened August 4, 1957. Designed by John E. Wallace. Outdoor exercise yards opened summer of 1958. Paid for out of bond issue funds.

Fish Pond (59, C-5)

Erected 1964. Circular concrete. Donated by Mr. and Mrs. Sidney S. Cohen.
Inscription on bronze plaque: "This fish pond was given to the children of St. Louis by Mr. and Mrs. Sidney S. Cohen 1964."

Great Ape Facility (60, C-6)

Ground breaking December 13, 1983. Under construction in 1985. Designed by Peckham, Guyton, Albers, and Viets, Inc. Expected to cost $3 million.

Haglin, Christopher, Memorial Drinking Fountain (61, C-6)

Erected 1969. Bronze on brick pedestal. Designed by William C. Severson, using animals and insects modeled by Haglin's classmates at Ladue Elementary School, later Reed School.

Donated by parents, friends, and classmates of Christopher Paul Haglin who died of natural causes on June 28, 1967, at the age of eleven.

Inscription: "Love is understanding. To the children of St. Louis from Chris and all who loved him." (For previous structure at this location, see Portland Building.)

Mark Twain Drinking Fountain (57, C-6)

Dedicated July 23, 1940. Sculptor Franz Vittor. Bronze statue about 18" high on granite base with semicircular drinking pool. Base by Breen-Thomas Monument Co. of St. Louis. Donated by Miss Ora Hill as memorial to her parents.

Inscription on base: " 'To be good is noble; but to show others how to be good is nobler and no trouble.' Mark Twain [facsimile signature] In loving memory of Dr. James McGee Hill and Rebecca Ellen by their daughter Ora Hill."

Located near center of zoo. Later moved to Aquatic House and then to Whittaker wing of Bird House.

Maschmeyer, Jessie Tennille, Memorial Fountain (Bird Charmer) (55, C-6)

Erected April 18, 1932. Sculptor Walker Hancock. Bronze, on granite base with two drinking bowls. Cost about $12,000. Donated in bequest by Augustus Maschmeyer as memorial to his first wife.

Inscription on front (west) base: "Jessie Tennille Maschmeyer Memorial"; on back of base: "The gift of Augustus Maschmeyer"; near bottom of statue, north side: "Walker Hancock"; east side: "Roman Bronze Works, N Y."

Primate House (62, B-6)

Construction began November 1923. Opened January 12, 1925. Total cost of building exceeded $200,000. Architect John E. Wallace. Renovated at cost of more than $845,000 and reopened June 1977. Renovation architects, Peckham, Guyton, Albers, and Viets, Inc., received outstanding award from Institute of Business Designers and ⟨Interior Design⟩ magazine.

Reptile House (63, B-5)

Opened September 3, 1927. Cost almost $195,000. Architect John E. Wallace. Reopened August 19, 1978, as Herpetarium after renovation costing almost $1 million.

Small Mammal Pits (64, C-6)

Built 1929–30. Construction supervised by C. H. Johnson of Detroit who had worked under Victor Borchert, builder of the Bear Pits.

Vierheller, George P., Fountain; Vierheller Statue (65, D-6)

Dedicated November 23, 1962. Sculptor Richard Frazier. Fountain by Gyo Obata. Bronze statue on concrete base. Circular fountain and pool with brick edging. Cost about $5,000. Donors Mr. and Mrs. Howard F. Baer.

Inscription on bronze plaque on fountain: "This fountain is dedicated to George Philip Vierheller 1882–1966 the first director and devoted builder of the St. Louis Zoo serving from 1919 until his retirement in 1962 he unselfishly gave of himself, to the renown of his institution, and his city."

Inscription on bronze plaque on base of statue: "George Philip Vierheller 1882–1966 The first director and devoted builder of this zoo. Serving from 1919 to 1962, he unselfishly gave of himself to the renown of his institution and his city."

Statue signed on base: "R. Frazier 1962."

Statue later removed from fountain and re-erected near Kiener Gate.

Yalem, Charles H., Children's Zoo (66, C-5)

Ground breaking September 1967. Opened June 14, 1969. Cost more than $840,000. Charles H. Yalem donated $250,000. Designed by Hellmuth, Obata, and Kassabaum.

ZOO BUILDINGS AND STATUES REMOVED BY 1985†

Fighting Sea Lions; Fighting Polar Bears (54, B-6)

Sea Lions erected between June 12, 1917, and April 10, 1918. Bears erected between September 2, 1918, and April 17, 1922. Sculptor Frederick George Richard Roth. Reproduced by Eastman Plastic Relief Co. from statues shown at St. Louis World's Fair. Cost of reproduction, $2,700. Paid by zoo. Both later removed.

†All financed from city appropriations before 1916, from zoo funds afterward unless otherwise noted.

Great Ape House (60, C-6)

Completed August 1939. Designed by John E. Wallace. Federal funds covered 45 percent of construction cost. Demolished 1983. Replaced by Great Ape Facility.

Lion House (67, B-6)

Opened January 30, 1916, as general-purpose zoo building. Architect Tom P. Barnett. Cost, including heating system, slightly more than $15,000 of city funds. Decoration of elephant heads removed in 1919 after construction of elephant house. Building torn down in 1974 for construction of Big Cat Country.

Old Style Block House (68, F-9)

First zoo building in Forest Park, an "old style block house" built by the Forest Park Zoological Association in 1890–91 for the new herd of bison. Other buildings were added in 1892 when Fair Grounds zoological collection moved to Forest Park. Probably near Deer Lake. All of buildings and enclosures later torn down.

Portland Cement Building (61, C-6)

Built by company as display for World's Fair. Became city property when left after fair. Used by zoo to house small tropical birds, bakery, and zoo hospital. Demolished in 1960–61 when new zoo hospital built (at cost of about $200,000).

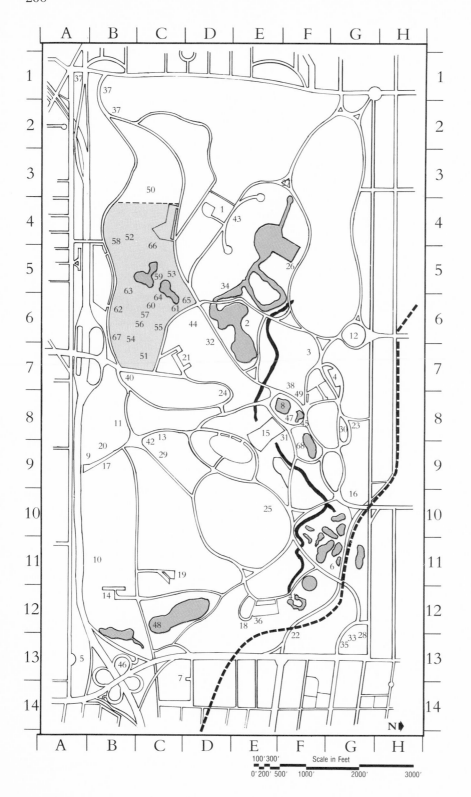

100' 300'   Scale in Feet

0' 200' 500'   1000'   2000'   3000'

Appendix 2. ROADS AND BODIES OF WATER

ROADS

Carr Lane Drive (1, C and D-8)*

William Carr Lane was the first mayor of St. Louis.

Clayton Avenue (2, C-14 to B-9)

Part of Clayton Road, the main route from downtown St. Louis toward Clayton, in St. Louis County, before the park began. Renamed Clayton Avenue in 1891. Park drive was cut off from rest of road on the west by construction of Highway 40 in the early 1960s.

Concourse Drive (3, D-8 to B-7)

Built before 1900 and named for the concourses, meeting places for carriages.

Confederate Drive (4, G-8 and G-9)

For the nearby Confederate Memorial.

Cricket Drive (5, G-8 and F-8)

For the nearby cricket field, site of cricket games since the 1890s.

Deer Lake Drive (6, F-9)

For nearby Deer Lake, an early zoo location before all the animals were consolidated near the bird cage in the early 1900s.

Faulkner Drive (7, C-12 and D-12)

Built about 1906; named for William R. Faulkner, the driving force behind construction of the Mounted Police Station, which the road served.

Fine Arts Drive (8, E-3 to D-5)

The St. Louis Art Museum was built as the Palace of Fine Arts for the 1904 fair. Road built by LPEC as part of park reconstruction.

Government Drive (9, G-10 to B-2)

Road passes Government Hill, which was the site of the U.S. Government and Missouri pavilions at the fair. LPEC built western portion of Government Drive, renamed eastern section, which had been part of Grand Drive.

Grand Drive (10, G-2 to G-12)

The first named street in the park, shown on the 1876 plan for the park. The grand drive that circled the park.

Jefferson Drive (11, F-11 to C-13)

Named in the early 1890s for Thomas Jefferson.

Lagoon Drive (12, G-2 to F-8)

The Lagoon is the body of water between Post-Dispatch Lake and the Grand Basin. Road probably built by LPEC during reconstruction of Forest Park after St. Louis World's Fair.

Macklind Drive (13, D-9 and D-10)

Macklind Avenue dead-ends into Oakland Avenue nearby.

McKinley Drive (14, F-8 to A-9)

Probably named for William McKinley, who, as President of the United States, issued the proclamation for the Louisiana Purchase Exposition (the 1904 World's Fair). Part of McKinley Drive had been section of Grand Drive.

Municipal Opera Drive (15, F-8 to F-10)

Runs in front of the Municipal Theatre. Formerly Theatre Drive. Renamed in 1968.

---

*The names of the roads and bodies of water are followed by the number and location on the locator map on p. 272.

River des Peres Drive (16, E-6 to E-7)

For the River des Peres Lagoon.

Summit Drive (17, D-8 to E-9)

Named for the elevation.

Union Drive (18, F-10 to D-8)

An extension of Union Boulevard into the park.

Valley Drive (19, C-2 to C-4)

Named for the elevation.

Washington Drive (20, G-7 to C-7)

Named in the early 1890s for George Washington. Washington Drive was rebuilt in a new location after the World's Fair by the LPEC, but the name was retained. The bridge that carries Washington Drive over the Lagoon is named Washington Bridge.

Wells Drive (21, F-11 to B-1)

Rolla Wells, mayor of St. Louis from 1901 to 1909, was instrumental in getting the city ready for the fair. Park Commissioner Scanlan, appointed by Wells, named the road, the western part of which was built as part of park restoration after fair, for Wells. The eastern part of Wells Drive was formerly part of Grand Drive.

West Pine Drive (22, G-12 and G-13)

Connects with West Pine Boulevard; built in 1940s to relieve traffic at the park's Lindell-Kingshighway entrance.

Bowl Lake (23, B-13)

Located in section of park called the bowl in the 1930s when the lake was built after the River des Peres was put underground.

BODIES OF WATER

Deer Lake (24, F-8)

Formerly Deer Paddock Lake. Near location of deer paddock, which was part of Forest Park zoo in 1890s.

Fish Hatchery Lakes (25, G-10 and G-11, F-10 and F-11)

Used as fish hatcheries and then as rearing ponds for fish hatched elsewhere from the 1870s through the 1950s. Sylvan Lake, one of the lakes built by Forest Park Commissioners in the 1870s, was broken up to make additional fish hatchery lakes. Sylvan Lake had been popular for boating and ice-skating.

Grand Basin (26, F-5 to E-4)

Name given during World's Fair to this body of water, which was extensively reshaped by LPEC.

Jefferson Lake (27, D-12 and C-12)

Near Jefferson Drive. Built in late 1930s when River des Peres put underground.

Lagoon (28, E-5 and E-6)

The body of water that connects Post-Dispatch Lake and the Grand Basin; built by the LPEC during park rebuilding after the 1904 World's Fair.

Lake Louie (29, F-12)

For Director of Parks, Recreation and Forestry Louis W. Buckowitz. On the original site of the River des Peres, then of the River des Peres Lagoon, reconstructed into present form in 1967.

Murphy Lake (30, G-11)

Lake was in existence before 1900. Called simply "Lake" on early maps. Named Murphy Lake by 1935. Origin of name unknown.

Pagoda Lake (31, F-8)

Island in this lake was site of park's first bandstand, also called the music pagoda. Bandstand torn down and later replaced with Nathan Frank Bandstand, but the lake name remained.

Post-Dispatch Lake (32, E-7 to D-6)

Named in honor of the newspaper's successful drive to collect money to dig a park lake extension in 1894. That extension was in about the present location of the Grand Basin, and the original lake, Peninsular Lake, was in about the present location of Post-Dispatch Lake. The newspaper often used the name Post-Dispatch Lake for the entire extended lake, which was drained and reshaped for the World's Fair. Only the Grand Basin was refilled for the fair. The lakes were modified into their present shape during park rebuilding following the World's Fair. As late as 1923, the *Post-Dispatch* called the lake section "the boat house lake."

River des Peres Lagoon (33, F-6 to F-11)

Over previous location of River des Peres, as modified by the LPEC, before the river was put into underground sewer pipes. Lagoon gradually shortened to its present length.

Round Lake (34, F-11)

Built by the Forest Park Commissioners in the 1870s. Called Round Pond in the early 1900s, when it had a central fountain. Park department employees installed a new fountain with more than 500 nozzles in 1916, a formal landscape around the edge in 1924.

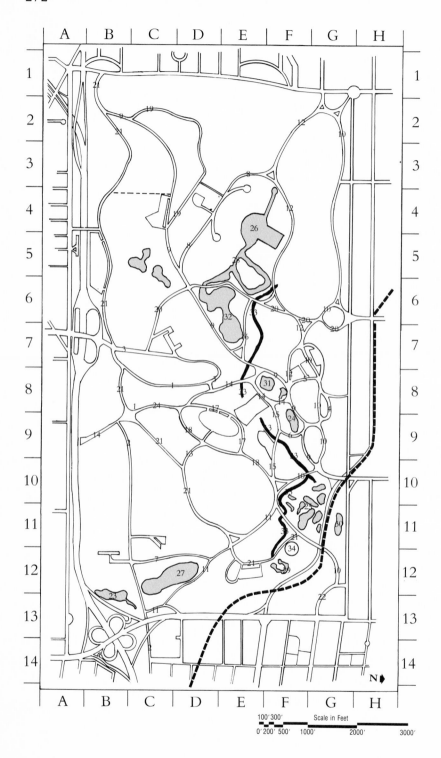

ROADS AND BODIES
OF WATER

Appendix 3. FOREST PARK ADMINISTRATORS

FOREST PARK COMMISSIONERS

1872–1873

Hiram W. Leffingwell, Chairman of Executive Committee
Levin H. Baker, President
Joseph Brown, Mayor of St. Louis
Joseph O'Neil, Presiding Justice of St. Louis County Court
Edwin O. Stanard
Dr. Thomas O'Reilly
Samuel Treat
Henry C. Haarstick
Robert Barth
Albert Todd, replaced by Charles Gibson before June 1872
Robert E. Carr
Peter G. Gerhart
John Withnell
D. A. January
Board declared unconstitutional in April 1873.

1874–1877

Andrew McKinley, President
Joseph O'Neil, then Chauncy F. Shultz, Presiding Justice of St. Louis County Court
Hiram W. Leffingwell
Peter G. Gerhart
John O'Fallon Farrar
Ansyl Phillips
John J. Fitzwilliam

1877–1914

In 1877 City of St. Louis took over park, which was under supervision of city Commissioner of Parks.

YEAR	MAYOR	COMMISSIONER OF PARKS
1877	Henry Overstolz (Ind)	Eugene F. Weigel
1878	"	"
1879	"	"
1880	"	"
1881	William L. Ewing (Rep)	"
1882	"	"

YEAR	MAYOR	COMMISSIONER OF PARKS
1883	"	"
1884	"	"
1885	David R. Francis (Dem)	"
1886	"	"
1887	"	Richard Klemm
1888	"	"
1889	Edward A. Noonan (Dem)	"
1890	"	"
1891	"	Jonathan P. Fechter
1892	"	"
1893	Cyrus P. Walbridge (Rep)	"
1894	"	"
1895	"	Franklin L. Ridgely
1896	"	"
1897	Henry Ziegenhein (Rep)	"
1898	"	"
1899	"	"
1900	"	"
1901	Rolla Wells (Dem)	"
1902	"	"
1903	"	Robert Aull
1904	"	"
1905	"	"
1906	"	"
1907	"	Philip C. Scanlan
1908	"	"
1909	Frederick H. Kriesmann (Rep)	"
1910	"	"
1911	"	"
1912	"	Dwight F. Davis
1913	Henry W. Kiel (Rep)	"
1914	"	"

1915–1959

Under new city charter parks were supervised by Commissioner of Parks and Recreation who was appointed by the Director of Public Welfare.

YEAR	MAYOR	DIRECTOR OF PUBLIC WELFARE	COMMISSIONER OF PARKS AND RECREATION
1915	Henry W. Kiel (Rep)	Emil Tolkacz	Dwight F. Davis
1916	"	"	Nelson Cunliff
1917	"	"	"
1918	"	John Schmoll	"
1919	"	"	"
1920	Henry W. Kiel (Rep)	John Schmoll	Fred W. Pape

YEAR	MAYOR	DIRECTOR OF PUBLIC WELFARE	COMMISSIONER OF PARKS AND RECREATION
1921	"	"	"
1922	"	Nelson Cunliff	"
1923	"	"	"
1924	"	"	"
1925	Victor J. Miller (Rep)	Harry Salisbury	"
1926	"	"	"
1927	"	"	"
1928	"	"	"
1929	"	"	"
1930	"	"	"
1931	"	"	"
1932	"	"	"
1933	Bernard F. Dickmann (Dem)	Joseph M. Darst	William A. Miller
1934	"	"	"
1935	"	"	"
1936	"	"	died 5/13/36
1937	"	"	Joseph J. Mestres
1938	"	"	"
1939	"	"	"
1940	"	"	"
1941	William Dee Becker (Rep)	"	"
1942	"	Henry S. Caulfield	Palmer B. Baumes
1943	Aloys P. Kaufmann (Rep)	"	"
1944	"	"	"
1945	"	"	"
1946	"	"	"
1947	"	"	"
1948	"	"	"
1949	Joseph M. Darst (Dem)	John O'Toole	"
1950	"	"	"
1951	"	"	"
1952	"	J. Glennon McKenna	"
1953	Raymond R. Tucker (Dem)	Virginia O'C. Brungard	"
1954	"	"	"
1955	"	"	"
1956	"	"	"
1957	"	"	"
1958	"	"	"
1959	"	"	"

1960–1984

Under charter amendments parks were under control of Department of Parks, Recreation and Forestry.

YEAR	MAYOR	DIRECTOR OF PARKS, RECREATION AND FORESTRY
1960	Raymond R. Tucker (Dem)	Virginia O'C. Brungard
1961	,,	,,
1962	,,	,,
1963	,,	,,
1964	,,	,,
1965	Alfonso J. Cervantes (Dem)	Louis W. Buckowitz
1966	,,	,,
1967	,,	,,
1968	,,	,,
1969	,,	,,
1970	,,	,,
1971	,,	,,
1972	,,	,,
1973	John H. Poelker (Dem)	Georgia L. Buckowitz
1974	,,	,,
1975	,,	,,
1976	,,	,,
1977	James F. Conway (Dem)	,,
1978	,,	,,
1979	,,	,,
1980	,,	,,
1981	Vincent C. Schoemehl, Jr. (Dem)	George M. Kinsey
1982	,,	,,
1983	,,	,,
1984	,,	,,
1985	,,	Nancy E. Rice

Board of Parks and Recreation

Norman R. Seay (1959–1964, 1965–1966)
Mrs. Harry Hilliker (1959–1966)
Jane Conzelman (1959–1963)
Charles H. Christel (1959–1963)
Edwin R. Culver III (1959–1966)
Philip C. McGrath (1959–1966)
Gerald P. Deppe (1964–1966)
C. C. Johnson Spink (1964–1966)
George M. Khoury (1966–1974)
H. Reid Derrick (1966–1969)
Jack W. Minton (1966–1968)
Arthur B. Baer (1966–1967)
Rev. Joseph W. Nicholson (1966–1971)

Russell E. Gardner, Jr. (1966–1967)
Mrs. Ruth Datche Falchero (1967–1979)
David Hess (1970–71)
Allen Ura (1970–81)
Fred C. Varney (1970–1980)
Wilbur A. Stuart (1971–1983)
Joseph Marino, Jr. (1971–)
Aurelia Dulle (1976–1983)
Theresa Garagnani (1974–1982)
Sylvia Elliott (1978–1984)
Joseph T. Goral (1978–)
Louis Knoepp (1983–)
William Krumm (1983–)
Josephine M. Lockhart (1984–)

NOTES

A manuscript of the complete notes for this book can be found in various libraries, including the University of Missouri-St. Louis. The bibliography in this book describes the sources for the work and gives some indications for further reading.

Annual reports for fiscal years covering more than one calendar year are cited in these notes under the ending year. For example, PC 1904 means the annual report of the commissioner of parks for the fiscal year 1903–4.

LIST OF ABBREVIATIONS

AAA: St. Louis Amateur Athletic Association or Triple A

AR: annual report

BPI: St. Louis Board of Public Improvements

BPS: St. Louis Board of Public Service

Bull: *Bulletin*

Chrono: chronological file

Comp: comptroller

Dem: *St. Louis Democrat*

Dis: *St. Louis Dispatch*

Exec Comm Mins: executive committee minutes

FLO: Frederick Law Olmsted

FPC: *Report of the Commissioners of Forest Park, 1875* (St. Louis 1876)

FPU: Forest Park University

GD: *St. Louis Globe-Democrat*

Griff: *The Government of St. Louis: The Summary Report of the Mayor's Advisory Committee on City Survey and Audit, conducted by Griffenhagen & Associates under the supervision of the Governmental Research Institute February 20, 1941*

GS: annual report of the general superintendent of parks

H&C: William Hyde and Howard L. Conard, *Encyclopedia of the History of St. Louis* (St. Louis:Southern History Co. 1899 4 vols.)

Jour: journal

LPEC: Louisiana Purchase Exposition Company

Mag: magazine section

MHS: Missouri Historical Society

MM: *Mayor's Message with Accompanying Documents to the Municipal Assembly of the City of St. Louis*

Ord: ordinance

PC: annual report of the commissioner of parks until 1915, of the commissioner of parks and recreation until 1959, of the director of parks, recreation and forestry thereafter

PD: *St. Louis Post-Dispatch*

Pics: Pictures section

PWA: Public Works Administration

Rep: *Missouri Republican* until May 1888, *Republic* thereafter

R/UDAT: *Report of the Regional/Urban Design Assistance Team* (St. Louis:1976)

SC: annual report of the superintendent of construction

ST: *St. Louis Star-Times*

UMSL: University of Missouri-St. Louis

INTRODUCTION

1. Gunther Barth, *City People: The Rise of Modern City Culture in Nineteenth-Century America* (Oxford:Oxford University Press, paperback edition 1982), pp. 34–37.

CHAPTER 1.

1. Opening-day descriptions are from *GD*, June 25, 1876, p. 6 and *Dis*, June 24, 1876.

2. Tower Grove autograph album, 1862–1864; FLO Papers, Reel 1, p. 82; for Olmsted comment that his "visit to St. Louis was of great interest and value to me personally" see FLO Papers, Reel 2, p. 257, typed copy is Reel 2, p. 323.

3. Act to establish a public park for the use of the inhabitants of the city of St. Louis. February 15, 1864.

4. *Rep*, April 1, 1864; *Dem*, April 1, 1864, p. 4.

5. The various plans and objections are described in *Dem*, October 21, 1870, p. 4; January 19, 1871, p. 1; February 5, 1871, p. 4; February 6, 1871, p. 2; February 8, 1871, pp. 2, 4; February 9, 1871, p. 1; February 13, 1871, p. 2. Text of bill is in *Dem*, January 28, 1871, p. 2. Indirect evidence for objections that park was too far appears in *Dem*, August 3, 1873, p. 4, FPC, p. 56.

6. Act to establish Forest Park March 25, 1872. Descriptions and comment can be found in *Rep*, March 31, 1872, p. 3; Napton Diary, p. 727, in MHS Chrono.

7. Griswold, Forsyth, and Skinker sales are in St. Louis deed books: b.457 p. 496, b462 p. 342, b463 p. 185.

8. *Dem*, June 30, 1972, p. 2.

9. *Dem*, May 23, 1872, p. 3; May 24, 1872, p. 1; June 2, 1872, p. 1.

10. Jamison v. Griswold, 2 Missouri Appeal Reports (1876), pp. 150–56.

11. The city limits extension controversy is covered in *Dem*, June 7, 1873, p. 4; November 30, 1873, p. 4; December 28, 1873, p. 4.

12. Chouteau v. Leffingwell, 54 Missouri Reports (1873) pp. 475–77. *Dem*, July 13, 1873, p. 4.

13. *Dem*, August 3, 1873, p. 4; August 31, 1873, p. 4; September 24, 1873, p. 4.

14. An act to establish "Forest Park," in the county of St. Louis, etc., February 15, 1874. The following year an amendment required that the interest be paid in gold.

15. Information about the survey is from *Dis*, April 27, 1874; May 25, 1874; Pitzman May 21, 1874 in City Library Forest Park Box.

16. Chouteau never lived on the land near Forest Park.

17. County Court of St. Louis County v. Griswold, order entered by Circuit Court of St. Louis County on January 9, 1875.

18. *ST*, August 31, 1931, pp. 1–2; September 6, 1949, p. 21; *GD*, July 1, 1923; *PD*, October 3, 1926.

19. For details on railroads see Joy v. St. Louis, 138 US Supreme Court (1891), pp. 1–51, see also FPC, pp. 13–16. Copy of agreement is in City Library Forest Park Box.

20. *Rep*, March 23, 1875, p. 3.

21. FPC. Details of plan and of early work are from this report.

22. *Rep*, March 23, 1875, p. 3.

23. Jour BPI, February 4, 1882. Arista C. Shewey, *Shewey's Pictorial St. Louis* (St. Louis: 1892), p. 182; Camille N. Dry and Richard J. Compton, *A Topographical Survey Drawn in Perspective, A.D. 1875*, plate 100, reprint (St. Louis: Knight Publishing Company, 1979).

24. *GD*, October 13, 1875, p. 8.

25. *GD*, June 12, 1876, p. 8.

CHAPTER 2

1. For story of separation see Thomas Barclay, *The St. Louis Home Rule Charter of 1876: Its Framing and Adoption* (Columbia, MO: University of Missouri Press, 1962). Quotations are from *Dis*, July 30, 1875, p. 1; *GD*, April 21, 1876, p.3; May 30, 1876, p.4; June 25, 1876; and 1875 Missouri Constitution, Article ix, Section 20.

2. *GD*, May 9, 1881, p. 2.

3. PC 1885, p. 283; *Rep*, May 1, 1879, p. 5; January 18, 1880, p. 6; *GD* May 1, 1881, p. 6.

4. *Rep* June 22, 1877, p. 5.

5. *GD*, June 8, 1881, p. 2.

6. *GD*, July 5, 1879, p. 7.

7. *PD*, July 4, 1883, p. 2.

8. PC 1885, p. 284.

9. MM 1877, p. 15; *PD*, November 21, 1898, p. 10; AR BPI 1878, p. 226.

10. PC 1879, p.2.

11. PC 1882, pp. 251–52. An appropriation of $5,000 on July 14, 1877, was apparently a loan to keep the park going until the county money arrived since it was returned to municipal revenue within three weeks of the transfer of funds from the county.

12. *Rep*, October 11, 1877, p. 5; Jour BPI, October 1, 1877.

13. PC 1884, p. 279.

14. Jour BPI, September 18, 1878, p. 463; October 21, 1878, p. 489.

15. PC 1884, p. 279.

16. PC 1879, pp. 3–4.

17. PC 1878, p. 296; 1879, p. 4.

18. *Rep*, March 21, 1880, p. 6.

19. PC 1880, p. 262; Larry Belusz, "Fish Hatcheries in Missouri," *Missouri Conservationist* 42:7 (July 1981).

20. Ord 12292, February 28, 1883.

21. FPC, p. 16; Ord 12551, November 17, 1883.

22. Jour BPI, April 12, 1878, p. 246.

CHAPTER 3

1. PC 1890, p. 273; James Cox, *St Louis through a Camera* (St. Louis: under the auspices of the Bureau of Information of the St. Louis Autumnal Festivities Association, 1892), pages not numbered. Ordinances on streetcar lines to Forest Park are 12888, October 6, 1884; 15445, February 20, 1890; 15601, April 4, 1890; 16089, April 3, 1891; 17072, March 4, 1893.

2. *PD*, May 23, 1893, p. 4.

3. *PD*, April 7, 1895, p. 20; May 5, 1895, p. 1.

4. *PD*, June 14, 1896.

5. PC 1896, p. 552.

6. AR, General Superintendent Repairs & Cleaning Streets to the Street Commissioner in MM 1896, p. 516; Jour BPI, July 5, 1881; *PD*, August 30, 1895.

7. Ord 18410, April 6, 1896.

8. *PD*, September 17, 1894, p. 3.

9. Ord 13927, March 11, 1887; 17625 April 30, 1894.

10. *PD*, May 3, 1901, p. 7.

11. An explanation of the arrangement under which the club moved into the park appears in *GD*, September 14, 1901, p. 16. While just a newspaper article, this statement was not denied, it was made less than five years after the club moved into the park, and it reflected what happened at the time of the World's Fair.

12. Ord 17374, January 27, 1894.

13. *PD*, January 7, 1894, p. 1; June 17, 1894.

14. *PD*, December, 31, 1894, p. 8; January 2, 1895, p. 7.

15. Ord 14435, March 27, 1888.

16. *PD*, September 17, 1894, p. 3; December 31, 1894, p.8.

17. PC 1892, p. 21; 1890, p. 275; Ord 16877, August 12, 1892.

18. Ord 19412, July 13, 1898.

19. *GD*, September 5, 1890, p. 3.

20. PC 1891, pp. 268–69.

21. H&C, Vol. 2:809; *PD*, August 19, 1894, p. 23; Ord 16879, August 12, 1892; 16881 August 12, 1892.

22. Ord 19969, March 13, 1900; Mab Mulkey, "History of the St. Louis School of Fine Arts, 1879–1909: The Art Department of Washington University" (M.A. Thesis, Washington University, 1944), p. 187.

23. Mulkey, p. 19; State ex rel. Board of Control of St. Louis School and Museum of Fine Arts v. City of St. Louis 216 Missouri Reports (En Banc. 1909) p. 58.

24. Ord 13217, March 11, 1885; 16002 March 6, 1891.

25. State ex rel Attorney General v. Schweickardt, 109 Missouri Reports (1891) pp. 496–518. Ord 16875, August 12, 1892; 17729 July 25, 1894.

26. Missouri Pharmaceutical Association program 1898 in City Library Art Room Forest Park File.

27. *PD*, July 14, 1894, p. 1; May 16, 1903, p. 4.

28. *GD*, May 14, 1898, p. 16; May 15, 1898, p. 9.

29. *PD*, August 9, 1896, p. 17.

30. PC 1886, p. 85; 1888, p. 259; 1889, p. 282; *GD*, June 23, 1885, p. 10.

31. PC 1893, p. 311; 1894, p. 365; *Mirror* (July 29, 1894), p. 6.

32. Jour BPI, June 6, 1890, p. 62; Police Commission AR 1891, p. 413.

33. Ord 16897, November 15, 1892; *GD*, October 5, 1901, p. 16.

34. *GD*, June 14, 1901, p. 9.

35. PC 1891, p. 269.

36. *PD*, July 27, 1894, p. 2.

37. PC 1900, p. 1.

38. PC 1897, 1900, p. 2.

39. PC 1889, p. 280.

40. Flyer MHS Archives August 2, 1896; H. B. Wandell, *The Story of a Great City in a Nutshell: 500 Facts about St. Louis* (St. Louis: 5th ed., 1900).

41. Brochure in MHS Archives.

42. Jour BPI October 10, 1897, p. 376; February 21, 1898, p. 586; October 28, 1898, p. 234.

43. FPU *Bull* (1897): 9–10.

44. PC 1893, p. 307; AR, President, BPI 1902, p. 628; AR, Health Commissioner in MM 1896, p. 142; AR, Chief Sanitary Officer in MM 1894, pp. 116, 142; *PD*, August 5, 1894, p. 1; August 19, 1894, p. 28; J. Thomas Scharf, *History of St. Louis City and County* (St. Louis: Louis H. Everts Co., 1883), p. 751.

45. PC in MM 1896, p. 551.

46. PC 1893, p. 311; *PD*, August 5, 1894, p. 20.

47. *Rep*, November 23, 1897, p. 4; PC 1896, p. 552; Jour BPI, June 8, 1886, p. 43. For an attempt at a donation of Pan statue and fountain for some park see Jour BPI, June 29, 1897, p. 263.

48. Cox, *Through a Camera*, npn; *Harper's* (September 24, 1901): 917.

CHAPTER 4

1. Ord 15390, January 22, 1890; *Rep*, January 11, 1870, p. 2.

2. *PD*, June 21, 1898, p. 6.

3. *GD*, May 10, 1901, p. 4.

4. Ord 20412, May 16, 1901; *GD*, May 12, 1901, Sec. 1, p. 8.

5. Description of selection process and arguments for and against the sites are in *Rep*, June 2, 1901, p. 1; *GD*, May 9, 1901,

p. 1; May 10, 1901, p. 4; June 2, 1901, Sec. 2, p. 9; June 6, 1901, p. 14; June 7, 1901, p. 7; Forest Park World's Fair Free Site Association, *Argument for Location of World's Fair in Western Forest Park*.

6. *Rep*, June 26, 1901, p. 2; *PD*, June 26, 1901, p. 1; *GD*, June 26, 1901, p. 6.

7. Information about the suit and the association comes from *GD*, July 26, 1901, p. 14; July 27, 1901, p. 12; August 2, 1901, p. 14; August 13, 1901, pp. 1, 14; *PD*, August 12, 1901; August 16, 1901, p. 2; *Rep*, July 28, 1901, p. 6; August 1, 1901, p. 2; August 15, 1901.

8. Mulkey *School of Fine Arts*, pp. 192–93.

9. Pamela G. Hemenway, *Cass Gilbert's Buildings at the Louisiana Purchase Exposition, 1904* (M.A. thesis, University of Missouri, 1970), pp. 22–24.

10. *GD*, October 19, 1901, p. 3; October 21, 1901, p. 3; November 4, 1901, p. 12; April 14, 1902, p. 1.

11. Ord 20412, May 16, 1901; Jour BPI, November 15, 1901, p. 140; November 23, 1901, p. 145; November 25, 1901, p. 148; November 30, 1901, p. 154; December 3, 1901, p. 156; January 4, 1902, p. 178; January 16, 1902, p. 184; January 28, 1902, p. 202; February 21, 1902, p. 230; February 4, 1902, p. 205; February 10, 1902, p. 218; February 14, 1902, p. 224; April 11, 1902, p. 4; April 18, 1902, p. 8; June 10, 1902, p. 60.

12. *GD*, November 24, 1901, Sec. 2, p. 16.

13. LPEC Exec Comm Mins, p. 8, June 6, 1901; see also LPEC Exec Comm Mins, January 15, 1902, p. 364.

14. *GD*, September 14, 1901, p. 16.

15. AR AAA 1902.

16. PC 1903, pp. 18–19.

17. BPI resolution in PC 1903, p. 4; LPEC Directors Minutes, pp. 546, 548, 638–39; Jour BPI, April 10, 1903, p. 302; March 18, 1904, p. 258.

18. *PD*, May 10, 1902, p. 9.

19. *PD*, June 7, 1902, p. 8; June 18, 1902, p. 1; W. Frauenthal Barney, *Barney's Information Guide to the City of St. Louis* (St. Louis: Barney's Information Guide Publishing Co., 1902), p. 31.

20. *GD*, July 11, 1904, p. 1.

21. *PD*, July 16, 1901, p. 4.

22. MM 1901, p. xiii; PC 1901, p. 609; 1904, pp. 4–5; 1905, pp. 3, 6–7; GS in PC 1904, p. 6. The "Remember the *Maine*" flagpole was almost certainly Busch's gift, since the *Maine* sank in 1898 and Ridgely reported in 1902 "no adequate flagstaff in Forest Park since the cyclone of 1896."

23. Barney, *Information Guide 1902*, p. 31; By the end of 1904 the force was down to 51.

24. Louisiana Purchase Exposition Free Information Service, *St. Louis Hotels, boarding and rooming houses* (St. Louis:1904), pp. 16–17.

25. *PD*, June 22, 1902, mag., p. 2.

26. Some boys went to the fair on days when children accompanied by an adult were admitted free, followed a woman they didn't know, and were considered by attendance-collectors to be with her. The previous two modern Olympics were Athens in 1896 and Paris in 1900.

CHAPTER 5

1. Francis's story of removing the fair and rebuilding the park is in David R. Francis, *The Universal Exposition of 1904*, 2 vols. (St. Louis: Louisiana Purchase Exposition Company, 1913), pp. 658–83. A series of documents about the process appear in

Journal of the House of Delegates 1905–06, pp. 1–8. Wells's view is in Rolla Wells, *Episodes of My Life*, (St. Louis, 1933), pp. 232–37. See *The St. Louis Guide* (1888), p. 34, in MHS Chrono for "magnificent forest."

2. Kessler On Public Parks at Kansas City, May 1892 in Kessler Papers, MHS; Kessler to LPEC Restoration Committee, October 28, 1904 in Kessler Papers; also LPEC Exec Comm Mins, p. 3257; Restoration of Forest Park in LPEC Collection, MHS Archives, Series 12, Subseries 1, Folder 2.

3. Kessler to Restoration Committee, October 28, 1904.

4. LPEC Exec Comm Mins, p. 3435 January 24, 1905; Jour BPI, January 20, 1905, p. 176.

5. *GD*, January 26, 1905, p. 6.

6. *GD*, July 11, 1905, p. 16.

7. *GD*, January 5, 1905, p. 1.

8. *PD*, August 15, 1906, p. 3.

9. AR Sewer Commissioner in MM, 1906, p. 154; GS in PC 1905 p. 27.

10. Ords 25550, 25551, 25552, January 25, 1911.

11. *Rep*, April 13, 1907, p. 9; *PD*, June 10, 1909, p. 2.

12. *GD*, October 4, 1906, p. 1.

13. An act providing for the establishment, maintenance, extension, and regulations of museums of art in cities of four hundred thousand inhabitants or more, and authorizing taxation for the same, March 7, 1907.

14. *GD*, March 25, 1907, p. 10; *PD*, April 3, 1907, p. 11.

15. For controversy and resolution see Jour BPI, November 22, 1907, p. 134; March 17, 1908, pp. 194–96; Kessler to Francis November 11, 1908 in LPEC Correspondence 1907– in MHS Archives; LPEC Minutes, April 9, 1907, p. 869; LPEC Exec Comm Mins, April 22, 1908, pp. 3919–24; Francis to LPEC Directors, September 15, 1908, in Francis Collection, September 1908, MHS Archives; *PD*, May 2, 1907, p. 8; PC 1908, p. 6.

16. Jour BPI, January 29, 1904, p. 206; February 12, 1904, p. 224; February 11, 1909, p. 194; BPI to Francis, October 23, 1908.

17. Jour BPI, May 1, 1908; *GD*, October 24, 1908, pp. 1, 8.

18. Board of Control of St. Louis School and Museum of Fine Arts v. St. Louis, 216 Missouri Reports (En Banc. 1909), pp. 47–99; Ord 24195, February 23, 1909; 24524, July 6, 1909; Mulkey, p. 219.

19. State ex rel. Bixby v. City of St. Louis, 216 Missouri Reports (En Banc 1912) pp. 231–50. Ord 26430, May 25, 1912.

20. Sundry Civil Service Act March 4, 1909, in Francis, vol. 1, p. 677.

21. Jour BPI, April 7, 1909, p. 230; Ord 24191, February 23, 1909.

22. The most detailed report on the design of the Jefferson Memorial is in LPEC Exec Comm Mins, March 21, 1916. For other information and relationship with MHS, see H&C, pp. 1308–9; Draft resolution attached to letter draft dated July 1901 in Kessler Papers Correspondence 1900–12 folder 1901 in MHS Archives; *Rep*, April 30, 1910, p. 1; *GD*, January 11, 1899, p. 2; Ord 22593, October 12, 1906.

23. Ord 25665, March 15, 1911; Francis, pp. 668–70; *GD*, May 1, 1913, pp. 2, 8.

24. Louisiana Purchase Historical Association Articles of Association Section 4–5.

25. Smithsonian AR 1901, pp. lxv, lxvi; 1905, p. 69; Ord 22020, April 6, 1905; AR Comp 1906, p. 32; 1911, p. 170; *GD*, March 12, 1905, p. 13; August 14, 1905, p. 4.

26. *GD*, August 27, 1910, p. 2.

27. GS in PC 1911, p. 14; *PD*, April 14, 1911, p.4.

28. *PD*, July 22, 1907, p. 8; August 18, 1907; June 24, 1911, p. 6; *GD*, January 8, 1905, p. 16; January 31, 1905, p. 11; *Rep*, April 28, 1907, p. 4.

29. Ord 21060, March 17, 1903; 24832 February 26, 1910.

30. PC 1910, p. 4; Ord 24444, 24445, June 21, 1909; 48374 April 4, 1910; Jour BPI, March 11, 1910, p. 232; June 21, 1910, p. 308; December 20, 1910, p. 404.

31. *PD*, October 7, 1906 mag, p. 1.

32. *PD*, April 1, 1907, p. 3; April 7, 1911, p. 4.

33. *PD*, July 28, 1911, p. 9.

34. *PD*, October 13, 1907, mag, p. 6; October 23, 1907, pp. 1–2.

35. Walter B. Stevens, editor, *St. Louis: One Hundred Years in a Week: Celebration of the Centennial of Incorporation, October Third to Ninth, Nineteen Hundred and Nine* (St. Louis: St. Louis Centennial Association), pp. 99, 113, 148; *PD*, October 8, 1909, pp. 1–3.

36. Ord 24387, March 30, 1909; City Deed Book 2368, p. 31; *GD*, October 16, 1904, p. 6.

37. *PD*, June 25, 1911, p. 7.

38. Ord 25072, March 30, 1910; PC 1917 pic.

CHAPTER 6

1. PC 1915, p. 3, *PD*, May 21, 1911, p. 1B.

2. By 1911 Forest Park had a five-mile bridle path (a conversion of the seldom-used bicycle path), a boat house on the lagoon, and five football fields.

3. *PD*, June 30, 1911, p. 14; July 7, 1912, Sec. 3, p. 1.

4. *GD*, November 21, 1915, p. 11; PC 1914, p. 5.

5. City Plan Commission, *Problems of St. Louis* (St. Louis, 1917), p. 84; James Neal Primm, *Lion of the Valley: St. Louis, Missouri* The Western Urban History Series, vol. 13 (Boulder, Colo.: Pruett Publishing Company, 1981), pp. 436–39.

6. State ex. rel. Howard v. Pape cause number 67616, order entered denying writ of mandamus June 24, 1928, *PD* October 1, 1917, p. 1; August 16, 1923, p. 3.

7. GS in PC 1913, p. 17.

8. PC 1914, p. 5.

9. *PD*, March 15, 1915, p. 12.

10. *GD*, July 20, 1901, p. 5.

11. *Playground Magazine* (December 1922):537.

12. Donald Bright Oster, "Nights of Fantasy: The St. Louis Pageant and Masque of 1914," *MHS Bull* (April 1975):175–205; PC 1914, p. 10.

13. 1914 City Charter Article VIII, Section 1, Article XII, Section 6.

14. PC 1917, p. 7; for permanent construction of the theatre see *Rep*, April 15, 1917, pt. 6, p. 1; *GD*, May 20, 1917, Mag, p. 3; *PD*, April 15, 1917, p. 10b.

15. *PD*, June 6, 1917, p. 3.

16. Jour BPS, July 6, 1917, p. 592.

17. Jour BPS, May 8, 1917, p. 560; "Putting Over the Big Show" in City Library Art Room St. Louis Fashion Pageant folder; *GD*, July 31, 1919, p. 2.

18. *PD*, July 29, 1917, p. 11b.

19. Jour BPS, October 7, 1924; May 15, 1925; May 22, 1925; May 26, 1925; *GD*, August 3, 1919, p. 2b; May 23, 1925, p. 13; Visit St. Louis Committee, *Forest Park*, p. 44.

20. *PD*, April 8, 1918, p. 4; May 12, 1918, p. 1.

21. *GD*, May 25, 1919, p. 8c.

22. *GD*, June 20, 1927, pp. 1, 2.

23. AR MHS in PC 1938, p. 43; *PD*, December 11, 1930, p. 2B.

24. See *PD*, May 1, 1922, p. 7, for suggestion of tax support.

25. PC 1912, pp. 10, 11.

26. PC 1913, pp. 9–10; *Star*, August 17, 1912, p. 3; *Rep*, October 6, 1913, p. 1.

27. *PD*, December 2, 1913, p. 1; Ord 27287, December 2, 1913.

28. *PD*, July 11, 1914, p. 6; Ord 28151, July 14, 1915.

29. An act providing for the establishment, maintenance, extension, and regulations of zoological parks in cities of 400,000 inhabitants or more, and authorizing taxation for the same, March 23, 1915; Ord 29743, August 1, 1917. The ordinance also revised zoo boundaries slightly.

30. *GD*, November 6, 1916, p. 14.

31. See *American City* 3 (1925):252 for a favorable article on zoo construction.

32. *PD*, July 5, 1912, p. 12.

33. *Star*, September 21, 1916, p. 3.

34. Cass Gilbert to W. K. Bixby, April 24, 1916; August 15, 1916; August 25, 1916; Samuel Sherer to Bixby, May 14, 1923, all in Bixby Papers, MHS archives.

35. *Journal of American Institute of Architects* 5 (January-December 1917):117–18; Jour BPS, December 21, 1917, p. 673; January 9, 1917, p. 494; March 15, 1918, p. 713; June 25, 1918, npn; February 18, 1919; January 6, 1920; June 3, 1924; July 29, 1924; September 26, 1924; Ord 33198, June 30, 1924.

36. PC 1912, pp. 5, 8; 1913, p. 7.

37. *PD*, November 14, 1912, p. 1; Ord 53930, December 16, 1912.

38. *Star*, June 11, 1930. Moffitt spelled *Moffat*, *Moffatt*, or *Moffit* in some sources.

39. PC 1927, p. 10.

40. Jour BPS, January 12, 1917, p. 496; August 29, 1917; October 7, 1924.

41. *PD*, August 1, 1916, p. 13; *Star*, July 14, 1927, p. 4.

42. *Star*, July 20, 1912, p. 2.

43. *GD*, July 5, 1921, p. 2.

44. *GD*, April 5, 1915, p. 4.

45. AR Department of Streets 1916, pp. 11, 12; Jour BPS, December 7, 1915; July 7, 1916.

46. *GD*, November 25, 1915, p. 4; Jour BPS, July 25, 1916; October 27, 1916; June 22, 1921; April 16, 1926; September 7, 1926; Ord 35965, April 26, 1927; 37793, July 9, 1929; Jour BPS August 22, 1916; p. 414; May 31, 1929; March 11, 1930; April 29, 1930; Ord 37825, July 10, 1929; Jour BPS, May 9, 1916, p. 356; May 4, 1926; March 16, 1928; December 27, 1928; March 12, 1929; Ord 37448, March 5, 1929.

47. PC 1912, pp. 6–7.

48. *PD*, March 24, 1928, p. 1.

49. City Plan Commission, *Recreation in St. Louis* (St. Louis: 1917), pp. 35, 39; City Plan Commission, *Problems of St. Louis* (St. Louis: 1912), pp. 80, 88, 90, 122–24.

50. State ex. rel. Zoological Board of Control v. City of St. Louis, 318 Missouri Reports (En Banc. 1928), pp. 910–28.

51. Ord 30759, April 13, 1920; 32975, April 9, 1924; SC in PC 1925, p. 14.

52. Ord 26751, December 10, 1912; 26863 February 1, 1913; Capps v. City of St. Louis, 158 Southwestern Reporter (Missouri Supreme Court 1913), pp. 616–24; *PD*, October 29, 1922, p. 1.

53. *Engineering News Record*, July 24, 1930, p. 124; August 21, 1930, pp. 296, 299–300.

54. *PD*, September 13, 1935, p. 2D; GS in PC 1930, p. 19.

55. *PD*, June 4, 1914, p. 1.

56. Kathleen M. Harleman, Susan K. Tepas, and Georgiane Stuart, *The Neighborhood: A History of Skinker-DeBaliviere* (St. Louis: Skinker-DeBaliviere Community Council, 1973), pp. 31–33, 38–39.

57. For information on Park Plaza name, plans see Cass Gilbert to W. K. Bixby, October 26, 1916; June 1, 1918 in Bixby Papers at MHS.

58. Isaac T. Cook to Louis Nolte January 17, 1922, in Cook records at Washington University archives.

59. *GD*, December 11, 1918, p. 4; Jour BPS, January 14, 1919; AR, U.S. Post Master General, 1920, pp. 58, 60–61; 1921, p. 46.

60. Jour BPS, July 26, 1921.

61. *PD*, August 3, 1919, p. 3.

62. *GD*, May 19, 1918, p. 26; May 21, 1918, pp. 9–10.

63. Young v. Cunliff, order entered dismissing the case by the Circuit Court of the city of St. Louis on November 10, 1922, cause number B26744; *GD*, July 14, 1925, p. 14.

64. *PD*, October 9, 1921, p. 7B. See *PD*, May 1, 1923, p. 18, for complaint the club was excluding nonmembers.

65. *PD*, September 5, 1926, pp. 1–2; *Star*, September 8, 1926, pp. 8, 15.

66. *PD*, September 23, 1929, p. 22.

67. *PD*, June 5, 1929, p. 24.

68. *Star*, August 24, 1929, p. 6; *PD*, June 8, 1929, p. 4.

69. *PD*, October 3, 1929, p. 24.

70. *PD*, April 12, 1930, p. 4A.

CHAPTER 7

1. *PD*, July 8, 1936, p. 3A; July 9, 1936, p. 3A.

2. AR, Sergeant of Guard in PC 1938, p. 37.

3. *PD*, February 21, 1932, p. 3A.

4. *PD*, March 27, 1935, p. 10A.

5. *PD*, April 1, 1935, p. 26; April 16, 1935, p. 2C; Jour BPS, September 17, 1935; October 22, 1935; October 29, 1935.

6. *Architectural Forum* 12 (1937 supplement):22.

7. *Star*, April 13, 1932, p. 14.

8. *PD*, August 28, 1938, pp. 1, 3B.

9. *PD*, July 12, 1936, p. 2H. Art museum attendance increased in 1933–34, though there was no bus service for most of the summer. It declined in 1934–35, though not as low as it had been in 1930–31, and in 1938–39, with a newly-acquired Egyptian cat statue on display, attendance set a new record.

10. AR, Comp, 1941; Jour BPS, August 3, 1938; September 20, 1938; September 27, 1938; October 18, 1938; October 25, 1938; November 15, 1938; November 29, 1938; PWA Docket 1526; Jour BPS June 2, 1936; July 7, 1936.

11. *PD*, August 31, 1938, pp. 5A, 1D.

12. *Collier's* article reprinted in *PD*, September 5, 1942, p. 4A; *Fortune* (July 1945) vol 32, no. 1, p. 117.

13. Visit St. Louis Committee, *Forest Park and Its History* (St. Louis Chamber of Commerce and the City of St. Louis, 1943), p. 5.

14. *PD*, August 26, 1940, p. 3B; September 5, 1942, p. 2B.

15. *PD*, November 10, 1939, p. 3A.

16. St. Louis Revised Code 1936, Sec 4299; Ord 34087, June 24, 1925; 42307 April 11, 1942; 43533 March 26, 1946.

17. *PD*, August 27, 1944, p. 1D; SC in PC 1939, p. 1.

18. *PD*, July 5, 1940, p. 3A; June 8, 1941, p. 4A.

19. *PD*, July 5, 1942, pp. 1, 4, 5A.

20. *ST*, May 6, 1941, p. 5; May 9, 1941, p. 11.

21. *PD*, March 14, 1937, p. 8I.

22. *PD*, April 5, 1942, p. 3A; April 6, 1942, p. 3C.

23. Jour BPS, February 28, 1933; March 14, 1933; April 14, 1933; April 18, 1933.

24. PC 1929, p. 6; *PD*, August 23, 1929, p. 29.

25. Jour BPS, January 12, 1934.

26. Jour BPS, May 28, 1934.

27. *Scientific American* 153:6 (December 1935):298.

28. Ord 40615, July 9, 1935; *PD*, January 10, 1936, p. 2C; July 9, 1936, p. 2C.

29. *PD*, April 22, 1943.

30. PC 1887 in MM, p. 283.

31. AR, Forester in PC 1934, p. 2.

32. AR, Forester in PC 1942, p. 1; AR, Superintendent of Golf, 1944, p. 1.

33. *PD*, October 22, 1935, p. 2C.

34. *PD*, July 5, 1936, p. 5F.

35. Ord 41153, July 8, 1937.

CHAPTER 8

1. *GD*, February 2, 1984, p. 8D.

2. *GD*, May 27, 1970, p. 13A. The Department of Parks, Recreation and Forestry included the three divisions named. Somewhat confusingly, the title of Commissioner of Parks, formerly used for the head of the department, was assigned to the head of the division of parks. For several years, newspapers often called the division heads "supervisors" rather than "commissioners" to avoid confusion.

3. Harleman, et al., *The Neighborhood*, p. 39; City Plan Commission, *Population* (St. Louis: 1964), pp. 17–22.

4. *Argus*, August 3, 1945, p. 4.

5. *Argus*, August 9, 1946, p. 1.

6. Hudlin v. Baumes, order entered dismissing the case on July 17, 1945, by the Circuit Court of the city of St. Louis, cause number 88154C.

7. *Argus*, July 20, 1945, p. 8.

8. *Argus*, June 11, 1948, p. 12.

9. *Review of the Program of the St. Louis Urban League and the Social and Economic Conditions of the Negro Population of St. Louis, Mo. conducted for the Social Planning Council of St. Louis and St. Louis County by the National Urban League, New York City* (September–October 1948) in UMSL archives, pp. 109–10; "Negro Attitude Survey" (1949) in UMSL archives, p. 20; George Schermer, *The Fairground Park Incident* (July 27, 1948) in UMSL archives, p. 10.

10. Schermer, pp. 11, 32.

11. *GD*, August 20, 1951, p. 3C.

12. BPS, permit 57157, approved March 3, 1959.

13. *PD*, April 8, 1968, pp. 1, 3A.

14. St. Louis Research Groups, Inc., *User Demand Study* (draft ca. 1978), pp. 71–75; Numbers of blacks are probably understated since the study was based on interviews with drivers of private vehicles and those who arrived in park by bus or on foot were not included in the count. Still, observation on a typical day put black proportion under 1/3.

15. Ord 51519, December 11, 1962.

16. Flyer for Triple A election, September 14, 1963 (in possession of Frank A. Thompson, Jr.); *PD*, April 14, 1964, p. 5C.

17. Triple A also paid the city $5.00 for each tennis member,

a new membership classification.

18. *User*, p. 13; After the zoo installed turnstiles, gate counts were 1980–81, 1,794,237; 1981–82, 2,015,639; 1982–83, 2,095,416; 1983–84, 1,902,612.

19. *PD*, March 29, 1970, p. 3G; February 7, 1964, p. 3A.

20. Beginning in 1978 the Zoo Parent Program offered benefits to those who wished to contribute the cost of feeding an animal for a year.

21. In 1983 voters approved propositions doubling the zoo and art museum support to 8 cents, increasing the science museum's tax and giving tax support for the first time to the Missouri Botanical Garden.

22. Susan Croce Kelly, "Zoos in Saint Louis" (M.A. Thesis, St. Louis University, 1973), pp. 114–15.

23. The chimp show was discontinued during the summer of 1983, and a few chimps added to the sea lion show. At the end of the 1983 season, the chimp arena was torn down to make way for a new Great Ape Facility, replacing the barred Great Ape House.

24. Jour BPS, January 22, 1952; March 23, 1954; April 20, 1954; April 27, 1954; May 4, 1954; May 11, 1954; June 11, 1957; July 16, 1957; July 30, 1957; September 20, 1957.

25. One of the authors clearly remembers the look on the guard's face when she and her family, short of cash, entered the exhibit of Bingham drawings without depositing the "suggested donation."

26. The art museum, too, like the zoo, benefited from the increased tax rate voted in 1983.

27. *User*, p. 12; *PD*, October 23, 1983, p. 5B.

28. Nonmembers had to pay a fee for use of the library and archives, however.

29. *MHS Bull* 22 (April 3, 1966):297–300.

30. *Time* (May 8, 1950) vol 55, no 19:36–37.

31. Ord 55529, February 24, 1970.

32. In 1968 the service used the much smaller Dwight Davis Tennis Center. It then returned to the Municipal Theatre in 1969 before disappearing.

33. *Time* (August 30, 1948), vol 52, no 9:50.

34. Indoor wintertime performances outside Forest Park began September 7, 1982.

35. *Architectural Forum* (August 1963):95–96.

36. Ord 52541 March 31, 1964.

37. Ord 49777 February 9, 1960; 55899, April 1, 1971.

38. Ord 47487, April 8, 1955.

39. Ord 52952, February 1, 1965.

40. *GD*, June 5, 1949, p. 4A; June 26, 1949, p. 2A; Ord 43256 July 3, 1945; 49008 June 26, 1948; 56219 June 13, 1972.

41. *Griff*, pp. 138–39, 144; Interview of Robert E. Reed by Catherine Anderson, September 6, 1983.

42. *PD*, April 15, 1967, p. 1.

43. Team Four, *Task Force Summary of Progress to Date*, December 1979, p. 17; "Master Plan," draft 7, 1983, pp. 5–19.

44. Interview of Leroy Tyus by Catherine Anderson, June 23, 1983, p. 4.

45. PC 1953, p. 13; 1955, p. 31.

46. In 1949 organizers cancelled a planned celebration of the park's seventy-fifth anniversary because St. Louisans were "generally reluctant to join in large crowds" at a time when polio was a major threat. (*GD*, August 27, 1949, p. 7C)

47. PC 1953, p. 15; 1949, p. 18; Missouri Botanical Garden report in Team Four, *Review of Available Data*, August 1979, p. 11.

48. *PD*, May 3, 1979.

49. *PD*, November 1, 1972, p. 17A.

50. PC 1950, p. 17.

51. *GD*, April 27, 1970, p. 1A.

52. *GD*, May 25, 1972, p. 13A; June 21, 1976, p. 4A; *PD*, June 19, 1972, p. 3A.

53. *PD*, July 5, 1968, p. 1A. The major Fourth of July celebration was in Forest Park in 1979 because of landscaping work at the Arch.

54. *PD*, September 23, 1974, p. 1B.

55. *GD*, July 7, 1970, p. 1A.

56. *GD*, December 30, 1971, p. 1A.

57. *GD*, May 13, 1975, p. 6A; June 21, 1976, pp. 1, 4A.

58. *PD*, November 3, 1959, p. 2C; January 31, 1961; February 12, 1961.

59. Kirkwood v. City of St. Louis, 351 Southwestern Reporter (Missouri Supreme Court 1961) pp. 781–88.

60. *PD*, October 26, 1959, p. 5A; Ord 52113 and 52115, November 12, 1963; 52943, December 29, 1964. The extra highway lanes were paved in 1983.

61. *PD*, December 15, 1958, p. 1.

62. *PD*, October 26, 1959, p. 4A; October 31, 1959; April 19, 1962, p. 2B.

63. *PD*, April 18, 1954, p. 17C.

64. *GD*, July 29–30, 1972, p. 12A.

65. Beginning in 1977 the Arena operated under the management of Ralston Purina Company as the Checkerdome, becoming the Arena again in 1983.

66. *GD*, May 1, 1969, p. 7A.

67. Ord 56576, July 17, 1963; *PD*, May 11, 1951, p. 3A; for metered parking on streets with little traffic after construction of Highway 40, see Ord 52271, December 30, 1963.

68. R/UDAT 3-2, 3-12, 4-1, 5-1.

69. Channel 4 editorial December 8, 1976PM; December 9, 1976AM; December 9, 1976PM; December 10, 1976AM; *PD*, November 2, 1976 1C; November 4, 1976.

70. *PD*, May 8, 1977.

71. St. Louis Children's Hospital v Conway and McKenna v. Poelker 582 Southwestern Reporter (Missouri Supreme Court 1979) pp. 687–91.

72. *PD*, December 20, 1977, p. 6B.

BIBLIOGRAPHY

This bibliography describes the major sources for this book and gives some indication for further reading. The vast majority of the works cited here are available at the Main St. Louis Public Library (which now includes the collection of the former Municipal Reference Library). Most of the other items can be found at the Missouri Historical Society, Washington University, St. Louis University, or one of the specialized collections, such as the Missouri Botanical Garden library.

GENERAL SOURCES

Most of the detailed information for this book came from official reports by park and city officials and from newspapers of the time. Each source has its advantages and disadvantages. Official reports are particularly useful for documenting physical changes in the park, especially new facilities, and official priorities. The reports, which give an administrator's view of the park, often discuss plans as well as accomplishments. Newspapers are invaluable for a user's view of the park. Detailed reports of special events, such as opening day or the Lindbergh reception, and feature articles about the numbers of people in the park on a fine spring day contribute a great deal to understanding of park usage. Various opinions about Forest Park found expression in newspaper editorials, letters to the editors, and, in the earlier years, in the news columns.

Reports

A complete set of all official city reports is available at the Main St. Louis Public Library. For the original plan of the park and an account of some of the early work, the *Report of the Commissioners of Forest Park, 1875* (St. Louis, 1876) is an essential source. After that, a major source for information about the entire city, not just the parks, is "The Mayor's Message with Accompanying Documents to the Municipal Assembly of the City of Saint Louis" issued annually (except for 1898, 1899, and 1900) through 1915. After 1915 the annual reports of the Division of Parks and Recreation and then the Department of Parks, Recreation and Forestry were issued annually through 1968 with only a few years missing, and another annual report appeared in 1979. In some years these reports included information about the art museum, the Missouri

Historical Society, the Municipal Athletic Association, the Municipal Theatre Association, and the zoo. After 1960 the reports were considerably less detailed than they had been. Juanita June Dempsey, "History of Parks and Recreation; City of St. Louis: 1812–1958" (M.A. Thesis, University of Missouri, Columbia, 1983) contains a digest of park department reports and a list of ordinances affecting parks.

The comptroller's report, still issued annually, contains valuable financial information. For bond issue votes, see "St. Louis Bond Issue Results: 1923–1955" (1955) (at Main St. Louis Public Library). (The Municipal Reference Library had an edition updated through 1978.) At various intervals the St. Louis auditor issued lists of city employees, which give a picture of staffing patterns. These reports are still available for the years 1889, 1891, 1895, 1899, 1902, 1904, 1905, 1907, and 1913. "The Government of the City of St. Louis," the summary report of the Mayor's Advisory Committee on City Survey and Audit, conducted by Griffenhagen and Associates under the supervision of the Governmental Research Institute (February 20, 1941) available at Washington University contains an analysis of city operations, including the park department. Unfortunately for the researcher, neither the comptroller nor the park department reported Forest Park expenditures separately after 1958.

The journals of the board of public improvements (later the board of public service) are also extremely valuable, especially for permits issued, and would be even more so if they were indexed. (The office of the board of public service maintains cards that index board actions. Some are dated as early as 1906, but the references are most complete after about 1940.) The journals must be read, however, with the understanding that not everything the board authorized in fact occurred.

For city ordinances see Elliot C. Bennett, *Index, St. Louis City Ordinances from Incorporation in 1822 to 1903* (St. Louis: William H. O'Brien Printing and Publishing Co., n.d.), then index in city register's office. Compilations of ordinances were issued as the combined code or the revised code in various years, including 1901, 1914, 1926, 1936, 1948, 1960, and 1980. *The Scheme for the Separation and Re-Organization of the Governments of St. Louis City and St. Louis County and the Charter for the City of St. Louis* (St. Louis: 1877) is important in understanding the city-county separation and early city administration. The 1914 revised charter replaced the 1876 charter.

Newspapers and Periodicals

Much of the information for this book came from reading microfilms of several St. Louis newspapers—the *Democrat* and the *Globe-Democrat*, the *Dispatch* and the *Post-Dispatch*, the *Republican* and the *Republic*, the *Argus*, and the *Star-Times*. An index covers the period from 1975 to 1979 in the *Post-Dispatch*, the *Globe-Democrat*, the *Argus*, and several other publications. A published index to the *Post-Dispatch* continues to be available. For the early years researchers read the papers around important dates, then scanned years or just the summer months for sample years during each period. For the period from the late 1920s until the present, both the *Post-Dispatch* and the *Globe-Democrat* graciously offered the use of their morgue index files, not open to the public, which saved a great deal of work. The Missouri Historical Society owns scrapbooks of newspaper clippings on a variety of subjects (the dates are not always reliable), and its name and chronological files index some newspaper articles. The clippings at the Mercantile Library were not particularly useful for this work. The authors of this book maintained a file of clippings about Forest Park, mostly from St. Louis newspapers, beginning in May 1977. Late in the research for this book, we were able to use a scrapbook of clippings, mostly from 1923, kept by Nelson Cunliff while he was president of the board of public service, which was quite helpful. The scrapbook is now available on microfilm at the University of Missouri-St. Louis archives.

Newspaper reports, as noted above, are most useful for detailed contemporary reports of events and of public opinion. In the nineteenth and early twentieth centuries, the papers often ignored stories they didn't wish to cover. A diligent search of the *Westliche Post*, for example, failed to disclose any mention of Forest Park until opening day. In general, the *Post-Dispatch* provided more coverage of Forest Park in that period than did the *Globe-Democrat*. For the World's Fair, however, the *Globe-Democrat* is the paper of choice. The *Republican* carried detailed reports of meetings of the St. Louis County Court, which are especially useful for Forest Park questions in the 1870s. In both newspapers and general-circulation periodicals, historical articles almost always contain major inaccuracies.

For national periodicals, *The Reader's Guide to Periodical Literature* is essential. *American City* carried articles about city administration, usually from the administrator's point of view. Special interest magazines have been noted under various subjects. Locally, two publications of the Missouri Historical Society (MHS), *Glimpses of the Past*, and *Bulletin*, contained helpful articles of varying levels of scholarship. MHS maintains indexes to its publications.

Graphics

Maps, drawings, and photographs are often useful but must be used carefully. For example, maps of St. Louis between 1876 and 1901 used the plan for Forest Park as if everything had been built, which is misleading. Often only one section of a map was updated before the map was reissued.

Photographs are sometimes unidentified or undated, or, even worse, misidentified or misdated. Photographs can often be found in books, especially *Art Work of St. Louis* (St. Louis: W. H. Parish Publishing Co., 1895) and the park department annual reports. However, the year the book was published is not always the date the photograph was taken.

The Main St. Louis Public Library has a particularly useful map collection in its history and genealogy room and a number of photographs in the art room, organized but undated, some of which are noted below. Pictorial collections normally open to the public that were useful for this work were MHS, the State Historical Society of Missouri in Columbia, the Swekosky Collection of the of School Sisters of Notre Dame, the St. Louis Art Museum, the Missouri Botanical Garden, the St. Louis Police Library, the Missouri Department of Conservation in Jefferson City, and the EROS Data Center of the United States Department of the Interior's Geological Survey in Sioux Falls, South Dakota. Collections not normally open to the public that were useful for this book included those of the *Globe-Democrat*, the *Post-Dispatch*, the St. Louis Department of Parks, Recreation and Forestry, the St. Louis Zoo, the Municipal Theatre Association, the McDonnell Planetarium, the St. Louis Area Boy Scout Council, Barnes Hospital, the Laclede Gas Company, Mary Institute, Horner and Shifrin, Inc., and the Forest Park pictures taken by Philip Loughlin, assisted by Cicely Drennan.

Court Cases

Forest Park has been involved in a number of court cases. Among the most interesting are the following:

- First Forest Park act unconstitutional (State of Missouri ex rel. Chouteau v. Leffingwell, 54 Missouri Reports (1873) pp. 458–477)
- Second Forest Park act constitutional (County Court of St. Louis County v. Griswold 58 Missouri Reports (1874), pp. 175–201)
- Appoints appraisers, sets price for land (County Court of St. Louis County v. Griswold, order entered by Circuit Court of St. Louis County on January 9, 1875) in city library Forest Park box; land transfer in city deed book 521, pp. 183–92)
- Disposition of Forest Park bonds given Griswold under 1872 act (Jamison v. Griswold, 2 Missouri Appeal Reports (1876), pp. 150–56)
- The contested election over city-county separation; second case rules scheme and charter were approved and gives corrected vote totals (Barnes v. Gottschalk, 3 Missouri Appeal Reports (1876), pp. 111–37; and State ex rel. Beach v. Sutton, 3 Missouri Appeal Reports (1877) pp. 388–421)

- Disposition of railroad right-of-way following insolvency of Wabash, contains history of right-of-way to that time (Joy v. St. Louis, 138 U.S. Supreme Court [1891], pp. 1–51)
- Lease of Cottage valid (State ex rel. Attorney General v. Schweickardt, 109 Missouri Reports [1891] pp. 496–518)
- Tax to support art museum unconstitutional because is branch of Washington University (State ex rel. Board of Control of St. Louis School and Museum of Fine Arts v. City of St. Louis, 216 Missouri Reports (En Banc 1909) pp. 47–99)
- Tax to support art museum with board appointed by mayor constitutional (State ex rel. Bixby v. City of St. Louis 241 Missouri Reports [En Banc 1912] pp. 231–250)
- City must pay damages to parents of child drowned in River des Peres (Capps v. City of St. Louis, 158 Southwestern Reporter (Missouri Supreme Court, 1913) pp. 616–24)
- City may use park space for activities such as airfield, tourist camp, Triple A, etc. (Young v. Cunliff, order entered dismissing case by the Circuit Court of the City of St. Louis on November 10, 1922, Cause Number B26744)
- Court refuses to order city to issue golf permits to blacks (State ex rel. Howard v. Pape, order entered denying writ of mandamus by Circuit Court of the City of St. Louis on June 4, 1928, Cause Number 67616)
- Zoo tax constitutional (State ex rel. Zoological Board of Control v. City of St. Louis, 318 Missouri Reports (En Banc 1928) pp. 910–28) A similar case concerning the library tax (State ex rel. Carpenter v. City of St. Louis, 318 Missouri Reports (En Banc 1928), pp. 870–910)
- Municipal Tennis Association may refuse to allow Richard Hudlin to play in municipal tournament (Hudlin v. Baumes, order entered dismissing the case on July 17, 1945, by the Circuit Court of the City of St. Louis, Cause Number 88154C)
- City may build Forest Park Parkway (Kirkwood v. City of St. Louis, 351 Southwestern Reporter (Missouri Supreme Court 1961) pp. 781–88)
- Grant of air space over Kingshighway for hospital building addition improper (St. Louis Children's Hospital v. Conway, 582 Southwestern Reporter [Missouri Supreme Court En Banc 1979] pp. 687–91)
- Objection to hospital addition moot (McKenna v. Poelker 582 Southwestern Reporter (Missouri Supreme Court En Banc 1979) p. 691)

Missouri Laws

Missouri laws consulted for this work include:
- An act to establish a public park for the use of the inhabitants of the city of St. Louis. February 15, 1864
- An act to establish Forest Park. March 25, 1872
- An act to amend an act entitled, "An act to revise the charter of the city of Saint Louis, and to extend the limits thereof," approved March 4, 1870, so as to further extend limits of said city, and provide for the government thereof. March 30, 1872

- An act to repeal an act entitled "An act to amend an act entitled 'an act to revise the charter of the city of St. Louis, and to extend the limits thereof,' approved March 4, 1870, so as to further extend the limits of said city, and to provide for the government thereof," approved March 30, 1872, and to adjust certain taxes and expenditures within the new extended limits of the city created by said act. February 4, 1874
- An act to establish "Forest Park" in the county of St. Louis, to provide for the establishment and government thereof, and to provide for the issue of bonds by the county court of St. Louis County for the purposes of said park, and for the purchase and condemnation of lands for the same. March 25, 1874
- An act to amend section 4 of an act entitled "An act to establish 'Forest Park' in the county of St. Louis, to provide for the issue of bonds by the county court of St. Louis County for the purposes of said Park, and for the purchase and condemnation of lands for the same," approved March 25, 1874. February 2, 1875
- An act providing for the establishment, maintenance, extension and regulations of museums of art in cities of four hundred thousand inhabitants or more, and authorizing taxation for the same, with emergency clause. March 7, 1907
- An act providing for the establishment, maintenance, extension and regulations of zoological parks in cities of four hundred thousand inhabitants, or more, and authorizing taxation for the same, with emergency clause. March 23, 1915
- Metropolitan Park and Museum District (Missouri Revised Statutes 1978 Sections 184.350–384)
- Metropolitan Park and Museum District as revised 1983 (Cumulative Supplement to the Revised Statutes of 1978 Sections 184.351–362)

SOURCES FOR PARTICULAR SUBJECTS

Forest Park

Publications specifically about Forest Park are quite scanty. "The History of the Acquisition, Development and Restoration of Forest Park, 1870–1910," by Kevin Corrigan Kearns (Ph.D. Diss., St. Louis University, 1966, in the MHS library), only covers the legal difficulties in establishing the park in the 1870s and the controversy over restoration following the World's Fair, with nothing on the 1880s and 1890s. *Forest Park and Its History* by the Visit St. Louis Committee (Sponsored by the St. Louis Chamber of Commerce and the City of St. Louis, 1943) is episodic and uncritical, but particularly useful for matters its authors could remember. Andrew Mahaddie, "Forest Park, St. Louis" (M.A. Thesis, Washington University, 1966), was not helpful for this book.

The Regional/Urban Design Assistance Team report (St. Louis 1976) gives the team's findings. Various reports and drafts of the Forest Park Master Plan Task Force are unpublished and not available to·the public, but copies belonging to Caroline Loughlin were used for Chapter 8. The historical comments in these reports are not always reliable. In the art room at the city library is D. B. Neuman's unpublished research on the park keeper's house. The first four volumes of the MHS seven-volume scrapbook "Art in St. Louis: Park and Recreation" contain some helpful clippings through the 1960s. For clippings beginning in 1967 see MHS scrapbook "St. Louis Parks and Recreation." There are a number of clippings with the photographs in the Main St. Louis Public Library art room.

For early park history, in addition to the 1876 commissioners' report, consult materials in the box labeled "St. Louis Forest Park Materials" located in the humanities room of the Main St. Louis Public Library. Materials include some financial statements from 1875 and 1876, information on several of the court cases, information from the St. Louis County Court records, and the tripartite agreement about the railroad right-of-way. The John G. Priest scrapbook at MHS contains interesting newspaper clippings about the survey and purchase of the park land in 1875. June Wilkinson Dahl, *A History of Kirkwood* (Kirkwood Historical Society, 1965), contains some information about Hiram W. Leffingwell.

Richard Longstreth, "From Farm to Campus: Planning, Politics and the Agricultural College Idea in Kansas" (manuscript copy in possession of the authors of this book c. 1985) contains information about the later achievements of Maximilian G. Kern, and a little about him before he arrived in St. Louis. Maximilian G. Kern, *Rural Taste in Western Towns and Country Districts in its Relation to the Principles of the Art of Landscape Gardening* (Columbia, Mo.: Herald Printing House, 1884), gives Kern's views at that date. G. M. Kern, *Practical Landscape Gardening, with reference to the Improvement of Rural Residences, Giving the General Principles of the Art; with Full Directions for Planting Shade Trees, Shrubbery and Flowers, and Laying Out Grounds* (Cincinnati: 1855), is almost certainly by the same man. Both books are in the Missouri Botanical Garden library.

Art and Architecture

For more information see some clippings in MHS scrapbooks "Art and Historic Markers" (2 vols.) and "Art in St. Louis: Parks and Recreation" (7 vols.); *Art Work of St. Louis*, 12 vols. (St. Louis: W. H. Parish Publishing Co., 1895); Ora Hill, *Mark Twain Drinking Fountain Scrapbook* (at St. Louis Public Library); Mary Jane Kirtz, "Sculpture at the Missouri Botanical Garden" (at the Missouri Botanical Garden library 1983); George McCue, *Building Art in St. Louis: Two Centuries* (2d ed., St. Louis Chapter, American Institute of Architects, 1967; 3d ed., St. Louis: Knight Publishing Co., 1981); Mary Powell, "Public Art in St. Louis: Sculpture, Architecture, Mural Decorations, Stained Glass" *St. Louis Public Library Monthly Bulletin* 23:7–8(July–August 1925), 2d ed.,

originally published in St. Louis Public Library Monthly Bulletin vol. 18, no. 8, August 1920; and St. Louis Beautification Commission and America the Beautiful Fund, *Special Report on Public Art to Alfonso J. Cervantes, Mayor, City of St. Louis* (St. Louis, 1969). See also Main St. Louis Public Library art room collection about St. Louis statues and fountains.

Aviation

See James J. Horgan, *City of Flight: The History of Aviation in St. Louis* (Gerald, Mo.: Patrice Press, 1984). Also two MHS *Bulletin* articles, Horgan, "The International Aeronautic Tournament of 1907" 21:3 (April 1965), and Maj. Albert Bond and Maj. William B. Robertson, "Early History of Aeronautics in St. Louis" 5:3 (June 1928):238. The MHS also has three sets of papers on aviation: Aeronautics Papers 1830–1979, Albert B. Lambert File, and the Robertson File. Numerous chronologies give incorrect dates for the Forest Park Aviation Field. For accurate information and a concise report on the early years of the airmail service, see *Report of the Postmaster General* (Washington, D.C.: Government Printing Office) for 1920 and 1921. St. Louis University library has several publications on aviation and the reference librarian called Parks College, which is part of the university but located in Cahokia, Illinois, for more information.

Crime and the Police

St. Louis Police Department annual reports, which are not generally included in the Mayor's Messages, give valuable information on crime statistics, on police procedures, and on the Forest Park substation and mounted police station. The St. Louis Police Library maintains a complete set of annual reports and a chronology file to the St. Louis Police Department history. The police library also holds *History of the Metropolitan Police Department of St. Louis, 1810–1910* (St. Louis Board of Police Commissioners, 1910), which gives a detailed description of the department in 1910. Eugene J. Watts, "Police Priorities in Twentieth Century St. Louis," *Journal of Social History* 14:4(Summer 1981):649–73, relies heavily on statistics.

Fish Hatcheries

A series of articles by Larry Belusz in the *Missouri Conservationist* entitled "Fish Hatcheries in Missouri" 42:7–9 (July, August, September 1981) gives a detailed history from 1878 to 1981.

Institutions

Art Museum. The art museum library and archives were especially useful. See Mab Mulkey, "History of the St. Louis School of Fine Arts, 1879–1909: The Art Department of Washington University" (M.A. Thesis, Washington University, 1944); Gerald R. Baum, 1978, "The History of the St. Louis Art Museum: The Public as Patron," in the archives of the St. Louis Art Museum; and Richard

P. Stephenson, "St. Louis City Art Museum and its Administrative Board of Control" (M.A. Thesis, St. Louis University, 1962). The museum issued a pamphlet at the time of the east wing renovation titled *The Architecture of the St. Louis Art Museum, 1904–1977* (St. Louis, St. Louis Art Museum, 1978). All of the above works are at the St. Louis Art Museum. The William K. Bixby Papers at the Missouri Historical Society were also helpful. Annual reports of the City Art Museum, later the St. Louis Art Museum, are very informative and are available at the Main St. Louis Public Library as well as the St. Louis Art Museum. Many of the sources under the World's Fair of 1904 section of this bibliography also contain information about the art museum building.

Missouri Historical Society. The most comprehensive account is George R. Brooks, "The First Century of the Missouri Historical Society," *Bulletin* 22:3(April 1966): 273–301. MHS staff maintains a newspaper scrapbook entitled "Missouri Historical Society." Documents about the Lindbergh Collection are not open to the public.

Municipal Theatre Association. Mary Kimbrough, *The Muny: St. Louis' Outdoor Theatre* (St. Louis: Bethany Press, 1978) focuses mostly on the shows and the stars. See also newspaper clippings in MHS scrapbook, "Municipal Opera."

The Zoo. See Susan Croce Kelly, "Zoos in St. Louis" (M.A. Thesis, St. Louis University, 1973). A booklet issued by the zoo in about 1981, *St. Louis Zoological Park: A Zoo Worth Knowing*, (St. Louis, c. 1981) contains some historical information. Earlier guide books to the zoo include *Official Illustrations of the St. Louis Zoological Park* (St. Louis: Zoological Society of St. Louis, 1926) and *St. Louis Zoo Album: An Illustrated Guide to the St. Louis Zoological Park and to the Classes Mammalia, Aves, Reptilia and Amphibia* (St. Louis: Zoological Subdistrict Commission of the Metropolitan Park and Museum District, revised 1976). The three-volume Mrs. Cortland Harris scrapbook at MHS contains clippings, mostly from the period 1910–1913. St. Louis Zoological Park annual reports, minutes of the board meetings, photograph files, and scrapbooks of newspaper clippings are maintained at the zoo but are not open to the public. However, annual reports from 1917 through 1941, financial reports from 1930 through 1940, scrapbooks from 1910 through 1940, and a few other documents are now available on microfilm at the UMSL archives. Marlin Perkins, *My Wild Kingdom: An Autobiography* (New York: E. P. Dutton, 1982), contains some information.

McDonnell Planetarium

A set of scrapbooks of programs and newspaper clippings was consulted at the planetarium and was helpful for this work. For a plan to combine the science museum and the planetarium, see St. Louis Museum of Science and Natural History, *A Community Plan for a New Science Center Serving the Children, Youth and Adults of St. Louis City and County* (c.1978, copy held by Caroline Loughlin).

Race Relations

Consult "Negro Segregation in St. Louis," *Literary Digest* 52:12(March 18, 1916):702. The State Historical Society of Missouri in Columbia has *Report of the Committee on the Problems of Negroes of the Missouri Conference for Social Welfare* (1914). The following are in the UMSL archives: Social Planning Council of St. Louis and St. Louis County, *Negro Attitude Survey of St. Louis* (February, 1949); National Urban League, *Review of the Program of the St. Louis Urban League and the Social and Economic Conditions of the Negro Population of St. Louis, Mo.*, conducted for the Social Planning Council of St. Louis and St. Louis County by the National Urban League, New York City (September–October, 1948); and George Schermer, *The Fairground Park Incident* (Detroit, Mich.: Mayor's Interracial Committee, July 27, 1948), which considers park and recreation facilities citywide. Material from six interviews with the authors was also used in the book. Reports on those interviews are in the possession of the authors.

Sewer Work

W. W. Horner published a complete account of the design and construction of the River des Peres sewer in the *Engineering News Record* (July 24, July 31, August 14, August 21, 1930). He also wrote an article on sewer design that mentioned the Forest Park Foul Water Sewer in *Engineering and Contracting* (September 13, 1911). The Metropolitan Sewer District (MSD) library also contains valuable photographs and information, including a chronology of River des Peres work and problems.

Special Events

Boy Scout Camping. William J. Brittain, *The Spirit of Scouting: Challenge and Triumph—65 Years of St. Louis Area Scouting: The Story of the St. Louis Area Council, Boy Scouts of America* (St. Louis Area Council, Boy Scouts of America, 1976), is the major source.

Centennial Week. Walter B. Stevens, ed., *St. Louis: One Hundred Years in a Week: Celebration of the Centennial of Incorporation, October Third to Ninth, Nineteen Hundred and Nine* (St. Louis Centennial Association, n.d.), is the official account.

Pageant and Masque. Donald Bright Oster, "Nights of Fantasy: The St. Louis Pageant and Masque of 1914," MHS *Bulletin* 31:3 (April 1975), is an excellent account of the event, the planning, and the motives of the various supporters, with footnotes and bibliography.

World's Fair of 1904: Louisiana Purchase Exposition. There are a number of publications about the Louisiana

Purchase Exposition. Those published around the time of the fair include Mark Bennitt, ed., *History of the Louisiana Purchase Exposition* (St. Louis: Universal Exposition Publishing Co., 1905), which is very good; J. W. Buel, ed., *Louisiana and the Fair*, 10 vols. (St. Louis: World's Progress Publishing Co., 1904), with its beautiful engravings; Forest Park World's Fair Free Site Association, "Argument for the Location of World's Fair in Western Forest Park" (at the Missouri Historical Society); David R. Francis, *The Universal Exposition of 1904*, 2 vols. (St. Louis: Louisiana Purchase Exposition Company, 1913), Francis's exhaustive account of the administrative side of the fair, including financial reports; John Wesley Hanson, *The Official History of the Fair* (1904); Louisiana Purchase Exposition Company, *Official Catalogue of Exhibits, Department of Art* (St. Louis: Official Catalogue Company, 1904); M. J. Lowenstein, compiler, *Official Guide to the Louisiana Purchase Exposition* (St. Louis: Official Guide Co., 1904); *The Greatest of Expositions: 1904 St. Louis World's Fair* (reissued by Hawthorn Publishing Company, Inc., St. Louis: 1979); H. B. Wandell, *The Story of a Great City in a Nutshell: 500 Facts about St. Louis* (1900, 1901). The New York Public Library has a three-volume scrapbook, "St. Louis Louisiana Purchase Exposition 1904: Photographs of Sculpture," which also contains a February 19, 1903, report to the Advisory Board of Sculpture, St. Louis World's Fair from Karl Bitter.

More modern publications include Dorothy Daniels Birk, *The World Came to St. Louis: A Visit to the 1904 World's Fair* (St. Louis: Bethany Press, 1979), as the title suggests a tour of the fair illustrated by photographs taken by the author's father; and Margaret Johanson Witherspoon, *Remembering the St. Louis World's Fair* (St. Louis: 1973), which contains an especially useful map of the fair with a tissue overlay of current streets and buildings. The Missouri Historical Society put together a collection of articles from its *Bulletin* as *Louisiana Purchase Exposition: The St. Louis World's Fair of 1904* (St. Louis: Missouri Historical Society, 1979). Pamela G. Hemenway, "Cass Gilbert's Buildings at the Louisiana Purchase Exposition, 1904" (M.A. Thesis, University of Missouri, 1970) is in the library at the St. Louis Art Museum and was quite helpful.

The papers and correspondence of the Louisiana Purchase Exposition Company are available at the Missouri Historical Society. The minutes of the executive committee are indexed and are particularly useful. The *World's Fair Bulletin*, published monthly by the World's Fair Publishing Co. (1901–1904), contains much detail and many pictures. MHS has numerous World's Fair scrapbooks.

George Kessler's papers at the MHS are helpful in understanding the restoration period. The Journal of the St. Louis Municipal Assembly House of Delegates 1905–1906 (pp. 1–7) documents disagreements between the city and the Louisiana Purchase Exposition Company. It is available at the Missouri Historical Society, and a complete set of the journals is at the Main St. Louis Public Library. The Louisiana Purchase Historical Association papers at MHS shed some light on that organization, as do some papers of William K. Bixby also at MHS. Rolla Wells, *Episodes of My Life* (St. Louis, 1933), gives the mayor's point of view.

Annual reports of the Smithsonian Institution in 1901, 1904, and 1905 contain information on that organization's display at the fair, including the bird cage. The 1901 report gives the text of the act of Congress authorizing the fair. For a look at World's Fairs from 1851 through 1975 see John Allwood, *The Great Exhibitions* (London: Cassell & Collier Macmillan, 1977).

Sports

Almost all the detailed information on sports in the park and on the St. Louis Amateur Athletic Association (Triple A) came from park commissioner reports and the newspapers. Triple A lost all its files in the 1976 fire. For Triple A information, see *St. Louis Amateur Athletic Association, Constitution, Bylaws and Report from Organization to June 1, 1899* and annual report for 1904–1905, both at the Missouri Historical Society.

For tennis, Davison Obear, *Sixty Years of Tennis in St. Louis: 1881–1941* (St. Louis, 1941), contains much detailed information but is uncritical and must be used with caution. For cycling, the Main St. Louis Public Library has a copy of St. Louis Cycling Club, *Handbook of Information and Constitution and Bylaws* (1910).

Whip and Spur and *Saddle and Bridle* magazines were helpful on horseback riding. The Thomas H. Rockwood scrapbook at the MHS has clippings and programs about horse racing by the Gentlemen's Driving Club.

The national *Playground* magazine has information on the playground movement and on St. Louis's playground festival. The New York Public Library holds a copy of the Annual Report of the St. Louis Playground Association for 1906 (miscatalogued as St. Louis Park and Playground Association), which gives valuable details on the work of this private association.

For an account of the beginnings of St. Louis golf clubs, see Henry J. Scherck, "Clubs and Fairways: Golf Grows Up in St. Louis," 2:3 *Gateway Heritage* (Winter 1981–82).

For general coverage of athletics in the United States see John Rickards Betts, *America's Sporting Heritage, 1850–1950* (Reading, Mass.: Addison-Wesley, 1974); R. E. Carlson, T. R. Deppe, and J. R. MacLean, *Recreation in American Life*, 2d ed. (Belmont, Calif.: Wadsworth, 1972); Hilmi Ibrahim and Jay Shivers, *Leisure: Emergence and Expansion* (Los Alamitos, Calif.: Hwong Publishing Co., 1979); Frank G. Menke, *The Encyclopedia of Sports*, 6th ed. (Garden City, N.Y.: Doubleday, 1977); Benjamin G. Rader, *American Sports: From the Age of Folk Games to the Age of Spectators* (Englewood Cliffs, N.J.: Prentice-Hall, 1983).

Transportation

For roads to and around the park see street department reports in Mayor's Messages, and City Plan Commission reports. The library at the AAA Automobile Club of Missouri was helpful. Articles on the Oakland Express Higway appeared in *St. Louis Commerce* magazine September 30, 1936, and *St. Louis Chamber of Commerce News* on various dates. See also Missouri State Highway Commission report for the period ending December 1, 1936, and *Scientific American* (December 1935).

For public transportation to the park, publications include American Street Railway, *Official Souvenir of the Local Committee of Arrangements of the Fifteenth Annual Convention of the American Street Railway Association* (1896); Berl Katz, *Saint Louis Cable Railways* (Bulletin 14 of the Electric Railway Historical Society, February 1965); and James Cox, ed., *Missouri at the World's Fair: An Official Catalogue* (1893). Woodward's *Map of St. Louis*, 1896 (Municipal Reference Library 23) shows all of the streetcar routes at that time. A proposal for a streetcar system in the park is explained in E. R. Kinsey, "Public Transportation within Forest Park," February 17, 1916, seen at the Municipal Reference Library. A later proposal, also never implemented, is found in FTM (Future Transportation Models of St. Louis, Inc.), "Plan for Forest Park Intra-Park Tram Service (c. 1977, copy in possession of Caroline Loughlin). The archives of two transit operators, the Public Service Company and the Bi-State Development Agency, are at the National Museum of Transport in St. Louis County and at the time of research for this book were uncatalogued and closed to the public.

Park Neighborhood

For a graphic representation of St. Louis at the time Forest Park opened, see Camille N. Dry and Richard J. Compton, *Pictorial St. Louis: A Topographical Survey drawn in Perspective, A. D. 1875* (reprint St. Louis: Knight Publishing Company, 1979). There is some written matter, but the real interest of this book is in the bird's eye view drawings of every street and building in the city at the time. (Note, however, that the Baker Ave. horsecar line shown on plates 100 and 101 was planned, but never built.) For buildings around the park at later dates, see the fire insurance maps: Alphonse Whipple & Co., C. T. Aubin, engineer, *Insurance Maps of St. Louis, Missouri, Special Risks* (St. Louis: Guest Banknote, printer, 1897), a very fragile set at Washington University archives; the Sanborn fire insurance maps of various dates at University of Missouri-Columbia; MHS, St. Louis; Washington University, St. Louis; and Library of Congress, Washington, D.C. For ownership of land around the park see Julius Pitzman, *Pitzman's New Atlas of the City and County of St. Louis, Mo.* (Philadelphia: A. B. Holcombe & Co., 1878); and G. M. Hopkins, *Atlas of the City of St. Louis, Missouri, 1883* (Washington, D.C.: Library of Congress, 1883). The city deed books give detailed information, but in a much less easily usable form.

The City Plan Commission issued a variety of reports and plans, some of which contain historical data and maps. For a list see *City Plan Commission of Saint Louis, Missouri: Reports Prepared 1910–1965* (St. Louis, 1965). U.S. census data are helpful on the growth of the neighborhoods. The collections in the Main St. Louis Public Library art room contain pictures and some clippings on neighborhoods, schools, and hospitals.

Books and other sources about sections of St. Louis include *The Bell Place Realty* (St. Louis, 1894); John Albury Bryan, "Private Places of St. Louis" (in the Main St. Louis Library art room, St. Louis, 1964); Arthur Newell Chamberlin III, *Mary Institute: The Story of a Hundred and Ten Years in the Pursuit of Excellence* (n.p., n.d., Mary Institute Upper School Library); Robert A. Cohn, *The History and Growth of St. Louis County*, 6th ed. (St. Louis County Office of Public Information, 1974); Harriet A. Davidson, "An Historical Perspective" in directory of Church of St. Michael and St. George (copy from 1984 in possession of authors of this book); Forest Park Addition: Deed to Westmoreland and Park Place, November 7, 1888 (City Deed Book 886, p16); William Barnaby Faherty, S. J., *Dream by the River: Two Centuries of Saint Louis Catholicism 1766–1980*, 2d ed. (St. Louis: River City Publishers, 1981), and *Better the Dream; Saint Louis: University and Community, 1818–1968* (St. Louis: St. Louis University, 1968), which have some information on St. Louis University High School, the new cathedral, and the hospitals; Forest Park University *Bulletins* at the Main St. Louis Public Library; Kathleen M. Harleman, Susan K. Tepas, and Georgiana Stuart, *The Neighborhood: A History of Skinker-DeBaliviere* (St. Louis: Skinker-DeBaliviere Community Council, 1973), a carefully researched and footnoted work; Hermann Hagedorn, *Brookings: A Biography* (New York: Macmillan, 1936); Julius K. Hunter, *Kingsbury Place: The First Two Hundred Years* (St. Louis: C. V. Mosby, 1982), which was a little beyond the area covered in this book; Kreigshauser Mortuary, "Suburban Spotlight" (at the St. Louis County Public Library Headquarters, in pamphlet file for Richmond Heights and Maplewood); Maplewood-Richmond Heights High School Senior English Class, "History of Richmond Heights" (at the Richmond Heights Public Library, 1939); Rev. P. J. O'Connor, *History of Cheltenham and St. James Parish 1860–1937* (St. Louis, 1937); Burford Pickens and Margaretta J. Darnall, *Washington University in St. Louis: Its Design and Architecture* (St. Louis: School of Architecture, Washington University, 1978); City of Richmond Heights, *50th Anniversary Souvenir Book* (1965); David Rodnick, *The Economic Development of St. Louis and the Surrounding Area, 1764–1914* (St. Louis, 1944); Dickson Terry, *Clayton: A History* (St. Louis: Von Hoffman Press, 1976), a very detailed history of Clayton; *Urban Oasis: 75 Years in Parkview, a St. Louis Private Place* (St. Louis: Boar's Head Press,

1979); and Norbury L. Wayman, *History of St. Louis Neighborhoods: Kingsbury* (St. Louis Community Development Agency, n.d.), and *History of St. Louis Neighborhoods: Central West End* (St. Louis: Planning and Programming Division of the Community Development Agency, 1978).

The MHS scrapbook "Colleges and Universities in Missouri" has information on the establishment of Forest Park Community College. H. A. Wheeler, "Clay Deposits," in *Missouri Geological Survey*, Vol. 11 (1896), gives details on clay mines in St. Louis area. "Summer Beer Gardens of St. Louis," MHS *Bulletin* 19:4, pt. 1(July 1953):391–95, gives information on the beginnings of the Forest Park Highlands. There were several articles in *City Beautiful* magazine about the Arena. Washington University archives yielded information on the Hi-Pointe area.

General St. Louis History and Descriptions

By far the best history of St. Louis available is James Neal Primm, *Lion of the Valley: St. Louis, Missouri* The Western Urban History Series, vol. 13 (Boulder, Colo.: Pruett Publishing Company, 1981). The index and bibliography make it particularly useful. Earlier histories that are not as scholarly and/or complete but contain useful information are William Barnaby Faherty, S.J., *The Saint Louis Portrait* The American Portrait Series (Tulsa, Okla.: Continental Heritage Press, 1978); McCune Gill, *A History of St. Louis* (St. Louis, Title Insurance Corporation of St. Louis, n.d.), and *The St. Louis Story: Library of American Lives* (St. Louis, Historical Record Association 3 vols., 1952); Norbury L. Wayman, "How St. Louis Grew: The History of its Appearance" (seen at the Community Development Agency, 1981); Frances Stadler, *St. Louis: History, 1962* (Radio KSD, St. Louis, 1962, at the Main St. Louis Public Library); and Harry M. Hagen, *This Is Our St. Louis* (St. Louis: Knight Publishing Company, 1970). Hagen, *Saint Louis: Portraits of the Past* (St. Louis: Riverside Press, 1976), is entirely photographs, many of them from the collection of Dr. William Swekosky, which give a sense of what the city was like in an earlier day. Parker T. Finch, "City Planning in St. Louis" (Senior Thesis, Princeton University, 1931, at the Main St. Louis Public Library), is very helpful on its special topic, and Rolla Wells, *Episodes of My Life* (St. Louis, 1933) gives one point of view on an interesting period around the time of the World's Fair.

For the city-county split, in addition to the scheme and charter, see Thomas Barclay, *The St. Louis Home Rule Charter of 1876: Its Framing and Adoption* (Columbia: University of Missouri Press, 1962); and Robert A. Cohn, *The History and Growth of St. Louis County*, 6th ed. (St. Louis County Office of Public Information, 1974).

C. H. Cornwell, "St. Louis Mayors: Brief Biographies, 1823–1965" (at the Main St. Louis Public Library, 1965), gives concise information about the various mayors

but is not footnoted. For an understanding of St. Louis politics around the turn of the century, the most useful source, besides Primm, was A. S. McConachie, "The Big Cinch: A Business Elite in the Life of a City, St. Louis, 1895–1915" (Ph.D. Diss., Washington University, 1976, available at Missouri Historical Society). Also useful was Julian S. Rommelkamp, "St. Louis in the Early Eighties," Missouri Historical Society *Bulletin* 19 (July 1963). See Lincoln Steffens, *The Shame of the Cities* (New York: Hill and Wang, 1957), for a muckraker's view.

Several histories or descriptions of St. Louis came out in the late nineteenth and early twentieth century. The best of these include William Hyde and Howard L. Conard, *Encyclopedia of the History of St. Louis*, 4 vols. (St. Louis: The Southern History Company, 1899); J. Thomas Scharf, *History of St. Louis City and County* (St. Louis: Louis H. Everts Co., 1883); and Walter B. Stevens, *St. Louis: The Fourth City, 1764–1909*, 3 vols. and index (St. Louis: S. J. Clarke Publishing Co., 1909); also issued by that company in 1911 as *St. Louis: The Fourth City, 1764–1911*.

For information, although often uncritical, about specific individuals and businesses, consult, in addition to Hyde and Conard, C. M. Baskett, editor, *Men of Affairs in St. Louis* (St. Louis: Press Club of St. Louis, 1915); *German Engineers of Early St. Louis and Their Works* (no author, n.p., n.d., ca. 1915, at Missouri Historical Society); Anne (Andre-Johnson) Johnson (Mrs. Charles P.), *Notable Women of St. Louis* (St. Louis, 1914); E. D. Kargau, *Mercantile, Industrial and Professional St. Louis* (St. Louis, 1902); Jno. E. Land, *St. Louis: Her Trade, Commerce and Industries* (St. Louis, 1882); John W. Leonard, *Book of St. Louisans* (St. Louis, 1906, 1912); or L. U. Reavis, *Saint Louis: The Future Great City of the World: Biographical Edition* (St. Louis, 1875). Edwards's annual St. Louis city directories (St. Louis: Southern Publishing Company) and later Gould's (St. Louis: David B. Gould & Co.) give home and office addresses for prominent St. Louisans, lists of hotels, hospitals, organizations, etc., and some editorial matter that is boosterish. The Missouri Historical Society name file indexes its scrapbooks of articles about prominent St. Louisans, especially obituaries, and its chronological file indexes some material by date. The St. Louis Municipal Archives at City Hall contain vast quantities of documents that might be more used if the index and working conditions made them more accessible.

Guidebooks, descriptions, and booster books about St. Louis often give descriptions of Forest Park, useful for identifying facilities available on a specific date. The books include (in alphabetical sequence by author) Karl Baedeker, ed., 1893, *The United States, with an Excursion to Mexico: A Handbook for Travelers*, 1893, reprint, 3d ed. 1893 (New York: DaCapo Press, 1971); The Business Men's League of St. Louis, *St. Louis Today* (St. Louis: Robert A. Reid, n.d.); Consolidated Illustrating Co., *St. Louis up to Date* (St. Louis, 1895); James Cox, *Old and*

New St. Louis (St. Louis, 1894), and his St. Louis through a Camera (St. Louis: Bureau of Information of the St. Louis Autumnal Festivities Association, 1892, also published in 1896 and 1901); Joseph A. Dacus and James W. Buel, A Tour of St. Louis; of the Inside Life of St. Louis (St. Louis, 1878); John Devoy, A History of the City of St. Louis and Vicinity, from the Earliest Times to the Present (St. Louis: 1898); Barney W. Frankenthal, Barney's Information Guide to the City of St. Louis (St. Louis: Barney's Information Guide Publishing Co., 1902, 1903, 1904, 1909); Idress Head, Saint Louis: Historical and Interesting Places (St. Louis, 1909); The Illustrated Guide of St. Louis (St. Louis: Philip Roeder, 1896); Andrew Morrison and J. H. C. Irwin, The Industries of St. Louis (St. Louis: J. M. Elstner & Co., 1885); George Washington Orear, Commercial and Architectural St. Louis (St. Louis, 1888); Ring, Why St. Louis Grows (St. Louis: n.d., early 1900s); St. Louis: 1894, Historical and Descriptive Review of St. Louis (St. Louis, 1894); St. Louis: The Coming Giant of America (St. Louis: Davis Realty Development Co., 1909); St. Louis of '91 (St. Louis: Traveler's Protective Association of America, Missouri Division, 1891); St. Louis Rotary Club special edition of Picturesque St. Louis (St. Louis: Finkenbiner-Reid Publishing Co., 1910); St. Louis Star Sayings, The City of St. Louis and its Resources (Star Sayings newspaper, St. Louis, 1893); Pictorial St. Louis, Past and Present (St. Louis: Arista C. Shewey, 1892); Philip Skrainka, M. D., St. Louis: Its History and Ideals (St. Louis, 1910); Western Commercial Traveler's Association, The St. Louis of Today (St. Louis Exposition Business Promotions, 1888); M. M. Yeakle, Sr., The City of Saint Louis: Its Progress and Prospects (St. Louis: J. Osmun, Yeakle & Co., 1889). See also the World's Fair section of this bibliography for guidebooks, many of which described the park and its environs.

Arthur Proetz's reminiscence, I Remember You, St. Louis (Zimerman-Patty Co., St. Louis, 1963), is interesting but not entirely reliable on details. Guidebooks and descriptions issued after World War I such as Anne Fuller Dillon and Martha Mullally Donnelly, The Complete St. Louis Guide (St. Louis, 1976; 2d ed., St. Louis: Gateway Publishing, 1984); George McCue, The Building Art in St. Louis: Two Centuries (2d ed., St. Louis Chapter, American Institute of Architects, 1967; 3d ed., St. Louis: Knight Publishing Co., 1981); Writer's Program of the Works Projects Administration in the State of Missouri, Missouri: A Guide to the "Show Me" State (Missouri State Highway Department, 1941; rev. ed., New York: Hastings House, 1954); St. Louis Chamber of Commerce, St. Louis as It Is Today (St. Louis: Industrial Club and St. Louis Chamber of Commerce, 1929); St. Louis Chapter, Theta Sigma Phi, The National Fraternity for Women in Journalism, St. Louis Guidebook: A Complete Reference with Illustrations and Maps (St. Louis: St. Louis Guidebook Publishing Corporation, 1964); St. Louis Visitors Guide (St. Louis: Convention and Visitors Bureau of Greater St. Louis, n.d., 1980s); and Shirley Seifert, The Key to St.

Louis (Philadelphia: J.B. Lippincott, 1963), provide descriptions at various dates. Norbury L. Wayman, A Pictorial History of St. Louis (St. Louis, 1968); N. B. Young, ed., Your St. Louis and Mine (St. Louis, 1937); and Albert Von Hoffman, All about St. Louis (St. Louis, 1923), were less helpful.

On The Growth of United States Cities

Books on urban development in the United States useful for this work include David R. Goldfield and Blaine A. Brownell, Urban America: From Downtown to No Town (Boston: Houghton Mifflin, 1979), and Paul Boyer, Urban Masses and Moral Order in America, 1820–1920 (Cambridge, Mass.: Harvard University Press, 1978). Gunther Barth, City People: The Rise of Modern City Culture in Nineteenth-Century America (New York: Oxford University Press, 1980), is a very readable account that describes the effects on the city and its residents of the growth of big city newspapers, department stores, professional sports teams, and vaudeville circuits. Another specialized account is Martin V. Melosi, ed., Pollution and Reform in American Cities, 1870–1930 (Austin: University of Texas Press, 1980). Grady Clay, Close-up: How to Read the American City (New York: Praeger, 1973), shows how to use physical clues to deduce the history and current "turf" arrangements in a modern city. Edward C. Banfield, The Unheavenly City Revisited (Boston: Little Brown, 1974), focuses on urban problems in the period following World War II and discusses corrective measures likely (and unlikely) to be successful.

Urban Parks

Most of the books on the growth of U.S. cities mention the role of urban parks in the nineteenth century and their intended benefits. For a more detailed treatment, see August Heckser, Urban Spaces: The Life of American Cities (New York: Harper & Row, 1977). Books about New York's Central Park, such as Elizabeth Barlow, The Central Park Book (New York: Central Park Task Force, 1977); and Henry Hope Reed and Sophia Duckworth, Central Park: A History and a Guide 2d ed., (New York: Potter, 1972), give general background information on urban parks. Another slant on Central Park is available through biographies of its designer, Frederick Law Olmsted, such as Albert Fein, Frederick Law Olmsted and the American Environmental Tradition (New York: George Braziller, 1972); Laura Wood Roper, FLO: A Biography of Frederick Law Olmsted (Baltimore: Johns Hopkins University Press, 1973); and Elizabeth Stevenson, Park Maker: A Life of Frederick Law Olmsted (New York: Macmillan, 1977). Some of Olmsted's professional papers are available, with connective material, in Frederick Law Olmsted, Forty Years of Landscape Architecture: Central Park, Frederick Law Olmsted, Jr., ed., and Theodora Kimball (New York: Putnam, 1928).

The same material is available with introductory biographical information in *Frederick Law Olmsted: Landscape Architect, 1822–1903* by the same author and editors (New York: Benjamin Blom, 1970, first published in 1922, 1928). Many of Olmsted's papers, journals, and letters are in the Library of Congress and can be borrowed on microfilm through interlibrary loan.

Histories of other urban parks include Robert C. Alberts, *The Shaping of the Point: Pittsburgh's Renaissance Park* (Pittsburgh: University of Pittsburgh Press, 1980); Raymond Clary, *The Making of Golden Gate Park: The Early Years, 1865–1906* (San Francisco: California Living Books, 1980); Carolyn Ingraham Galloway, untitled thesis on Audubon Park in New Orleans (M.A. Thesis, University of New Orleans, 1977); Sally K. Evans Reeves and William D. Reeves, *Historic City Park: New Orleans* (New Orleans: Friends of City Park, 1982); and Theodore B. White, *Fairmount, Philadelphia's Park: A History* (Philadelphia: Philadelphia Art Alliance Press, 1975). For a history of urban parks with a St. Louis slant, see Susan R. Lammert, "The Origin and Development of Landscape Parks in 19th Century St. Louis" (M.A. Thesis, Washington University, 1968).

INDEX

NOTE: A page number in italics indicates a picture on that page; a page number followed by a "c" indicates a caption on that page. A page number followed by an "m" indicates a map; if the map entry name is not the same as the index entry, the number of the map entry follows in parentheses. A map entry is indexed only if an item is new or changed.

CREDITS FOR ILLUSTRATIONS

The pictures and maps in this book were provided through the courtesy of the following institutions, organizations and individuals. Photographers' or artists' names, when known, and other information are in parentheses after figure number or name.

Barnes Hospital: 8–3, and in Appendix 1, Forest Park Parking Center, and Hudlin Memorial Marker

Boy Scouts of America, St. Louis Area Council: 6–34, 7–15 (Sievers Coml. Photographer, St. Louis), 7–28

Drennan, Cicely J. (also photographer): 8–10, 8–14, 8–49, and in Appendix 1, Baitcasting clubhouse

Drennan, Cicely J., and Catherine Anderson: 1–6, 1–14, 1–15, 3–29, 3–30, 4–4, 4–12, 4–20, 5–21, 6–47, 6–48, 7–32, 8–51, 8–52, and in Appendixes 1 and 2, maps

Horner & Shifrin, Inc., Design Engineers/Architects, St. Louis, Missouri: 6–39

Laclede Gas Company: 8–47

Loughlin, Dorothy Mudd: 4–3

Loughlin, Philip (also photographer): 1–7, 1–10, 1–12, 3–4, 5–16, 6–30, 6–33, 8–11, 8–20, 8–28, 8–32, 8–33, 8–42, 8–44, 8–48, and in Appendix 1, Davis Tennis Center Arena, Fire and Police Alarm Center, Park Department Office building, third Triple A clubhouse, Colonial Daughters Fountain, Davis Tennis Center Plaque, Centennial Marker, Triangular Fountain, Jahn Memorial, Kiel Marker, Lander Drinking Fountain, Langenberg Field Marker, Rosenbaum Tree Marker, St. Francis of Assisi statue, St. Louis Award (White Pine) statue, Mary Leighton Shields Sundial, Stupp Memorial Fountain, Vandeventer Place Gates, {Waves, Memories, Reflections}, Memorial to Frontier Women

Mary Institute Archives, The: 6–14 (Carrie P. Bribach)

Missouri Botanical Garden, The: in Appendix 1, O'Neil Fountain angel

Missouri Botanical Garden, The, Library: 1–3, 3–3, 3–27

Missouri Department of Conservation: 2–7, 3–12

Missouri Historical Society: title-page panorama of Charles Lindbergh (Sievers Photographers, Neg: Aviation 598), 1–8, 2–1 (L. Johnson & Co., Neg: Parks 229), 2–2 (Neg: Transportation 69), 2–6 (Neg: Parks 197), 2–8 (W. C. Persons, Neg: Parks 42a), 3–1 (Frank Starke, Neg: Sports 58), 3–2 ({Missouri at the World's Fair: An Official Catalog}, 1893, Neg: World's Fair 654), 3–7 (E. Boehl, Neg: Parks 81), 3–9 (Neg: Parks 208), 3–10 (E. Boehl, Neg: Parks 37), 3–11 (Neg: Parks 192), 3–14 (Kuehn), 3–19 (E. Boehl), 3–21 (Neg: Parks 210), 3–24 (A. Zeese & Sons, Cmp., Neg: Parks 219), 3–28 (A. Russell, Neg: Parks 201), 4–1 (Neg: World's Fair 657), 4–6 (Neg: World's Fair 656), 4–7 (Neg: World's Fair 45), 4–8 (Neg: World's Fair 653), 4–9, 4–11 (Neg: World's Fair 652), 4–14 (Park Commissioner Annual Report, 1904, Neg: Parks 212), 4–15 (Park Commissioner Annual Report, 1904, Neg: Parks 216), 4–16 (Park Commissioner Annual Report, 1904, Neg: Parks 217), 4–17

(Neg: World's Fair 655), 5–6 (Neg: World's Fair 56), 5–17, 5–18 (Neg: Aviation 498), 5–19 (Neg: Parks 157), 5–20 (World's Fair 699), 6–6 ({St. Louis Post-Dispatch}, Neg: Parks 211), 6–11, 6–12 (Neg: Parks 196), 6–16 (Pete Hangge Collection, Neg: Aviation 431), 6–17 (Mario Cavagnaro, Neg: Aviation 473), 6–18 (W. C. Persons, Neg: Missouri Historical Society 39), 6–19 (O. C. Conkling, Neg: Parks 227), 6–23 (O. C. Conkling, Neg: Parks 228), 6–26 (Neg: Transportation 26), 6–29 (W. C. Persons), 6–35 (W. C. Persons, Neg: Parks 222), 6–42 (Neg: Aviation 492), 7–1 (W. C. Persons, Neg: Parks 223), 7–5 (W. C. Persons, Neg: Parks 195), 7–16 (Pete Hangge/{Star-Times}, Neg: Parks 209), 7–18 (Pete Hangge Collection, Neg: Parks 200), 7–22 (O. C. Conkling, Neg: Parks 121), 7–23 (Pete Hangge/Star-Times, Neg: Parks 227), 8–16 (Lester Linck/ St. Louis Post-Dispatch, Neg: Missouri Historical Society 40), and in Appendix 1, Greenhouses (Park Commissioner Annual Report, 1897)

Municipal Theatre Association of St. Louis: 6–13, 7–14, and in Appendix 1, Municipal theatre

New York Public Library, The; Art, Prints, and Photographs Division; Astor, Lenox, and Tilden Foundations: 5–5

Pollak, Viola E. (also photographer): 5–7, and in Appendix 1, Frankenthal Memorial and Guggenheim Fountain

St. Louis Art Museum, The: 6–28 (Jules Guerin)

St. Louis Art Museum, The, Archives: 6–27, 8–15

St. Louis, City of; The Department of Parks, Recreation and Forestry: 5–9, 5–10, and in Appendix 1, Incinerator

St. Louis Globe-Democrat: 3–20 (Paul Ockrassa), 4–19, 6–37, 6–45 (Wings Photo Service), 6–46 (Associated Press), 7–3, 7–6, 7–7 (Durnin), 7–24, 7–25, 7–30, 7–31, 8–1, 8–2 (Howard Vogt), 8–4 (Bruce Bacon), 8–5, 8–6, 8–8, 8–17, 8–25, 8–31 (Paul T. Hodges), 8–34 (Ed Meyer), 8–37 (Paul T. Hodges), 8–39 (Ken Winn), 8–40 (T. V. Vessell), 8–41, 8–43 (Paul Ockrassa), 8–45 (Ed Meyer), 8–46 (J. E. Wood), 8–50 (Bob Moore), and in Appendix 1, Hangar building (Ken Winn), World's Fair Pavilion, and Jewish Tercentenary Flagpole

St. Louis Police Library: 3–17 (J. Dougall)

St. Louis Post-Dispatch: 6–2 (Geo. F. Heffernan), 6–8, 6–36, 6–43 (Geo. S. Pietzcker), 7–2, 7–13, 7–19, 7–20, 7–21, 7–26, 7–27, 7–29 (Victor Stevenson), 8–19 (Ed Burkhardt), 8–21, 8–22, 8–23 (Gene Rospeshil), 8–24, 8–26, 8–27, 8–29 (J. B. Forbes), 8–30, 8–35 (Steve Perille), 8–36, 8–38 (Robert C. Holt, Jr.), and in Appendix 1, McDonnell Planetarium

St. Louis Public Library: 1–1 (Camille Dry/Compton and Dry, Pictorial St. Louis: A Topographical Survey Drawn in Perspective, A. D. 1875), 1–2 (Frank Leslie's Illustrated Newspaper, 7/15/ 1876), 1–5 (Logan U. Reavis, Saint Louis, die Welt-Stadt der Zukunst), 1–11 (Shewey's Pictorial St. Louis, p. 182), 3–18, 3–22 (Art Work of St. Louis, W. H. Parish Publishing Co.), 3–23 (M. M. Yeakle, The City of St. Louis: Its Progress and Prospects), 3–25 (Shewey's Pictorial St. Louis), 5–1, 5–4, 6–3, 6–10, 6–20, 6–38